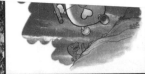

BOICHI

Ah, so happy... Ahh, so very happy... This book makes me so happy!

This story's got everything! Life in the great outdoors, a postapocalyptic setting, a scientist boy, primeval visuals and characters with the courage and conviction not to yield to an unfamiliar world. I seriously love it all, and drawing it is super fun!

RIICHIRO INAGAKI

What do you imagine when you think about scientists? Glasses, introverts, maybe a little mad...?

But in truth there can be scientists who are charmers and those who can be muscly too.

Our protagonist, Senku, is also be a bit different from the scientists we're used to imagining. He's one hot-blooded guy!

Get ready to cheer for him and his friends as they face this unprecedented challenge head-on!!

Boichi is a Korean-born artist currently living and working in Japan. His previous works include *Sun-Ken Rock* and *Terra Formars Asimov.*

Riichiro Inagaki is a Japanese manga writer from Tokyo. He is the writer for the sports manga series *Eyeshield 21*, which was serialized in *Weekly Shonen Jump.*

Dr.STONE

1

SHONEN JUMP Manga Edition

Story **RIICHIRO INAGAKI**
Art **BOICHI**

Translation/**CALEB COOK**
Touch-Up Art & Lettering/**STEPHEN DUTRO**
Design/**JULIAN [JR] ROBINSON**
Editor/**JOHN BAE**
Science Consultant/**KURARE**

Consulted Works:

- Dartnell, Lewis, *The Knowledge: How to Rebuild Civilization in the Aftermath of a Cataclysm*, translated by Erika Togo, Kawade Shobo Shinsha, 2015
- Davies, Barry, *The Complete SAS Survival Manual*, translated by Yoshito Takigawa, Toyo Shorin, 2001
- Kazama, Rinpei, *Shinboken Techo (Definitive Edition)*, Shufu to Seikatsu Sha, 2016
- McNab, Chris, *Special Forces Survival Guide*, translated by Atsuko Sumi, Hara Shobo, 2016
- Olsen, Larry Dean, *Outdoor Survival Skills*, translated by Katsuji Tani, A&F, 2014
- Weisman, Alan, *The World Without Us*, translated by Shinobu Onizawa, Hayakawa Publishing, 2009
- Wiseman, John, *SAS Survival Handbook, Revised Edition*, translated by Kazuhiro Takahashi and Hitoshi Tomokiyo, Namiki Shobo, 2009

Printed in Italy

Published by VIZ Media, LLC
P.O. Box 77010
San Francisco, CA 94107

10 9 8 7
First printing, September 2018
Seventh printing, December 2021

VIZ MEDIA
viz.com

SHONEN JUMP

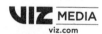

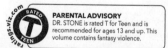

Dr.STONE

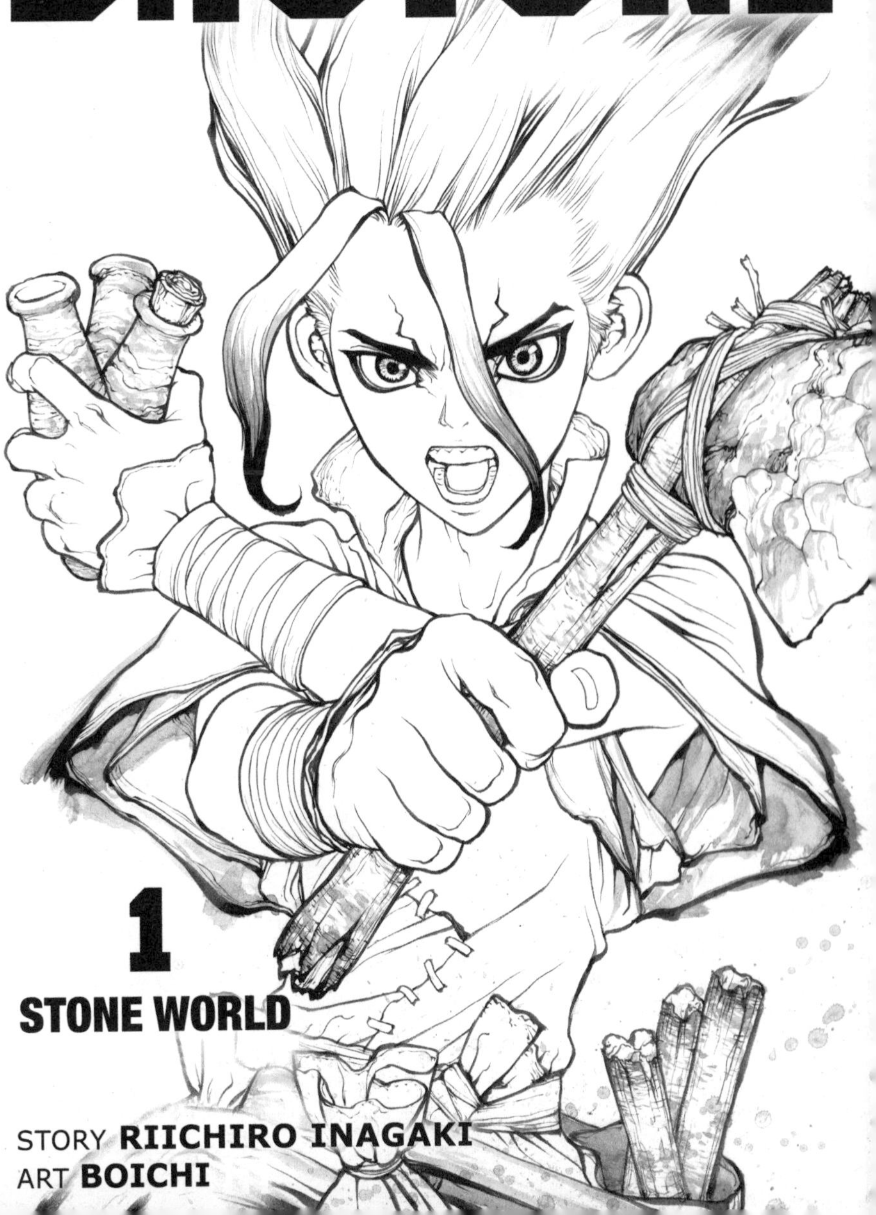

1

STONE WORLD

STORY **RIICHIRO INAGAKI**
ART **BOICHI**

CONTENTS

1
STONE WORLD

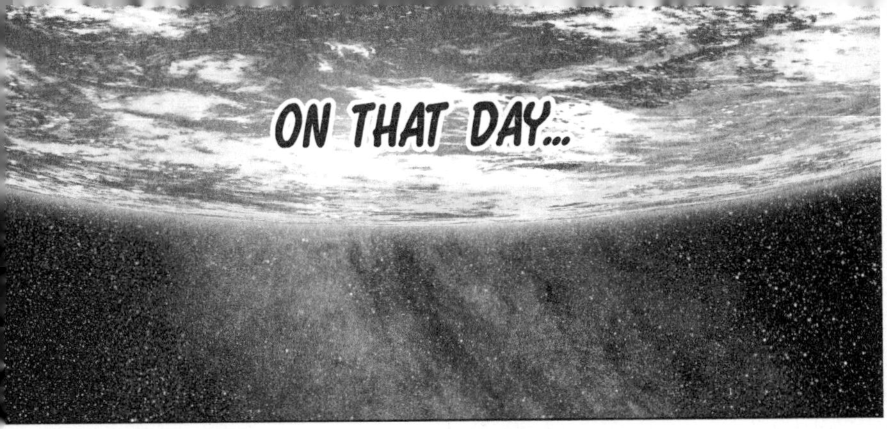
ON THAT DAY...
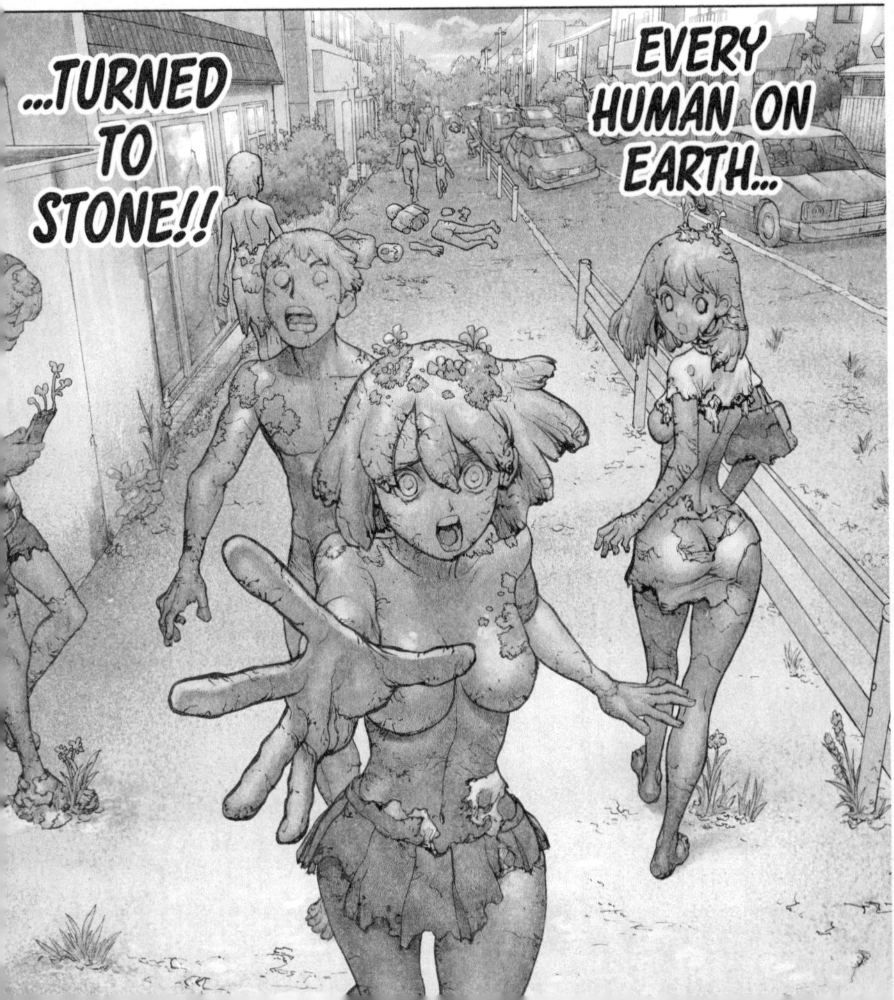
EVERY HUMAN ON EARTH...
...TURNED TO STONE!!

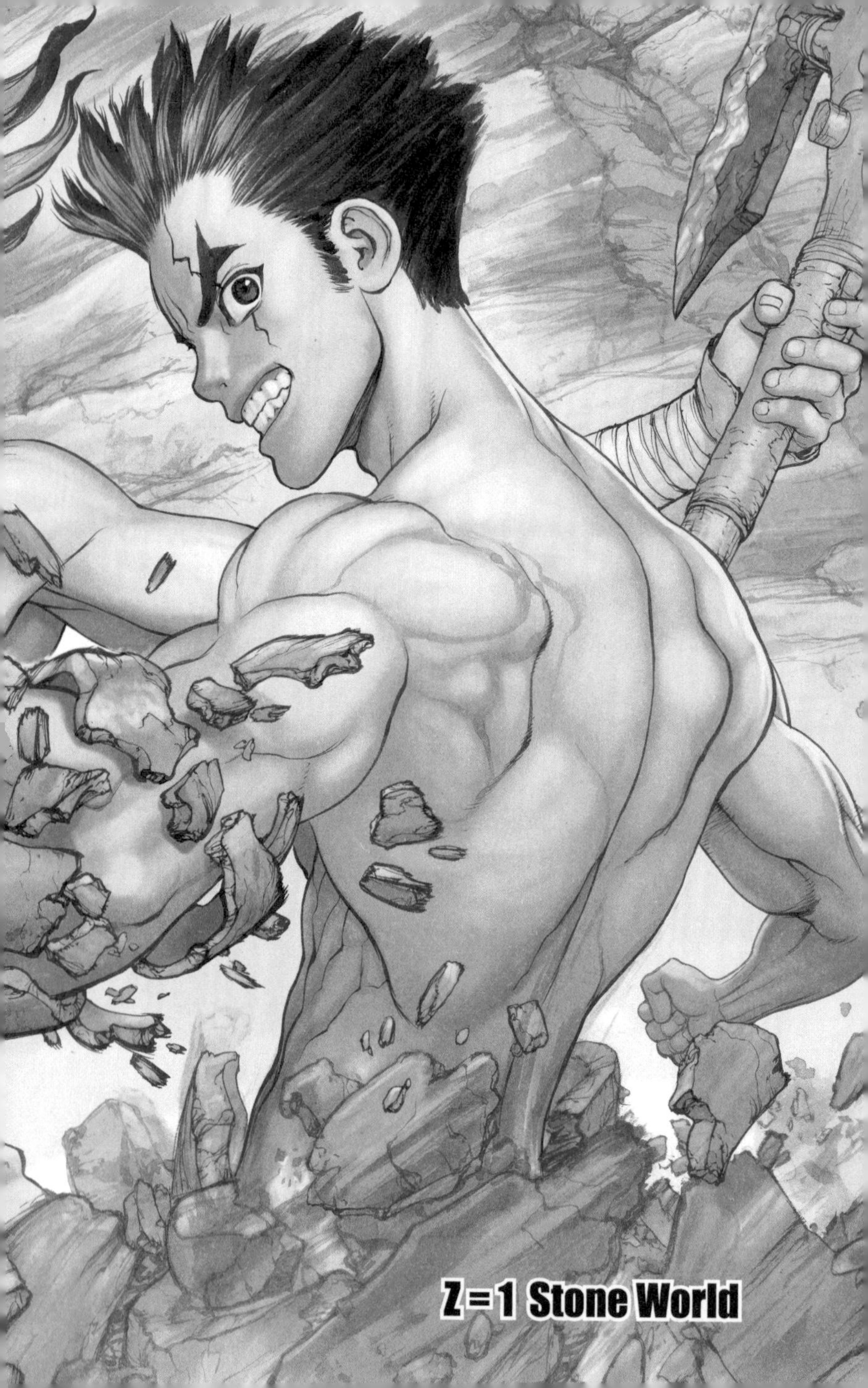
Z = 1 Stone World

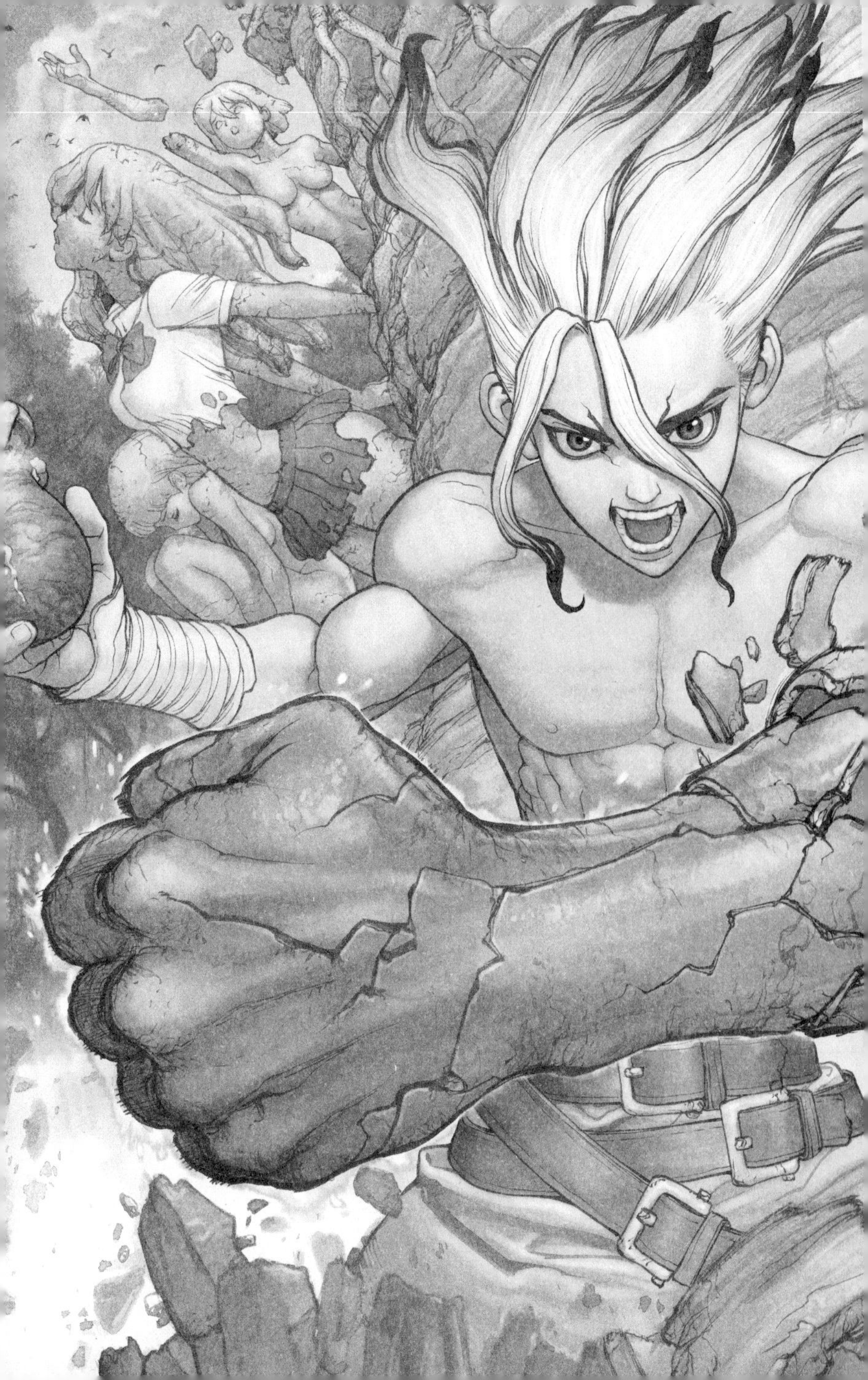

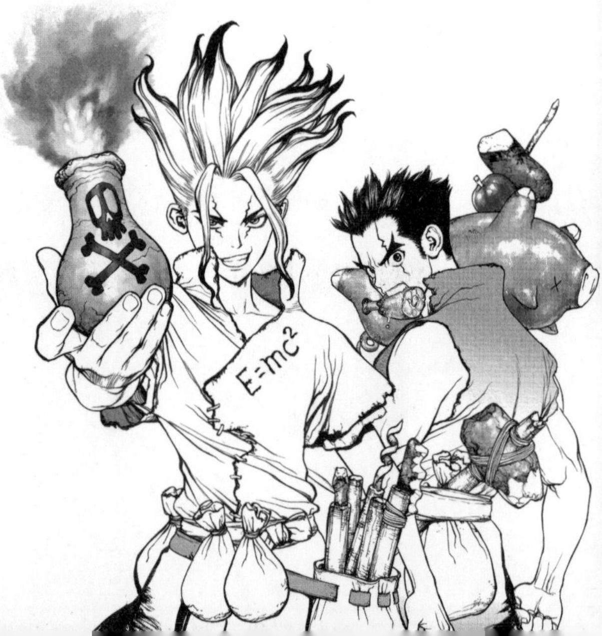
$E=mc^2$

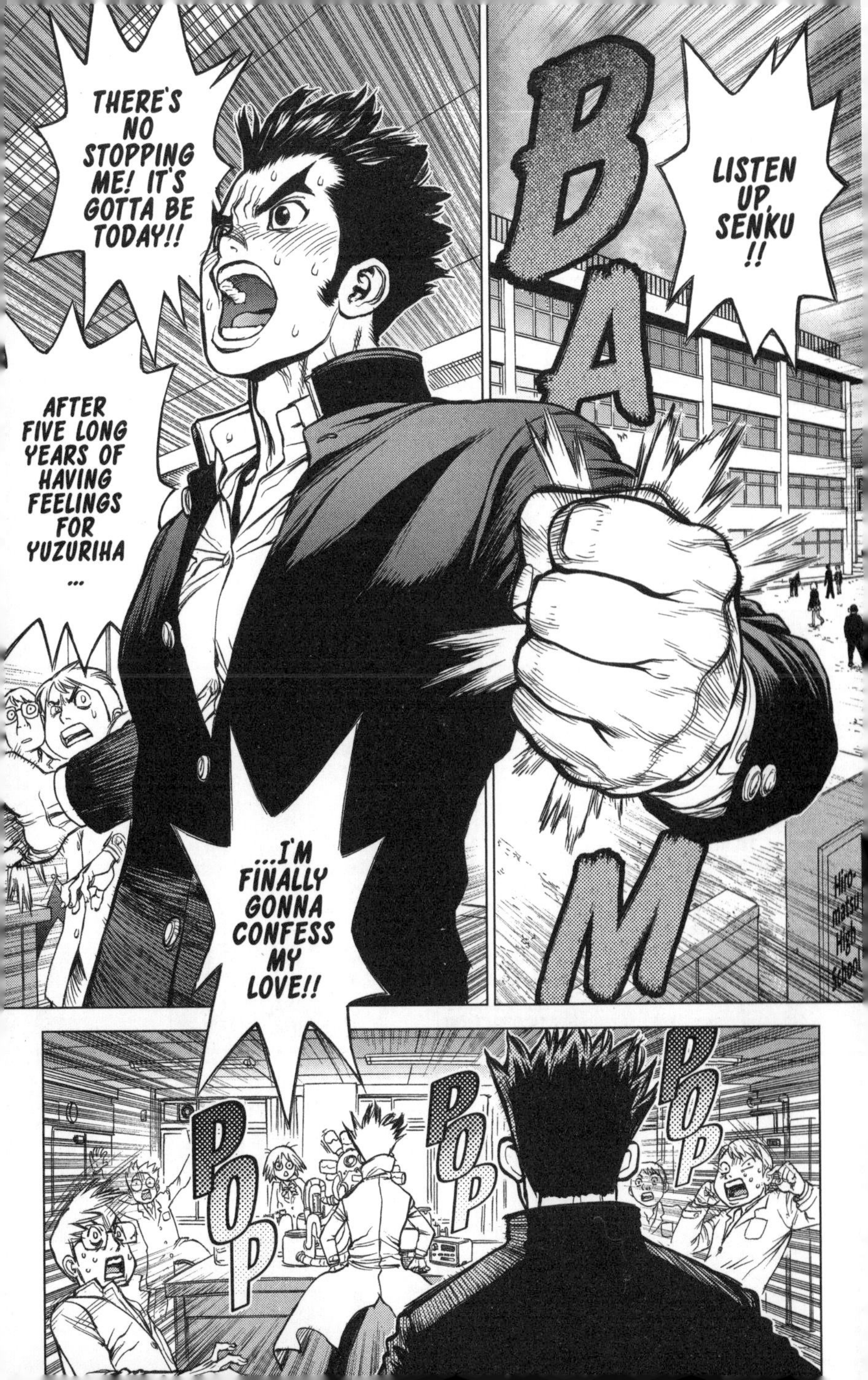
BAM
LISTEN UP, SENKU!!
Hiro-matsu High School
THERE'S NO STOPPING ME! IT'S GOTTA BE TODAY!!
AFTER FIVE LONG YEARS OF HAVING FEELINGS FOR YUZURIHA...
...I'M FINALLY GONNA CONFESS MY LOVE!!
POP
POP
POP

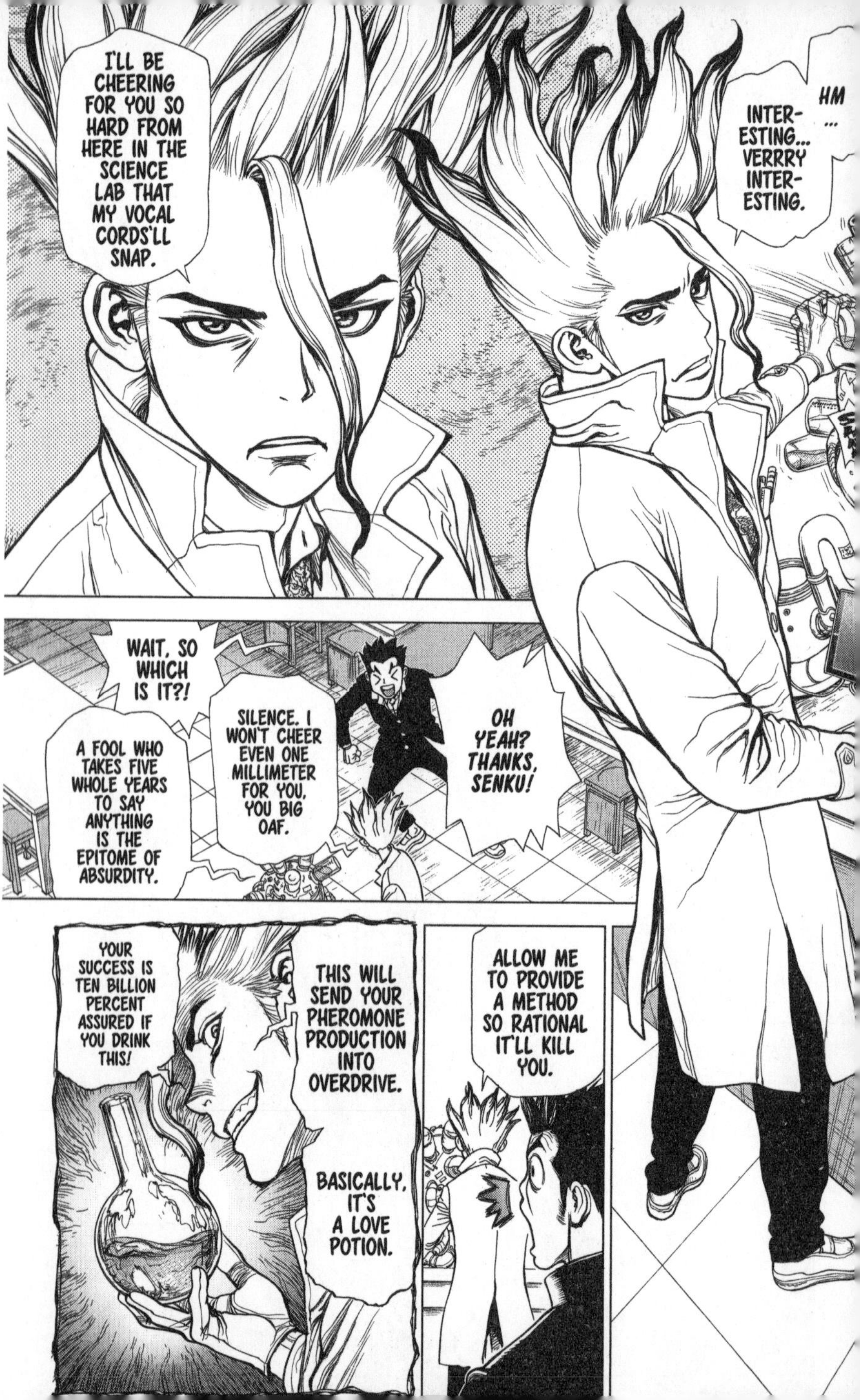
HM ...
INTERESTING... VERRRY INTERESTING.
I'LL BE CHEERING FOR YOU SO HARD FROM HERE IN THE SCIENCE LAB THAT MY VOCAL CORDS'LL SNAP.
OH YEAH? THANKS, SENKU!
SILENCE. I WON'T CHEER EVEN ONE MILLIMETER FOR YOU, YOU BIG OAF.
WAIT, SO WHICH IS IT?!
A FOOL WHO TAKES FIVE WHOLE YEARS TO SAY ANYTHING IS THE EPITOME OF ABSURDITY.
ALLOW ME TO PROVIDE A METHOD SO RATIONAL IT'LL KILL YOU.
THIS WILL SEND YOUR PHEROMONE PRODUCTION INTO OVERDRIVE.
YOUR SUCCESS IS TEN BILLION PERCENT ASSURED IF YOU DRINK THIS!
BASICALLY, IT'S A LOVE POTION.

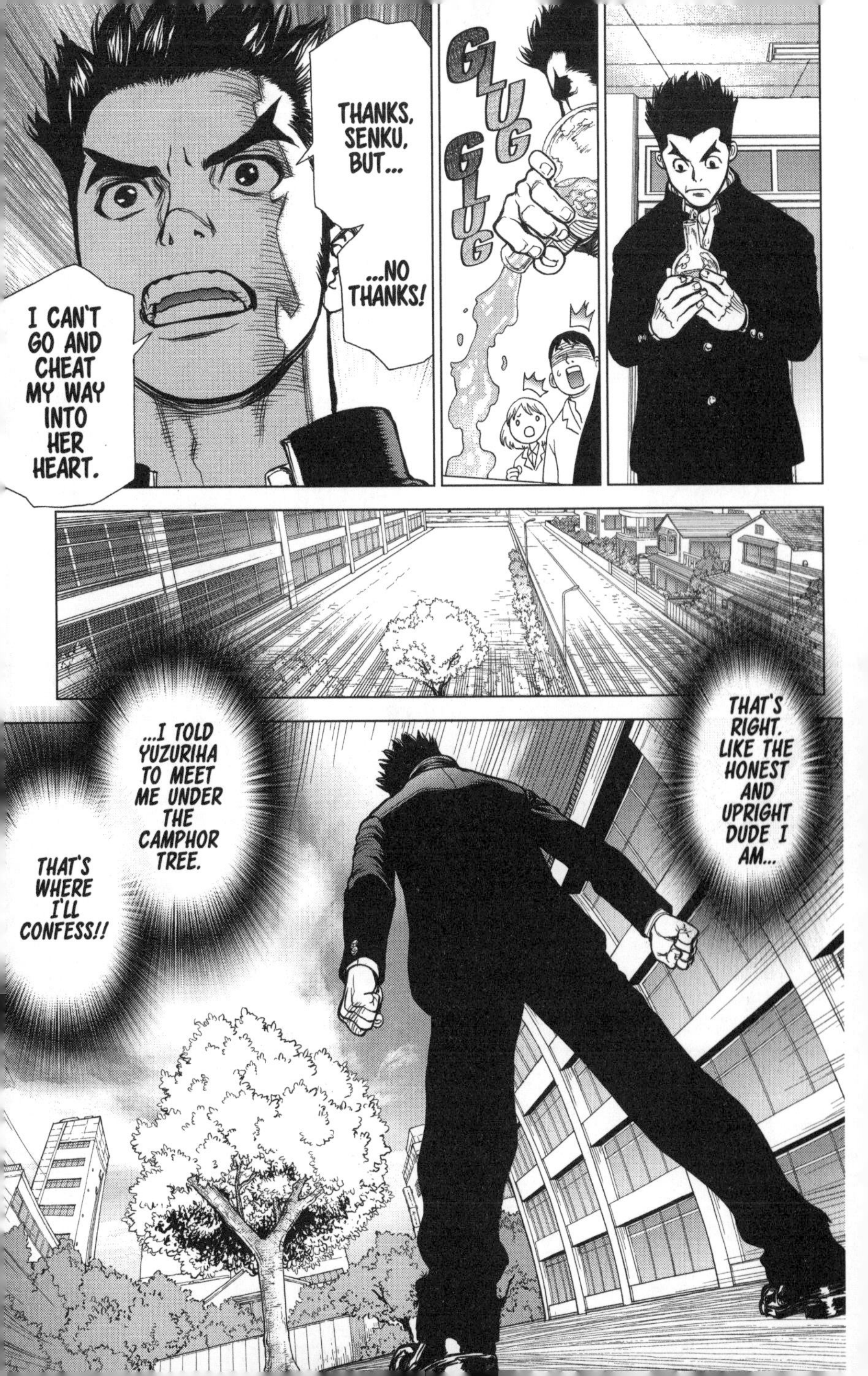
GLUG GLUG
THANKS, SENKU, BUT...
...NO THANKS!
I CAN'T GO AND CHEAT MY WAY INTO HER HEART.
THAT'S RIGHT. LIKE THE HONEST AND UPRIGHT DUDE I AM...
...I TOLD YUZURIHA TO MEET ME UNDER THE CAMPHOR TREE.
THAT'S WHERE I'LL CONFESS!!

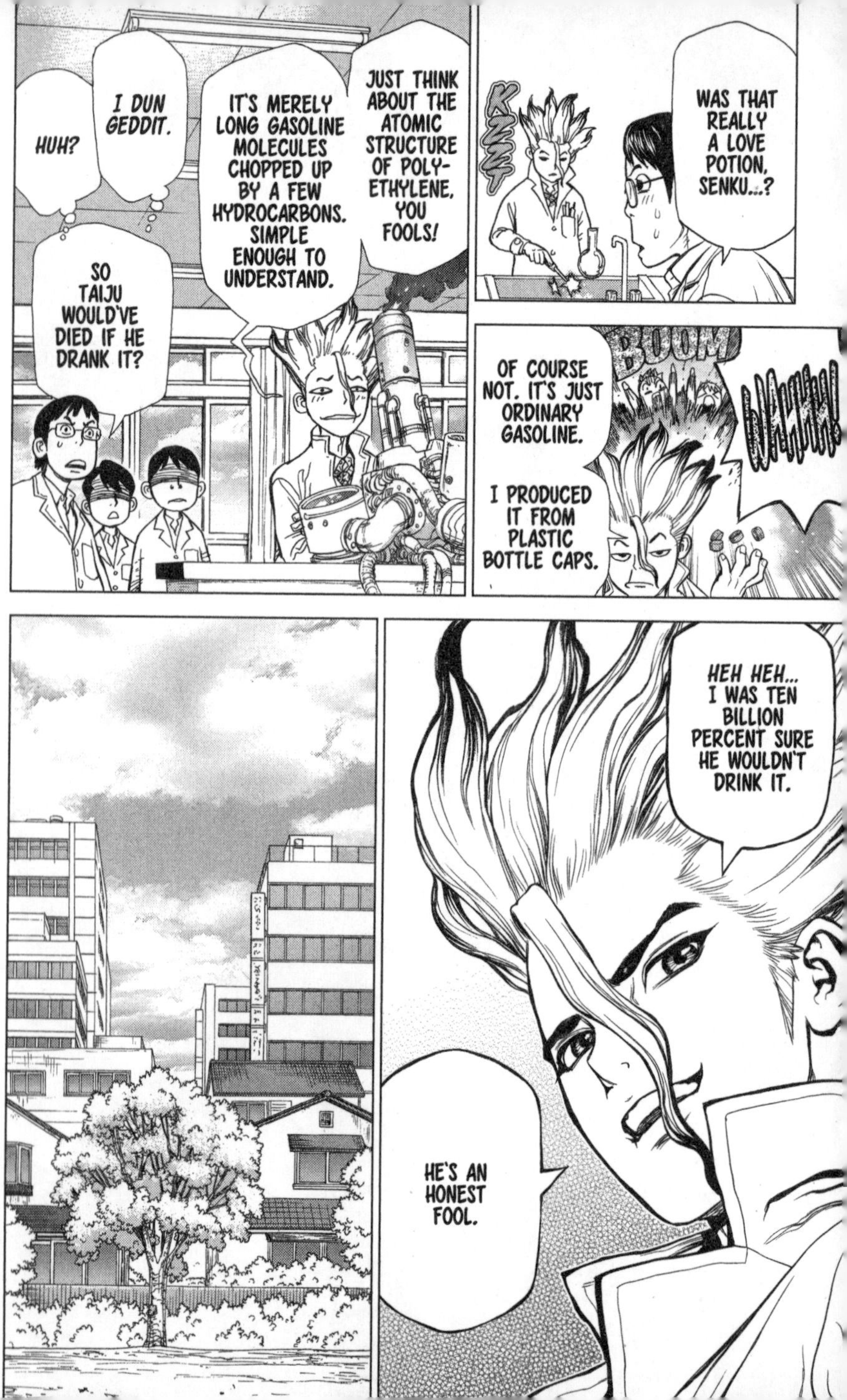
KZZT
WAS THAT REALLY A LOVE POTION, SENKU...?
BOOM
WAHHH!
OF COURSE NOT. IT'S JUST ORDINARY GASOLINE.
I PRODUCED IT FROM PLASTIC BOTTLE CAPS.
JUST THINK ABOUT THE ATOMIC STRUCTURE OF POLY-ETHYLENE, YOU FOOLS!
IT'S MERELY LONG GASOLINE MOLECULES CHOPPED UP BY A FEW HYDROCARBONS. SIMPLE ENOUGH TO UNDERSTAND.
I DUN GEDDIT.
HUH?
SO TAIJU WOULD'VE DIED IF HE DRANK IT?
HEH HEH... I WAS TEN BILLION PERCENT SURE HE WOULDN'T DRINK IT.
HE'S AN HONEST FOOL.

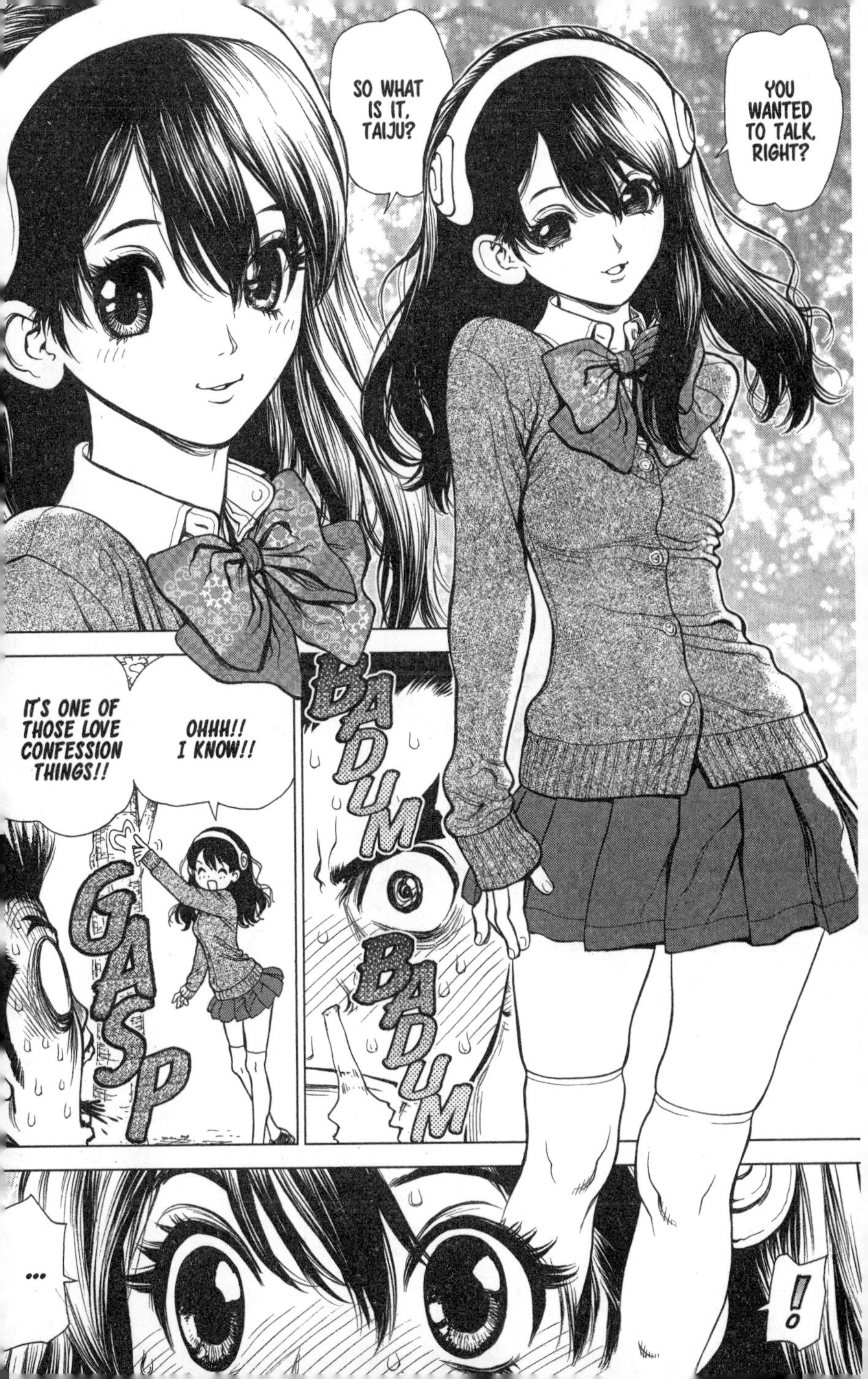
YOU WANTED TO TALK, RIGHT?
SO WHAT IS IT, TAIJU?
BADUM BADUM
OHHH!! I KNOW!!
IT'S ONE OF THOSE LOVE CONFESSION THINGS!!
GASP
!
...

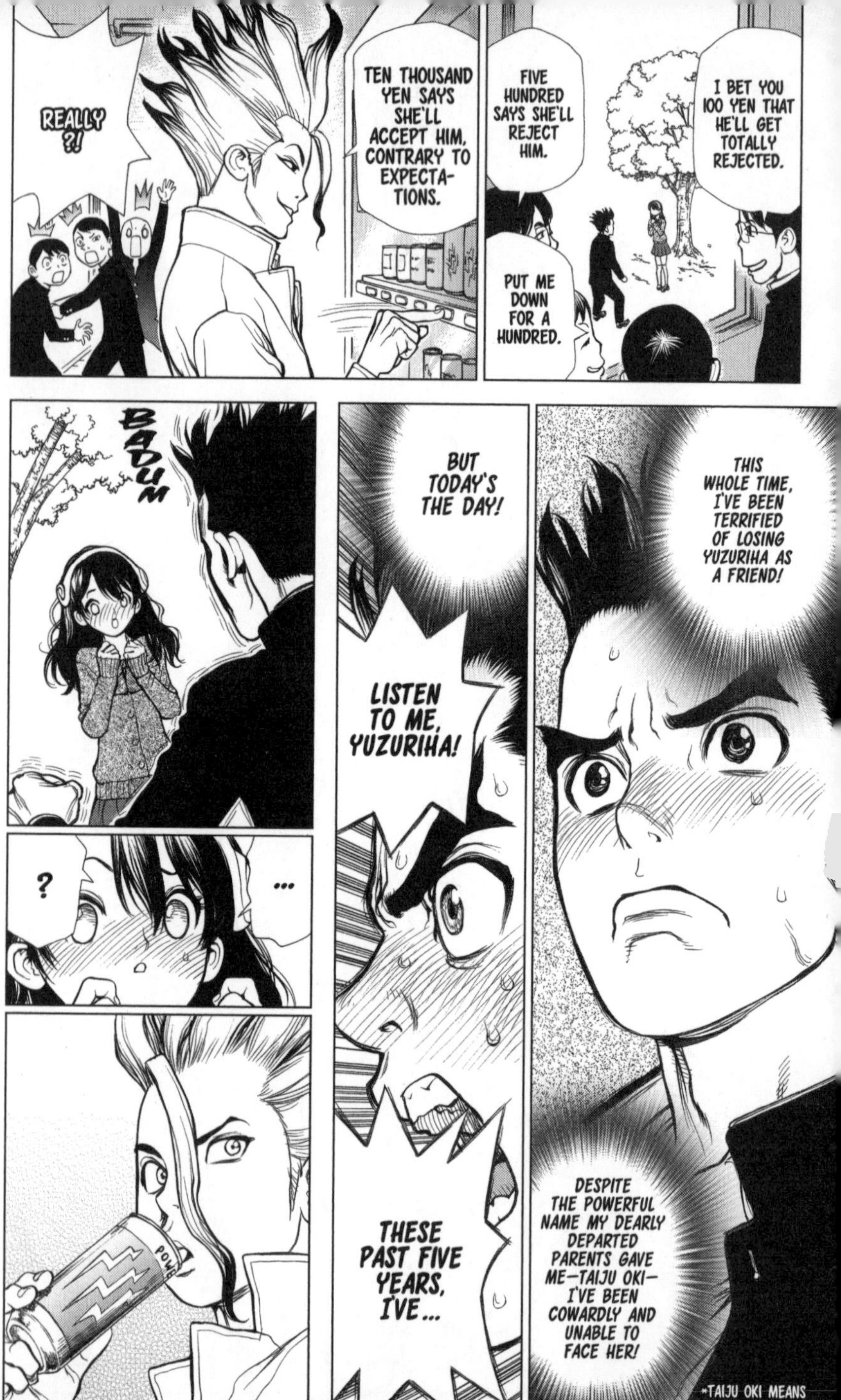
I BET YOU 100 YEN THAT HE'LL GET TOTALLY REJECTED.
FIVE HUNDRED SAYS SHE'LL REJECT HIM.
PUT ME DOWN FOR A HUNDRED.
TEN THOUSAND YEN SAYS SHE'LL ACCEPT HIM, CONTRARY TO EXPECTATIONS.
REALLY ?!
THIS WHOLE TIME, I'VE BEEN TERRIFIED OF LOSING YUZURIHA AS A FRIEND!
DESPITE THE POWERFUL NAME MY DEARLY DEPARTED PARENTS GAVE ME—TAIJU OKI—I'VE BEEN COWARDLY AND UNABLE TO FACE HER!
BUT TODAY'S THE DAY!
LISTEN TO ME, YUZURIHA!
THESE PAST FIVE YEARS, I'VE...
BADUM
...
?

*TAIJU OKI MEANS "BIG-TREE BIG-TREE."

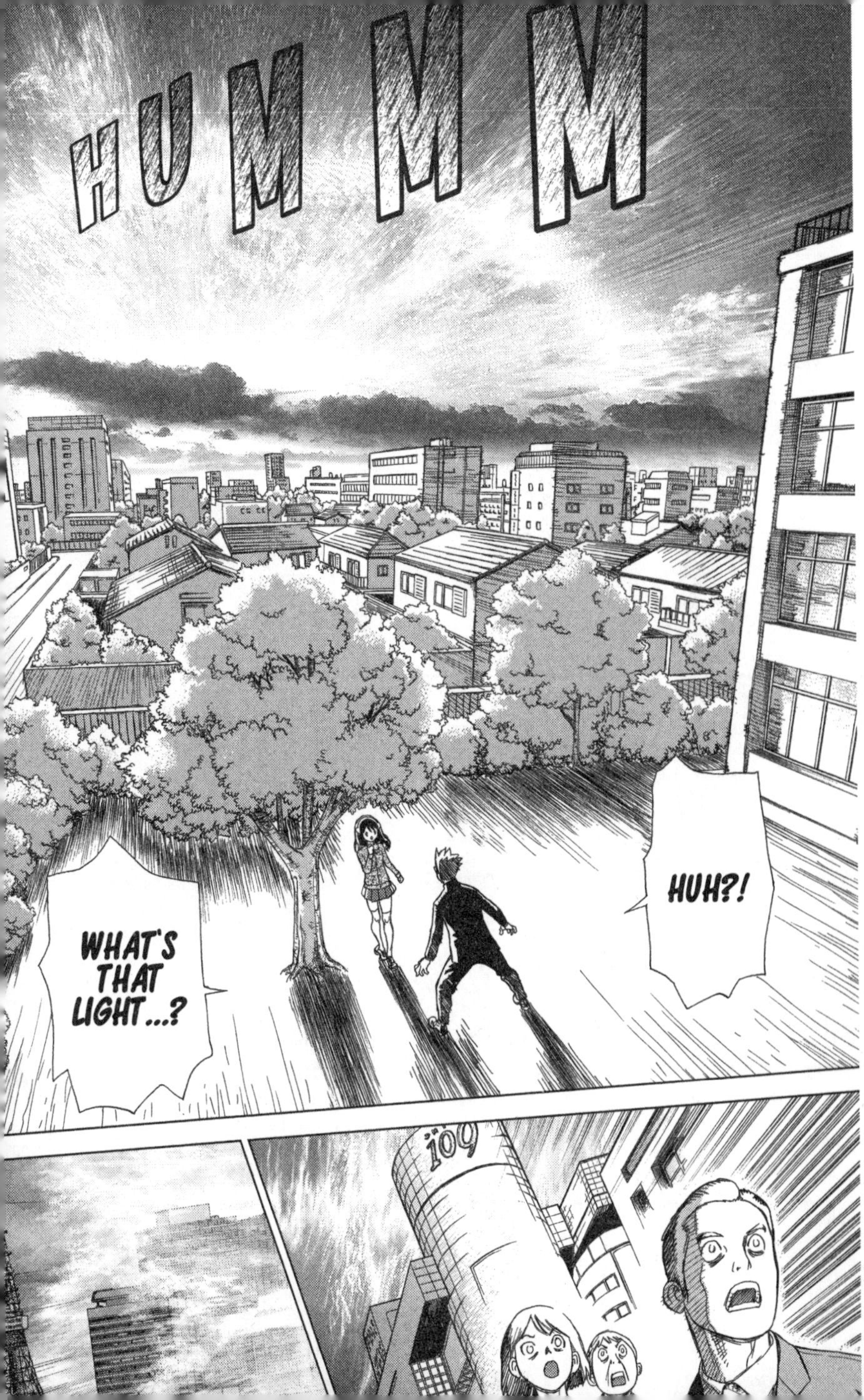
HUMMM
HUH?!
WHAT'S THAT LIGHT...?
109

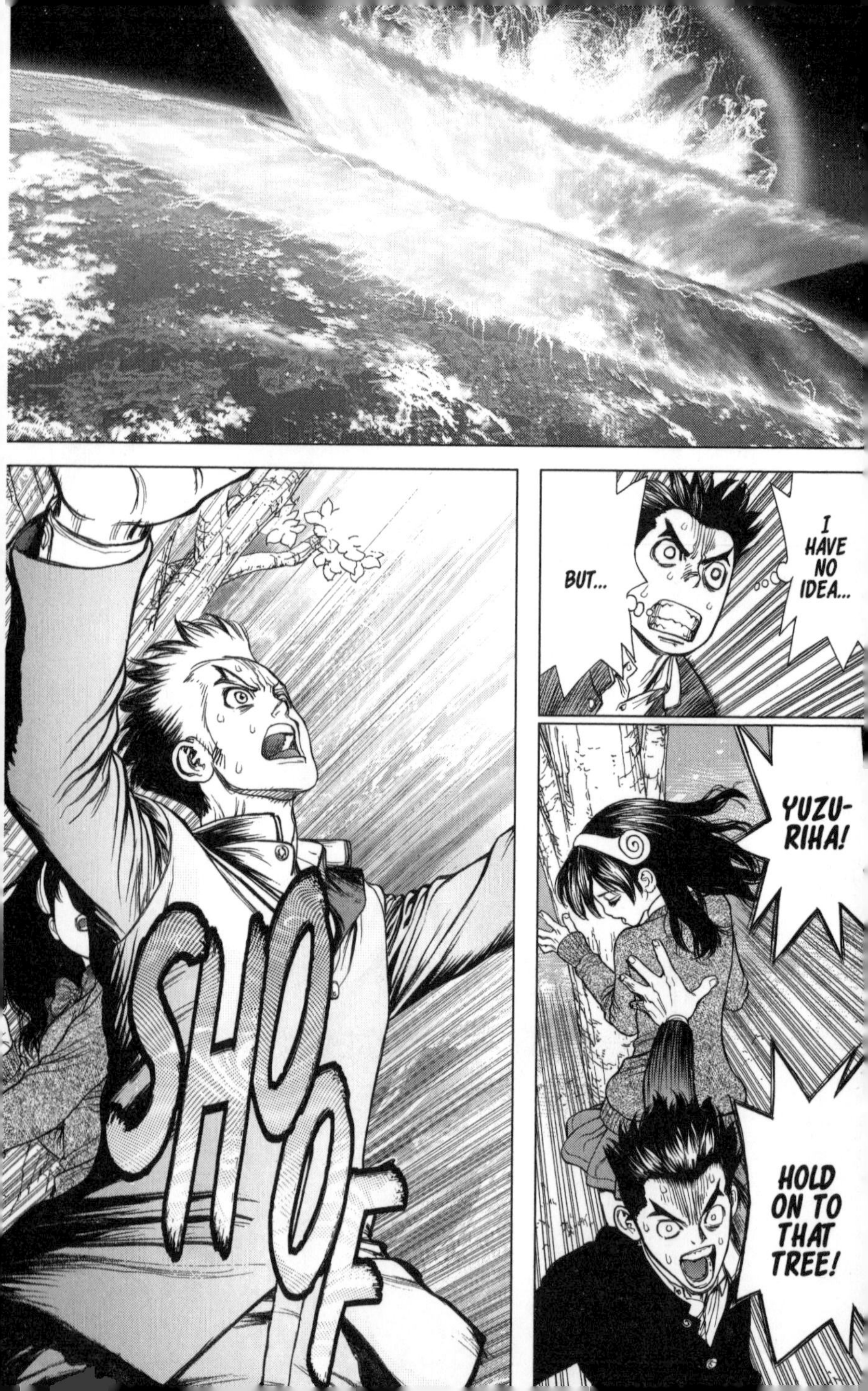
I HAVE NO IDEA...
BUT...
YUZURIHA!
HOLD ON TO THAT TREE!
SHOOF

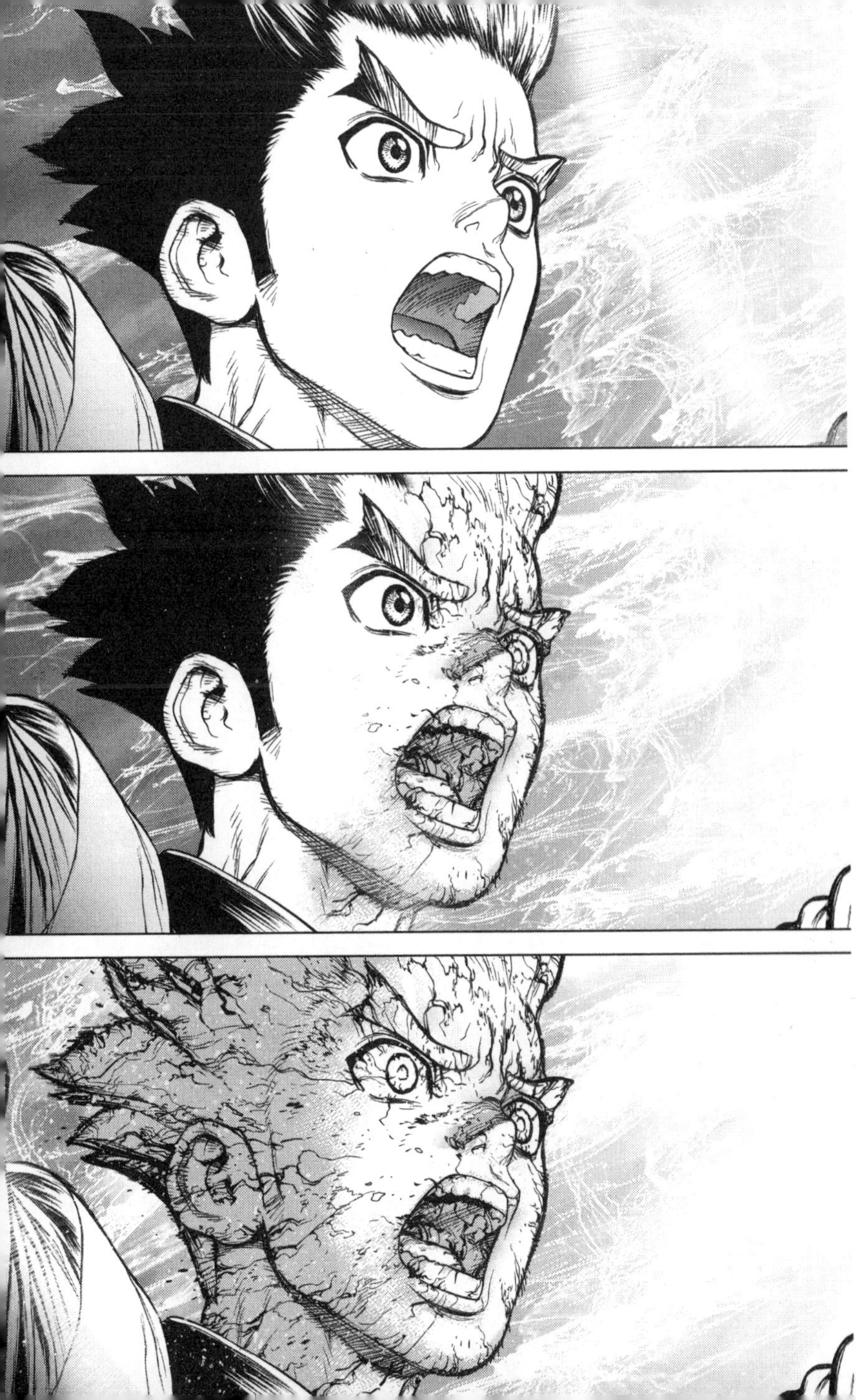

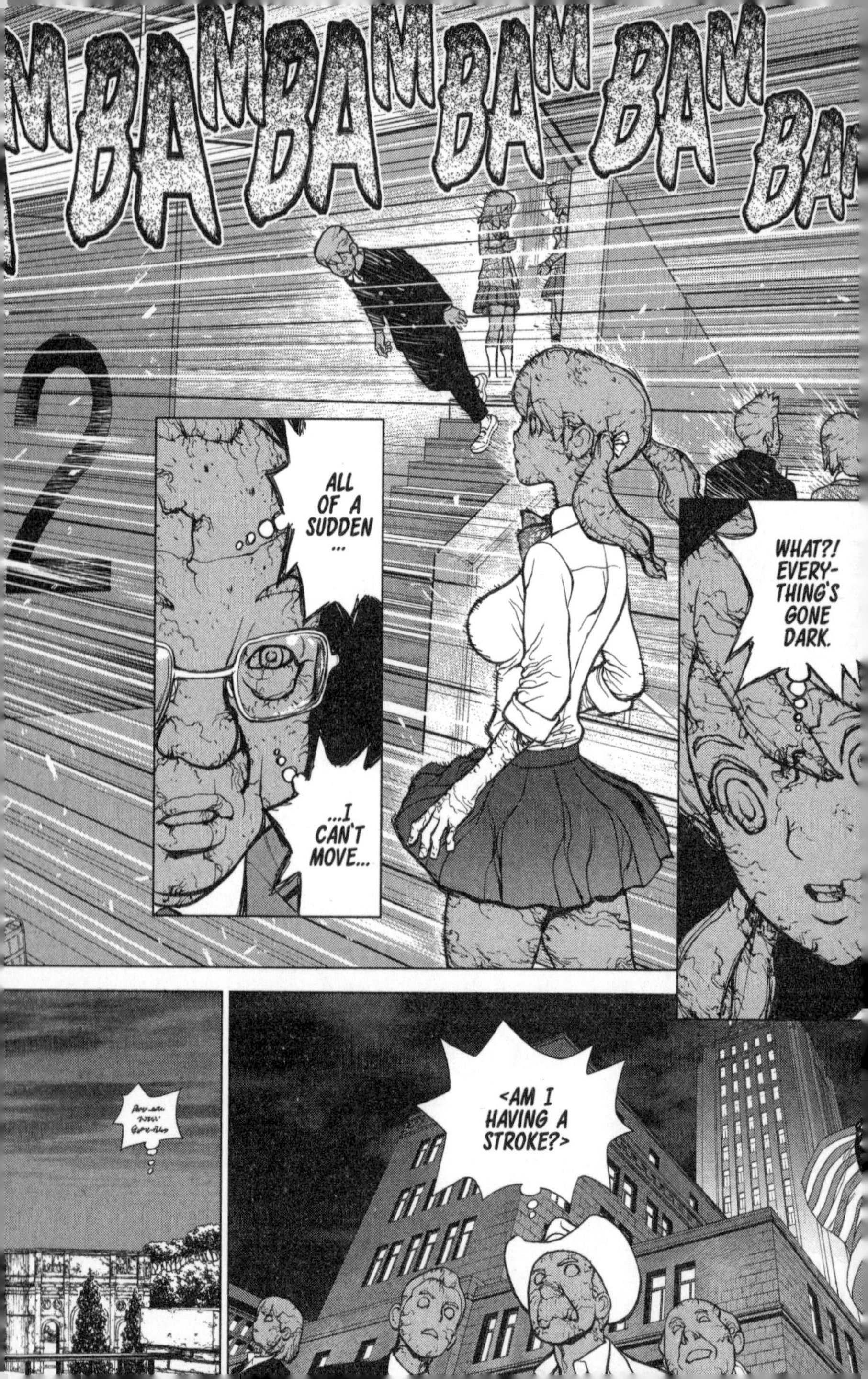
BAM BAM BAM BAM BAM
WHAT?! EVERYTHING'S GONE DARK.
ALL OF A SUDDEN...
...I CAN'T MOVE...
<AM I HAVING A STROKE?>

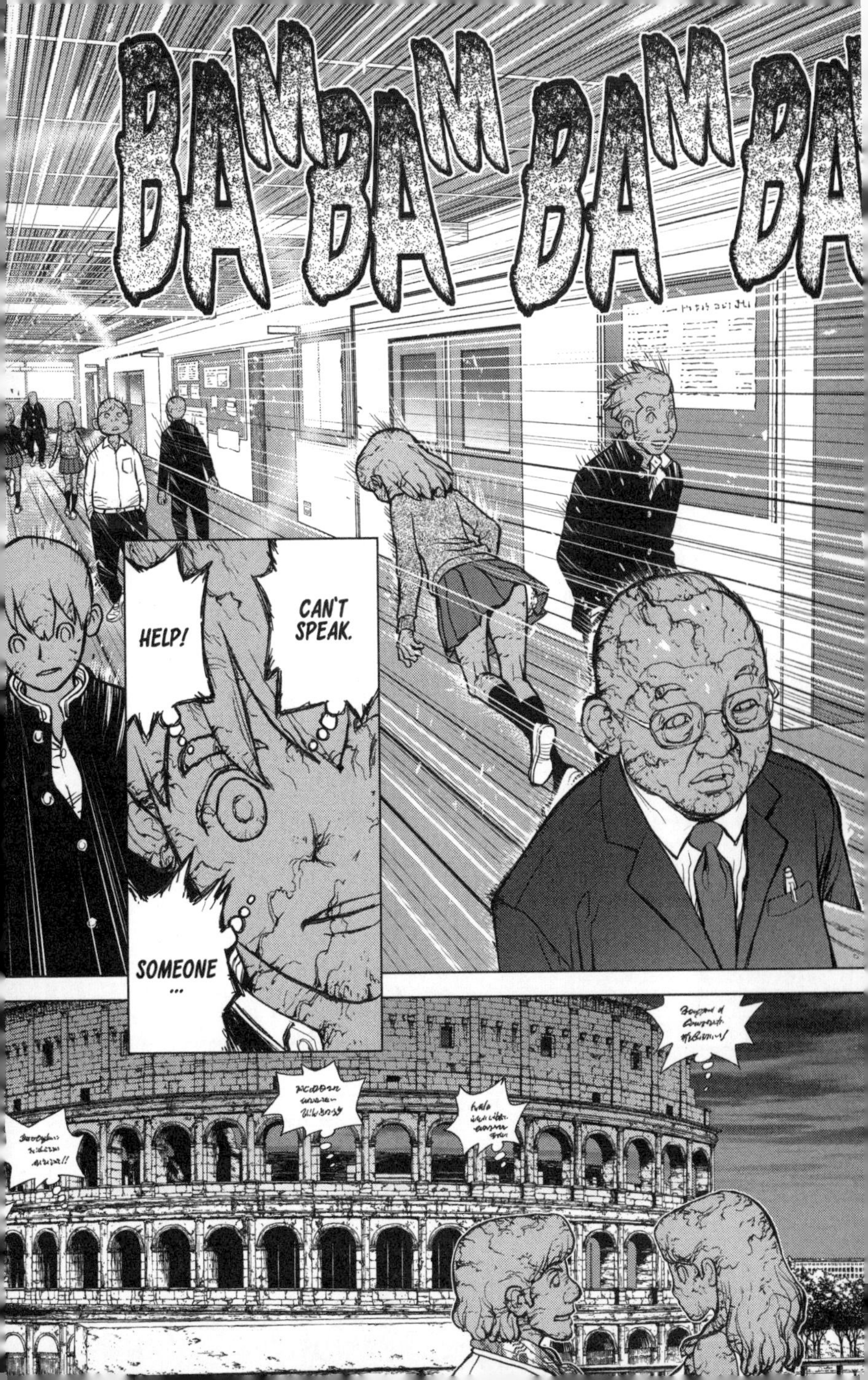
BAM BAM BAM BA
CAN'T SPEAK.
HELP!
SOMEONE ...

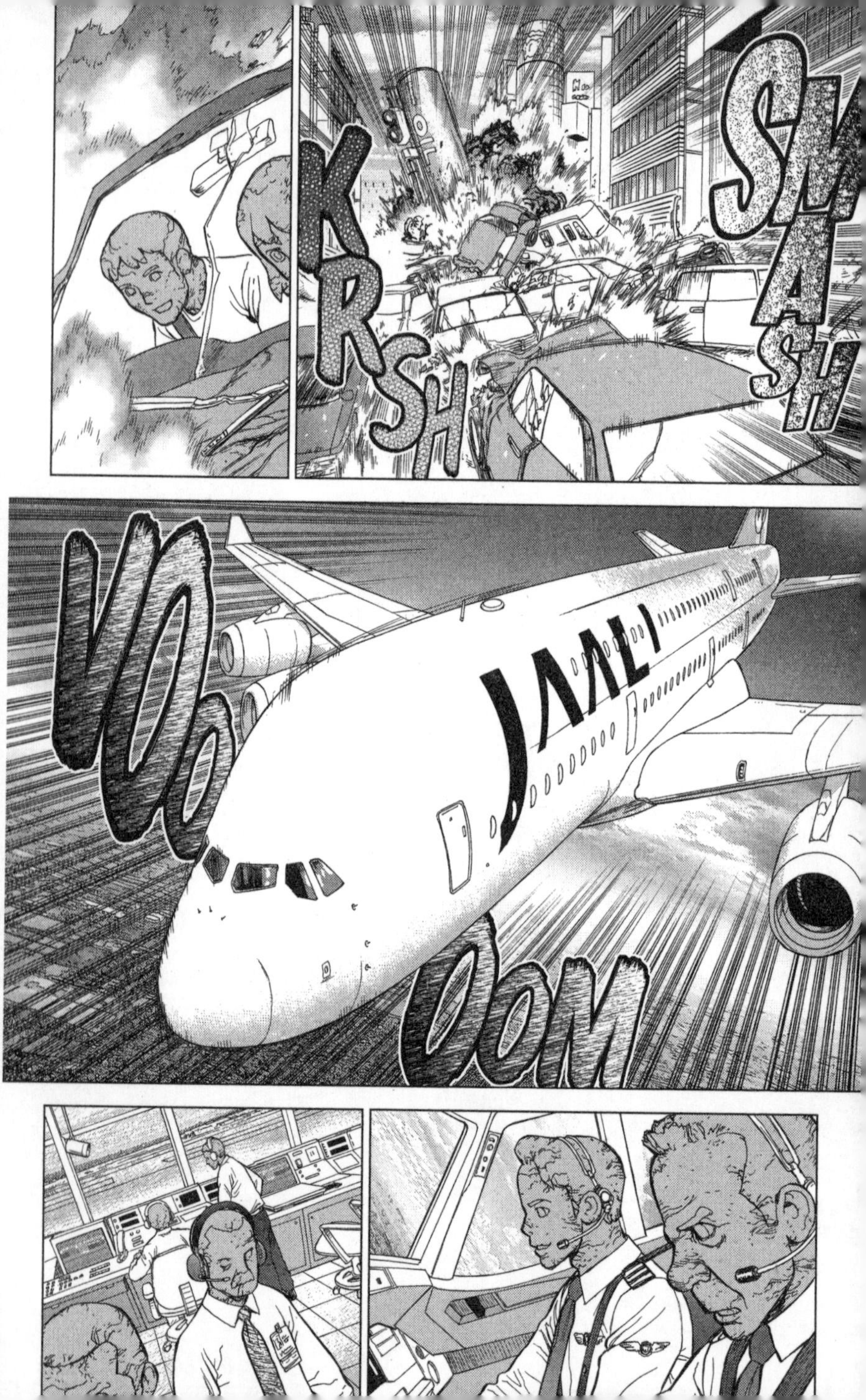
SMASH
KRSH
VOOO
OOM

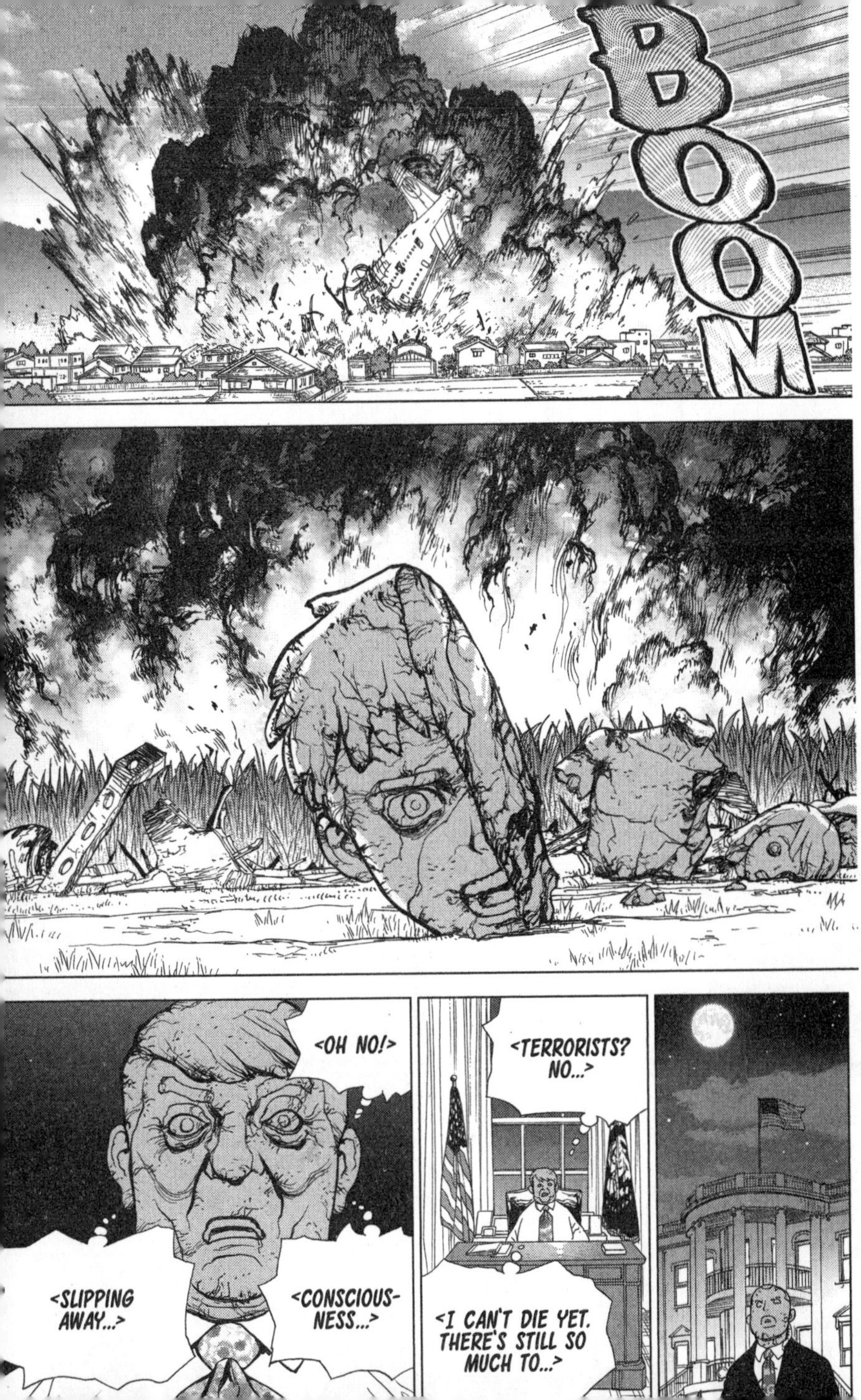
BOOM
<TERRORISTS? NO...>
<I CAN'T DIE YET. THERE'S STILL SO MUCH TO...>
<OH NO!>
<CONSCIOUS-NESS...>
<SLIPPING AWAY...>

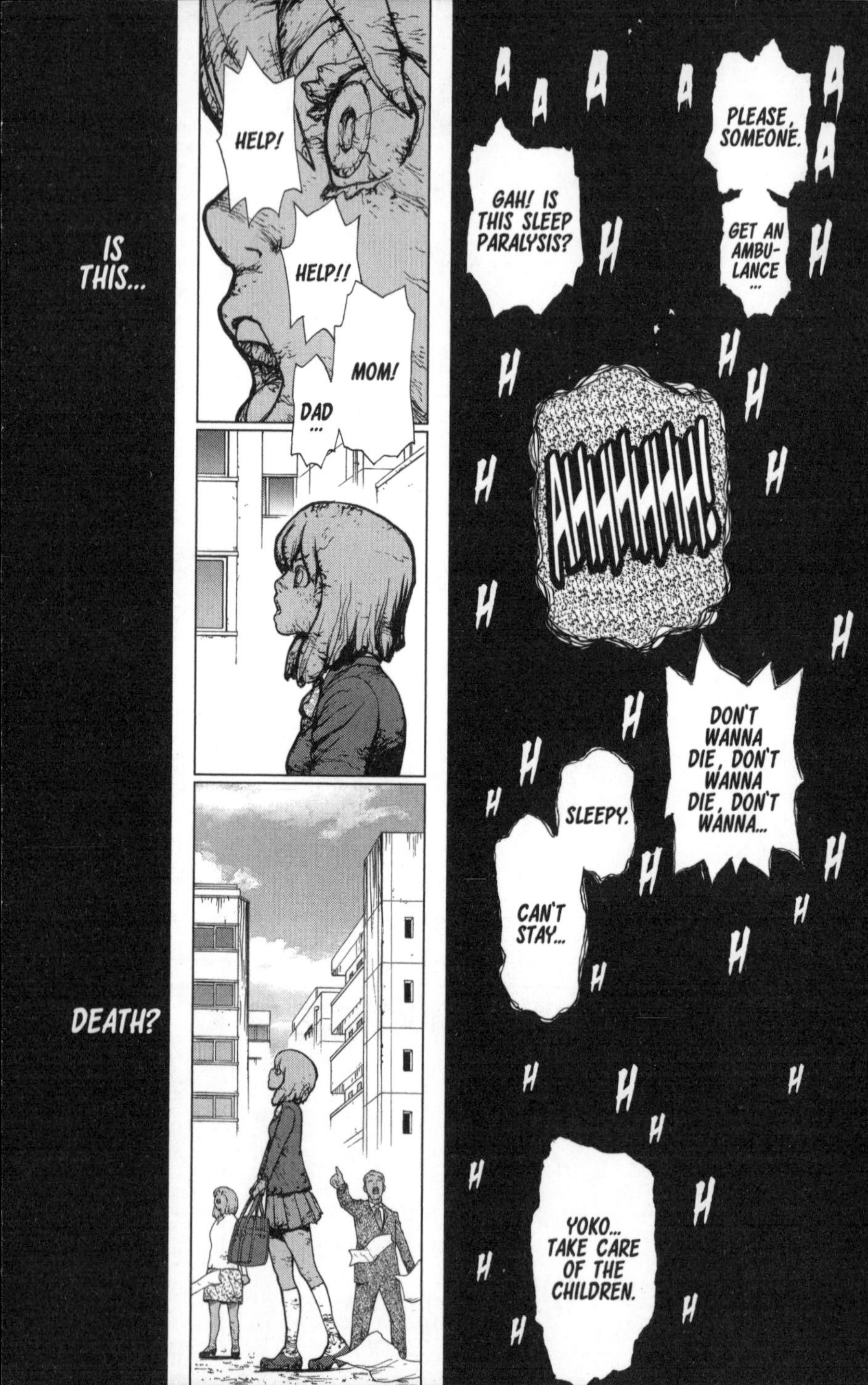
PLEASE, SOMEONE.
GAH! IS THIS SLEEP PARALYSIS?
GET AN AMBULANCE...
AHHHHHHH!
DON'T WANNA DIE, DON'T WANNA DIE, DON'T WANNA...
SLEEPY.
CAN'T STAY...
YOKO... TAKE CARE OF THE CHILDREN.
HELP!
HELP!!
MOM!
DAD...
IS THIS...
DEATH?

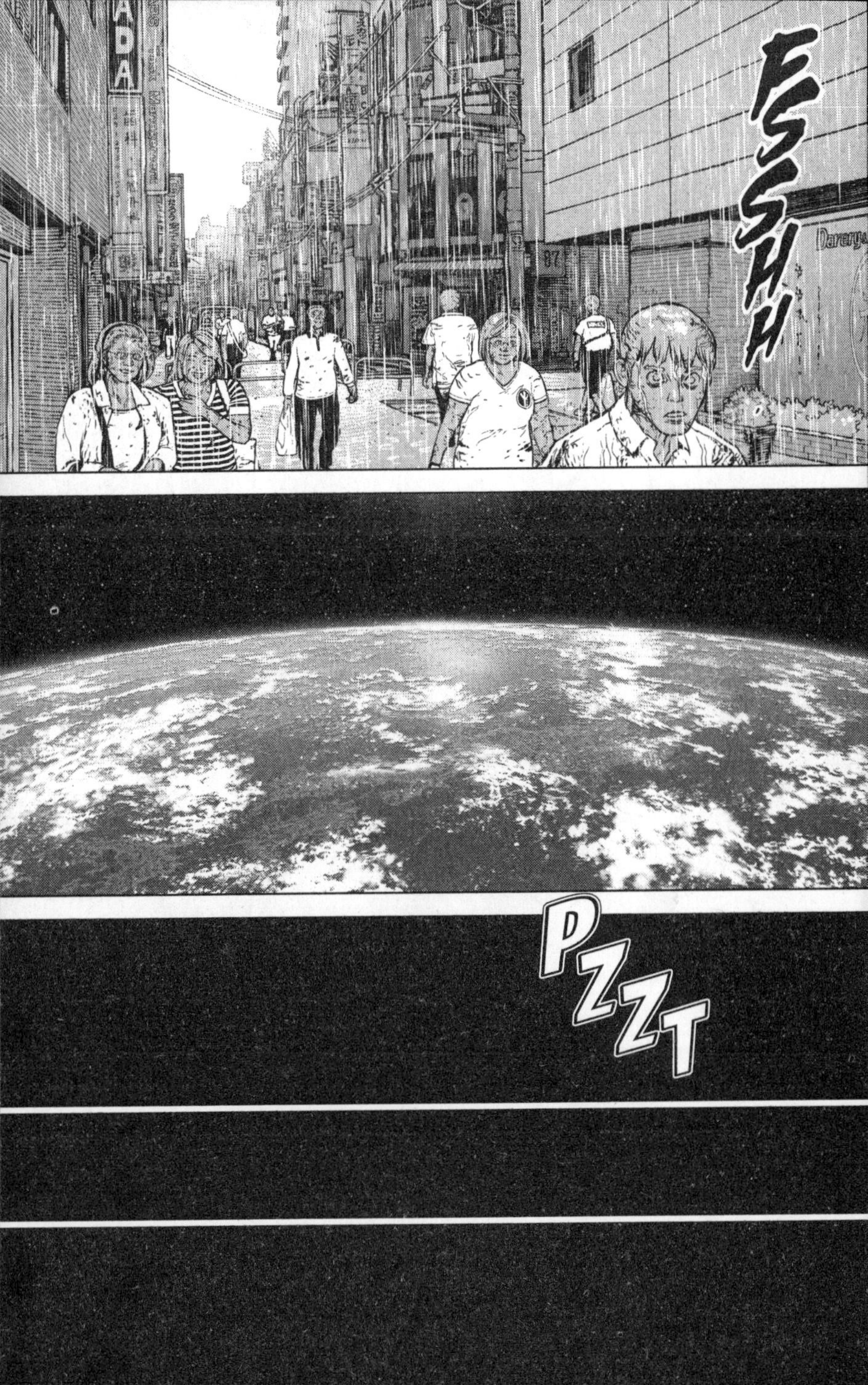
FSSHH
PZZT

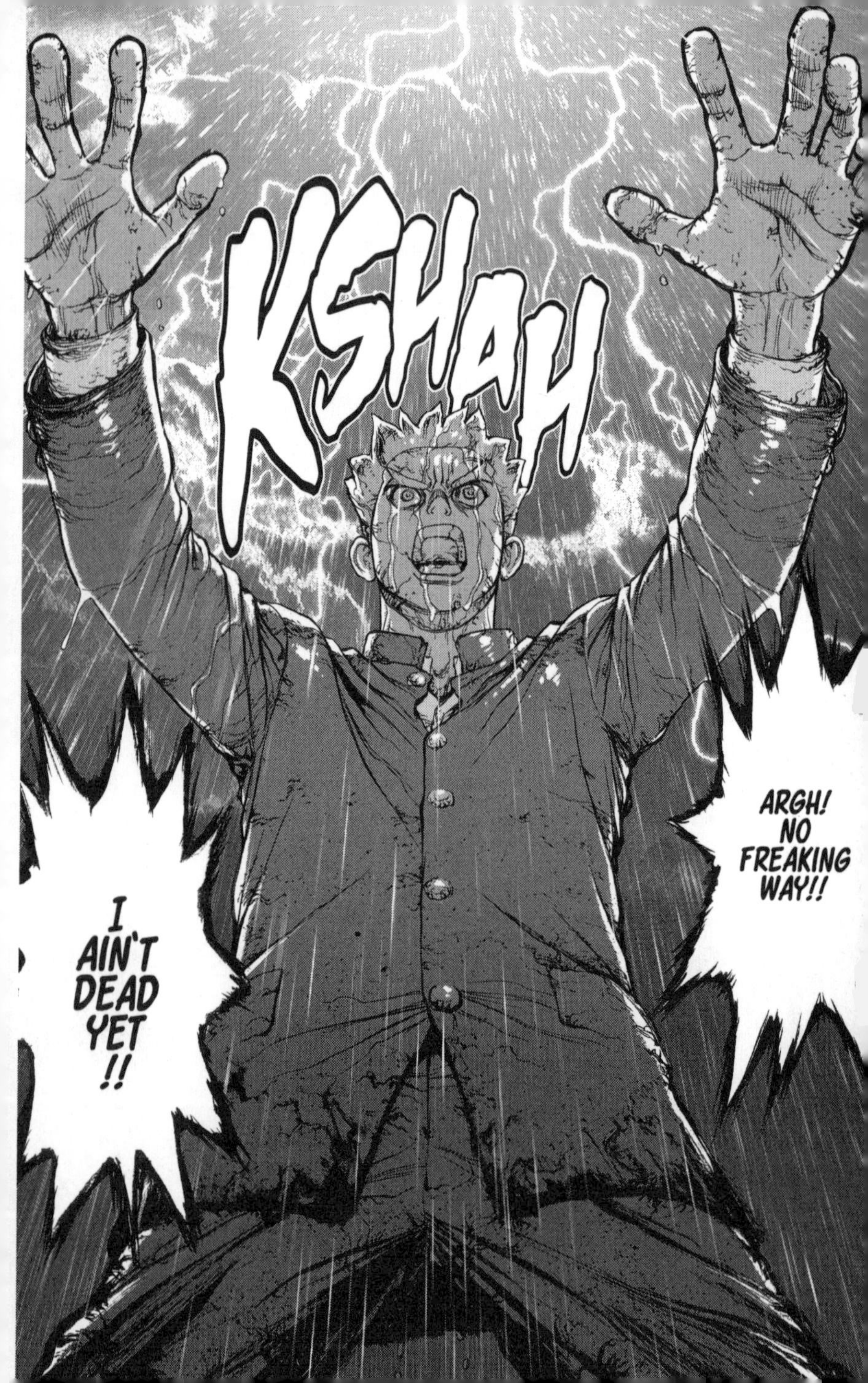
KSHAH
ARGH! NO FREAKING WAY!!
I AIN'T DEAD YET!!

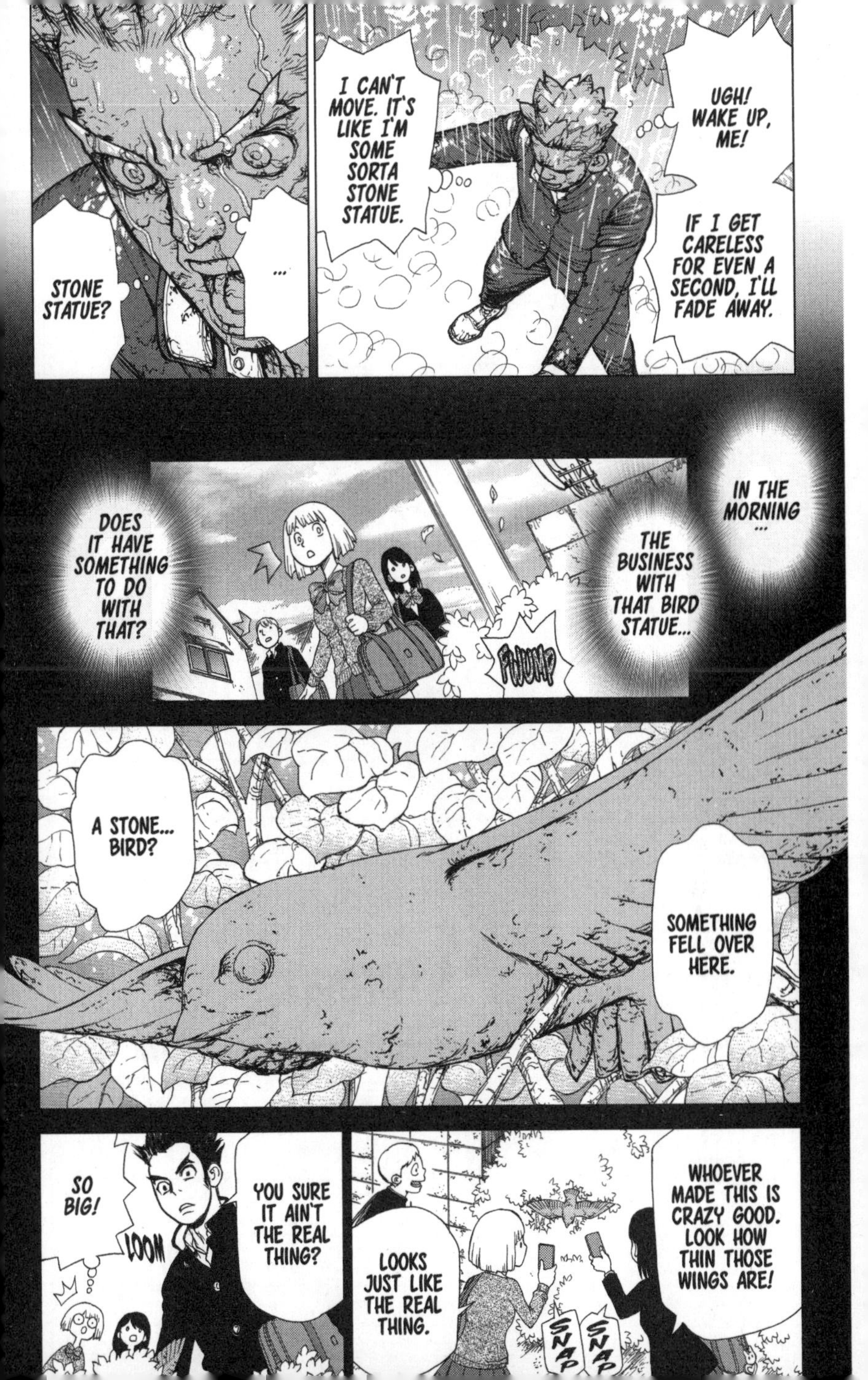
UGH! WAKE UP, ME!
IF I GET CARELESS FOR EVEN A SECOND, I'LL FADE AWAY.
I CAN'T MOVE. IT'S LIKE I'M SOME SORTA STONE STATUE.
...
STONE STATUE?
IN THE MORNING...
THE BUSINESS WITH THAT BIRD STATUE...
FWUMP
DOES IT HAVE SOMETHING TO DO WITH THAT?
SOMETHING FELL OVER HERE.
A STONE... BIRD?
WHOEVER MADE THIS IS CRAZY GOOD. LOOK HOW THIN THOSE WINGS ARE!
SNAP
SNAP
LOOKS JUST LIKE THE REAL THING.
YOU SURE IT AIN'T THE REAL THING?
LOOM
SO BIG!

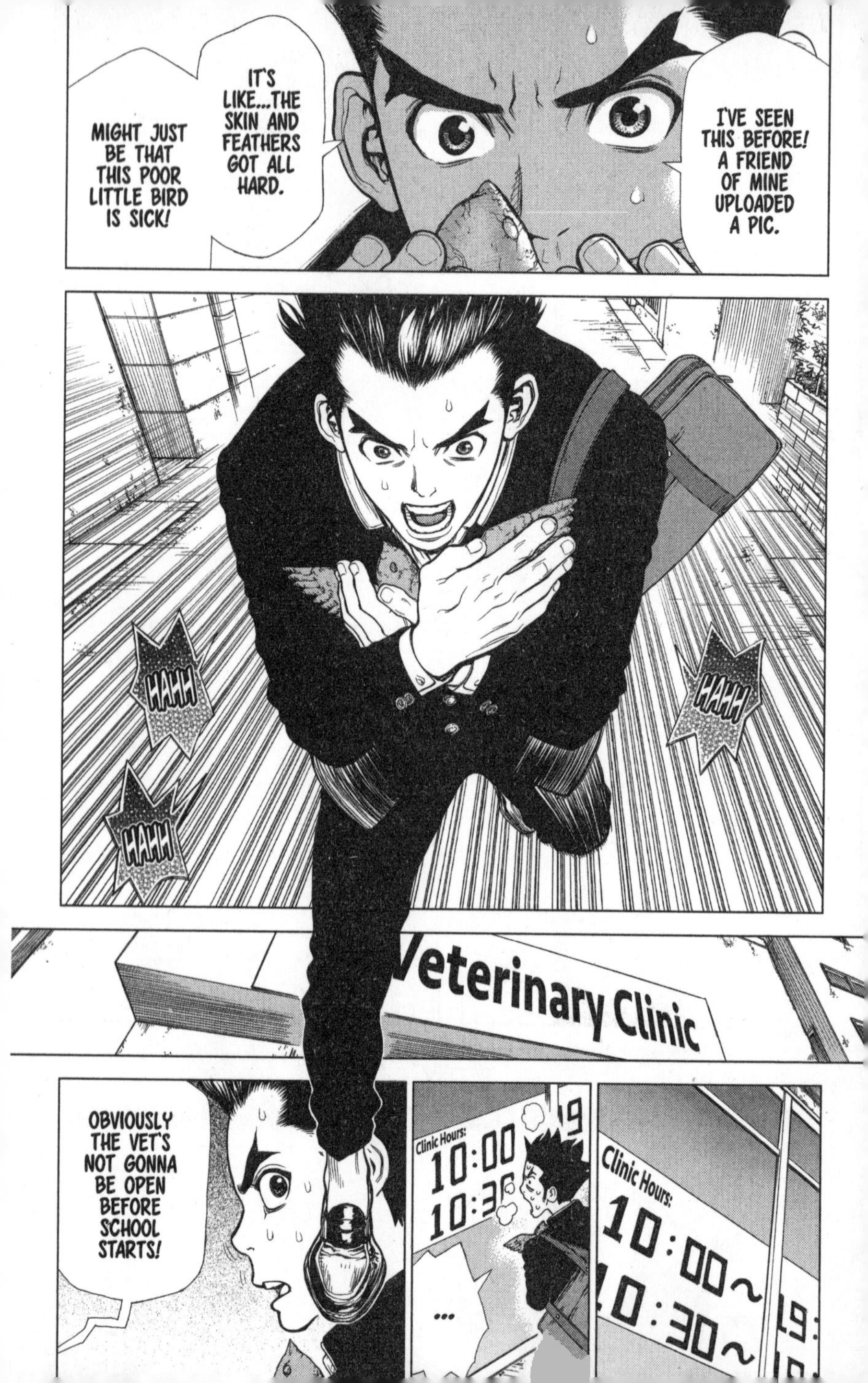
I'VE SEEN THIS BEFORE! A FRIEND OF MINE UPLOADED A PIC.
IT'S LIKE...THE SKIN AND FEATHERS GOT ALL HARD.
MIGHT JUST BE THAT THIS POOR LITTLE BIRD IS SICK!
HAHH
HAHH
HAHH
Veterinary Clinic
Clinic Hours:
10:00~
10:30~
Clinic Hours:
10:00
...
OBVIOUSLY THE VET'S NOT GONNA BE OPEN BEFORE SCHOOL STARTS!

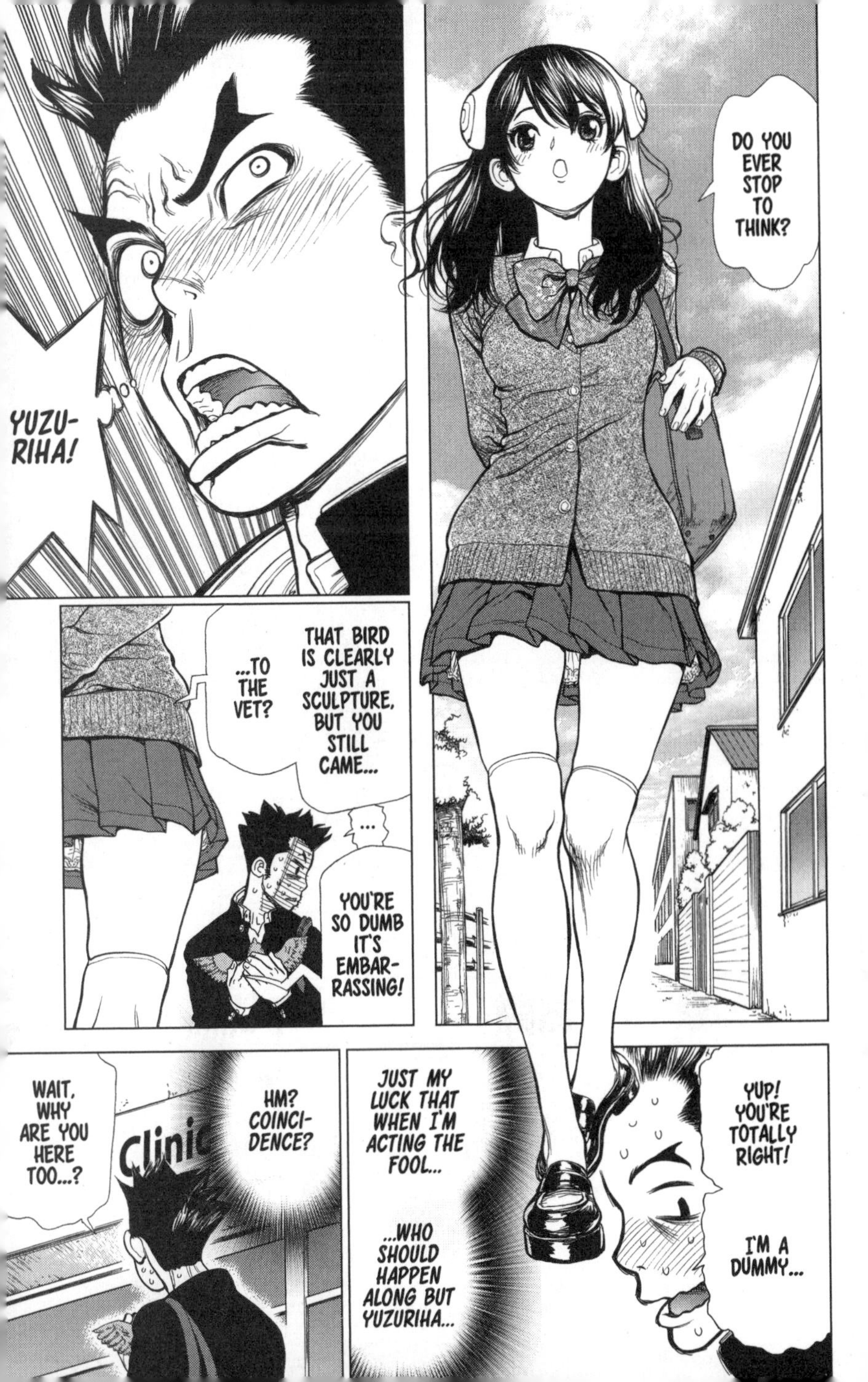
DO YOU EVER STOP TO THINK?
YUZU-RIHA!
THAT BIRD IS CLEARLY JUST A SCULPTURE, BUT YOU STILL CAME...
...TO THE VET?
...
YOU'RE SO DUMB IT'S EMBAR-RASSING!
YUP! YOU'RE TOTALLY RIGHT!
I'M A DUMMY...
JUST MY LUCK THAT WHEN I'M ACTING THE FOOL...
...WHO SHOULD HAPPEN ALONG BUT YUZURIHA...
HM? COINCI-DENCE?
Clinic
WAIT, WHY ARE YOU HERE TOO...?

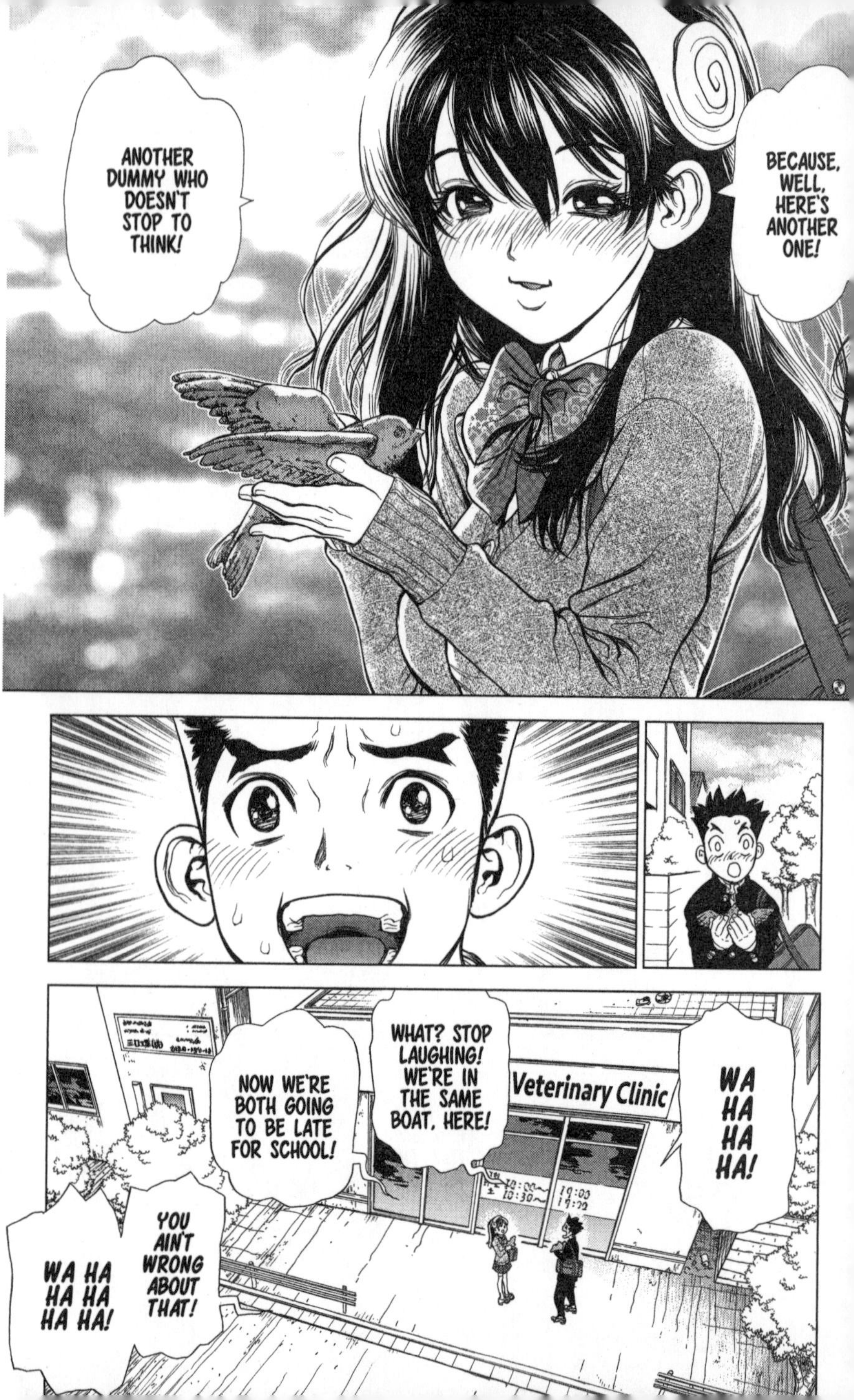
BECAUSE, WELL, HERE'S ANOTHER ONE!
ANOTHER DUMMY WHO DOESN'T STOP TO THINK!
WA HA HA HA!
Veterinary Clinic
WHAT? STOP LAUGHING! WE'RE IN THE SAME BOAT, HERE!
NOW WE'RE BOTH GOING TO BE LATE FOR SCHOOL!
YOU AIN'T WRONG ABOUT THAT!
WA HA HA HA HA HA!

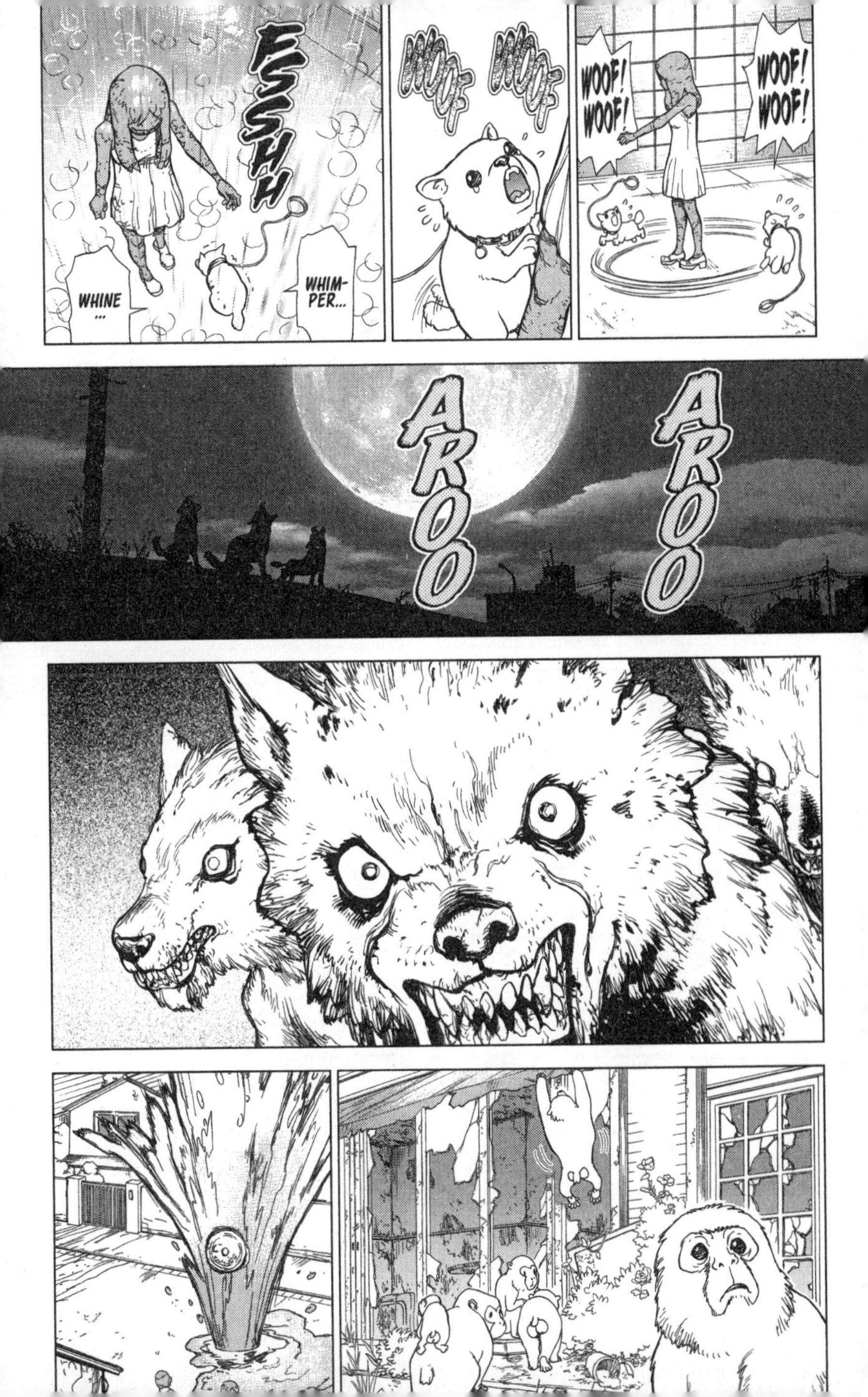
WOOF! WOOF!
WOOF! WOOF!
WOOF WOOF
FSSHH
WHIM-PER...
WHINE ...
AROO
AROO

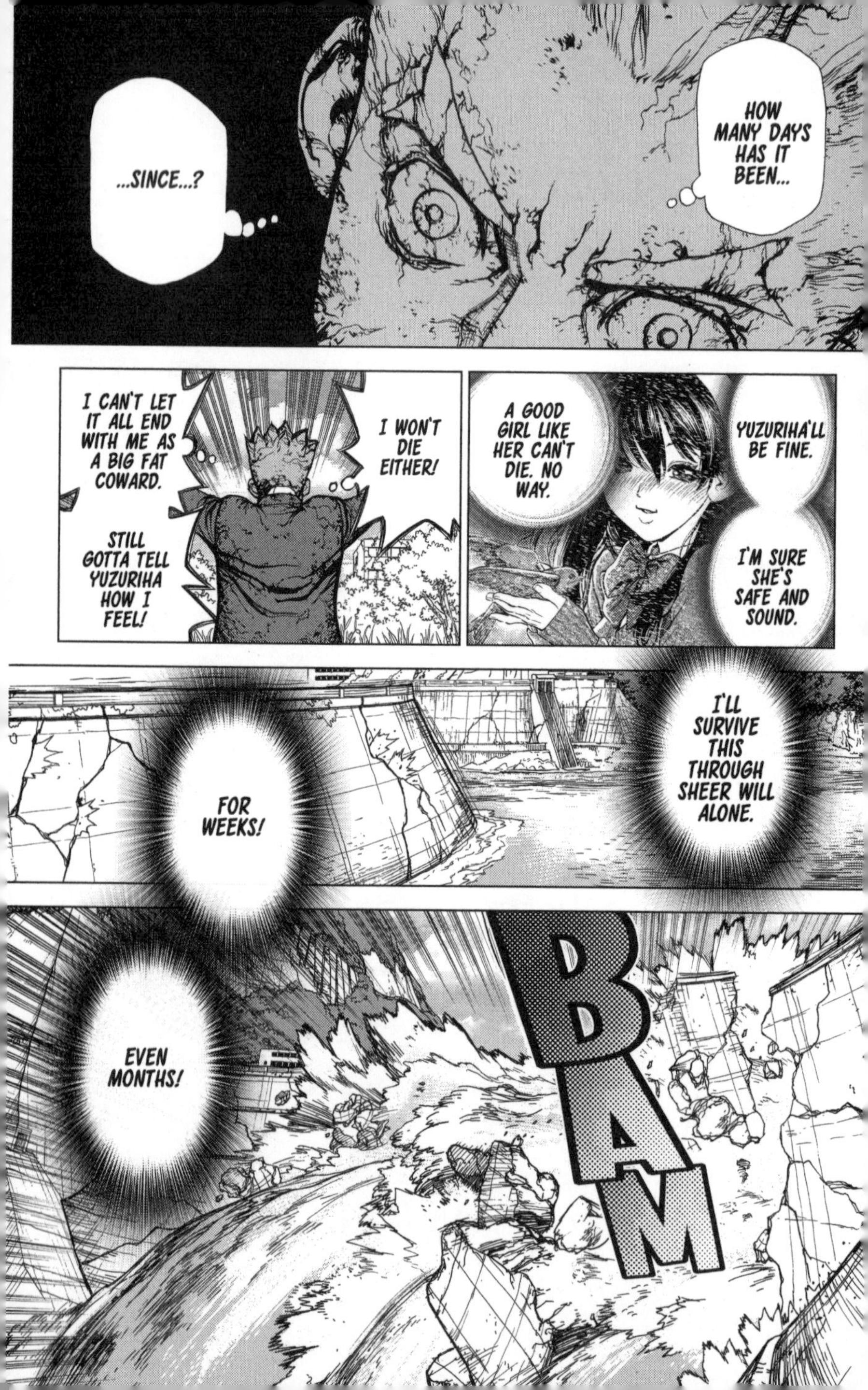
HOW MANY DAYS HAS IT BEEN...
...SINCE...?
YUZURIHA'LL BE FINE.
I'M SURE SHE'S SAFE AND SOUND.
A GOOD GIRL LIKE HER CAN'T DIE. NO WAY.
I WON'T DIE EITHER!
I CAN'T LET IT ALL END WITH ME AS A BIG FAT COWARD.
STILL GOTTA TELL YUZURIHA HOW I FEEL!
I'LL SURVIVE THIS THROUGH SHEER WILL ALONE.
FOR WEEKS!
BAM
EVEN MONTHS!

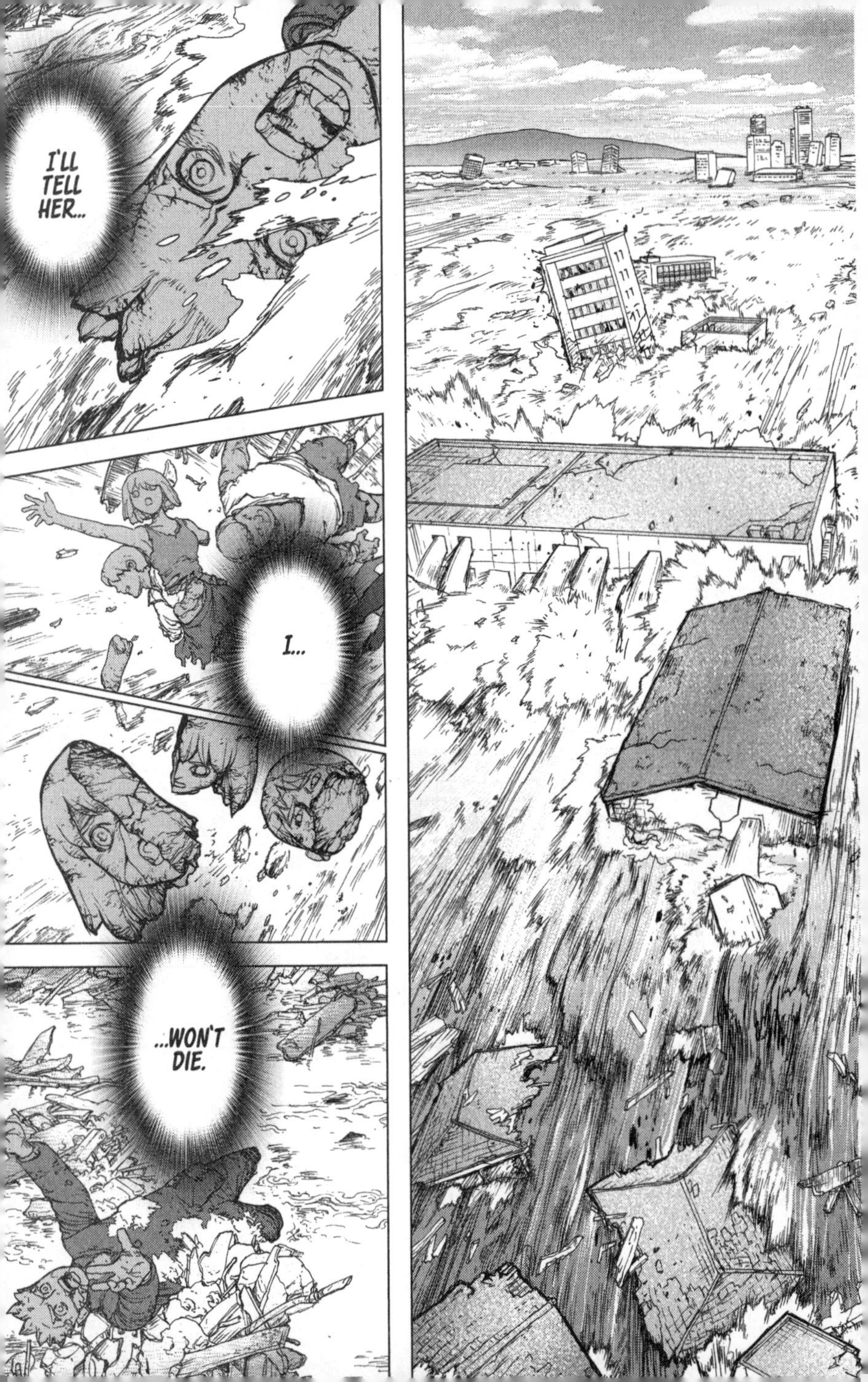
I'LL TELL HER...
I...
...WON'T DIE.

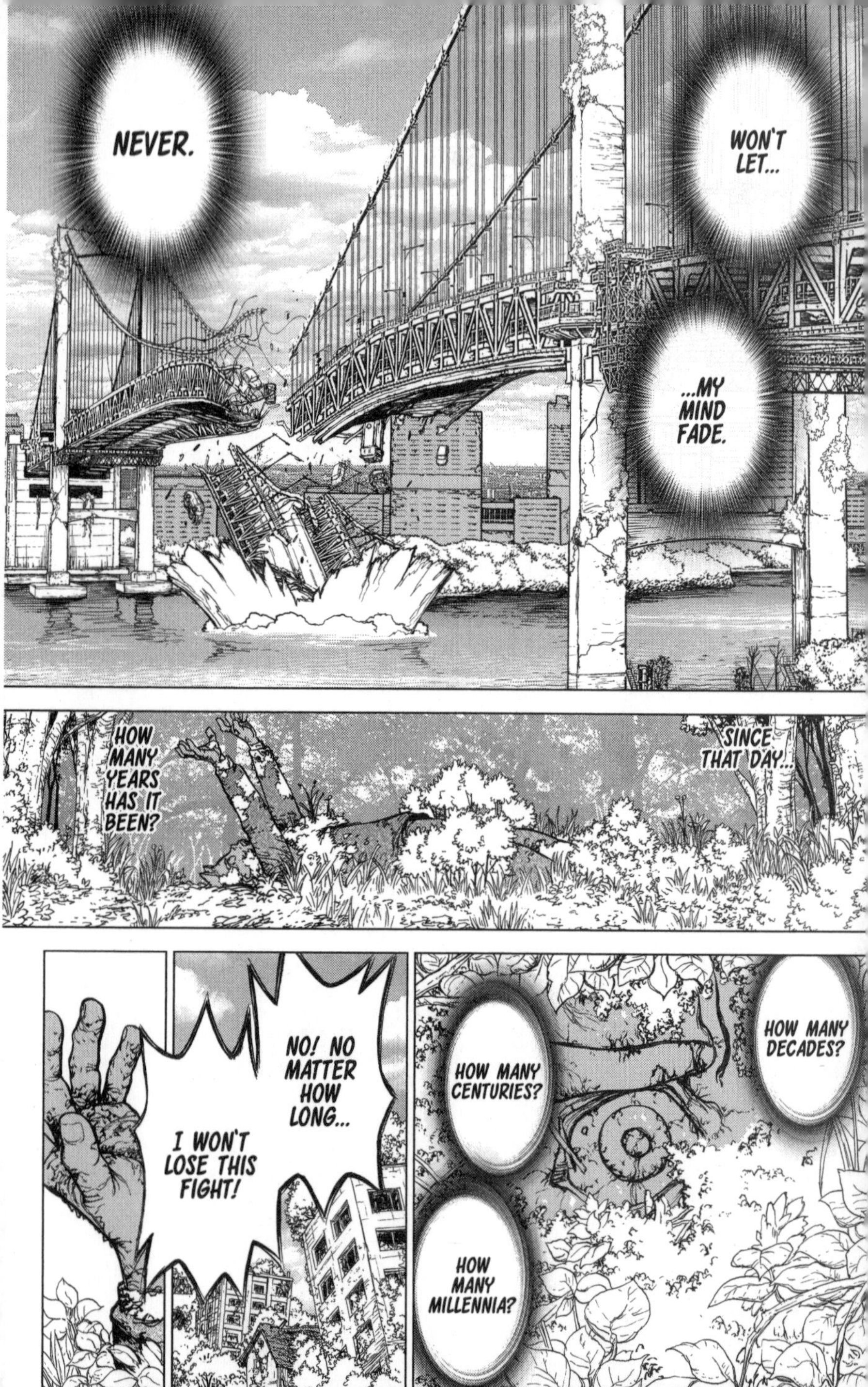
WON'T LET...
...MY MIND FADE.
NEVER.
SINCE THAT DAY...
HOW MANY YEARS HAS IT BEEN?
HOW MANY DECADES?
HOW MANY CENTURIES?
HOW MANY MILLENNIA?
NO! NO MATTER HOW LONG...
I WON'T LOSE THIS FIGHT!

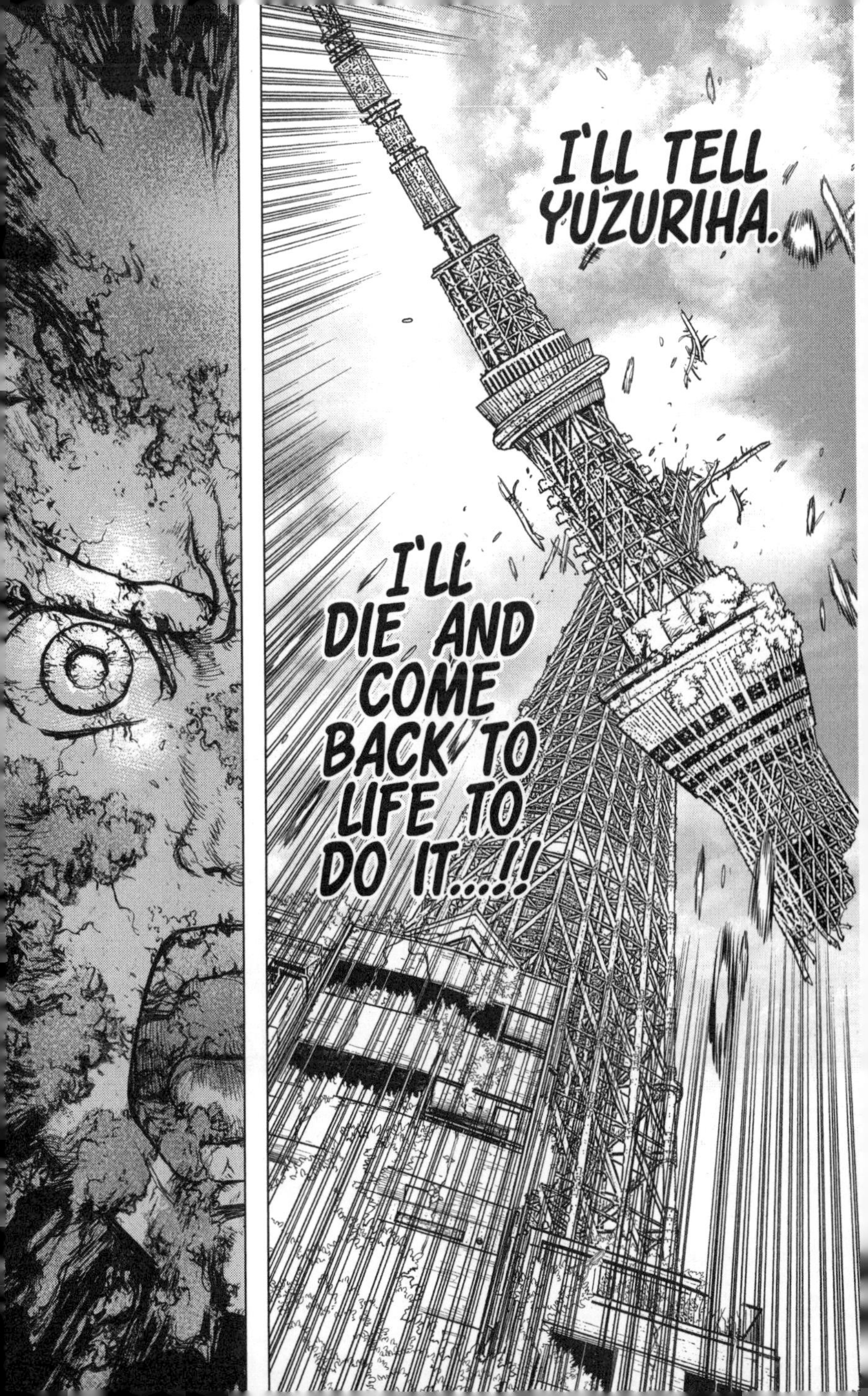
I'LL TELL YUZURIHA.
I'LL DIE AND COME BACK TO LIFE TO DO IT...!!

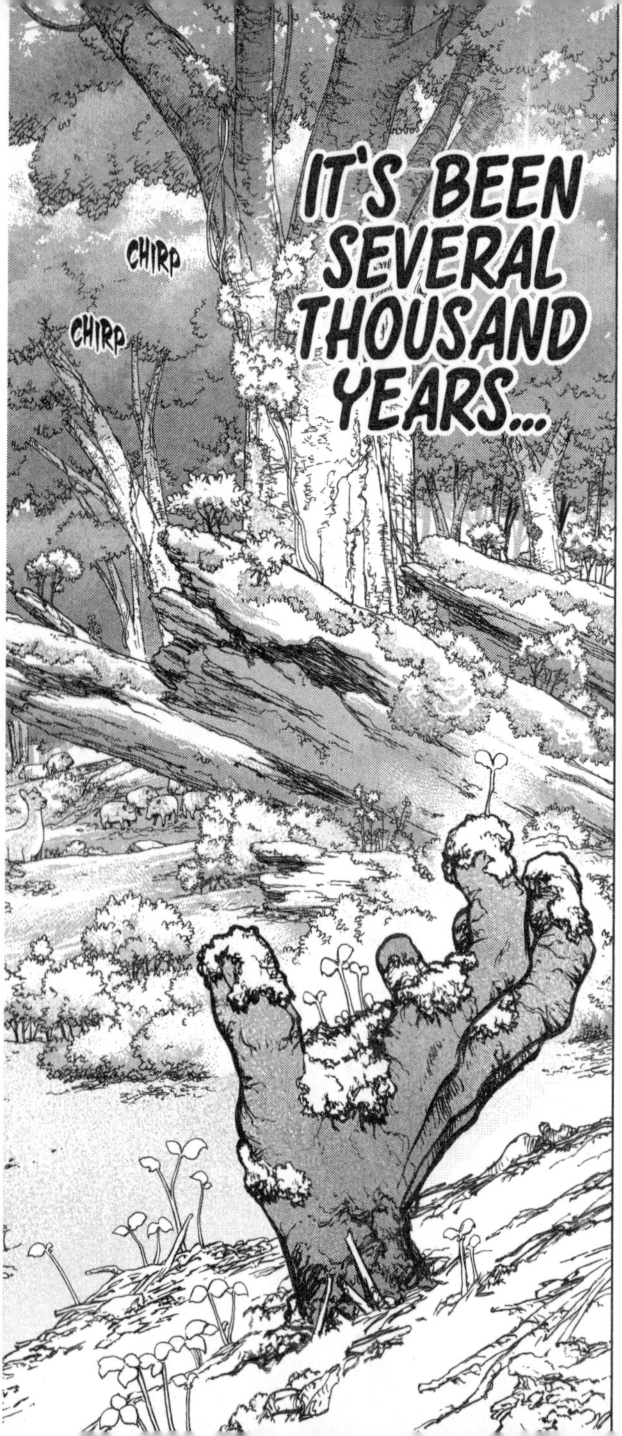
IT'S BEEN SEVERAL THOUSAND YEARS...
CHIRP
CHIRP

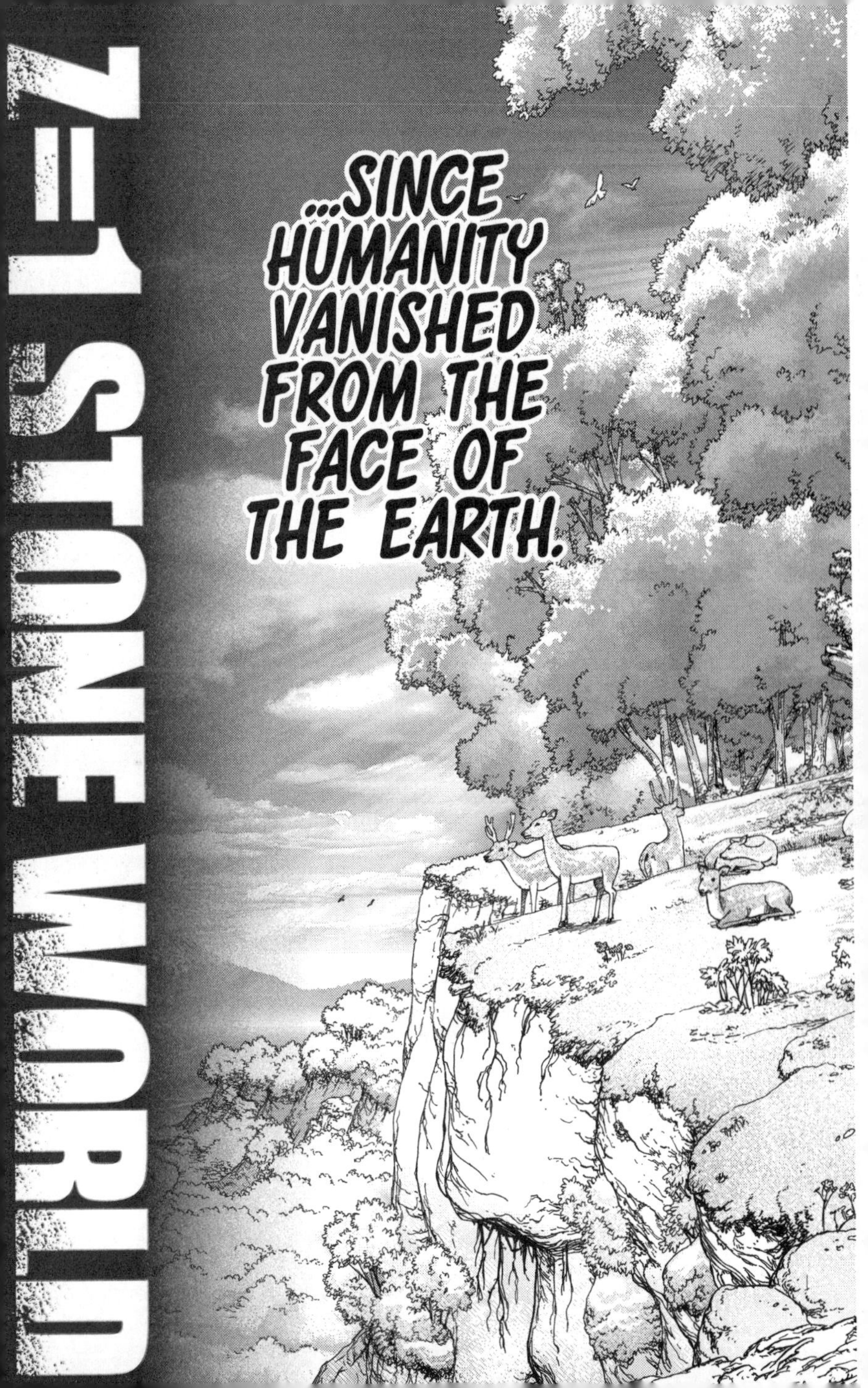
Z=1 STONE WORLD
...SINCE HUMANITY VANISHED FROM THE FACE OF THE EARTH.

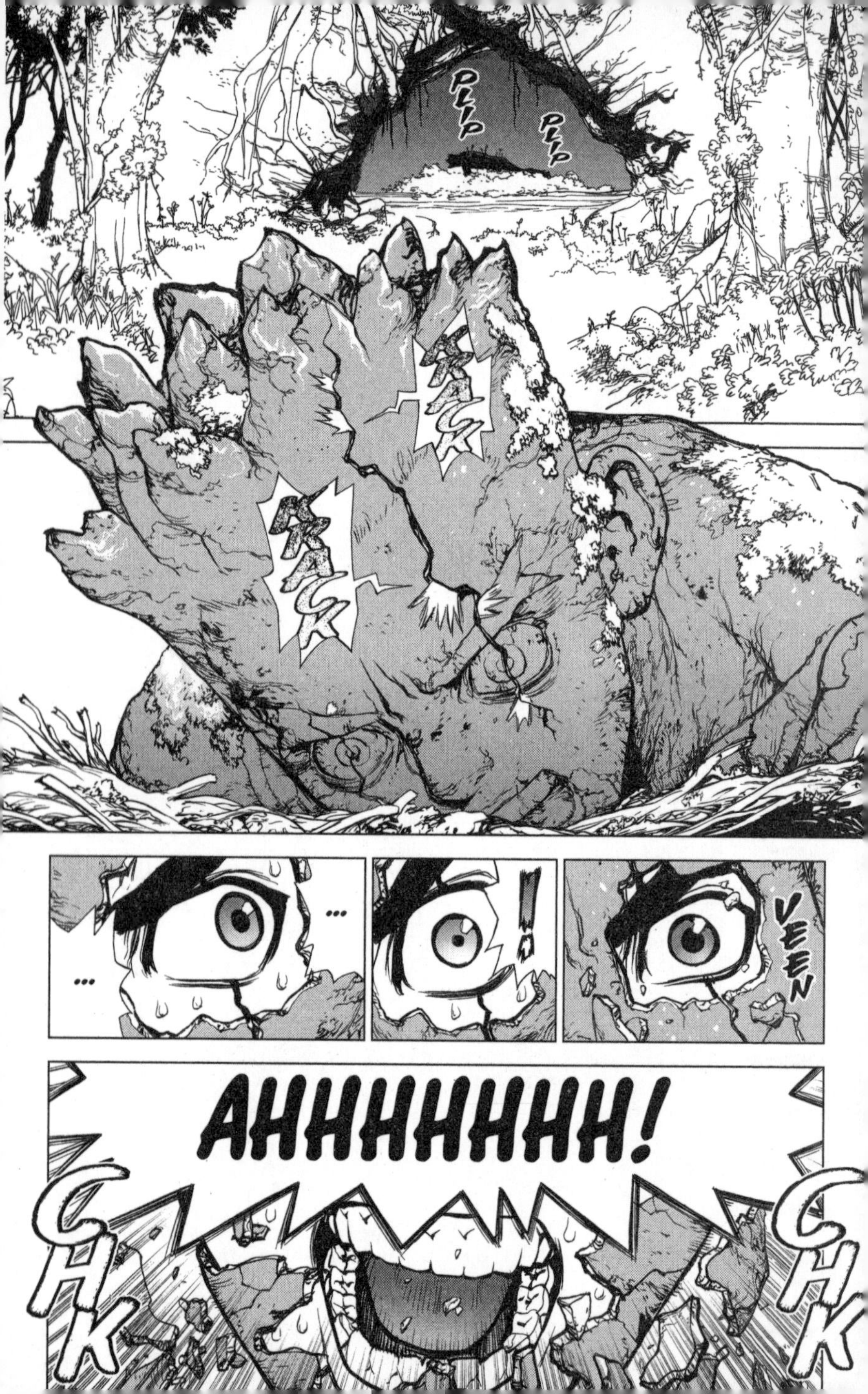
PLIP
PLIP
KRACK
KRACK
VEEN
!
...
...
AHHHHHHH!
CHK
CHK

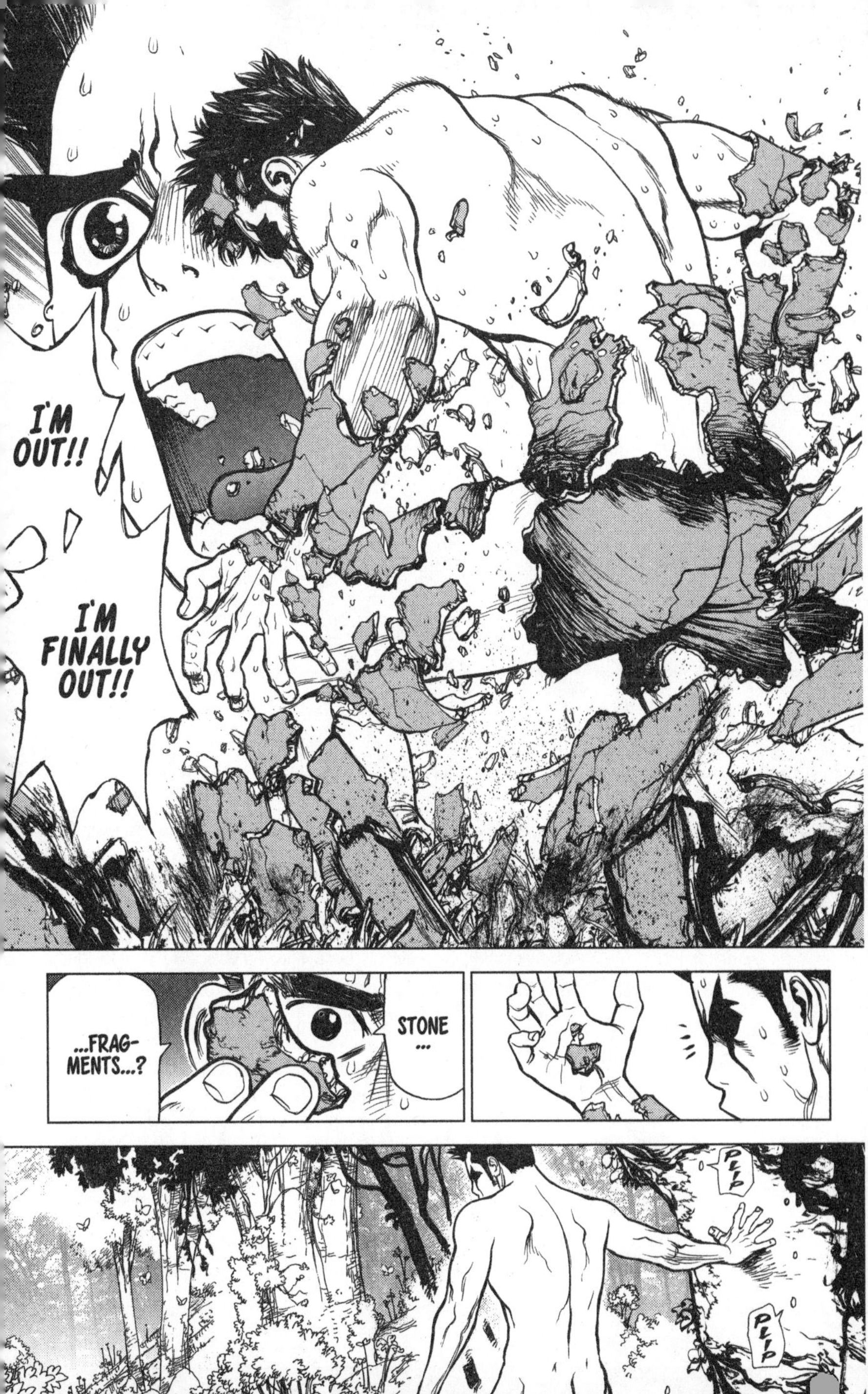
I'M OUT!!
I'M FINALLY OUT!!
STONE ...
...FRAG-MENTS...?
PEIP
PEIP

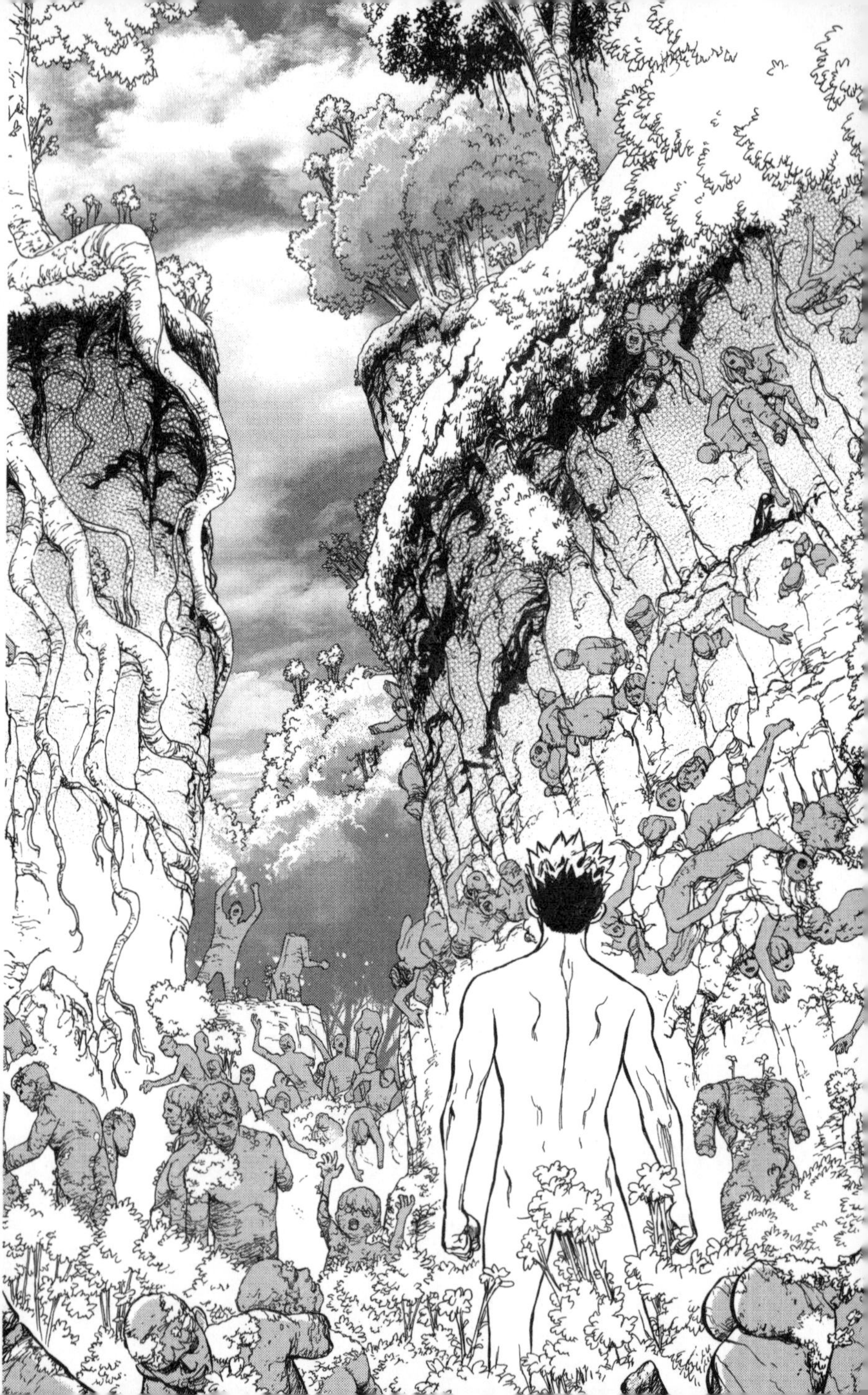

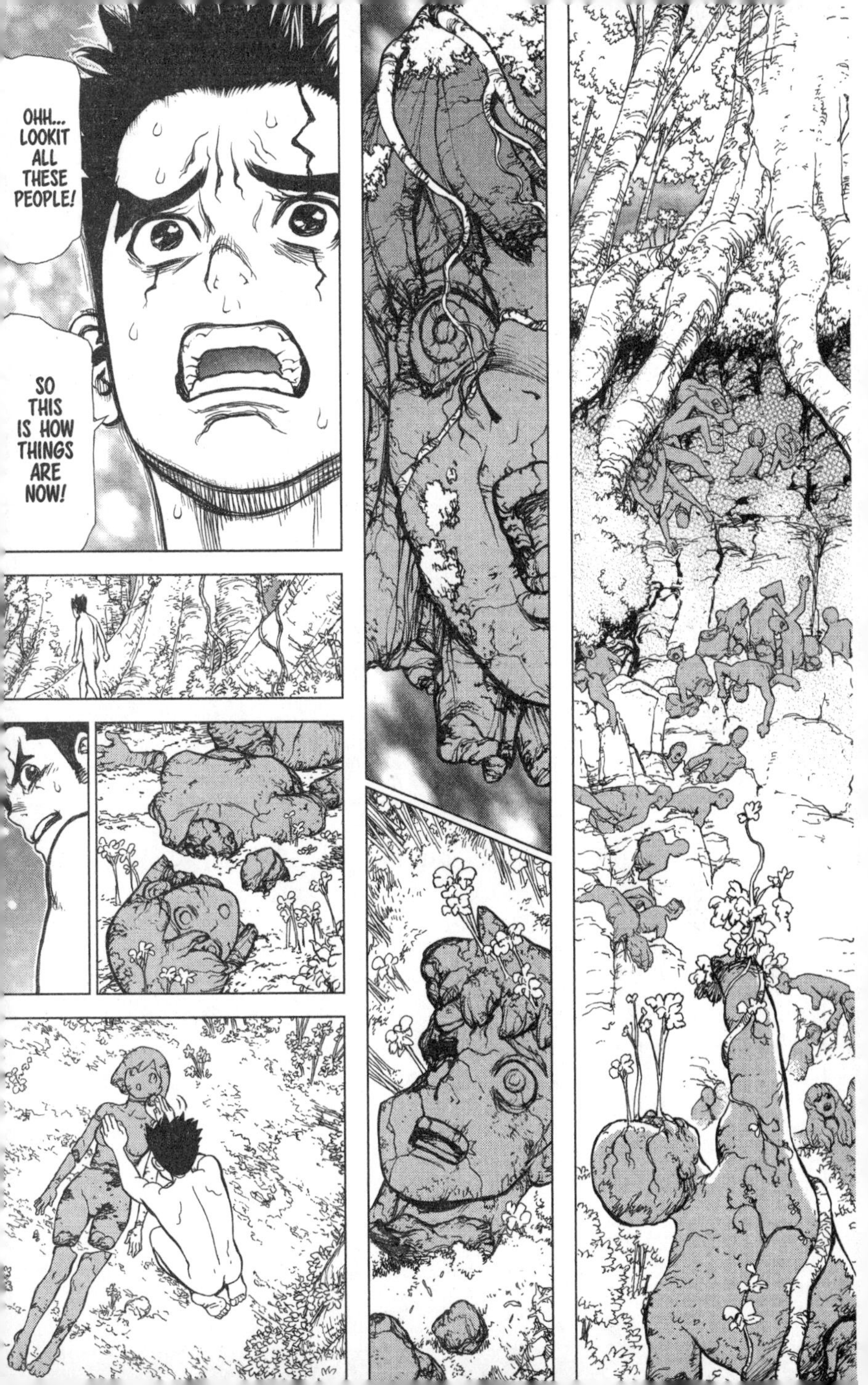
OHH... LOOKIT ALL THESE PEOPLE!
SO THIS IS HOW THINGS ARE NOW!

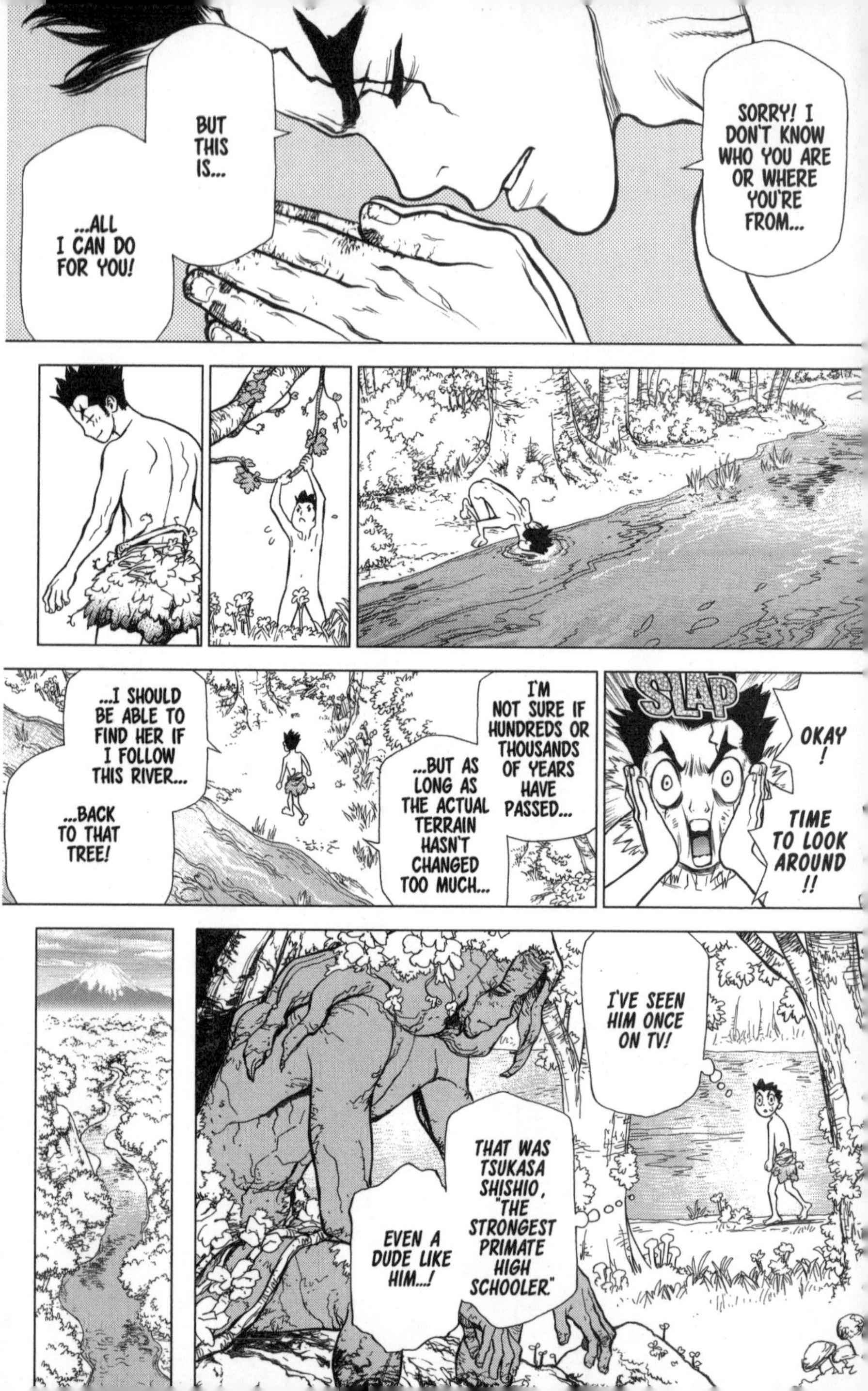
SORRY! I DON'T KNOW WHO YOU ARE OR WHERE YOU'RE FROM...
BUT THIS IS...
...ALL I CAN DO FOR YOU!
SLAP
OKAY! TIME TO LOOK AROUND!!
I'M NOT SURE IF HUNDREDS OR THOUSANDS OF YEARS HAVE PASSED...
...BUT AS LONG AS THE ACTUAL TERRAIN HASN'T CHANGED TOO MUCH...
...I SHOULD BE ABLE TO FIND HER IF I FOLLOW THIS RIVER...
...BACK TO THAT TREE!
I'VE SEEN HIM ONCE ON TV!
THAT WAS TSUKASA SHISHIO, "THE STRONGEST PRIMATE HIGH SCHOOLER."
EVEN A DUDE LIKE HIM...!

YUZURIHA.

RUSTLE

RUSTLE

THERE'S NO MISTAKE...

EVEN AFTER ALL THESE MILLENNIA...

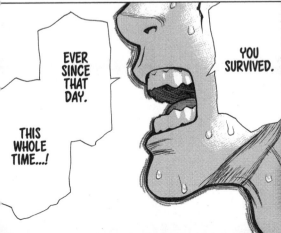

EVER SINCE THAT DAY.

THIS WHOLE TIME...!

YOU SURVIVED.

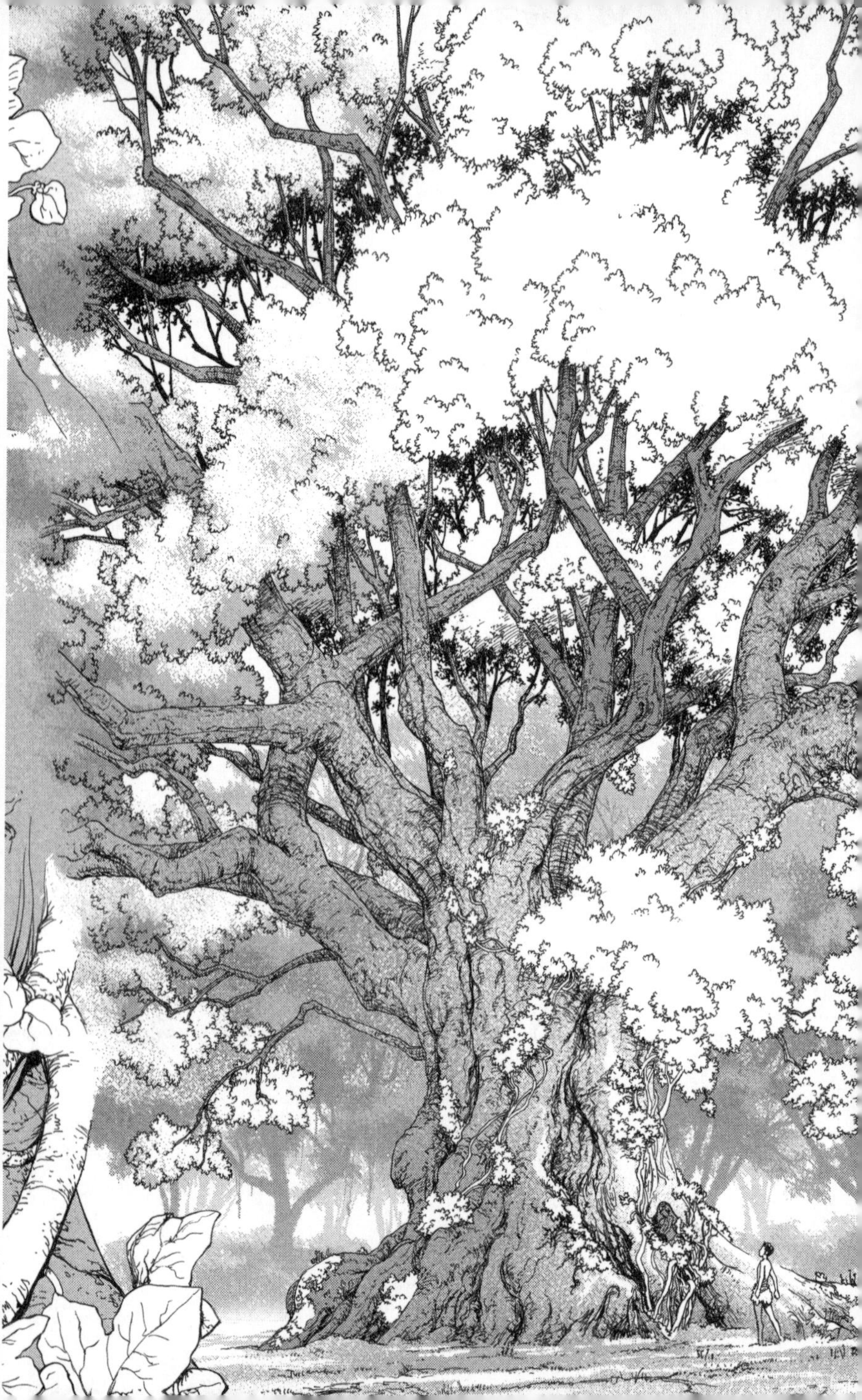

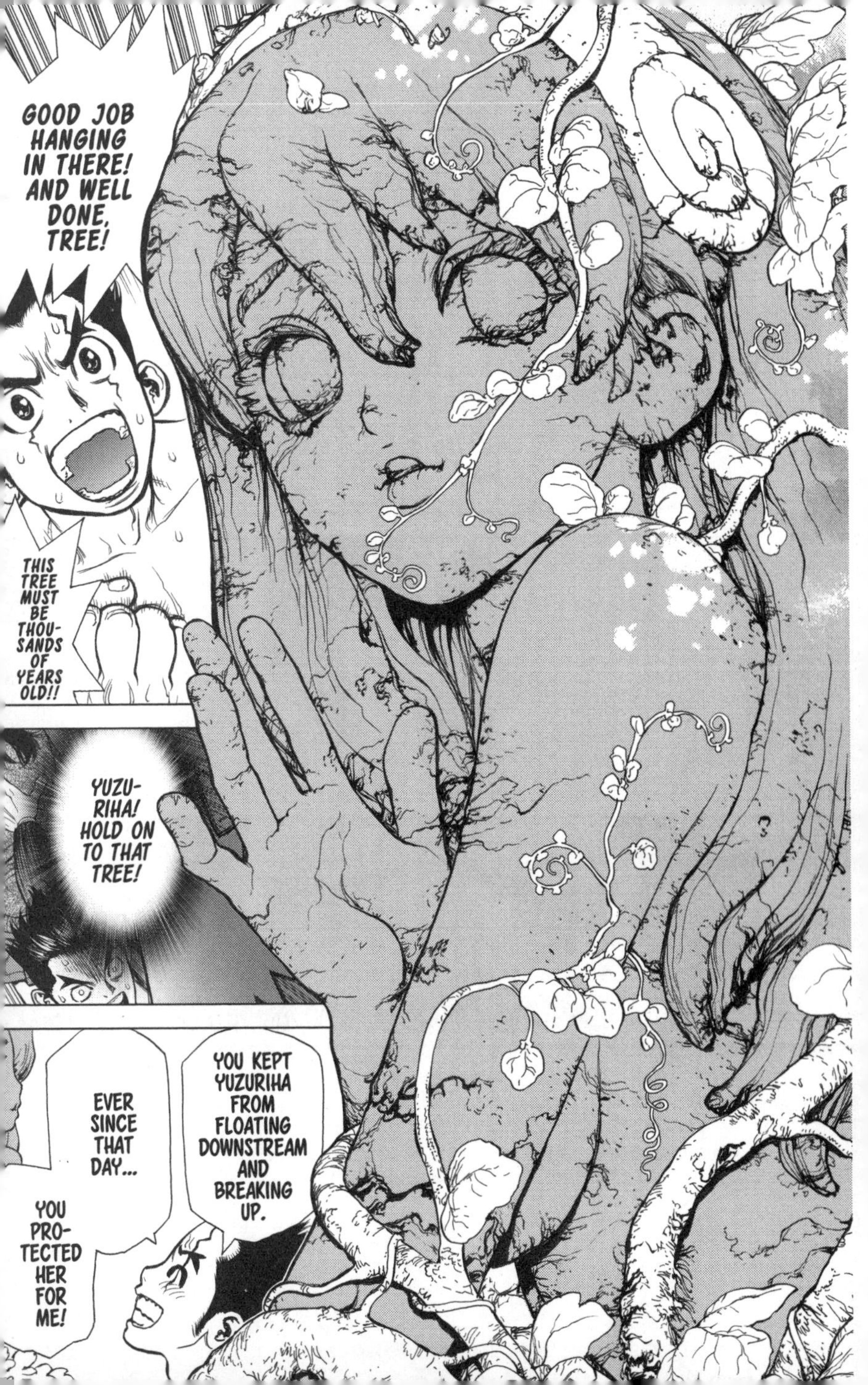
GOOD JOB HANGING IN THERE! AND WELL DONE, TREE!
THIS TREE MUST BE THOUSANDS OF YEARS OLD!!
YUZURIHA! HOLD ON TO THAT TREE!
YOU KEPT YUZURIHA FROM FLOATING DOWNSTREAM AND BREAKING UP.
EVER SINCE THAT DAY...
YOU PROTECTED HER FOR ME!

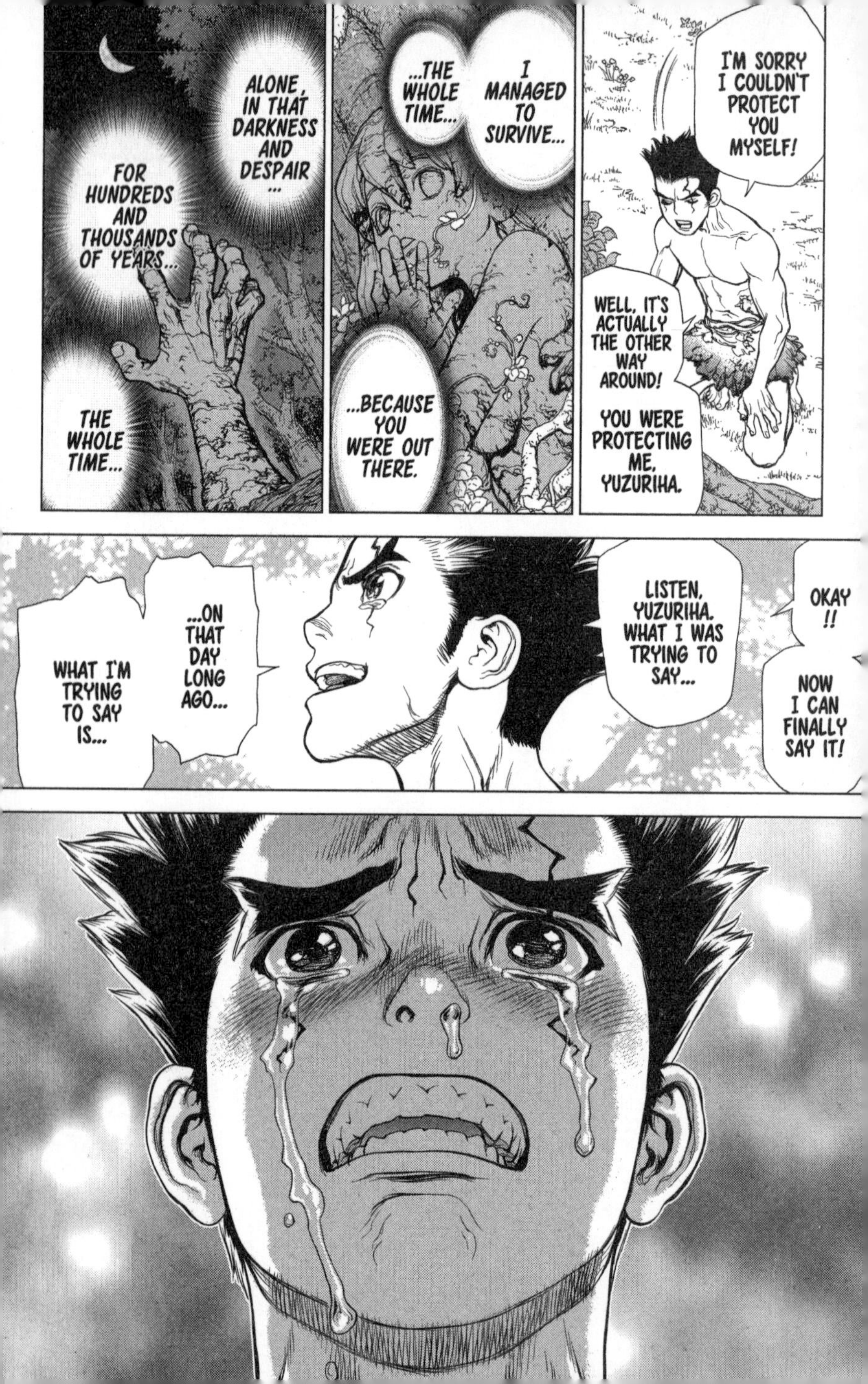
I'M SORRY I COULDN'T PROTECT YOU MYSELF!
WELL, IT'S ACTUALLY THE OTHER WAY AROUND!
YOU WERE PROTECTING ME, YUZURIHA.
I MANAGED TO SURVIVE...
...THE WHOLE TIME...
...BECAUSE YOU WERE OUT THERE.
ALONE, IN THAT DARKNESS AND DESPAIR...
FOR HUNDREDS AND THOUSANDS OF YEARS...
THE WHOLE TIME...
OKAY!!
NOW I CAN FINALLY SAY IT!
LISTEN, YUZURIHA. WHAT I WAS TRYING TO SAY...
...ON THAT DAY LONG AGO...
WHAT I'M TRYING TO SAY IS...

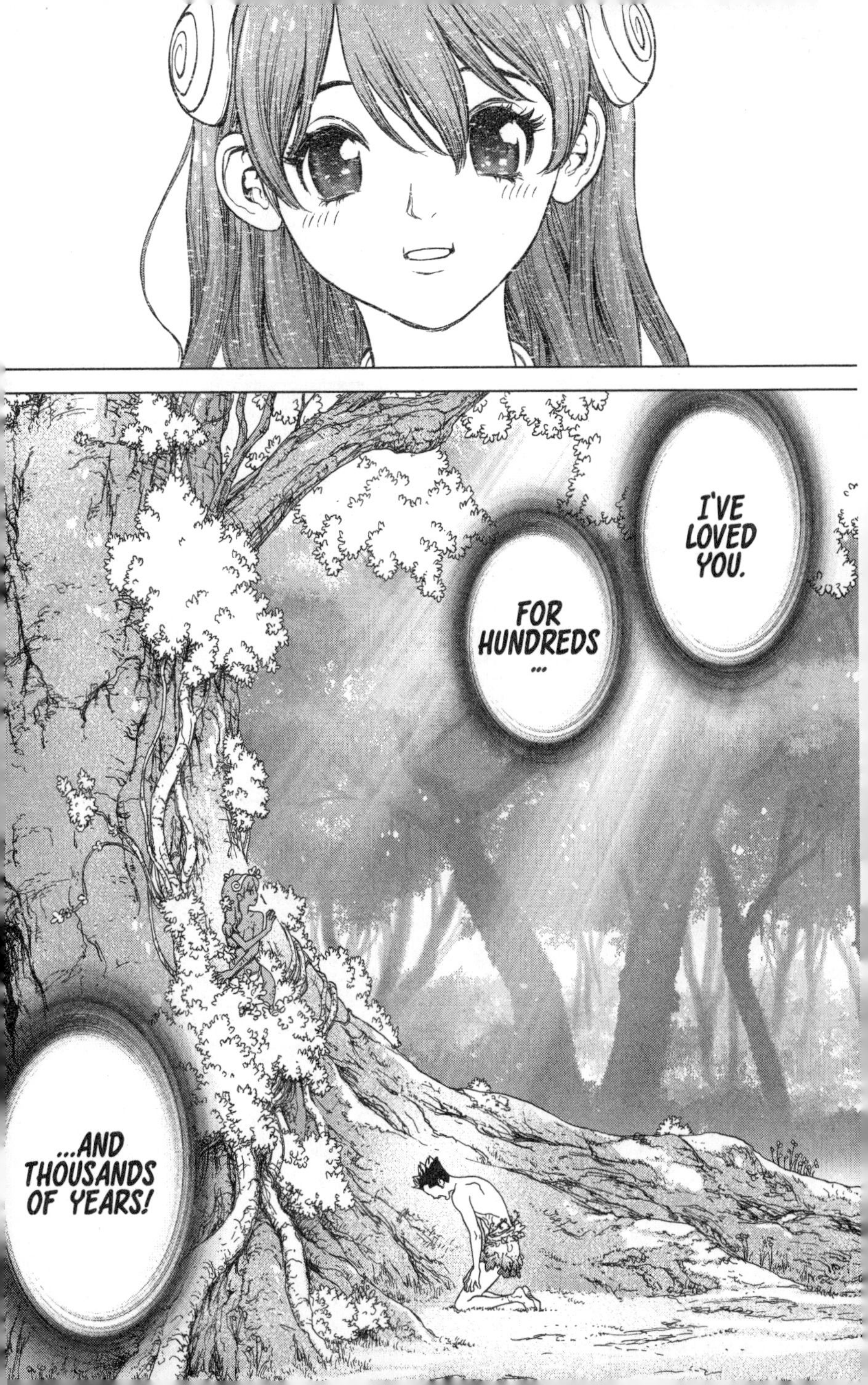
I'VE LOVED YOU.
FOR HUNDREDS...
...AND THOUSANDS OF YEARS!

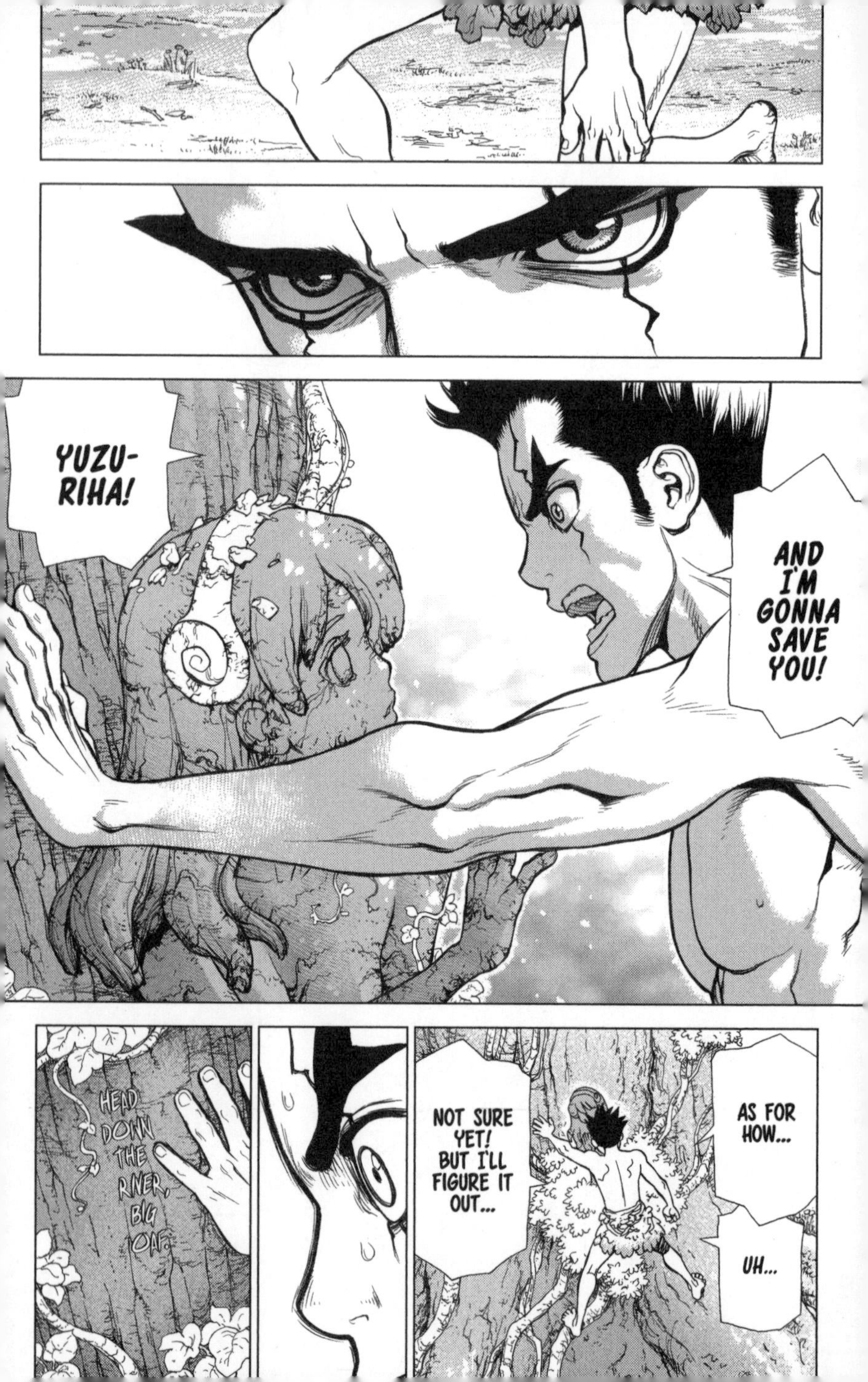
YUZU-RIHA!
AND I'M GONNA SAVE YOU!
AS FOR HOW...
UH...
NOT SURE YET! BUT I'LL FIGURE IT OUT...
HEAD DOWN THE RIVER, BIG OAF.

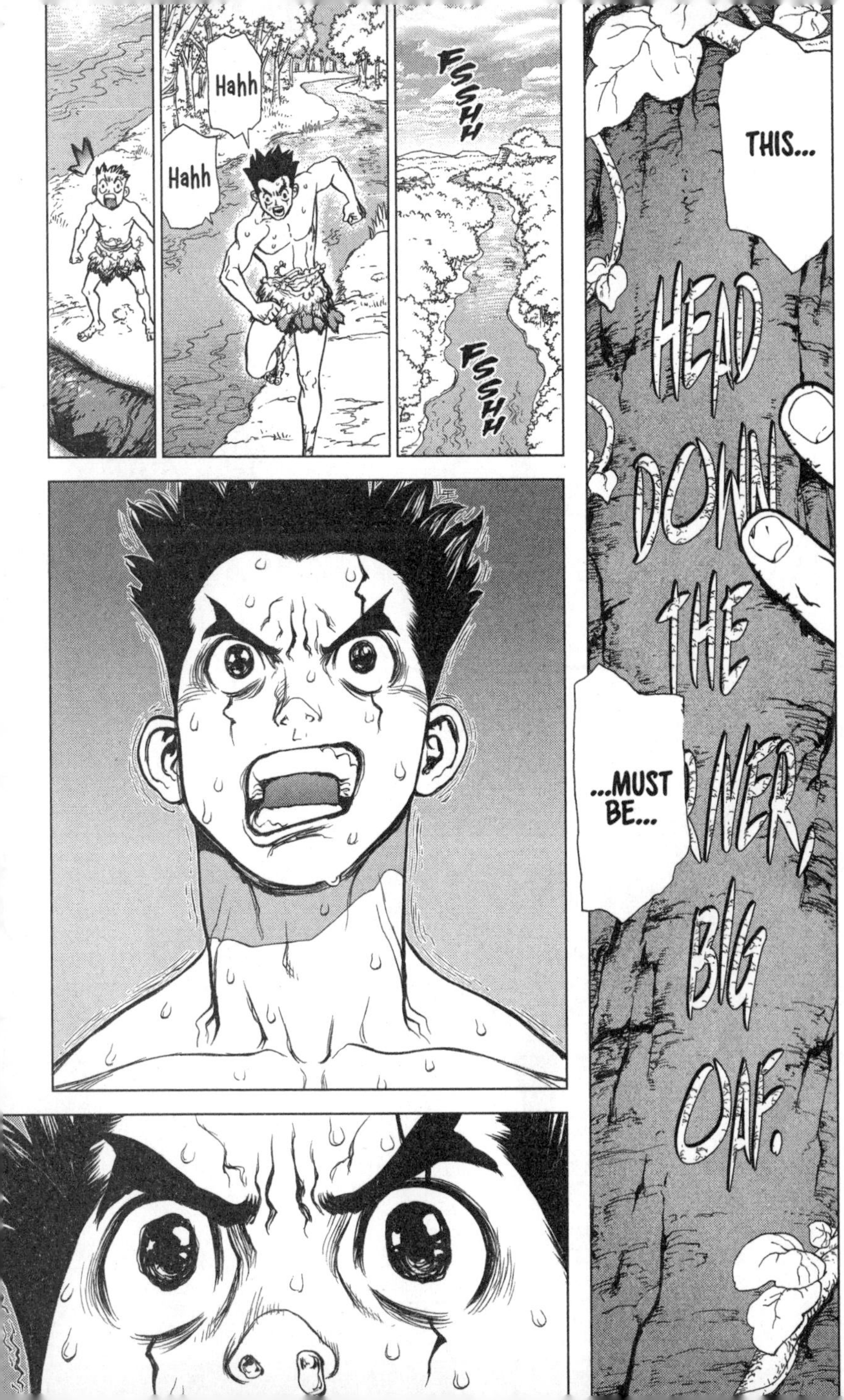
THIS...
HEAD DOWN THE RIVER, BIG OAF.
...MUST BE...
FSSHH
FSSHH
Hahh
Hahh

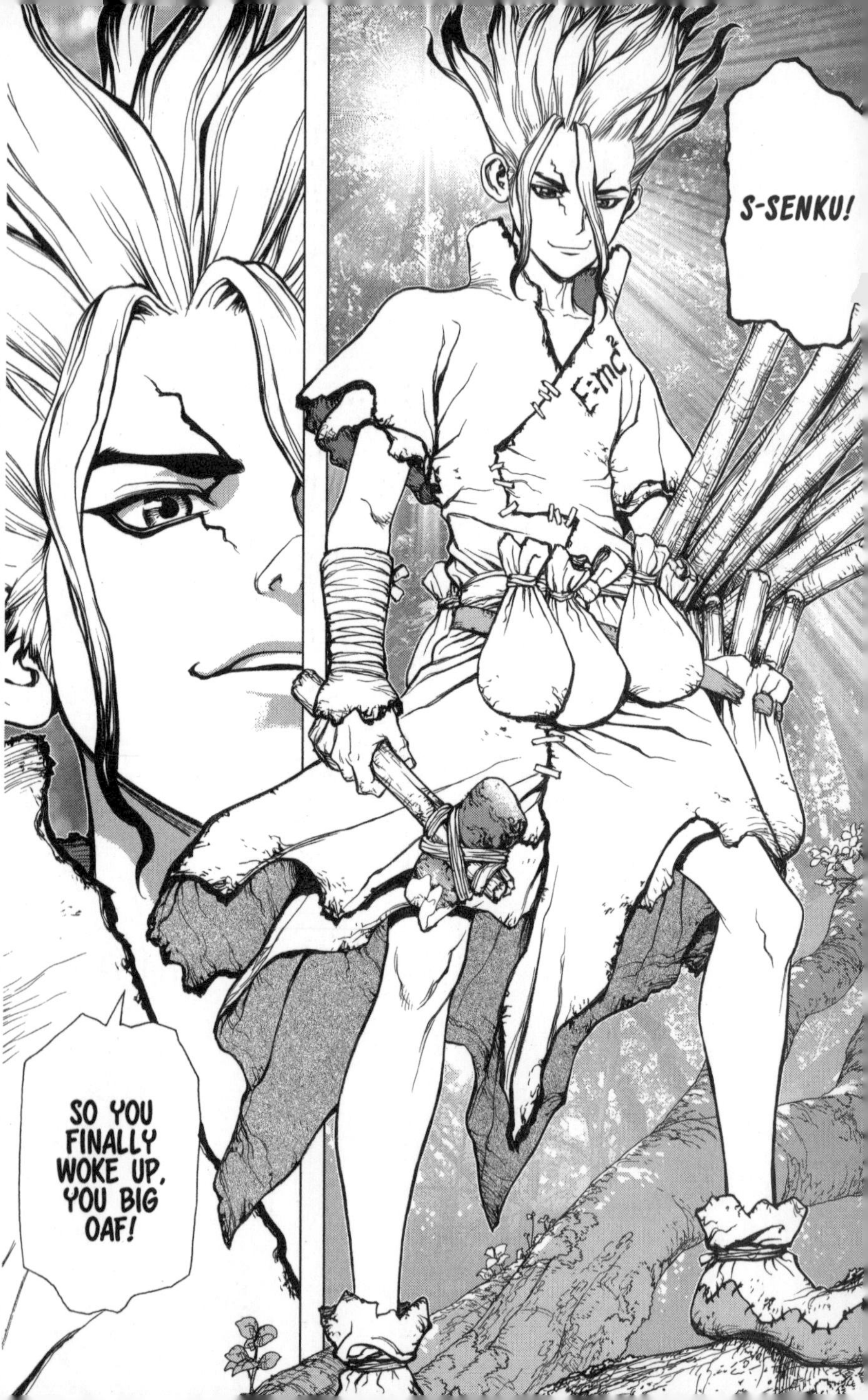
S-SENKU!
SO YOU FINALLY WOKE UP, YOU BIG OAF!

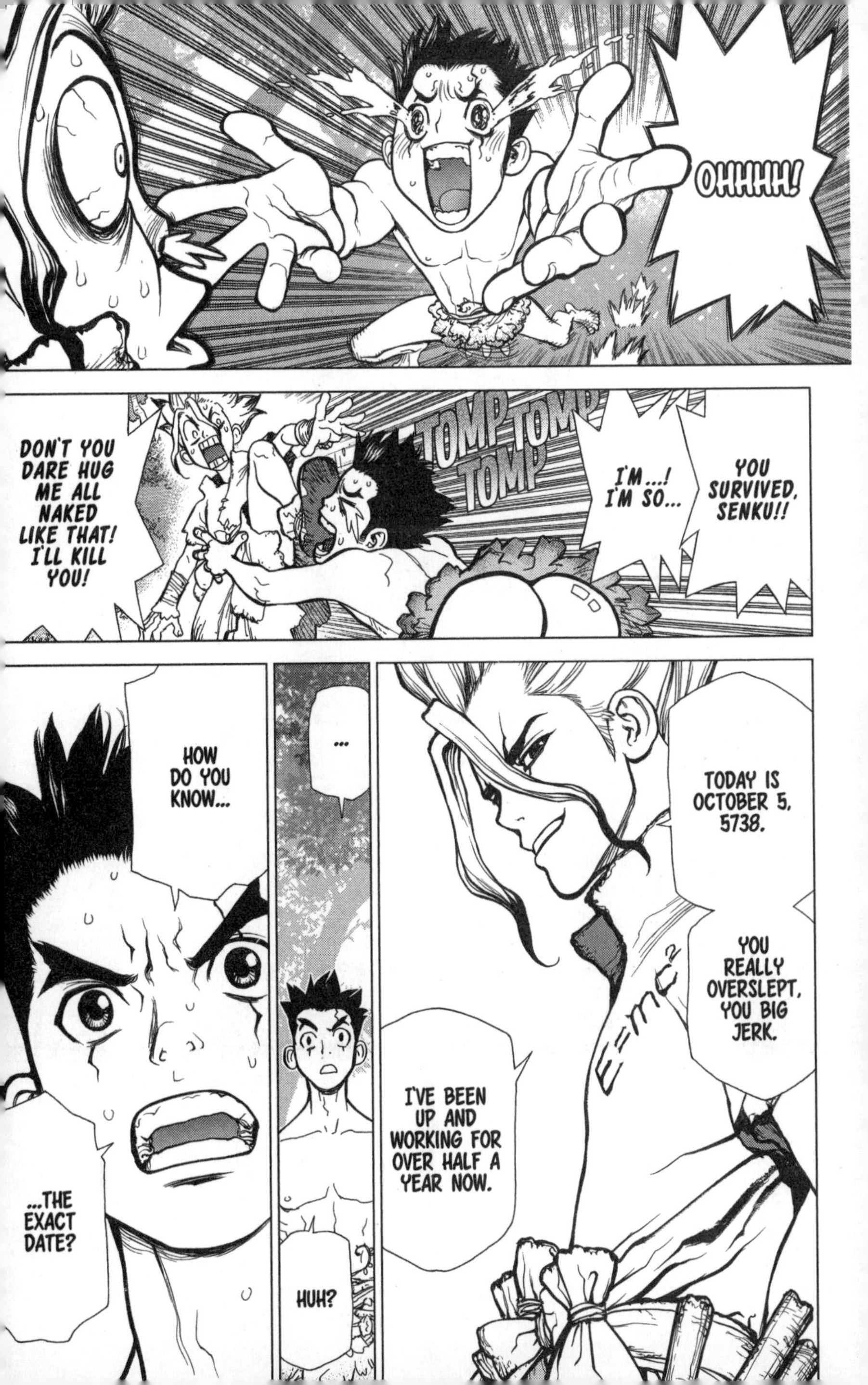
OHHHH!
YOU SURVIVED, SENKU!!
I'M...! I'M SO...
TOMP TOMP TOMP
DON'T YOU DARE HUG ME ALL NAKED LIKE THAT! I'LL KILL YOU!
TODAY IS OCTOBER 5, 5738.
YOU REALLY OVERSLEPT, YOU BIG JERK.
$E=mc^2$
I'VE BEEN UP AND WORKING FOR OVER HALF A YEAR NOW.
...
HUH?
HOW DO YOU KNOW...
...THE EXACT DATE?

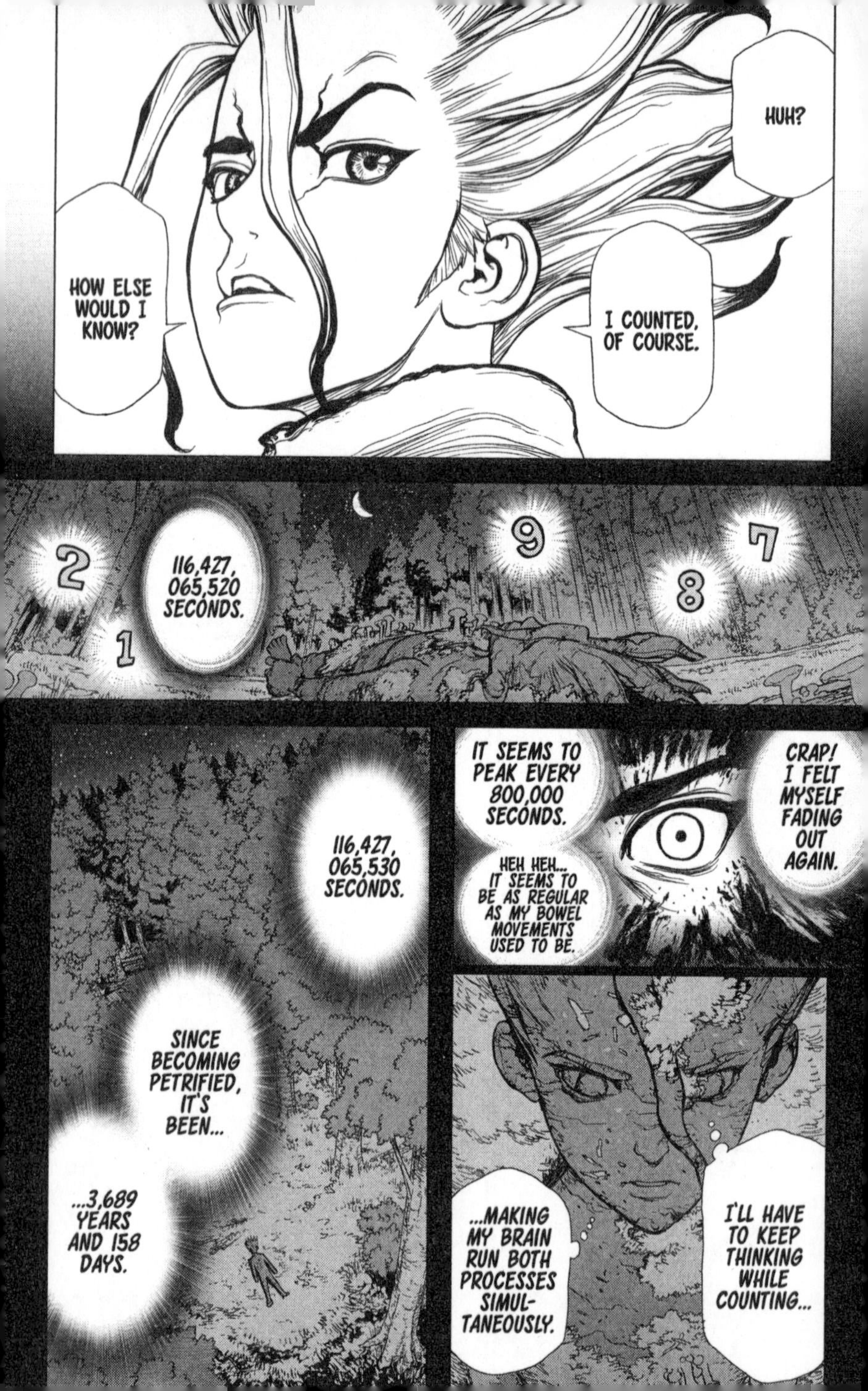
HUH?
I COUNTED, OF COURSE.
HOW ELSE WOULD I KNOW?
7
9
8
2
116,427, 065,520 SECONDS.
1
CRAP! I FELT MYSELF FADING OUT AGAIN.
IT SEEMS TO PEAK EVERY 800,000 SECONDS.
HEH HEH... IT SEEMS TO BE AS REGULAR AS MY BOWEL MOVEMENTS USED TO BE.
I'LL HAVE TO KEEP THINKING WHILE COUNTING...
...MAKING MY BRAIN RUN BOTH PROCESSES SIMUL-TANEOUSLY.
116,427, 065,530 SECONDS.
SINCE BECOMING PETRIFIED, IT'S BEEN...
...3,689 YEARS AND 158 DAYS.

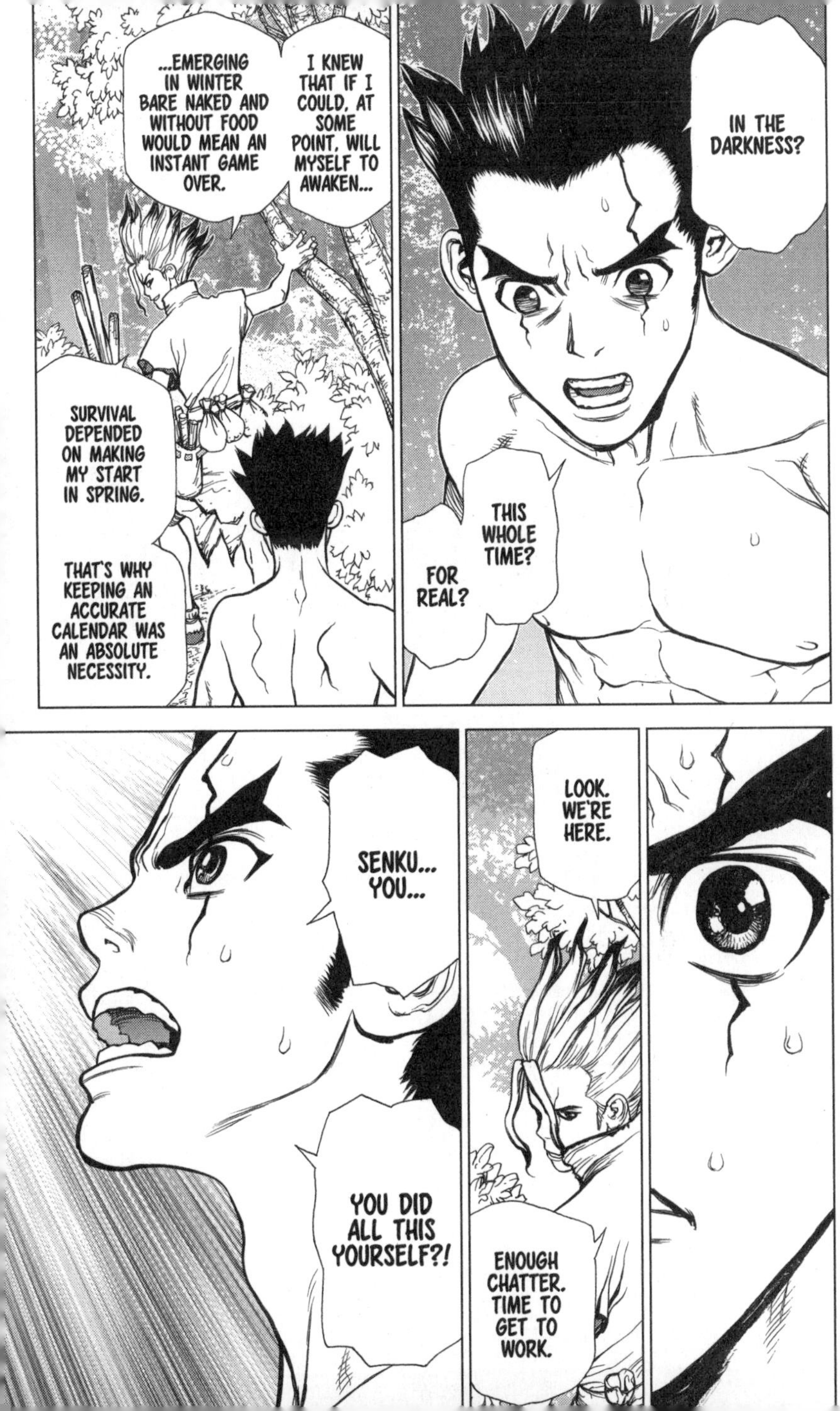
IN THE DARKNESS?
THIS WHOLE TIME?
FOR REAL?
I KNEW THAT IF I COULD, AT SOME POINT, WILL MYSELF TO AWAKEN...
...EMERGING IN WINTER BARE NAKED AND WITHOUT FOOD WOULD MEAN AN INSTANT GAME OVER.
SURVIVAL DEPENDED ON MAKING MY START IN SPRING.
THAT'S WHY KEEPING AN ACCURATE CALENDAR WAS AN ABSOLUTE NECESSITY.
LOOK. WE'RE HERE.
ENOUGH CHATTER. TIME TO GET TO WORK.
SENKU... YOU...
YOU DID ALL THIS YOURSELF?!

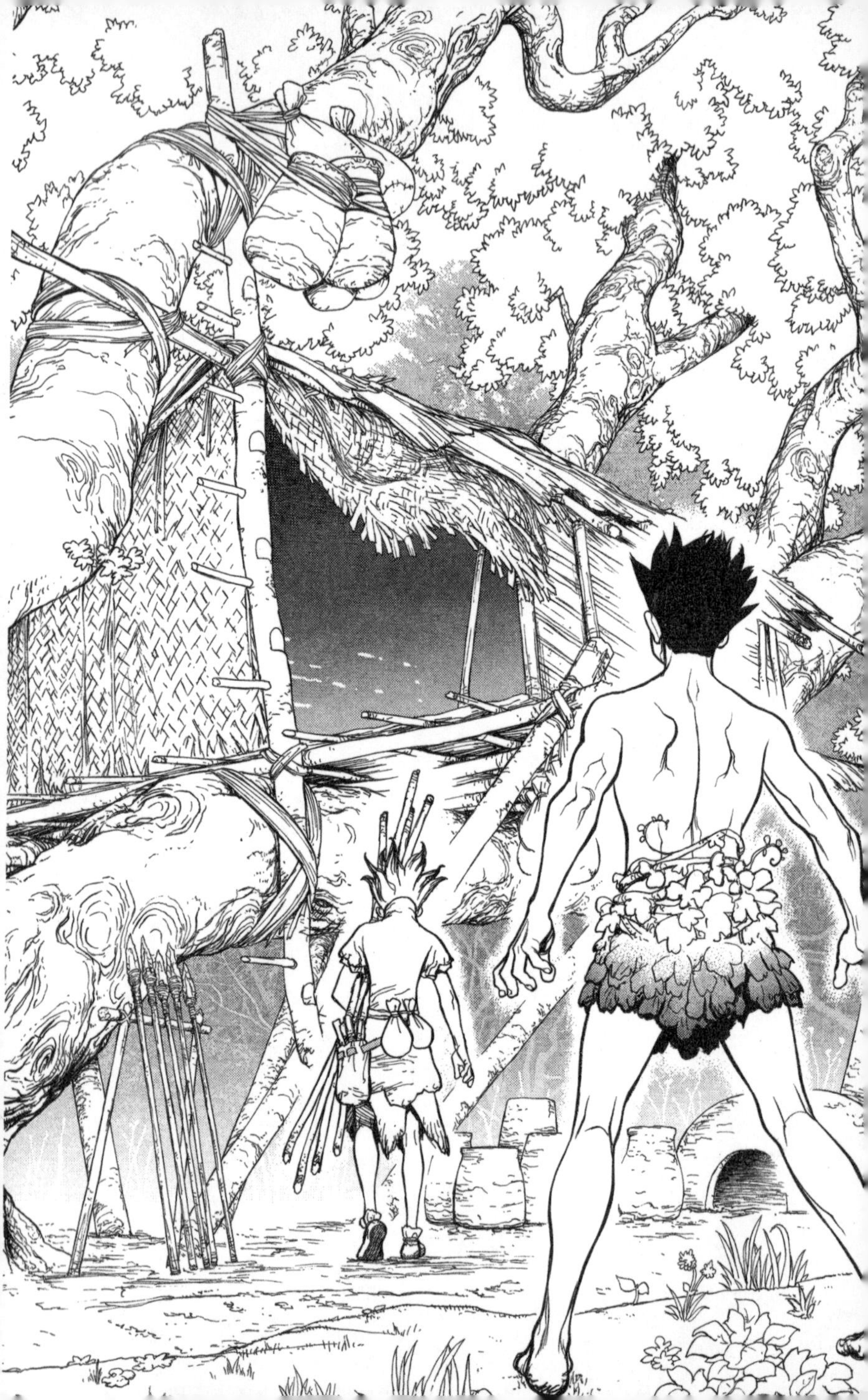

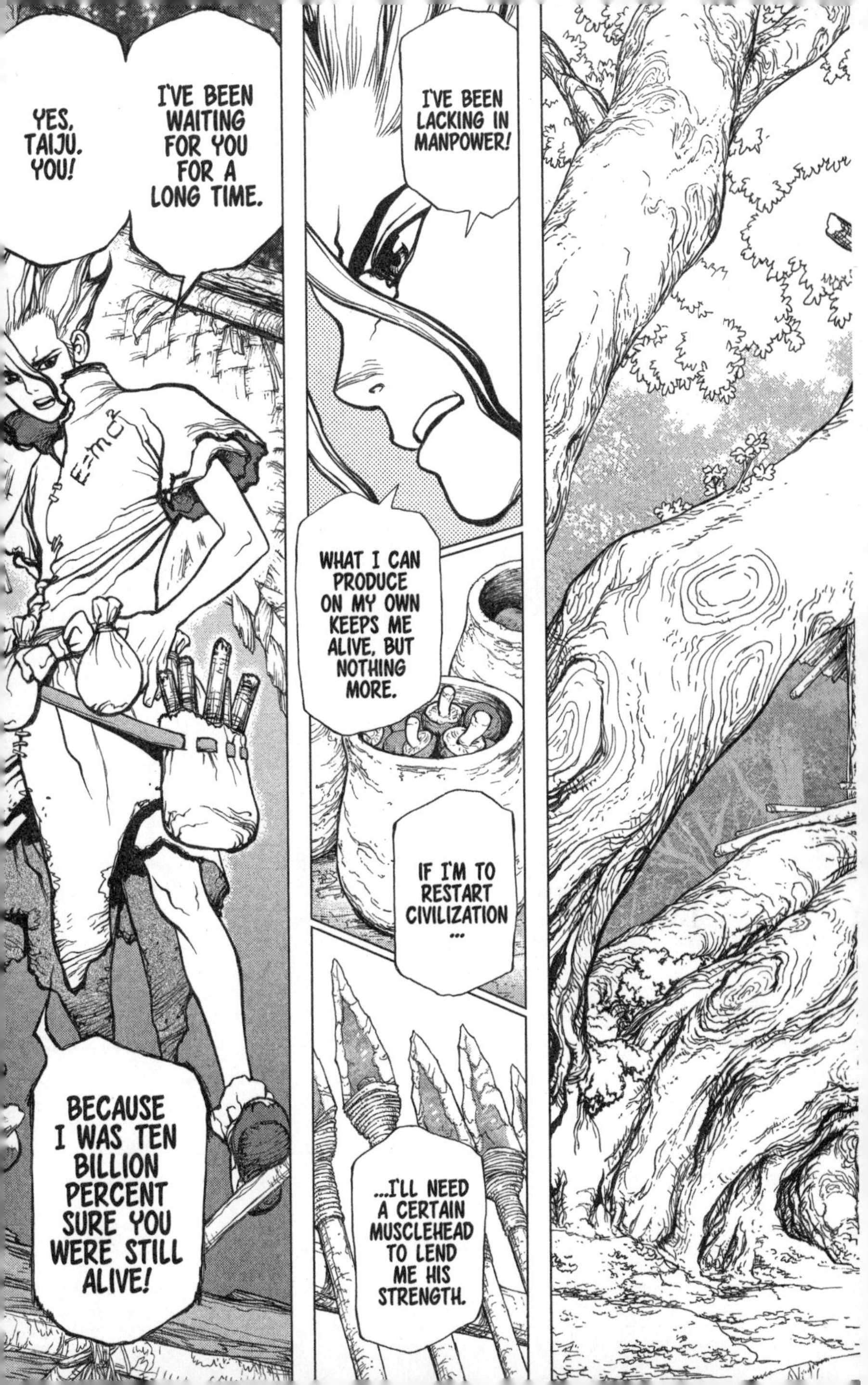
I'VE BEEN LACKING IN MANPOWER!
WHAT I CAN PRODUCE ON MY OWN KEEPS ME ALIVE, BUT NOTHING MORE.
IF I'M TO RESTART CIVILIZATION...
...I'LL NEED A CERTAIN MUSCLEHEAD TO LEND ME HIS STRENGTH.
I'VE BEEN WAITING FOR YOU FOR A LONG TIME.
YES, TAIJU. YOU!
BECAUSE I WAS TEN BILLION PERCENT SURE YOU WERE STILL ALIVE!

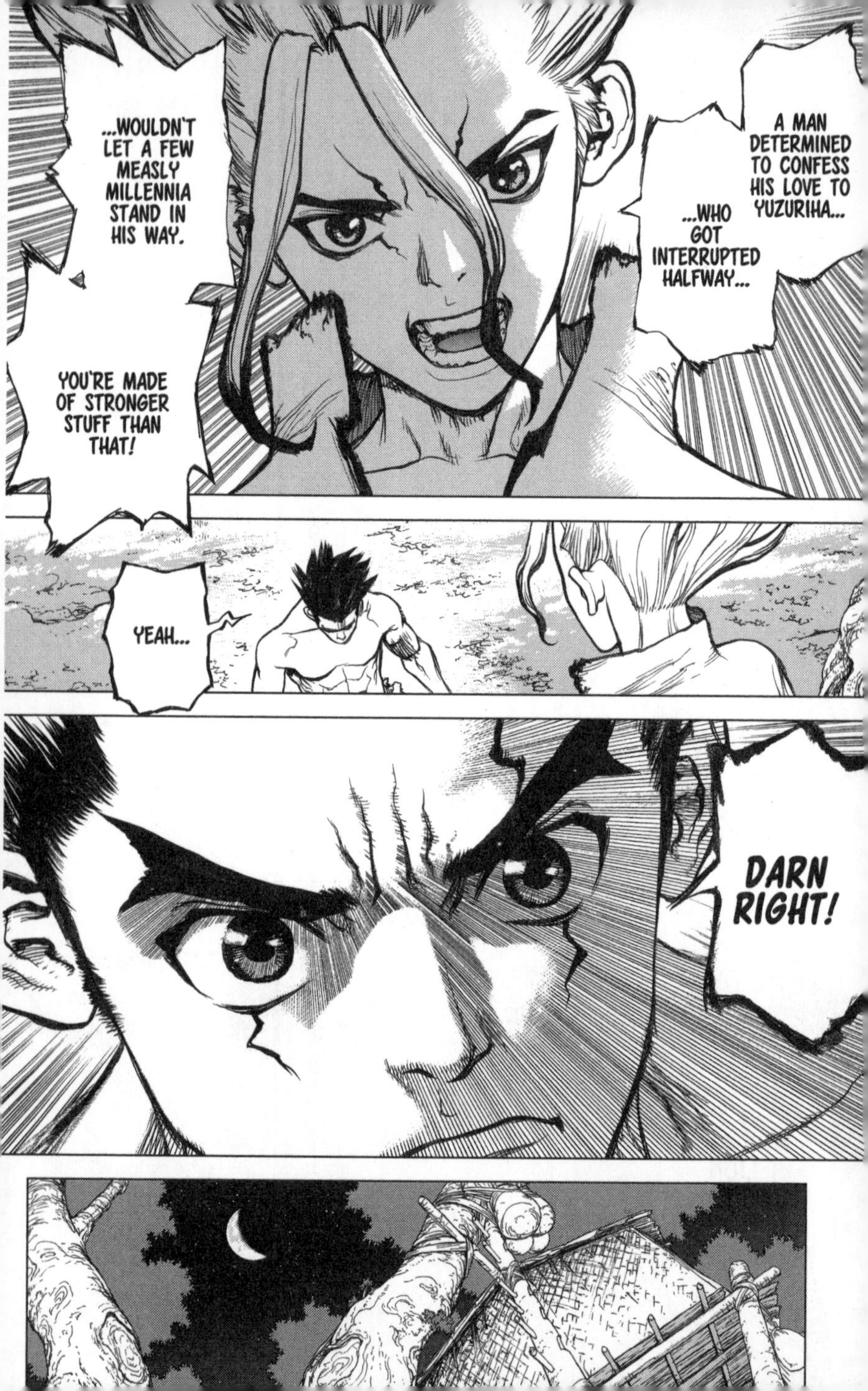
A MAN DETERMINED TO CONFESS HIS LOVE TO YUZURIHA...
...WHO GOT INTERRUPTED HALFWAY...
...WOULDN'T LET A FEW MEASLY MILLENNIA STAND IN HIS WAY.
YOU'RE MADE OF STRONGER STUFF THAN THAT!
YEAH...
DARN RIGHT!

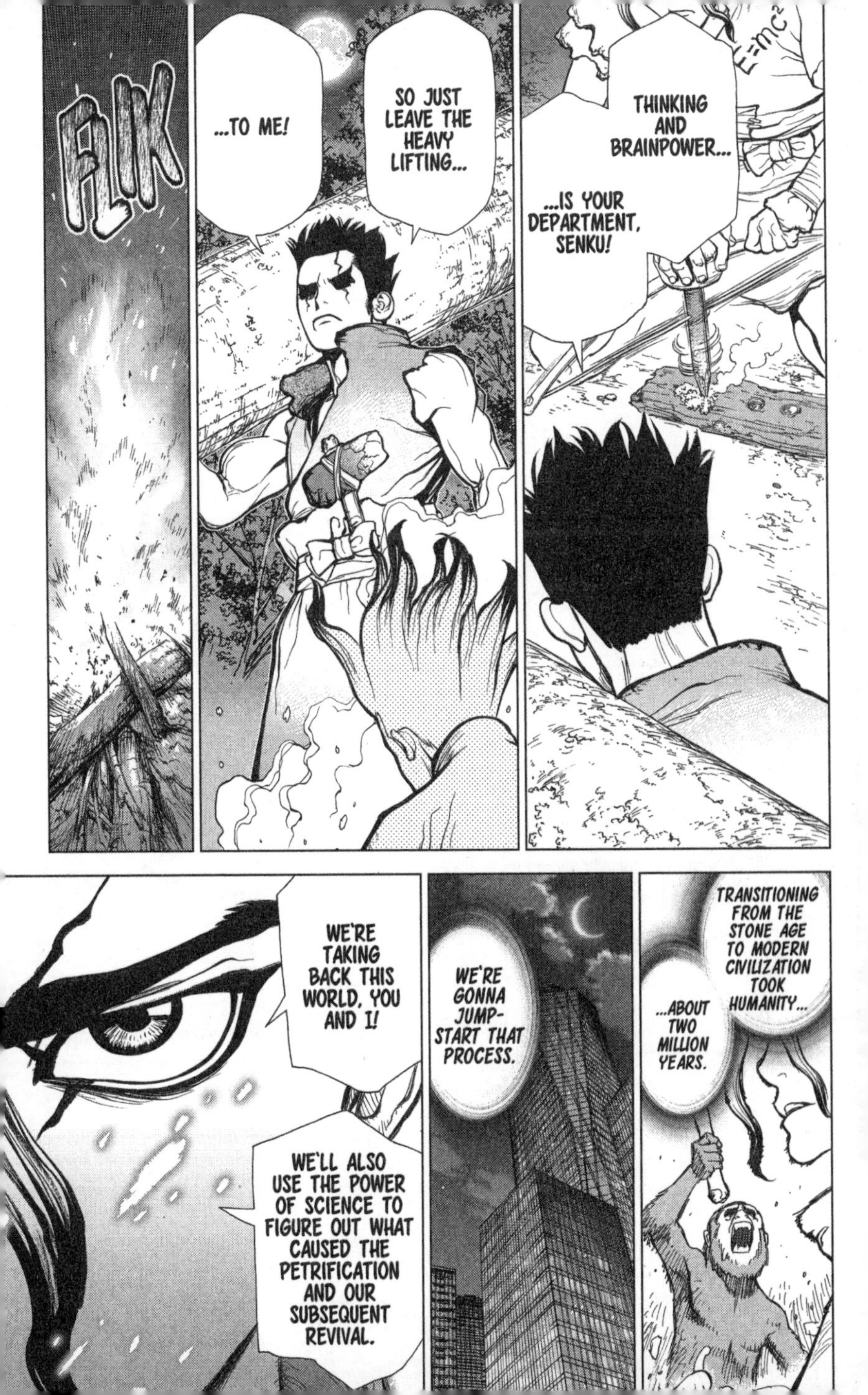
$E=mc^2$
THINKING AND BRAINPOWER...
...IS YOUR DEPARTMENT, SENKU!
SO JUST LEAVE THE HEAVY LIFTING...
...TO ME!
FLIK
TRANSITIONING FROM THE STONE AGE TO MODERN CIVILIZATION TOOK HUMANITY...
...ABOUT TWO MILLION YEARS.
WE'RE GONNA JUMP-START THAT PROCESS.
WE'RE TAKING BACK THIS WORLD, YOU AND I!
WE'LL ALSO USE THE POWER OF SCIENCE TO FIGURE OUT WHAT CAUSED THE PETRIFICATION AND OUR SUBSEQUENT REVIVAL.

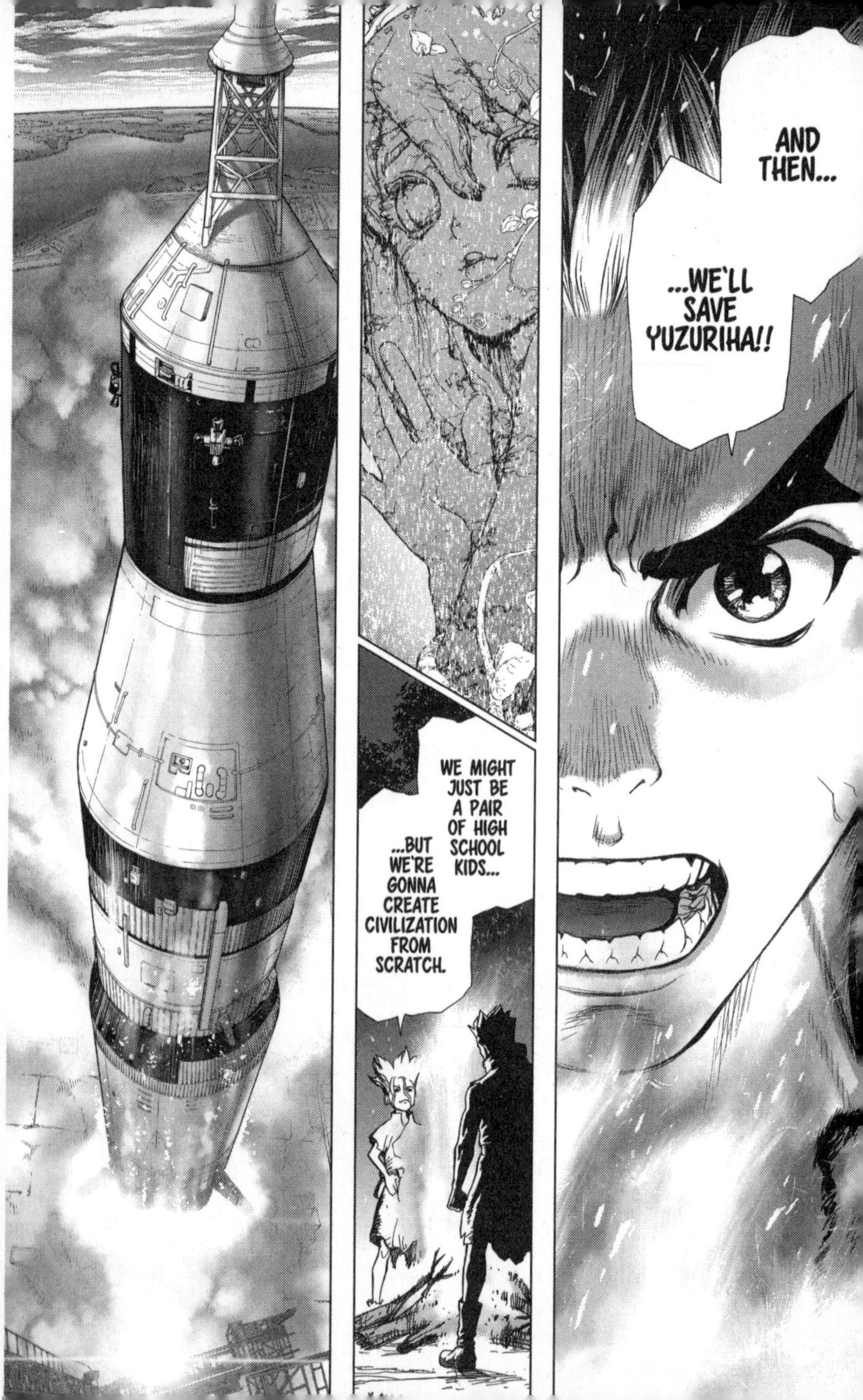
AND THEN...
...WE'LL SAVE YUZURIHA!!
WE MIGHT JUST BE A PAIR OF HIGH SCHOOL KIDS...
...BUT WE'RE GONNA CREATE CIVILIZATION FROM SCRATCH.

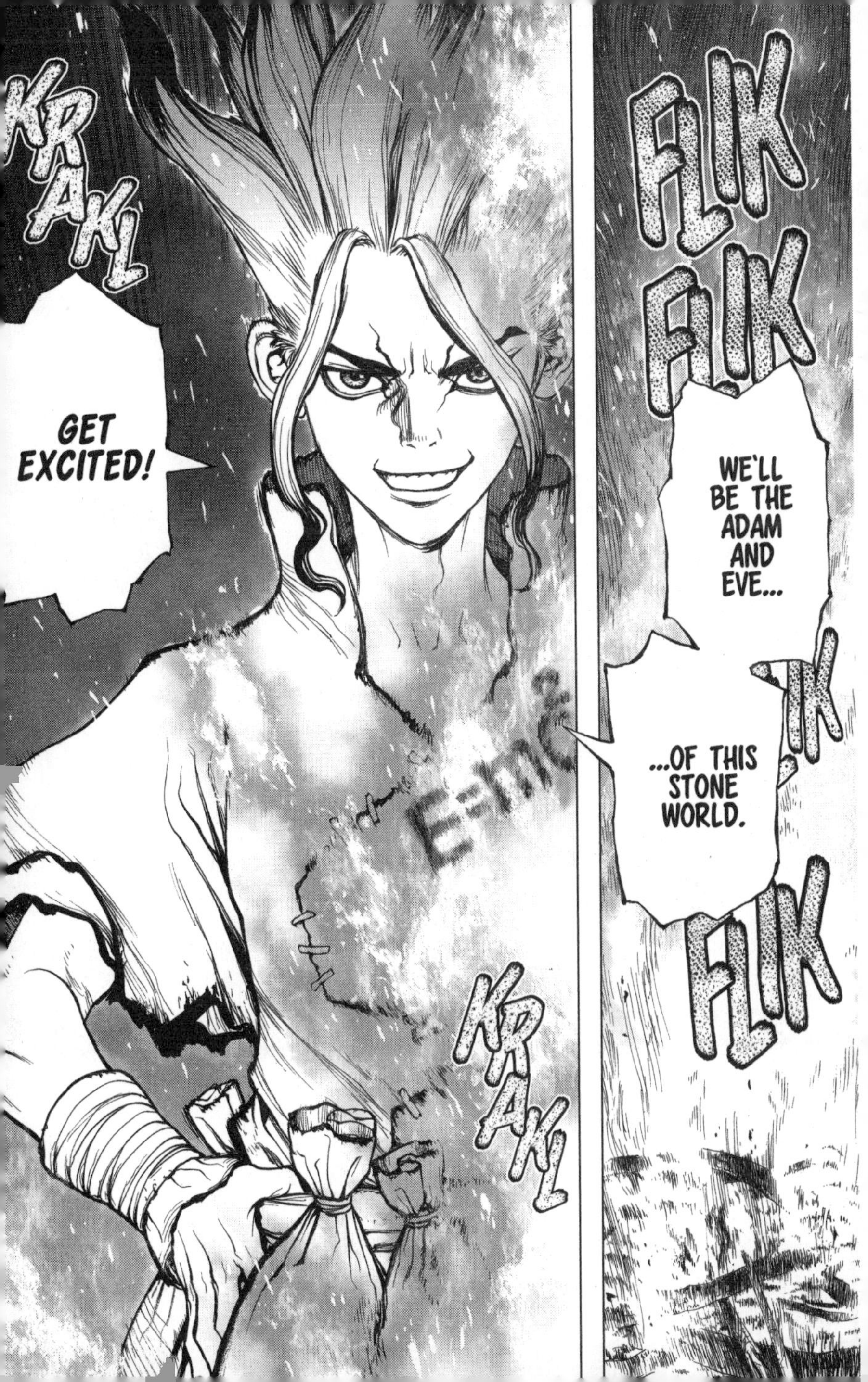
FLIK FLIK
WE'LL BE THE ADAM AND EVE...
...OF THIS STONE WORLD.
FLIK
KRAKL
GET EXCITED!
KRAKL

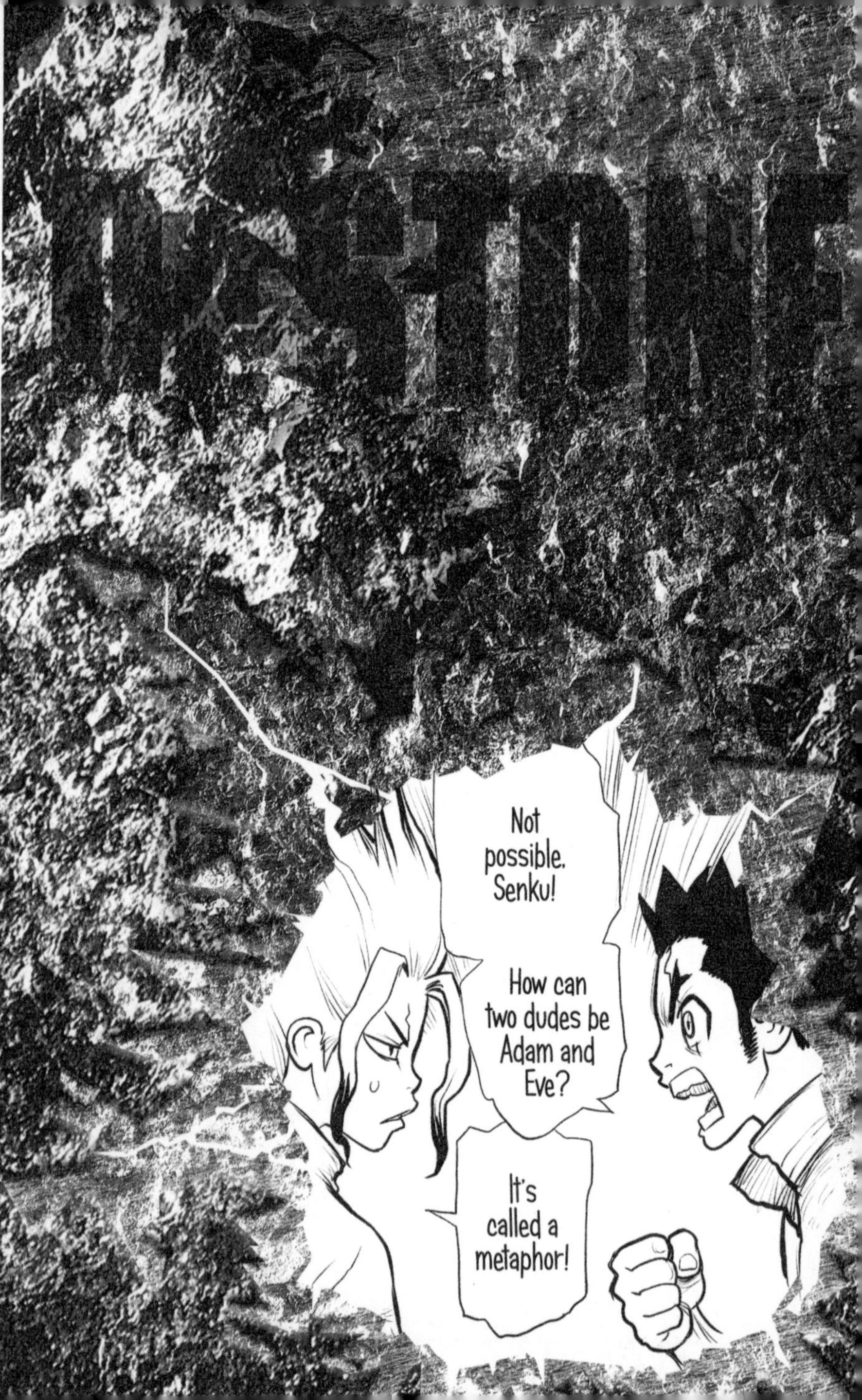
Not possible, Senku!
How can two dudes be Adam and Eve?
It's called a metaphor!

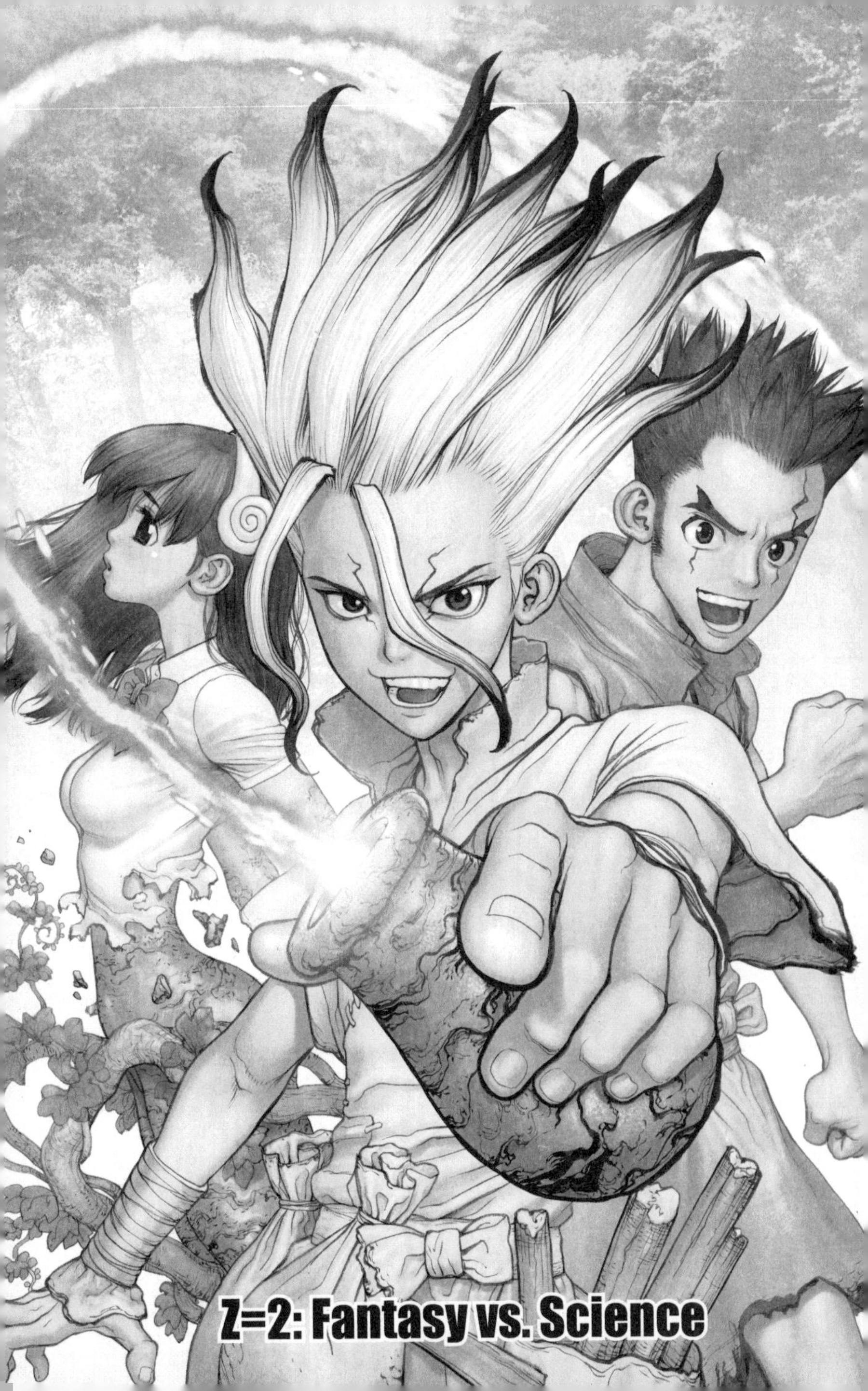
Z=2: Fantasy vs. Science

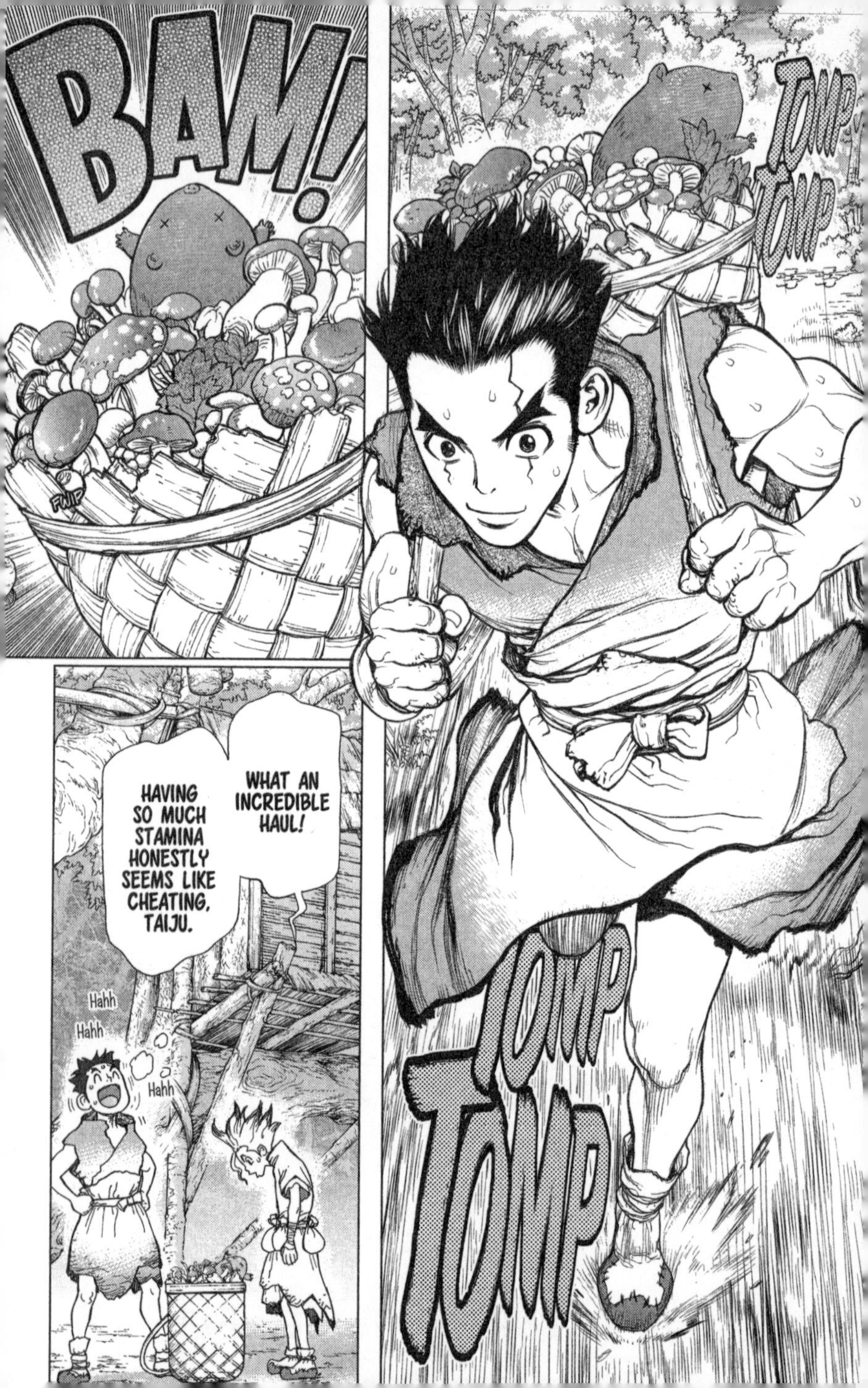
TOMP TOMP
BAM!
FWIP
TOMP TOMP
WHAT AN INCREDIBLE HAUL!
HAVING SO MUCH STAMINA HONESTLY SEEMS LIKE CHEATING, TAIJU.
Hahh
Hahh
Hahh

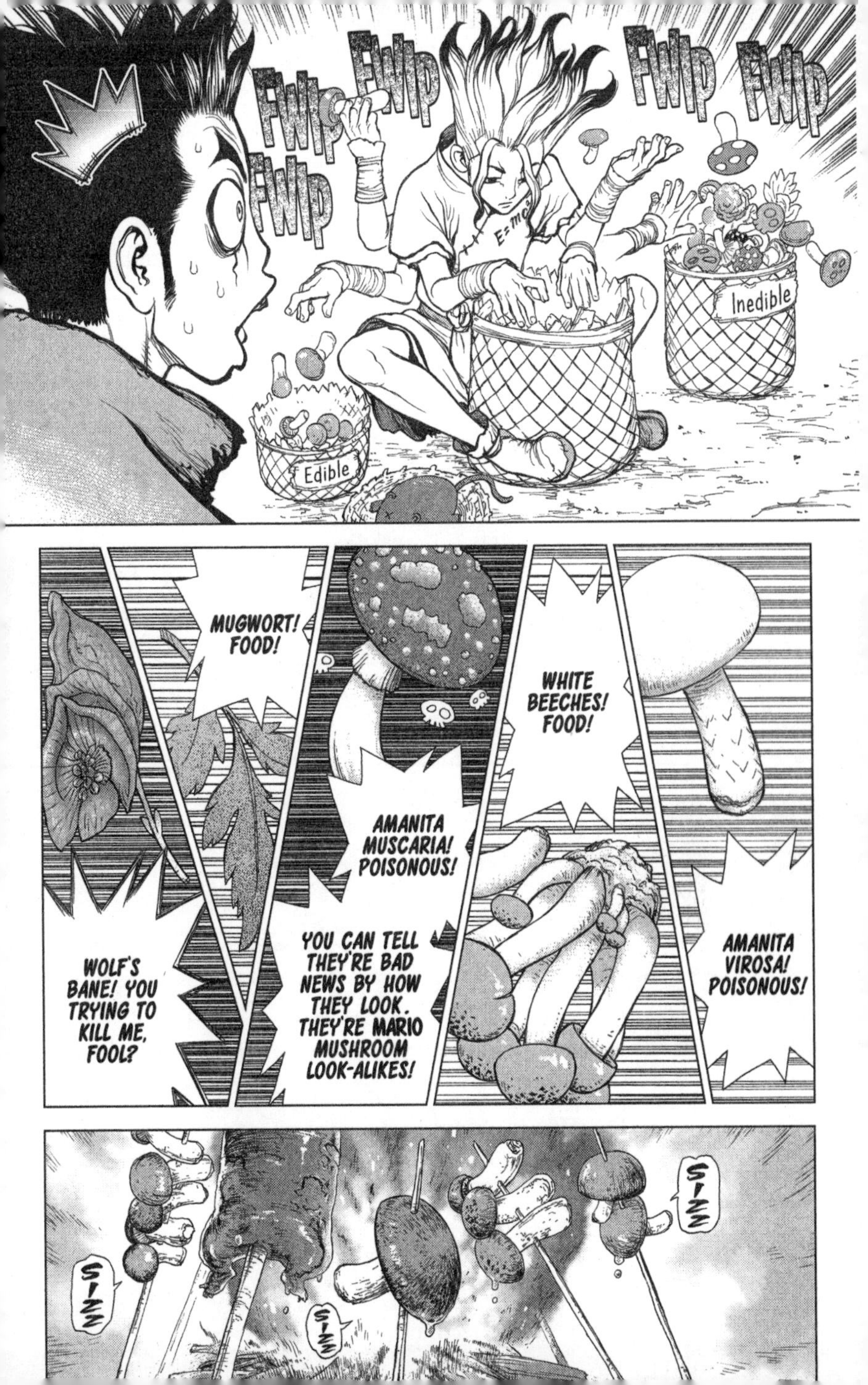

FWIP FWIP
FWIP FWIP
FWIP
Inedible
E=mc²
Edible
AMANITA VIROSA! POISONOUS!
WHITE BEECHES! FOOD!
AMANITA MUSCARIA! POISONOUS!
YOU CAN TELL THEY'RE BAD NEWS BY HOW THEY LOOK. THEY'RE MARIO MUSHROOM LOOK-ALIKES!
MUGWORT! FOOD!
WOLF'S BANE! YOU TRYING TO KILL ME, FOOL?
SIZZ
SIZZ
SIZZ

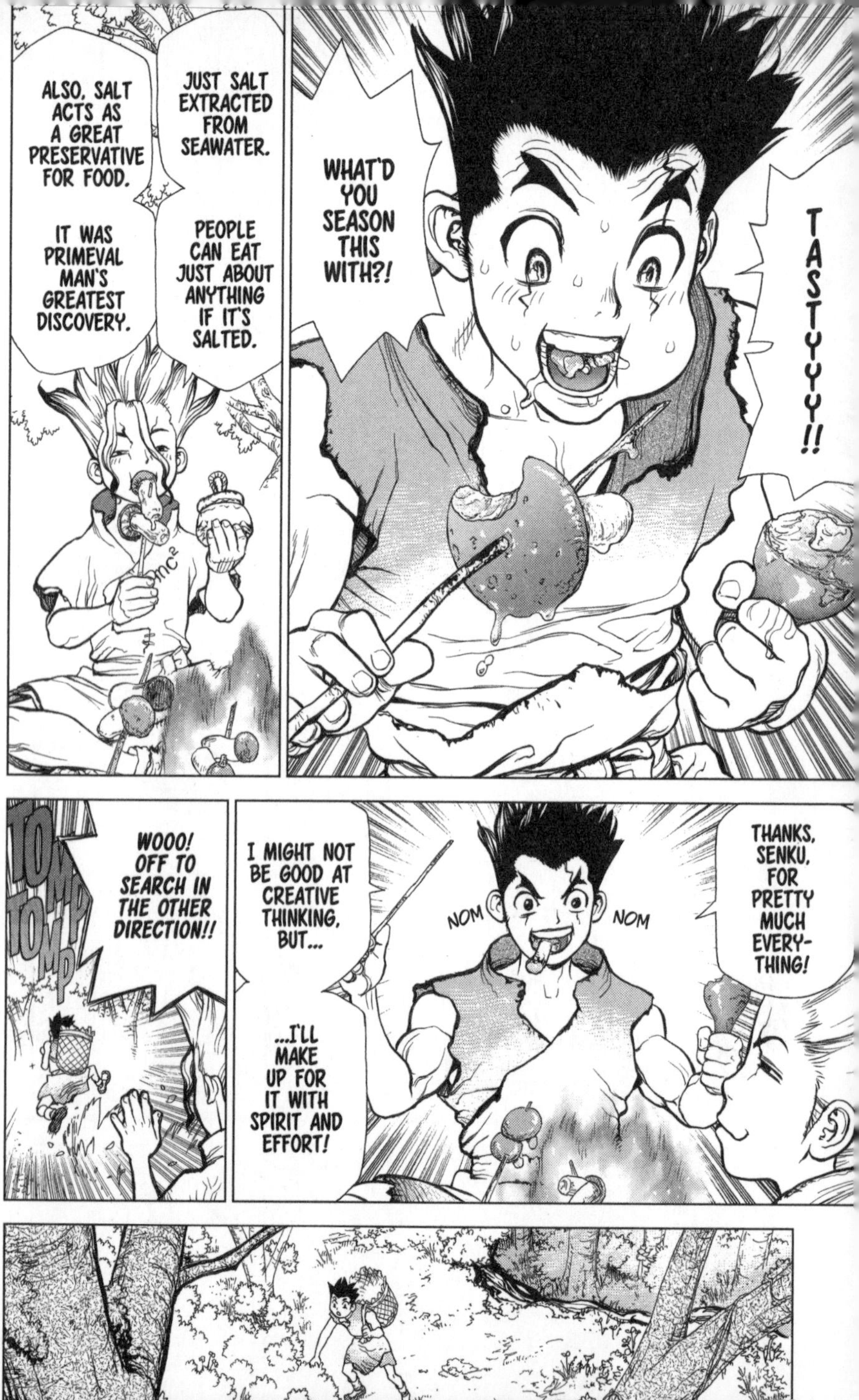
TASTYYYY!!
WHAT'D YOU SEASON THIS WITH?!
JUST SALT EXTRACTED FROM SEAWATER.
ALSO, SALT ACTS AS A GREAT PRESERVATIVE FOR FOOD.
PEOPLE CAN EAT JUST ABOUT ANYTHING IF IT'S SALTED.
IT WAS PRIMEVAL MAN'S GREATEST DISCOVERY.
THANKS, SENKU, FOR PRETTY MUCH EVERYTHING!
NOM NOM
I MIGHT NOT BE GOOD AT CREATIVE THINKING, BUT...
...I'LL MAKE UP FOR IT WITH SPIRIT AND EFFORT!
WOOO! OFF TO SEARCH IN THE OTHER DIRECTION!!
TOMP TOMP TOMP

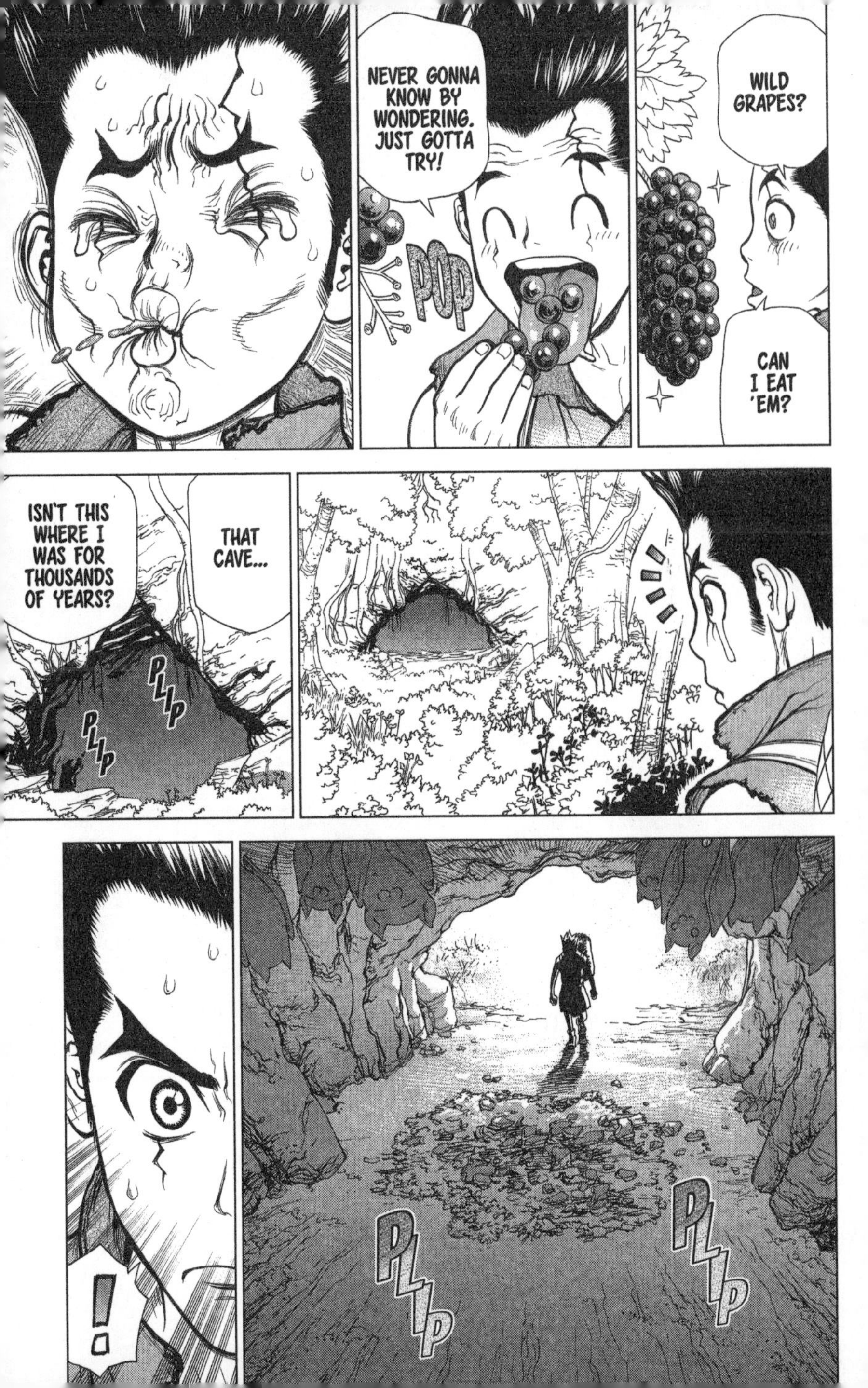
WILD GRAPES?
CAN I EAT 'EM?
NEVER GONNA KNOW BY WONDERING. JUST GOTTA TRY!
POP
THAT CAVE...
ISN'T THIS WHERE I WAS FOR THOUSANDS OF YEARS?
PLIP
PLIP
PLIP
PLIP
!

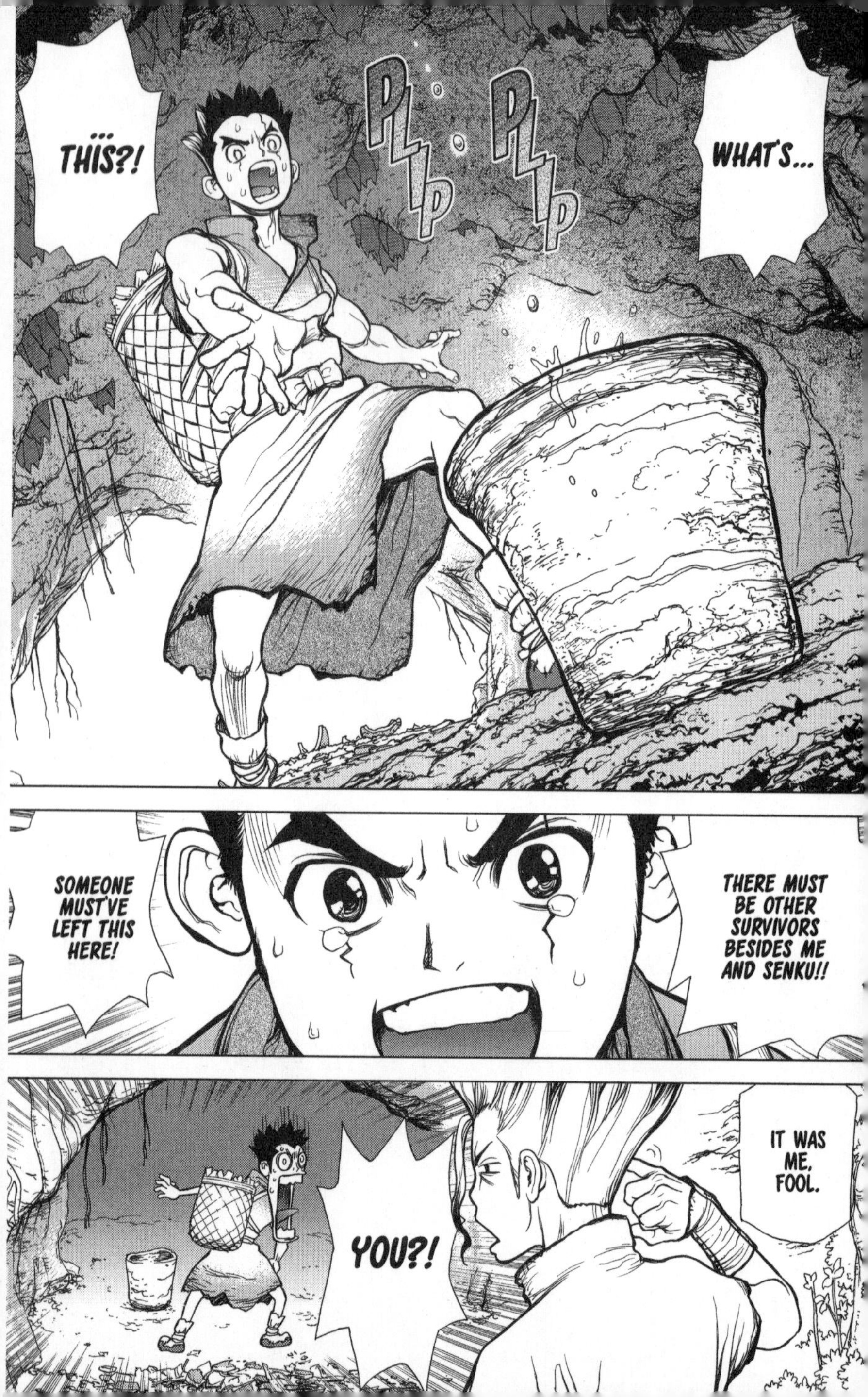
WHAT'S...
PLIP
PLIP
...THIS?!
THERE MUST BE OTHER SURVIVORS BESIDES ME AND SENKU!!
SOMEONE MUST'VE LEFT THIS HERE!
IT WAS ME, FOOL.
YOU?!

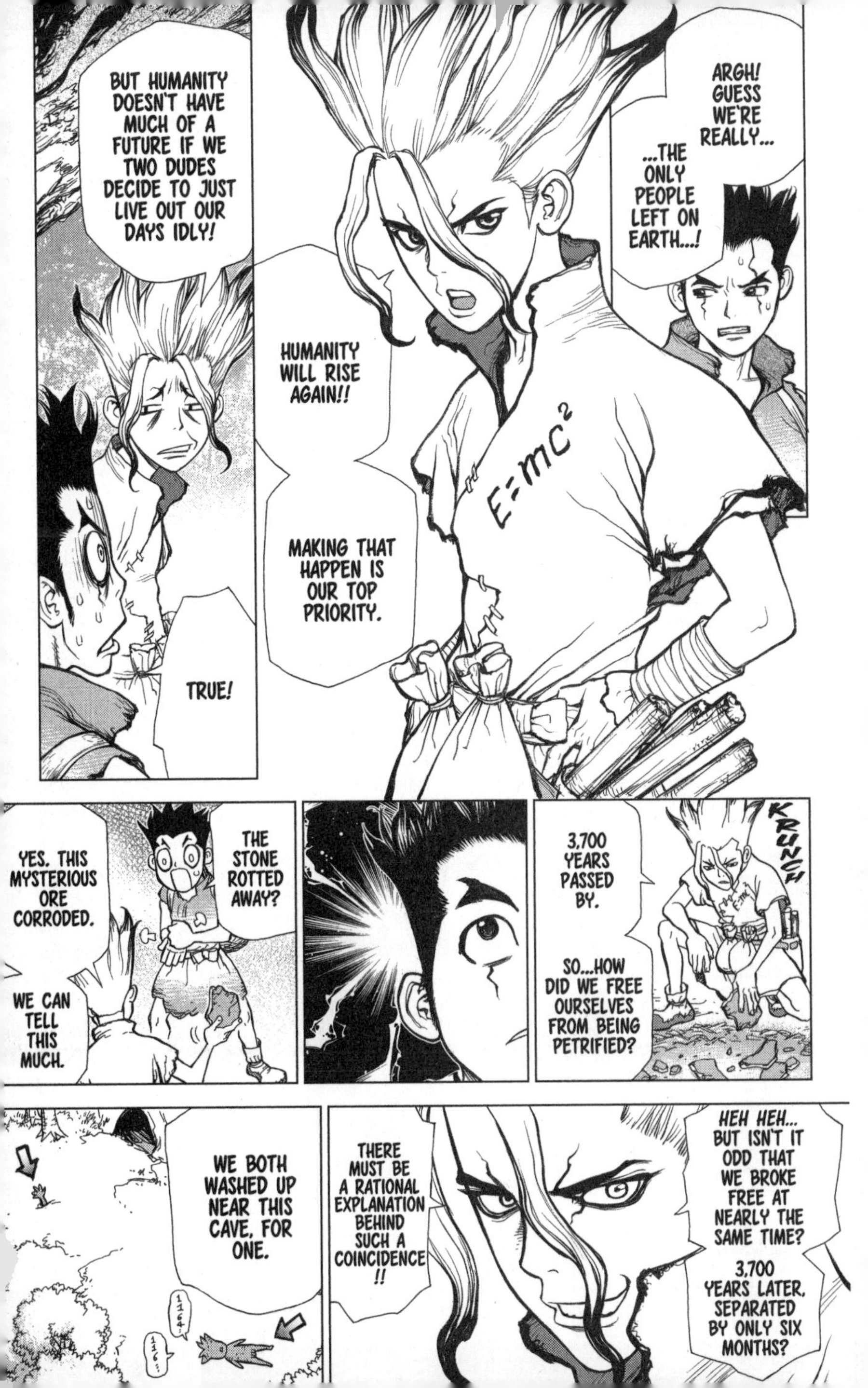
ARGH! GUESS WE'RE REALLY...
...THE ONLY PEOPLE LEFT ON EARTH...!
HUMANITY WILL RISE AGAIN!!
MAKING THAT HAPPEN IS OUR TOP PRIORITY.
BUT HUMANITY DOESN'T HAVE MUCH OF A FUTURE IF WE TWO DUDES DECIDE TO JUST LIVE OUT OUR DAYS IDLY!
TRUE!
KRUNCH
3,700 YEARS PASSED BY.
SO...HOW DID WE FREE OURSELVES FROM BEING PETRIFIED?
THE STONE ROTTED AWAY?
YES. THIS MYSTERIOUS ORE CORRODED.
WE CAN TELL THIS MUCH.
HEH HEH... BUT ISN'T IT ODD THAT WE BROKE FREE AT NEARLY THE SAME TIME?
3,700 YEARS LATER, SEPARATED BY ONLY SIX MONTHS?
THERE MUST BE A RATIONAL EXPLANATION BEHIND SUCH A COINCIDENCE!!
WE BOTH WASHED UP NEAR THIS CAVE, FOR ONE.

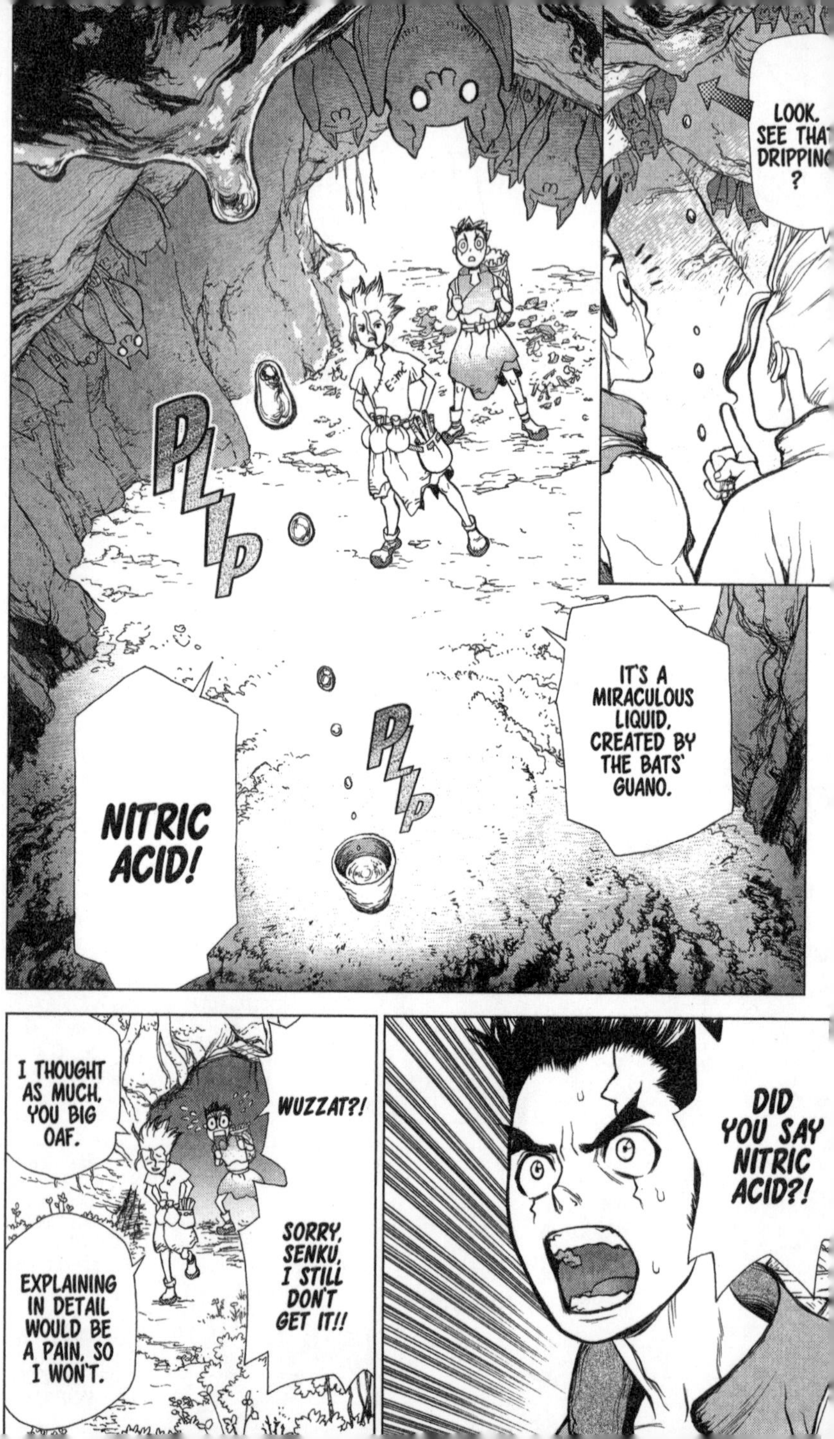
LOOK. SEE THAT DRIPPING?
PLIP
IT'S A MIRACULOUS LIQUID, CREATED BY THE BATS' GUANO.
NITRIC ACID!
PLIP
DID YOU SAY NITRIC ACID?!
WUZZAT?!
I THOUGHT AS MUCH, YOU BIG OAF.
SORRY, SENKU, I STILL DON'T GET IT!!
EXPLAINING IN DETAIL WOULD BE A PAIN, SO I WON'T.

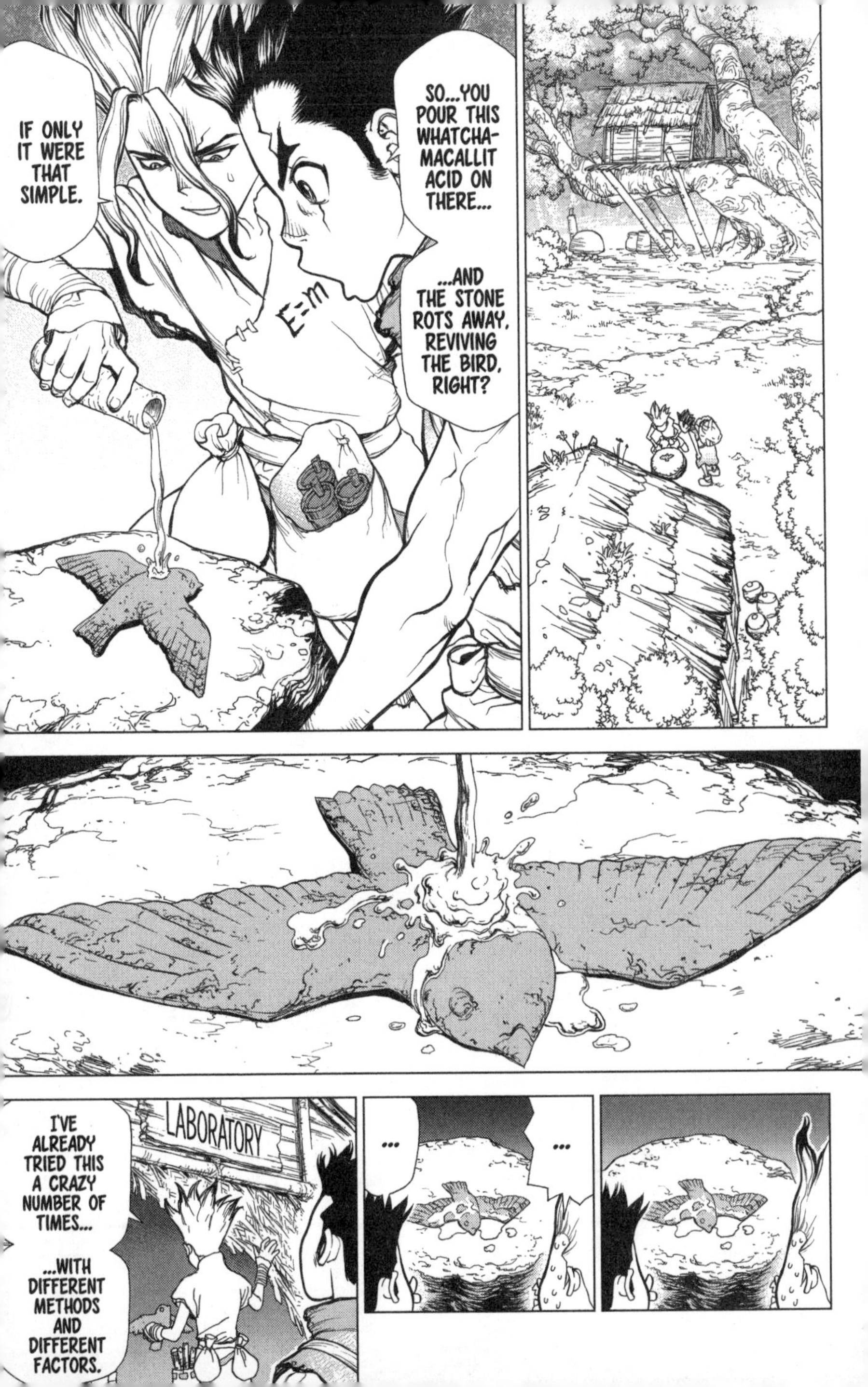
SO...YOU POUR THIS WHATCHAMACALLIT ACID ON THERE...
...AND THE STONE ROTS AWAY, REVIVING THE BIRD, RIGHT?
IF ONLY IT WERE THAT SIMPLE.
E=m
...
...
LABORATORY
I'VE ALREADY TRIED THIS A CRAZY NUMBER OF TIMES...
...WITH DIFFERENT METHODS AND DIFFERENT FACTORS.

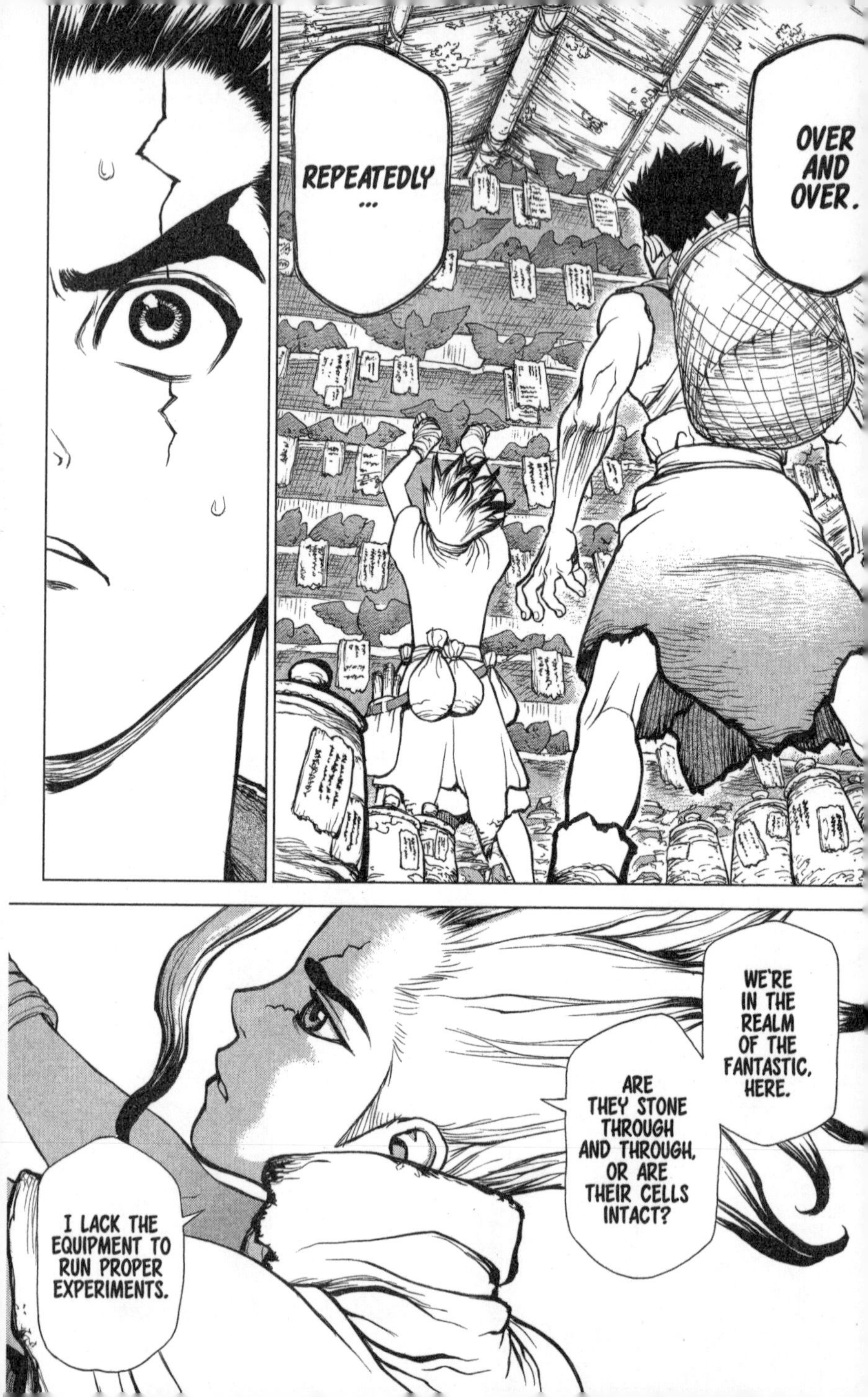
OVER AND OVER.
REPEATEDLY...
WE'RE IN THE REALM OF THE FANTASTIC, HERE.
ARE THEY STONE THROUGH AND THROUGH, OR ARE THEIR CELLS INTACT?
I LACK THE EQUIPMENT TO RUN PROPER EXPERIMENTS.

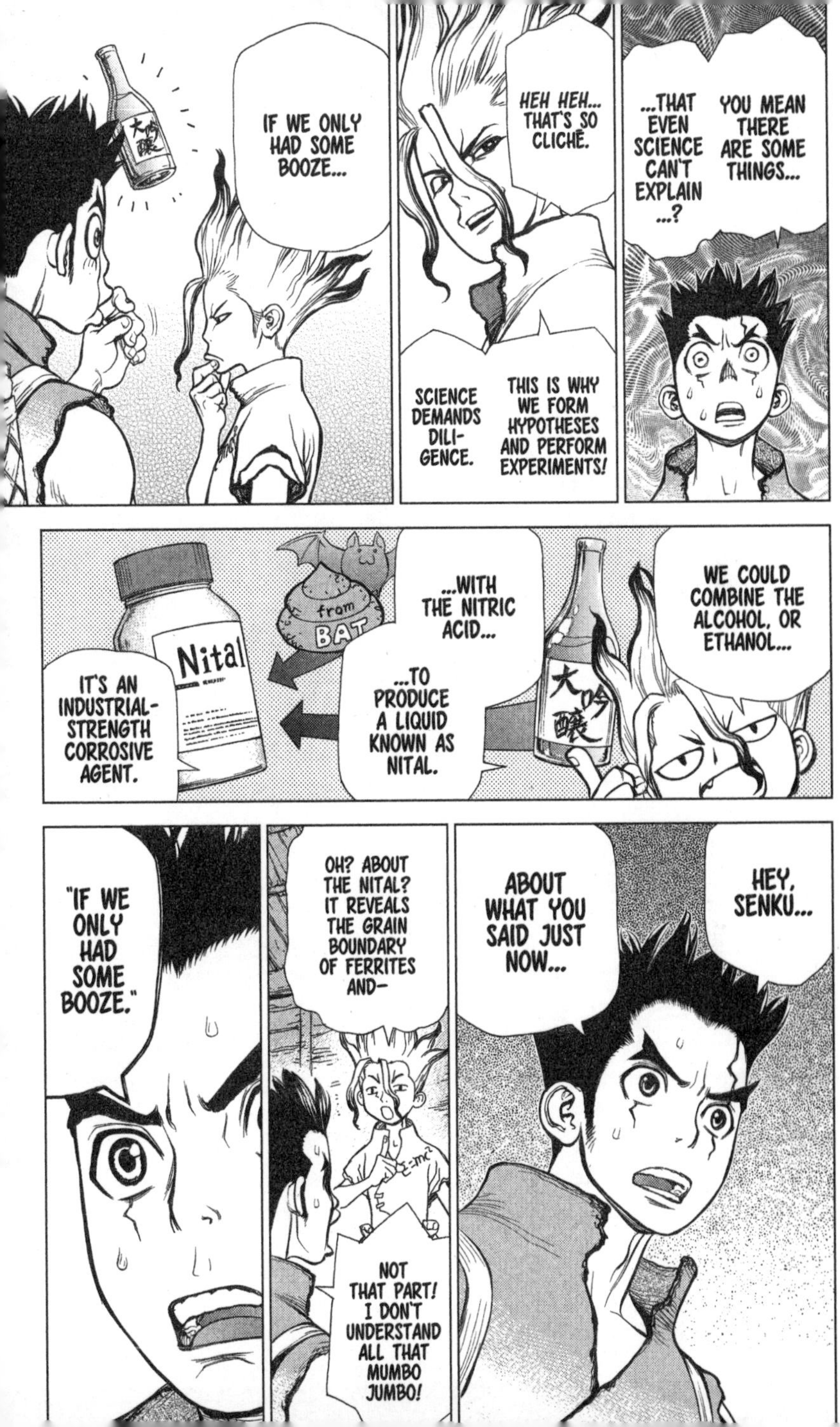
YOU MEAN THERE ARE SOME THINGS...
...THAT EVEN SCIENCE CAN'T EXPLAIN ...?
HEH HEH... THAT'S SO CLICHÉ.
THIS IS WHY WE FORM HYPOTHESES AND PERFORM EXPERIMENTS!
SCIENCE DEMANDS DILI-GENCE.
IF WE ONLY HAD SOME BOOZE...
大吟醸
WE COULD COMBINE THE ALCOHOL, OR ETHANOL...
大吟醸
...WITH THE NITRIC ACID...
from BAT
...TO PRODUCE A LIQUID KNOWN AS NITAL.
Nital
IT'S AN INDUSTRIAL-STRENGTH CORROSIVE AGENT.
HEY, SENKU...
ABOUT WHAT YOU SAID JUST NOW...
OH? ABOUT THE NITAL? IT REVEALS THE GRAIN BOUNDARY OF FERRITES AND–
E=mc²
NOT THAT PART! I DON'T UNDERSTAND ALL THAT MUMBO JUMBO!
"IF WE ONLY HAD SOME BOOZE."

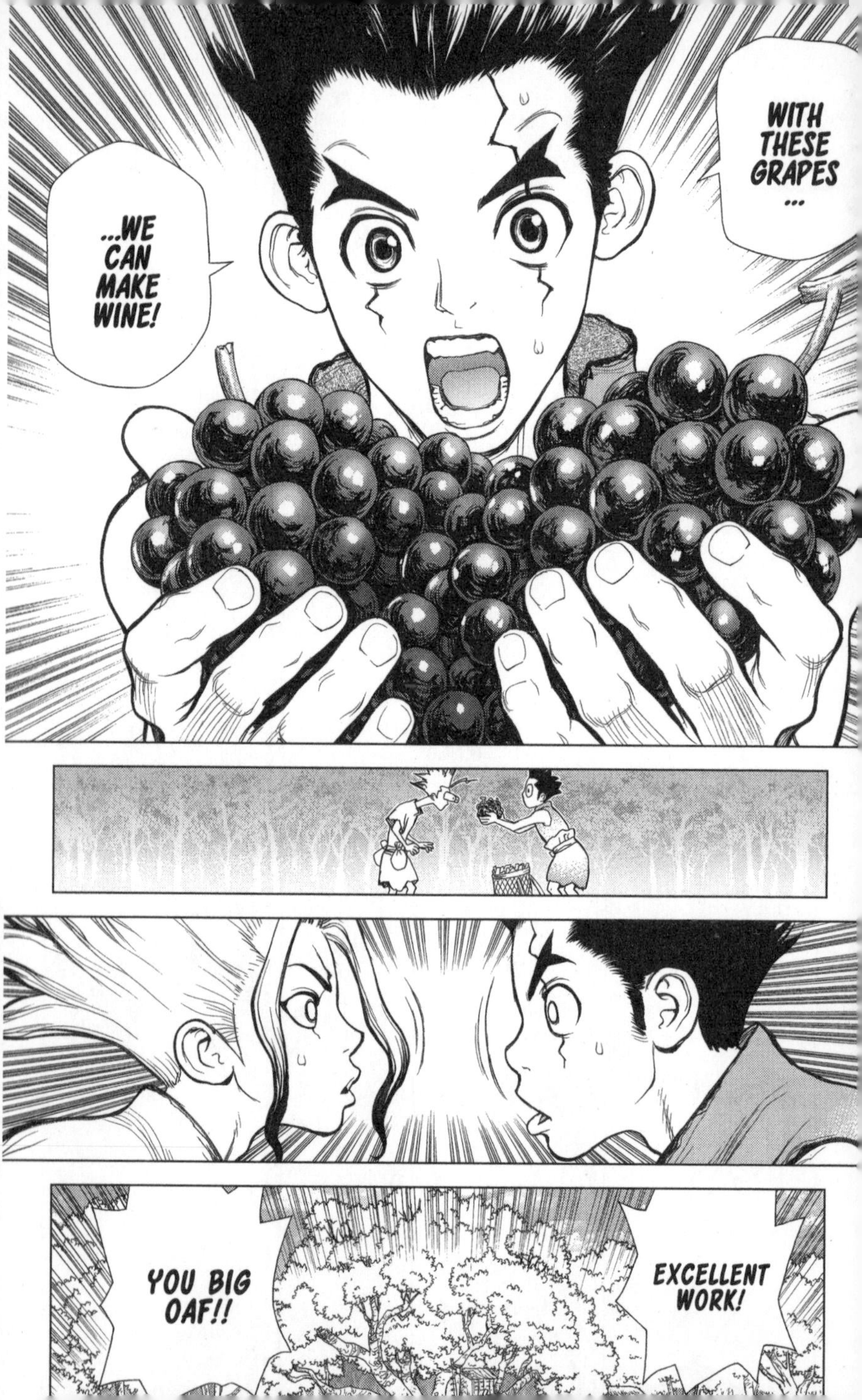
WITH THESE GRAPES ...
...WE CAN MAKE WINE!
EXCELLENT WORK!
YOU BIG OAF!!

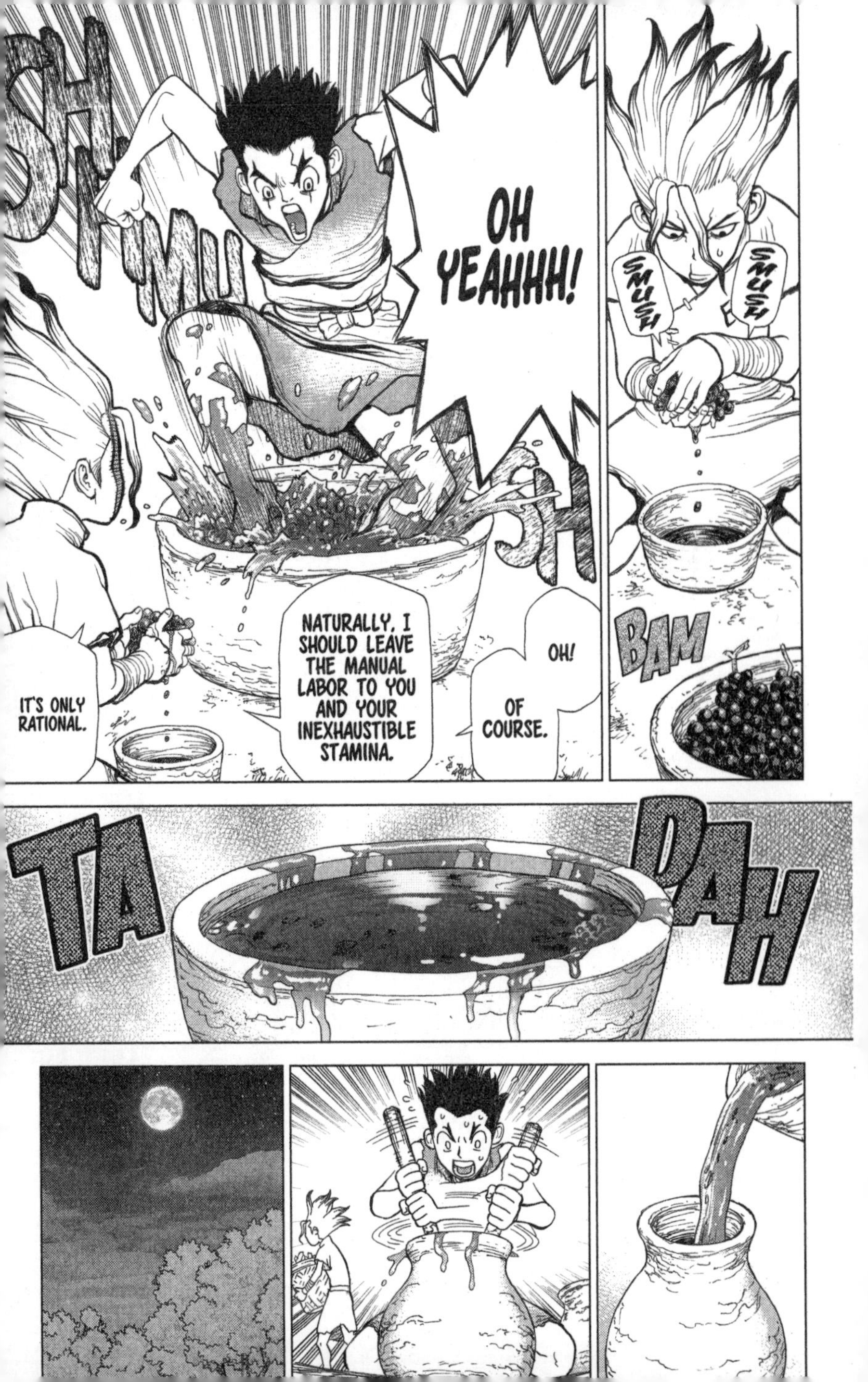
SMUSH
SMUSH
BAM
OH YEAHHH!
SHMUSH
OH!
OF COURSE.
NATURALLY, I SHOULD LEAVE THE MANUAL LABOR TO YOU AND YOUR INEXHAUSTIBLE STAMINA.
IT'S ONLY RATIONAL.
TA
DAH

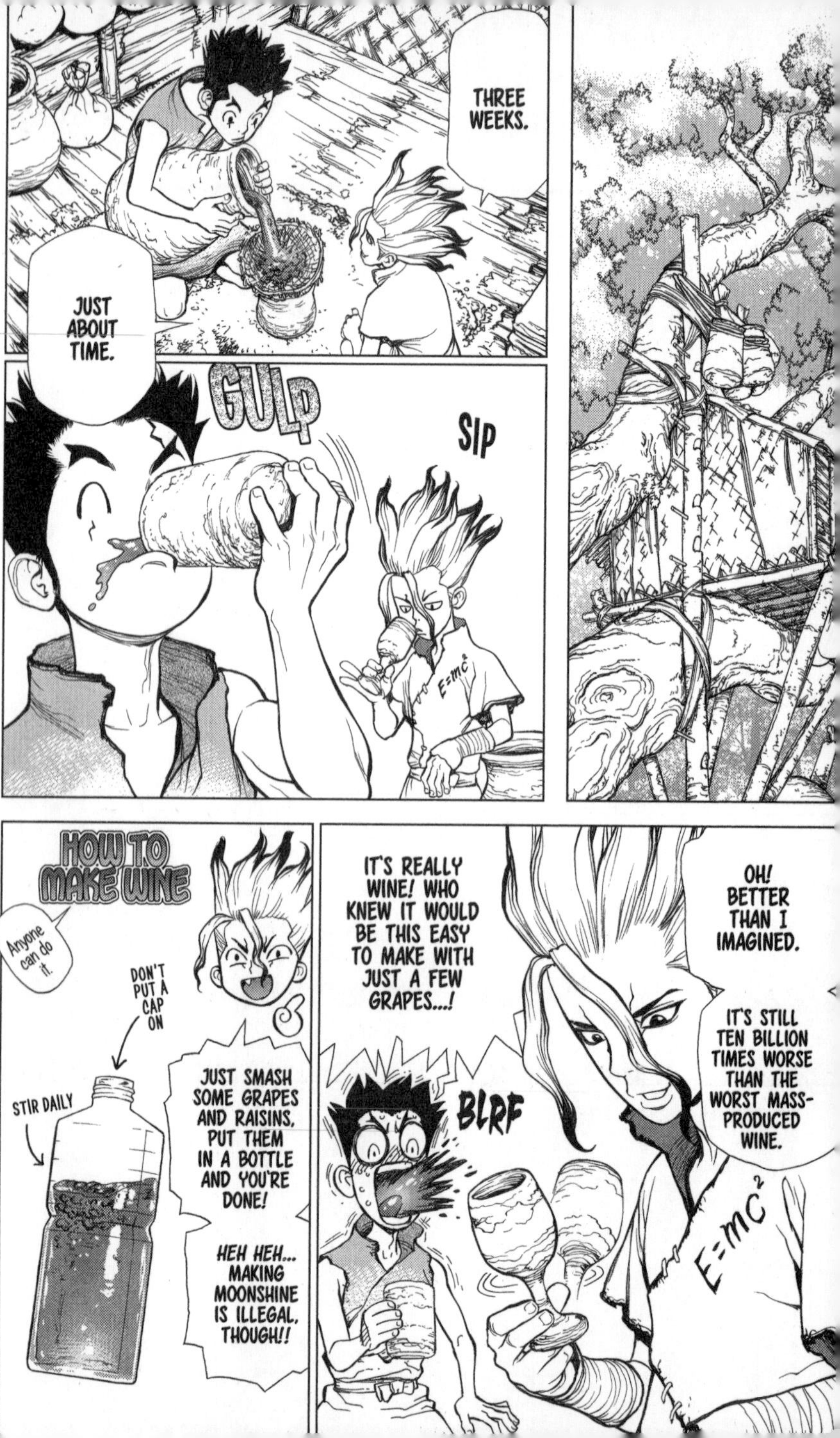

THREE WEEKS.
JUST ABOUT TIME.
GULP
SIP
OH! BETTER THAN I IMAGINED.
IT'S REALLY WINE! WHO KNEW IT WOULD BE THIS EASY TO MAKE WITH JUST A FEW GRAPES...!
IT'S STILL TEN BILLION TIMES WORSE THAN THE WORST MASS-PRODUCED WINE.
BLRF
E=mc²
HOW TO MAKE WINE
Anyone can do it.
DON'T PUT A CAP ON
STIR DAILY
JUST SMASH SOME GRAPES AND RAISINS, PUT THEM IN A BOTTLE AND YOU'RE DONE!
HEH HEH... MAKING MOONSHINE IS ILLEGAL, THOUGH!!

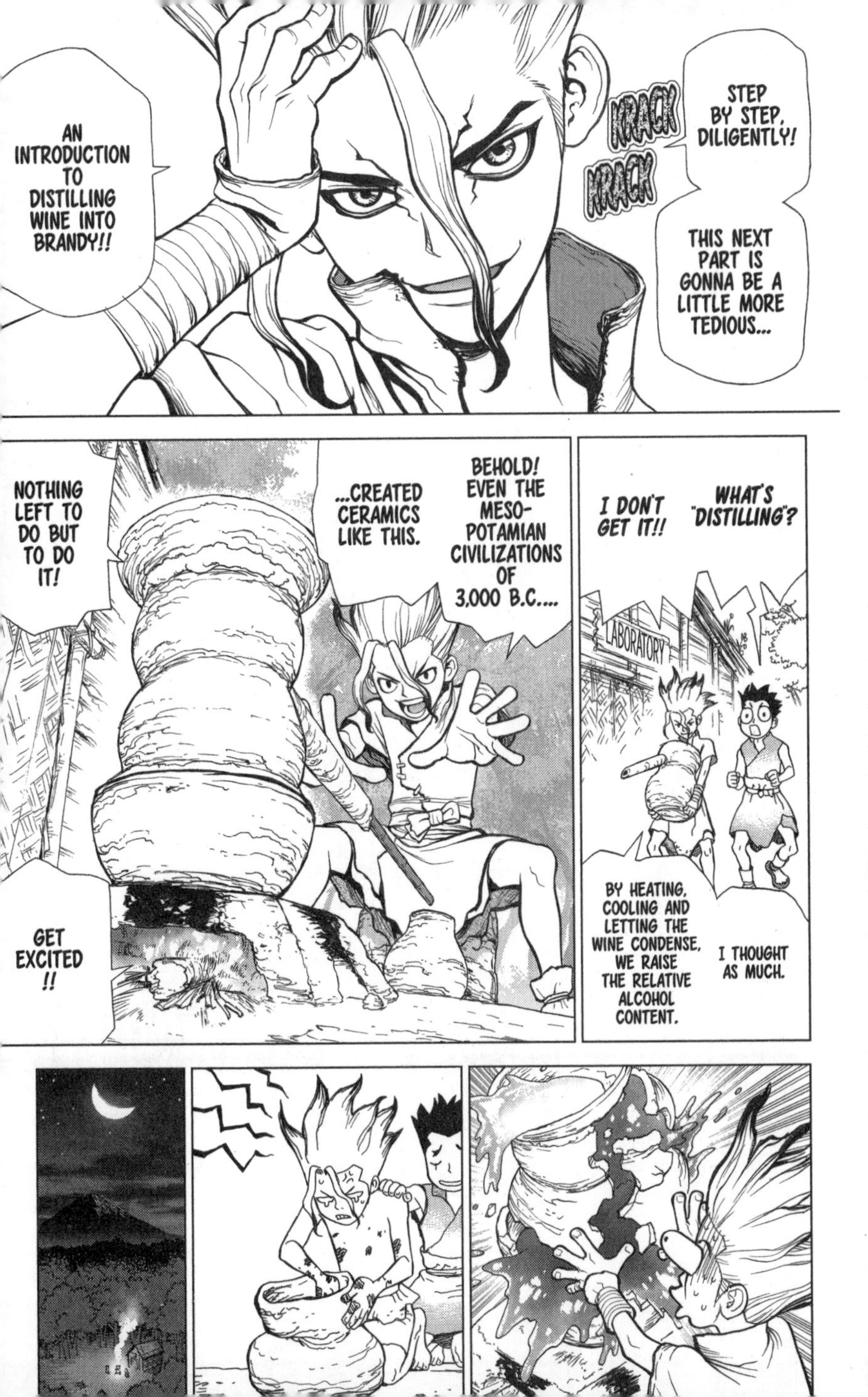
STEP BY STEP, DILIGENTLY!
KRACK
KRACK
THIS NEXT PART IS GONNA BE A LITTLE MORE TEDIOUS...
AN INTRODUCTION TO DISTILLING WINE INTO BRANDY!!
WHAT'S "DISTILLING"?
I DON'T GET IT!!
LABORATORY
I THOUGHT AS MUCH.
BY HEATING, COOLING AND LETTING THE WINE CONDENSE, WE RAISE THE RELATIVE ALCOHOL CONTENT.
BEHOLD! EVEN THE MESO-POTAMIAN CIVILIZATIONS OF 3,000 B.C....
...CREATED CERAMICS LIKE THIS.
NOTHING LEFT TO DO BUT TO DO IT!
GET EXCITED!!

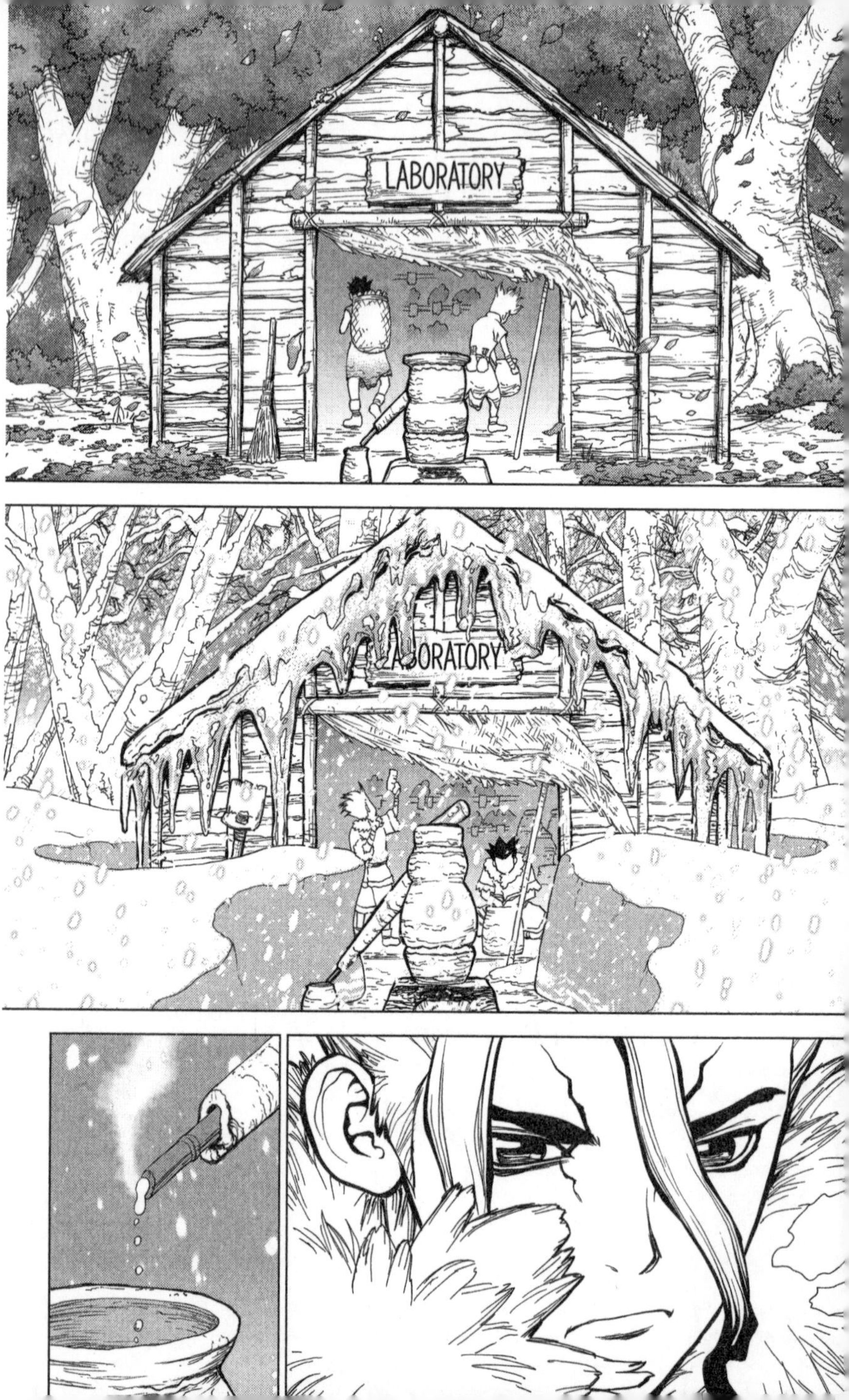
LABORATORY
LABORATORY

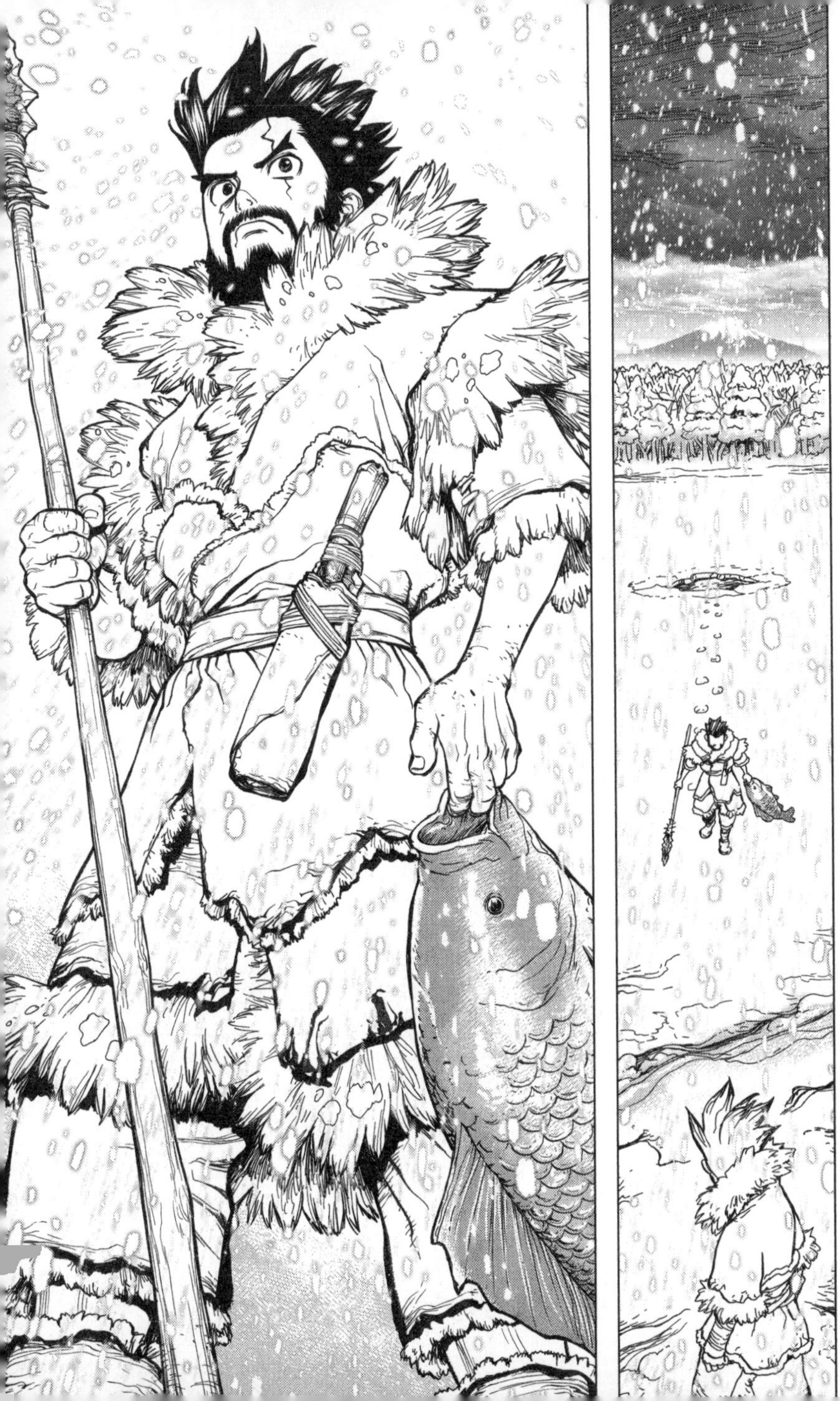

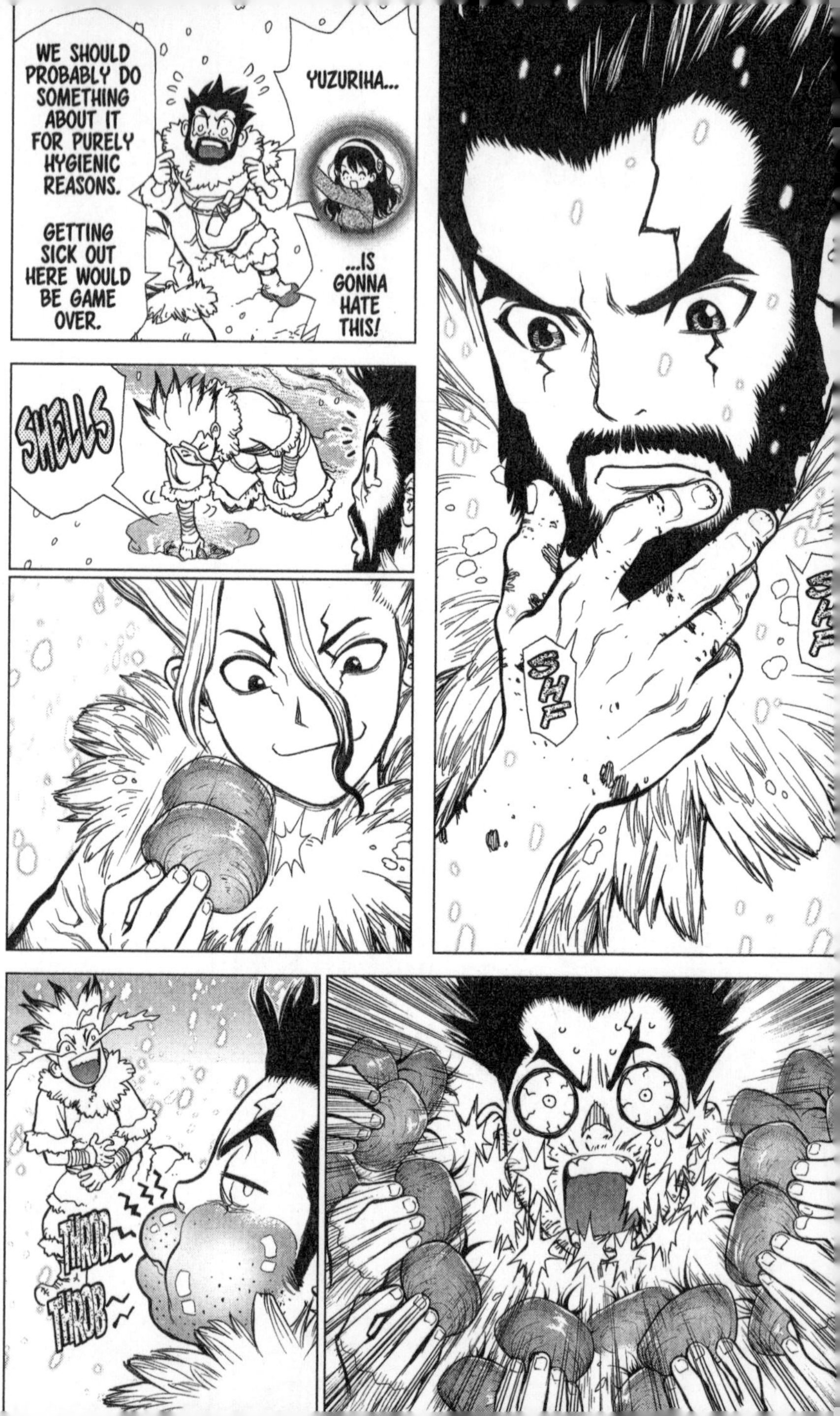
SHF
YUZURIHA...
...IS GONNA HATE THIS!
WE SHOULD PROBABLY DO SOMETHING ABOUT IT FOR PURELY HYGIENIC REASONS.
GETTING SICK OUT HERE WOULD BE GAME OVER.
SHELLS
THROB
THROB

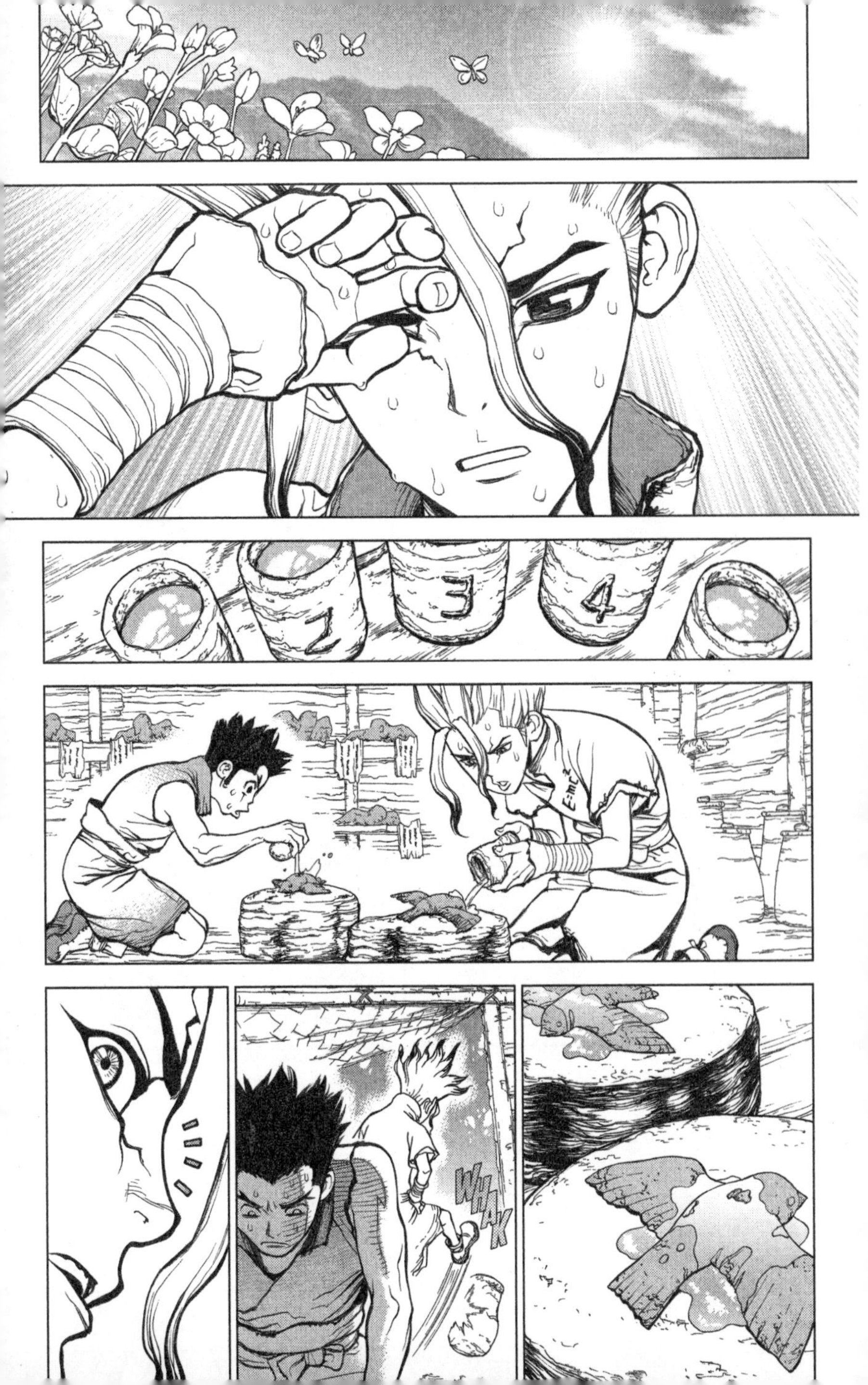
4
3
2
WHAK

FWIP

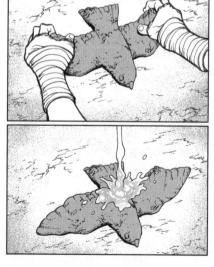

E=mc²

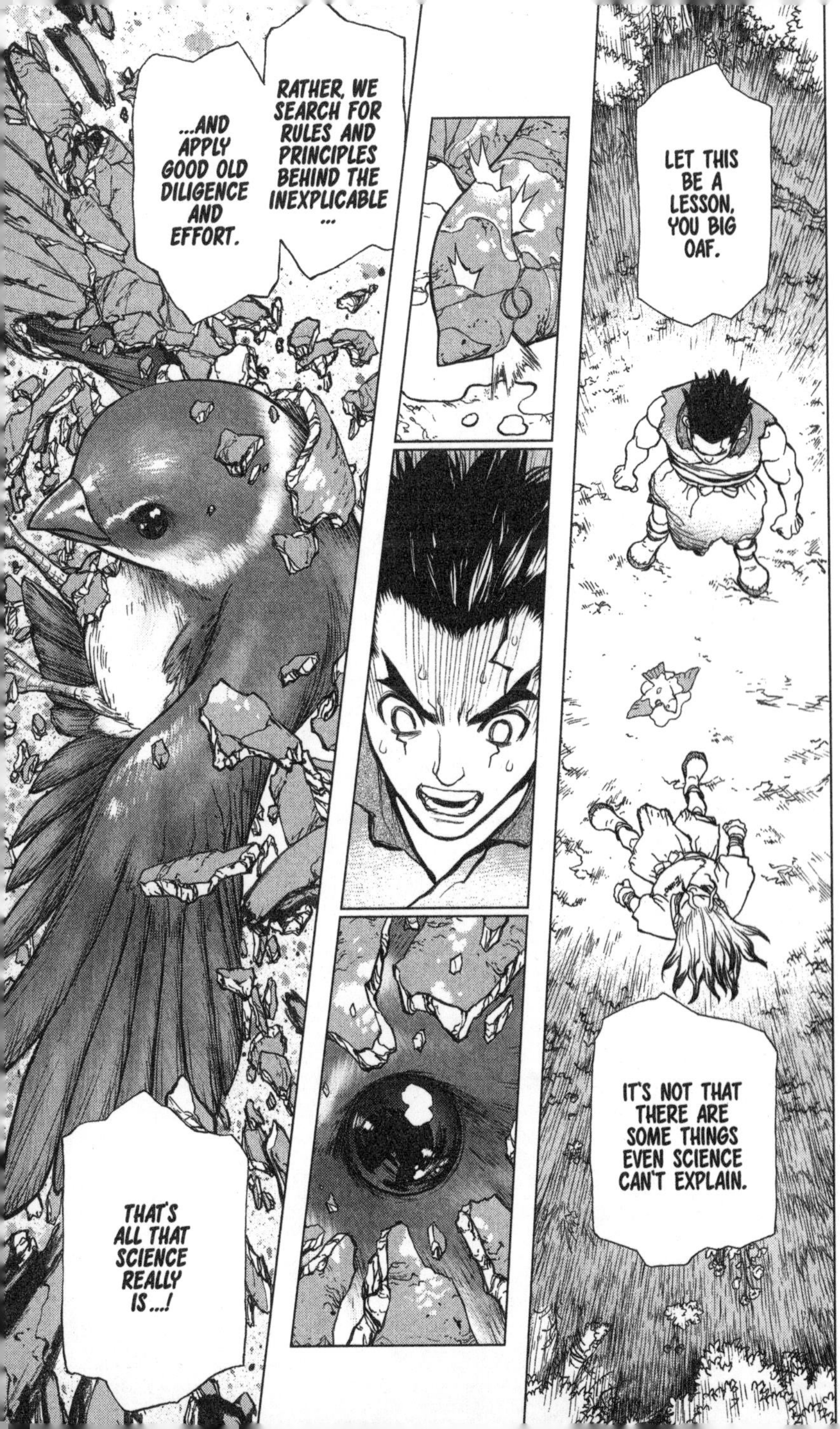
LET THIS BE A LESSON, YOU BIG OAF.
IT'S NOT THAT THERE ARE SOME THINGS EVEN SCIENCE CAN'T EXPLAIN.
RATHER, WE SEARCH FOR RULES AND PRINCIPLES BEHIND THE INEXPLICABLE...
...AND APPLY GOOD OLD DILIGENCE AND EFFORT.
THAT'S ALL THAT SCIENCE REALLY IS...!

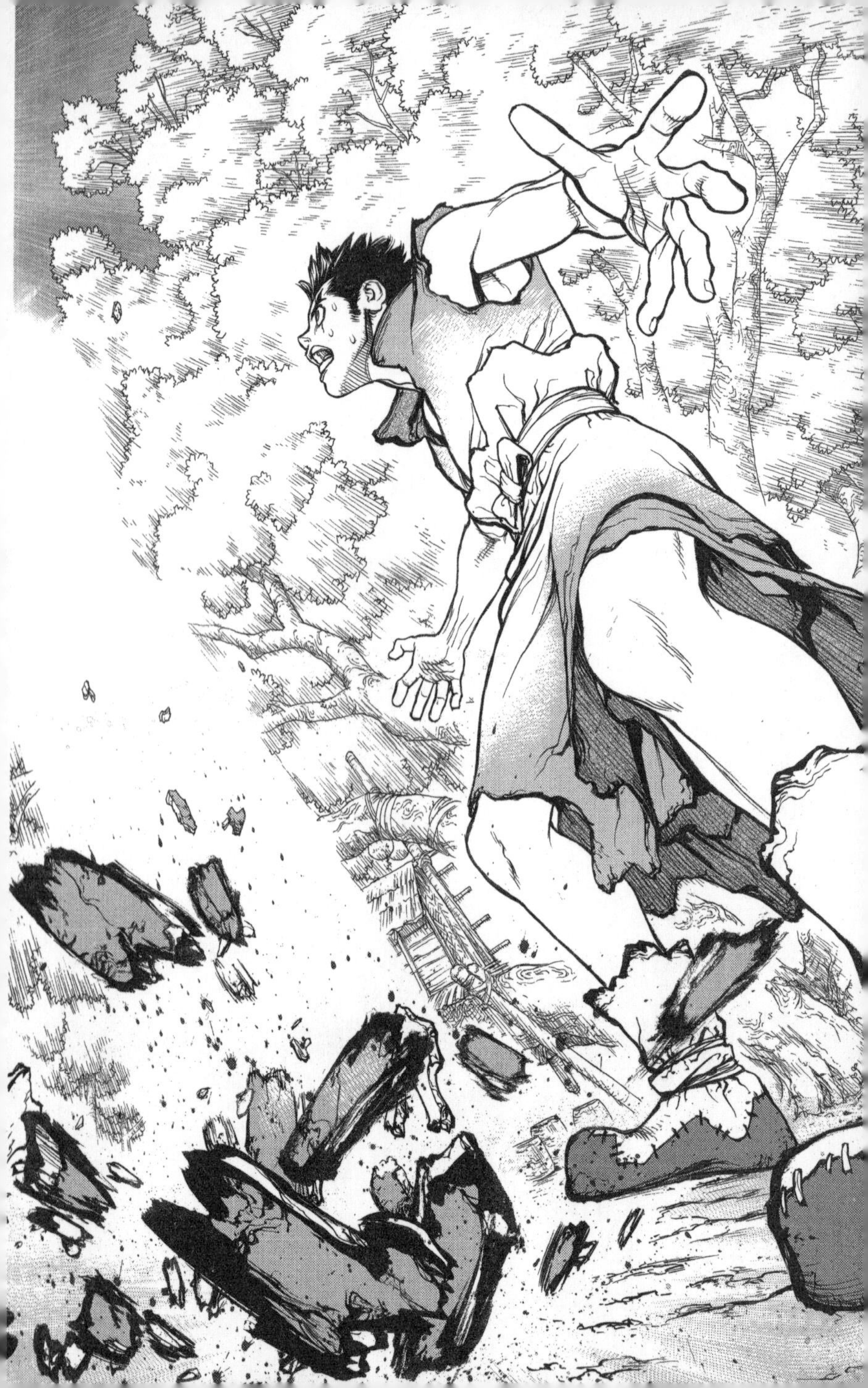

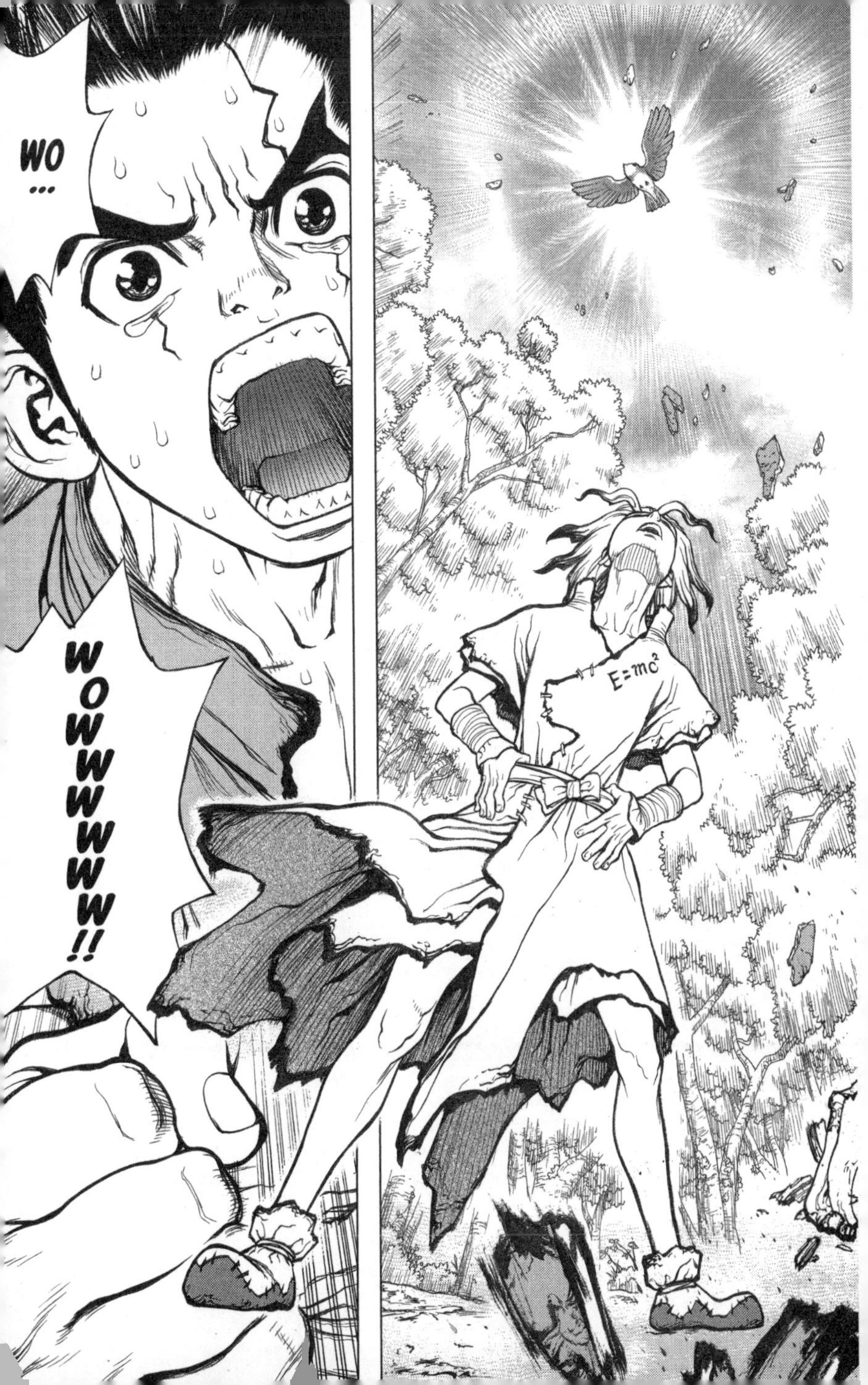
E=mc²
WO...
WOWWWWWWW!!

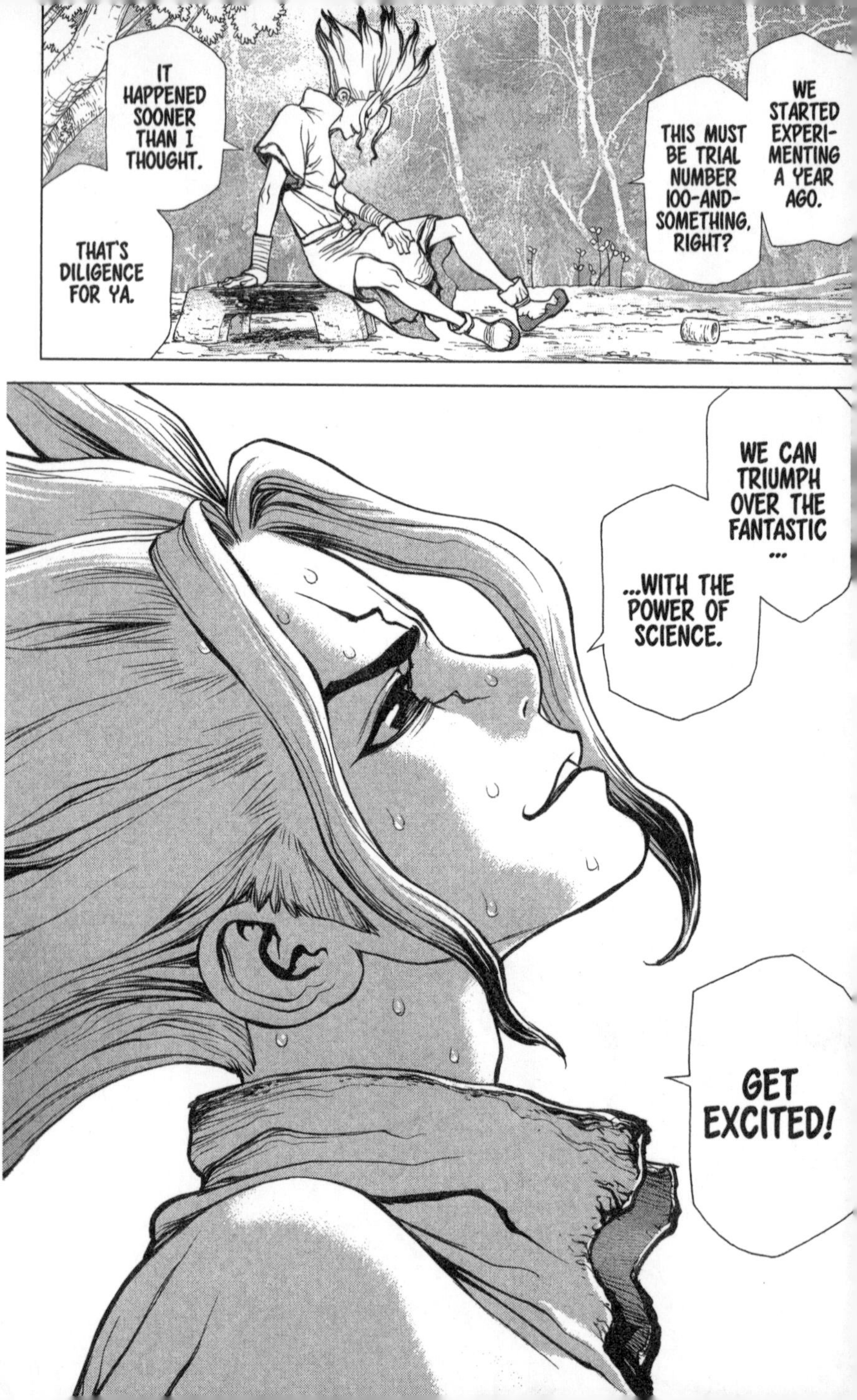
WE STARTED EXPERIMENTING A YEAR AGO.
THIS MUST BE TRIAL NUMBER 100-AND-SOMETHING, RIGHT?
IT HAPPENED SOONER THAN I THOUGHT.
THAT'S DILIGENCE FOR YA.
WE CAN TRIUMPH OVER THE FANTASTIC...
...WITH THE POWER OF SCIENCE.
GET EXCITED!

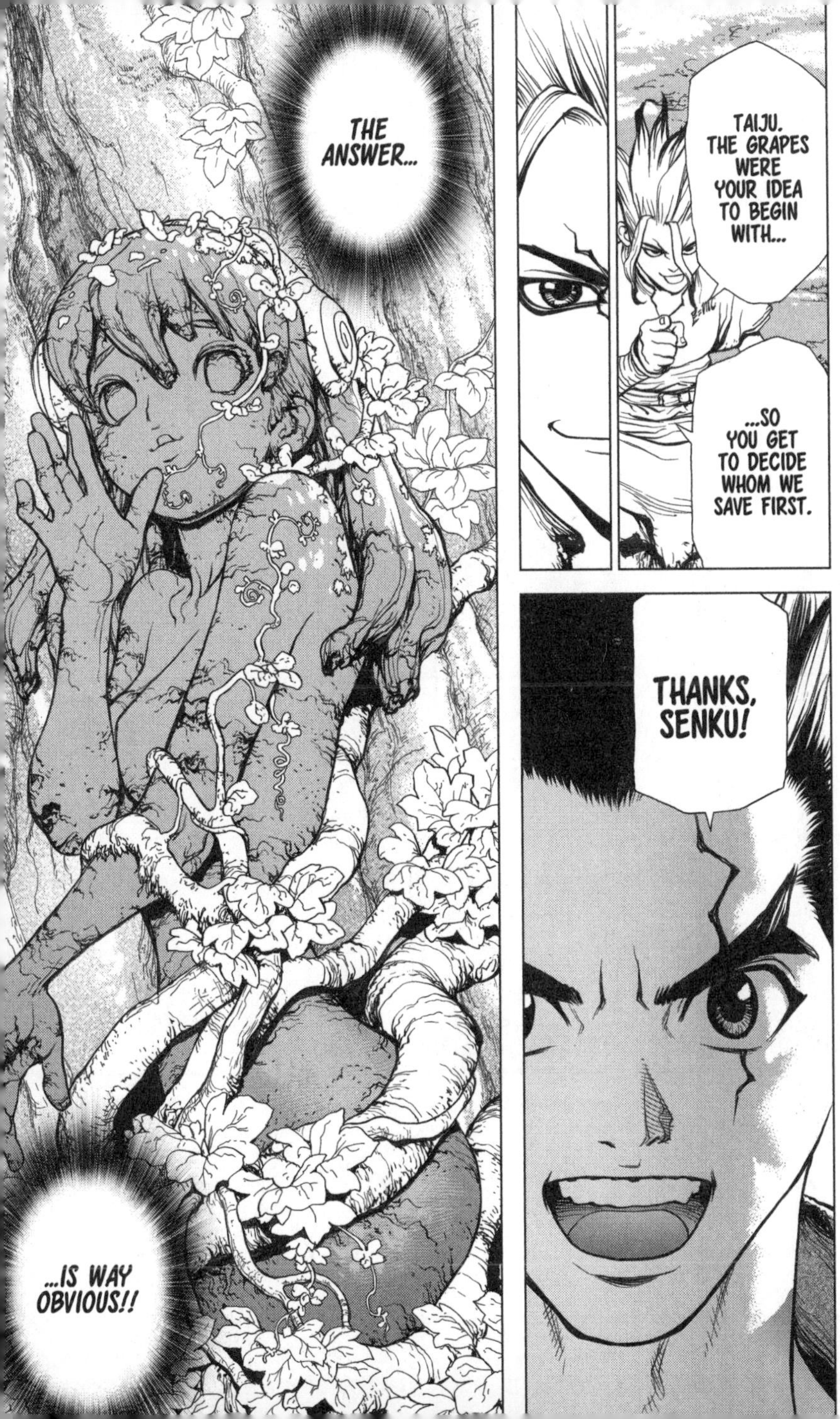
TAIJU. THE GRAPES WERE YOUR IDEA TO BEGIN WITH...
...SO YOU GET TO DECIDE WHOM WE SAVE FIRST.
THANKS, SENKU!
THE ANSWER...
...IS WAY OBVIOUS!!

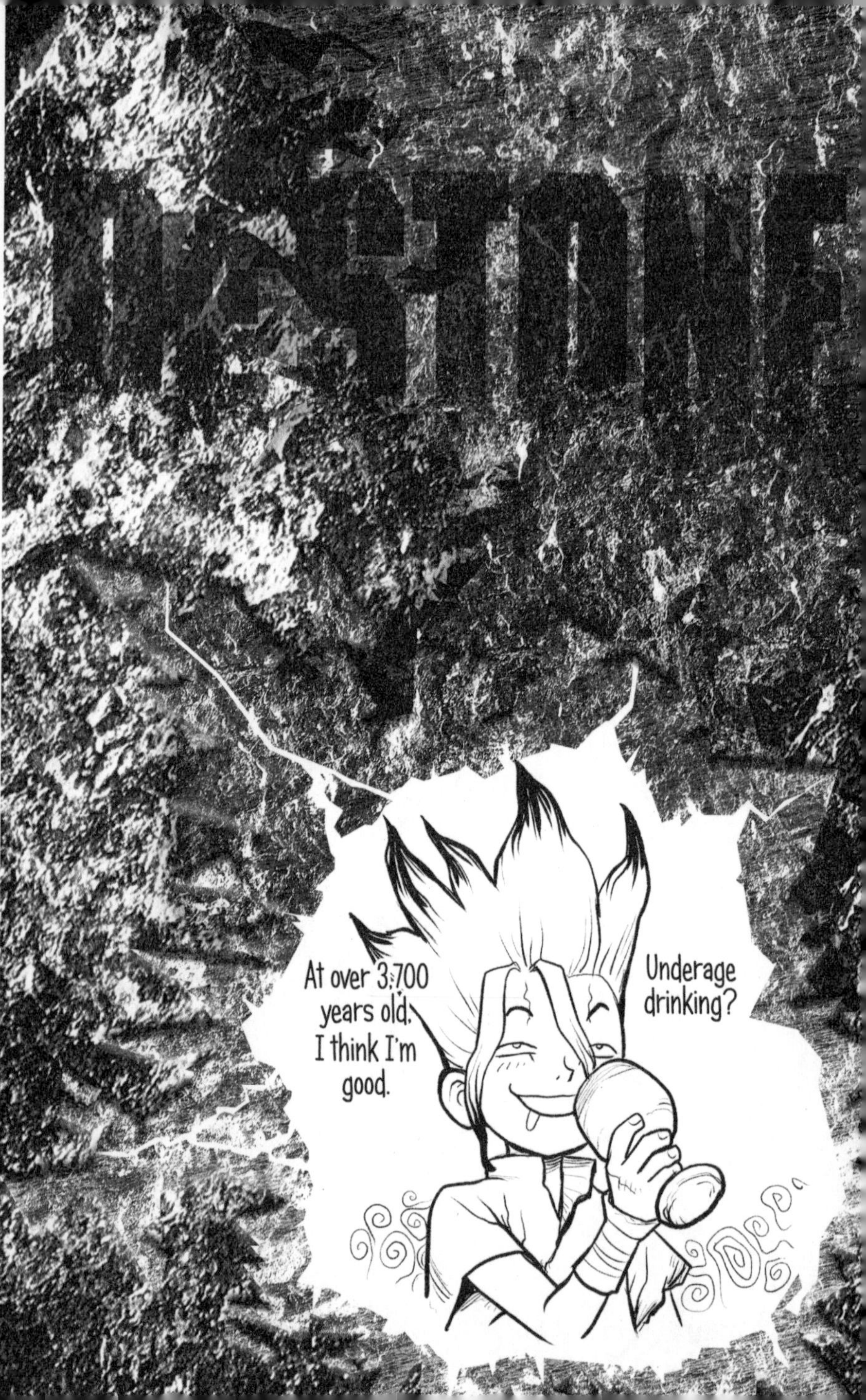
Underage drinking?
At over 3,700 years old, I think I'm good.

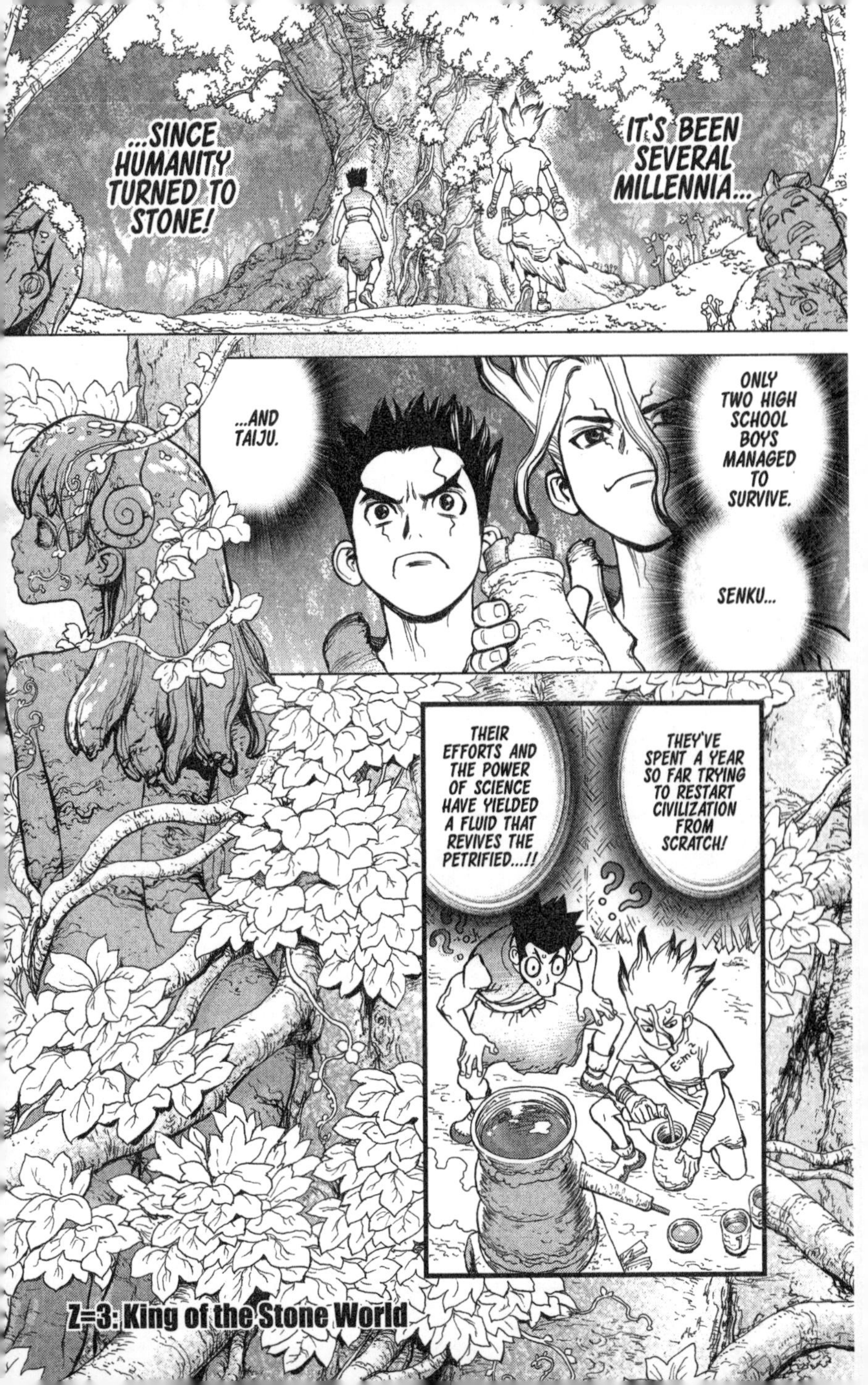
IT'S BEEN SEVERAL MILLENNIA...
...SINCE HUMANITY TURNED TO STONE!
ONLY TWO HIGH SCHOOL BOYS MANAGED TO SURVIVE.
SENKU...
...AND TAIJU.
THEY'VE SPENT A YEAR SO FAR TRYING TO RESTART CIVILIZATION FROM SCRATCH!
THEIR EFFORTS AND THE POWER OF SCIENCE HAVE YIELDED A FLUID THAT REVIVES THE PETRIFIED...!!
Z=3: King of the Stone World

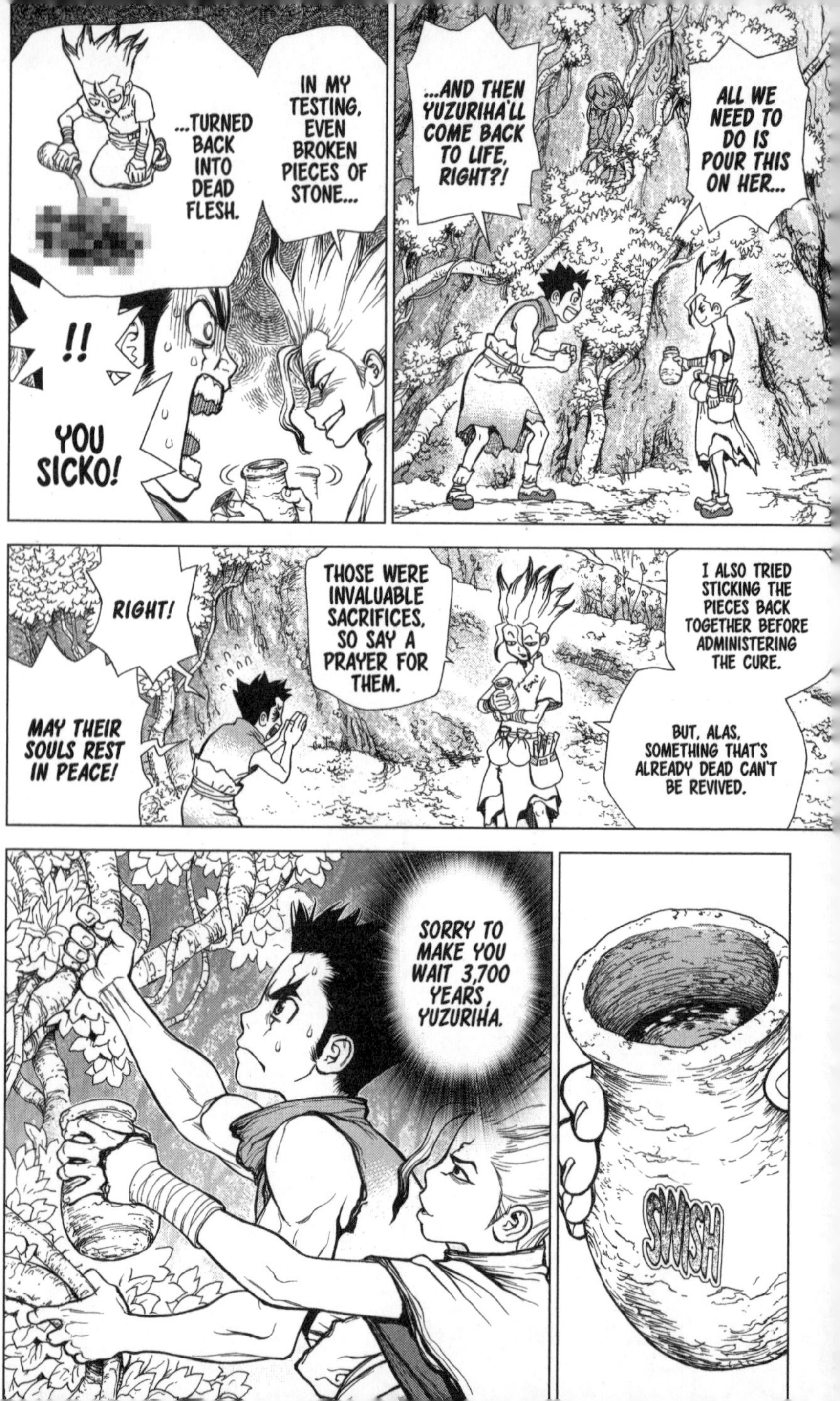
ALL WE NEED TO DO IS POUR THIS ON HER...
...AND THEN YUZURIHA'LL COME BACK TO LIFE, RIGHT?!
IN MY TESTING, EVEN BROKEN PIECES OF STONE...
...TURNED BACK INTO DEAD FLESH.
!!
YOU SICKO!
I ALSO TRIED STICKING THE PIECES BACK TOGETHER BEFORE ADMINISTERING THE CURE.
BUT, ALAS, SOMETHING THAT'S ALREADY DEAD CAN'T BE REVIVED.
THOSE WERE INVALUABLE SACRIFICES, SO SAY A PRAYER FOR THEM.
RIGHT!
MAY THEIR SOULS REST IN PEACE!
SWISH
SORRY TO MAKE YOU WAIT 3,700 YEARS, YUZURIHA.

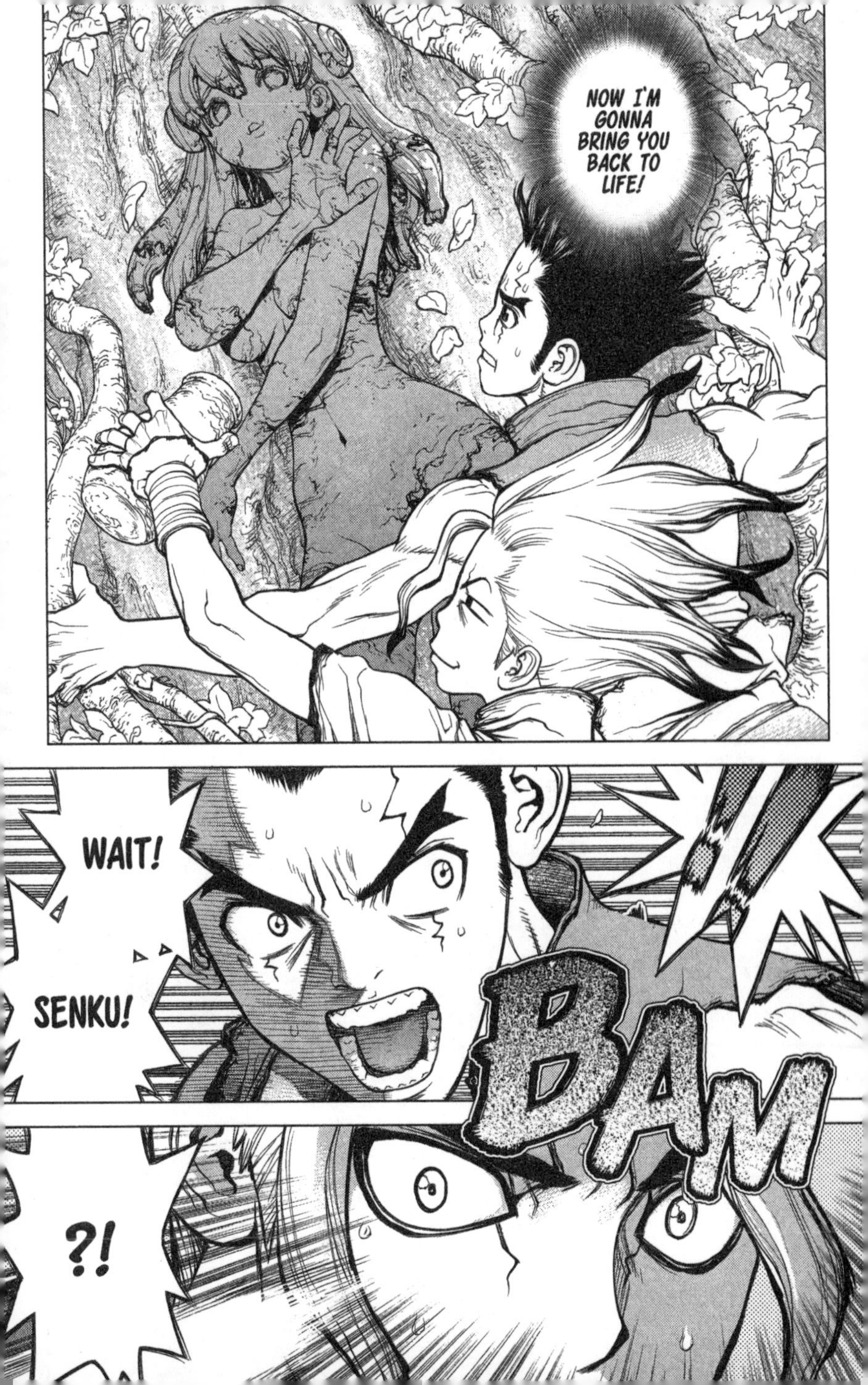
NOW I'M GONNA BRING YOU BACK TO LIFE!
BAM
WAIT!
SENKU!
?!

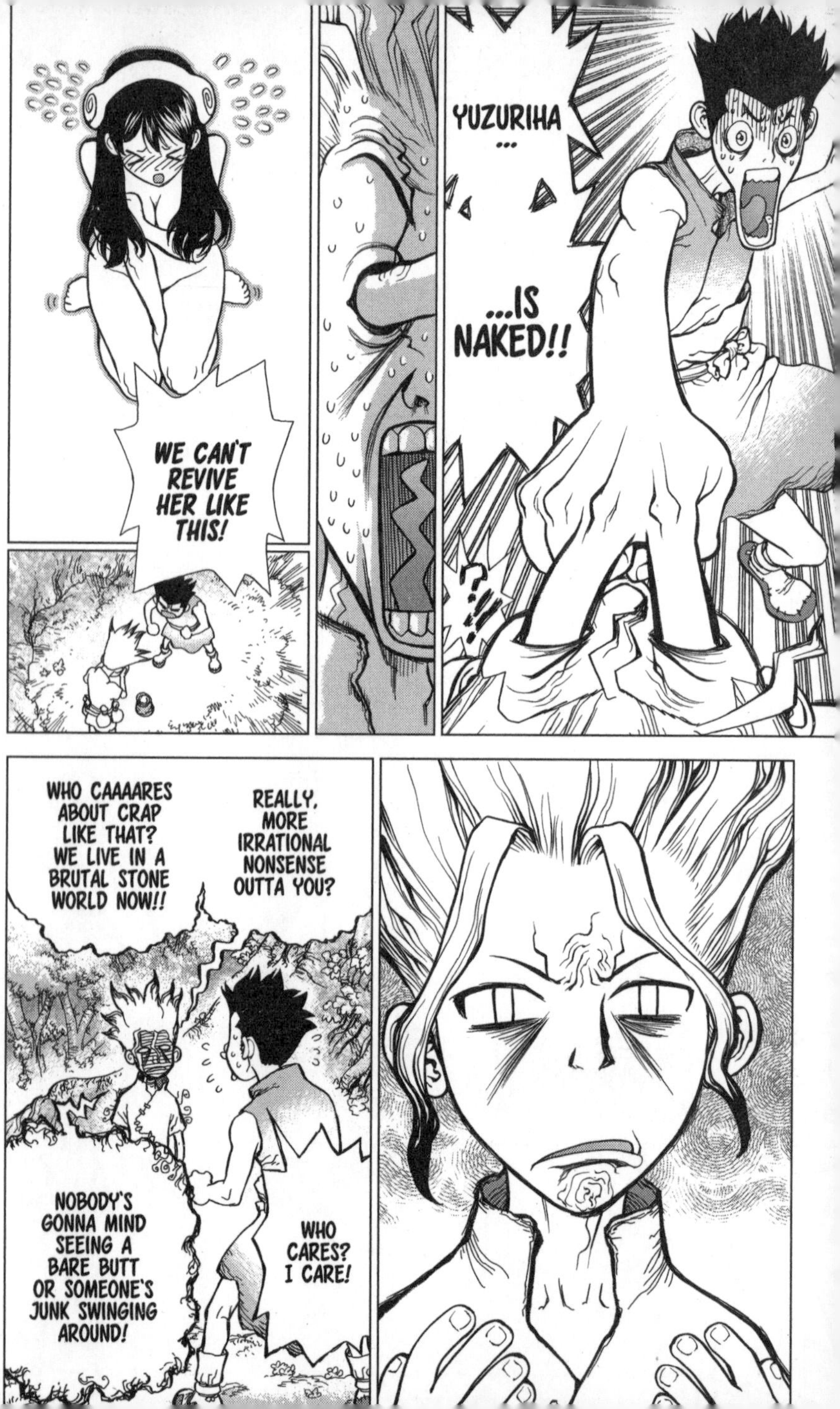
YUZURIHA ...
...IS NAKED!!
?!!
WE CAN'T REVIVE HER LIKE THIS!
REALLY, MORE IRRATIONAL NONSENSE OUTTA YOU?
WHO CAAAARES ABOUT CRAP LIKE THAT? WE LIVE IN A BRUTAL STONE WORLD NOW!!
WHO CARES? I CARE!
NOBODY'S GONNA MIND SEEING A BARE BUTT OR SOMEONE'S JUNK SWINGING AROUND!

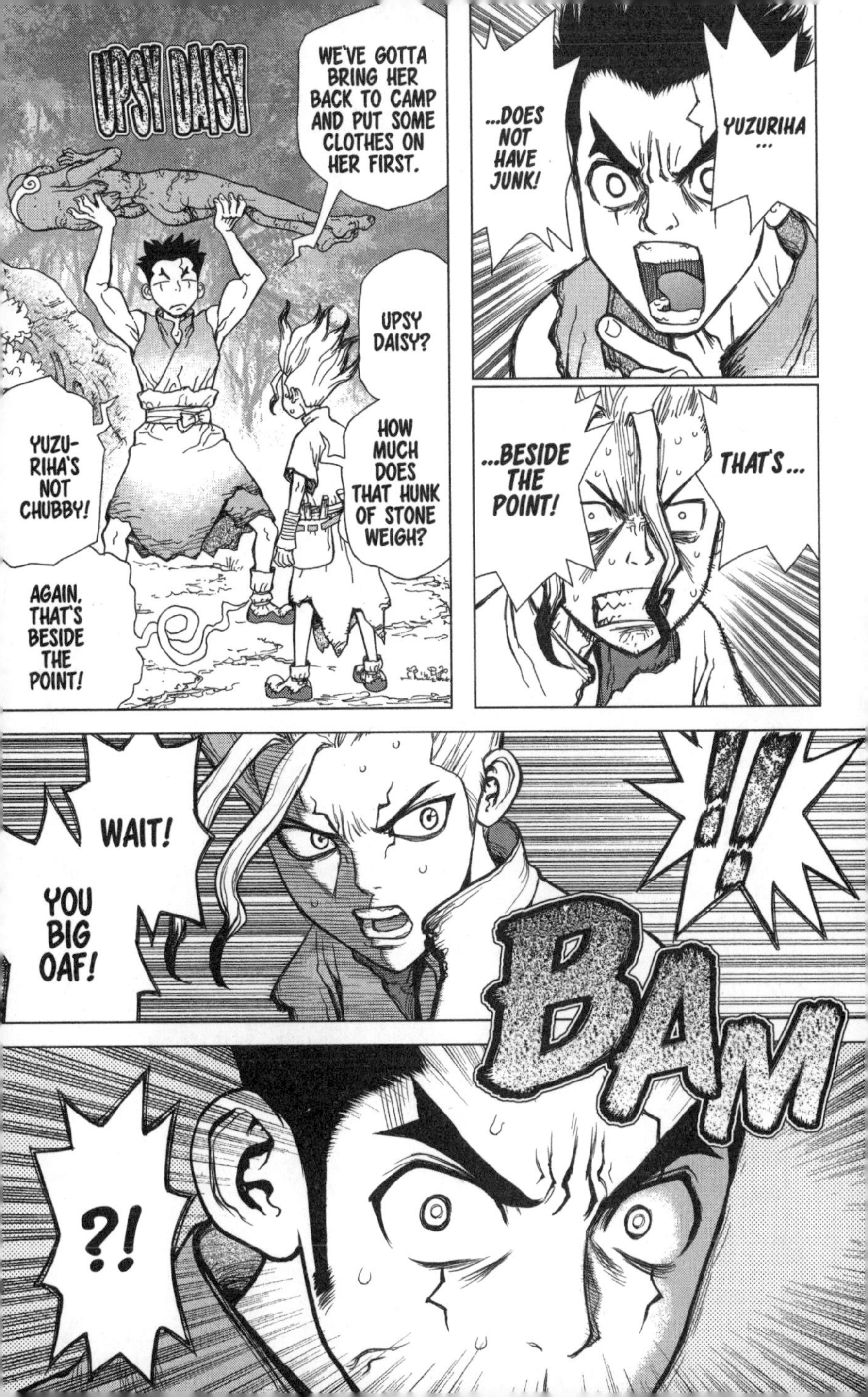
YUZURIHA ...
...DOES NOT HAVE JUNK!
THAT'S...
...BESIDE THE POINT!
WE'VE GOTTA BRING HER BACK TO CAMP AND PUT SOME CLOTHES ON HER FIRST.
UPSY DAISY
UPSY DAISY?
HOW MUCH DOES THAT HUNK OF STONE WEIGH?
YUZU-RIHA'S NOT CHUBBY!
AGAIN, THAT'S BESIDE THE POINT!
!!
WAIT!
YOU BIG OAF!
BAM
?!

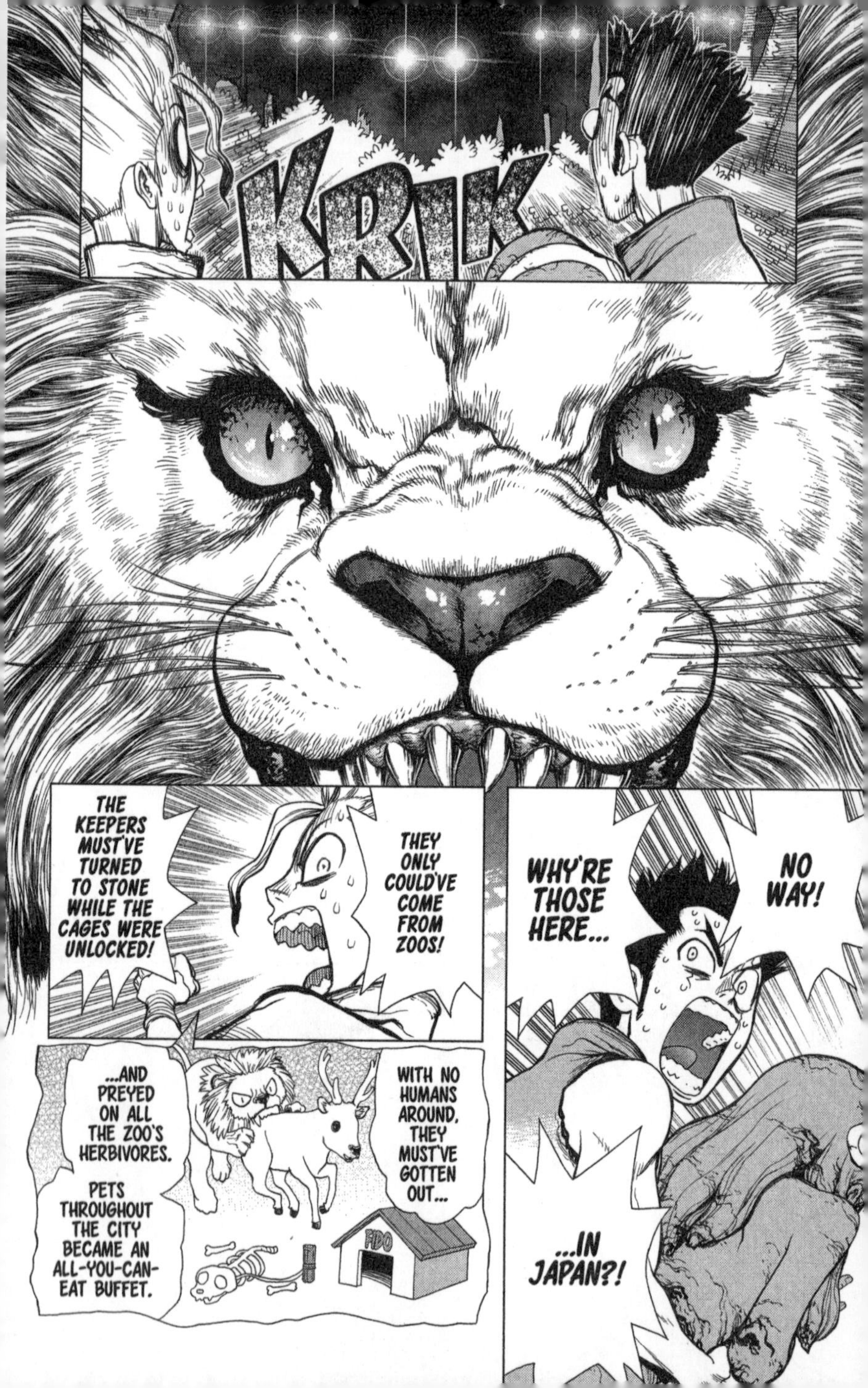
KRIK
NO WAY!
WHY'RE THOSE HERE...
...IN JAPAN?!
THEY ONLY COULD'VE COME FROM ZOOS!
THE KEEPERS MUST'VE TURNED TO STONE WHILE THE CAGES WERE UNLOCKED!
WITH NO HUMANS AROUND, THEY MUST'VE GOTTEN OUT...
...AND PREYED ON ALL THE ZOO'S HERBIVORES.
PETS THROUGHOUT THE CITY BECAME AN ALL-YOU-CAN-EAT BUFFET.
FIDO

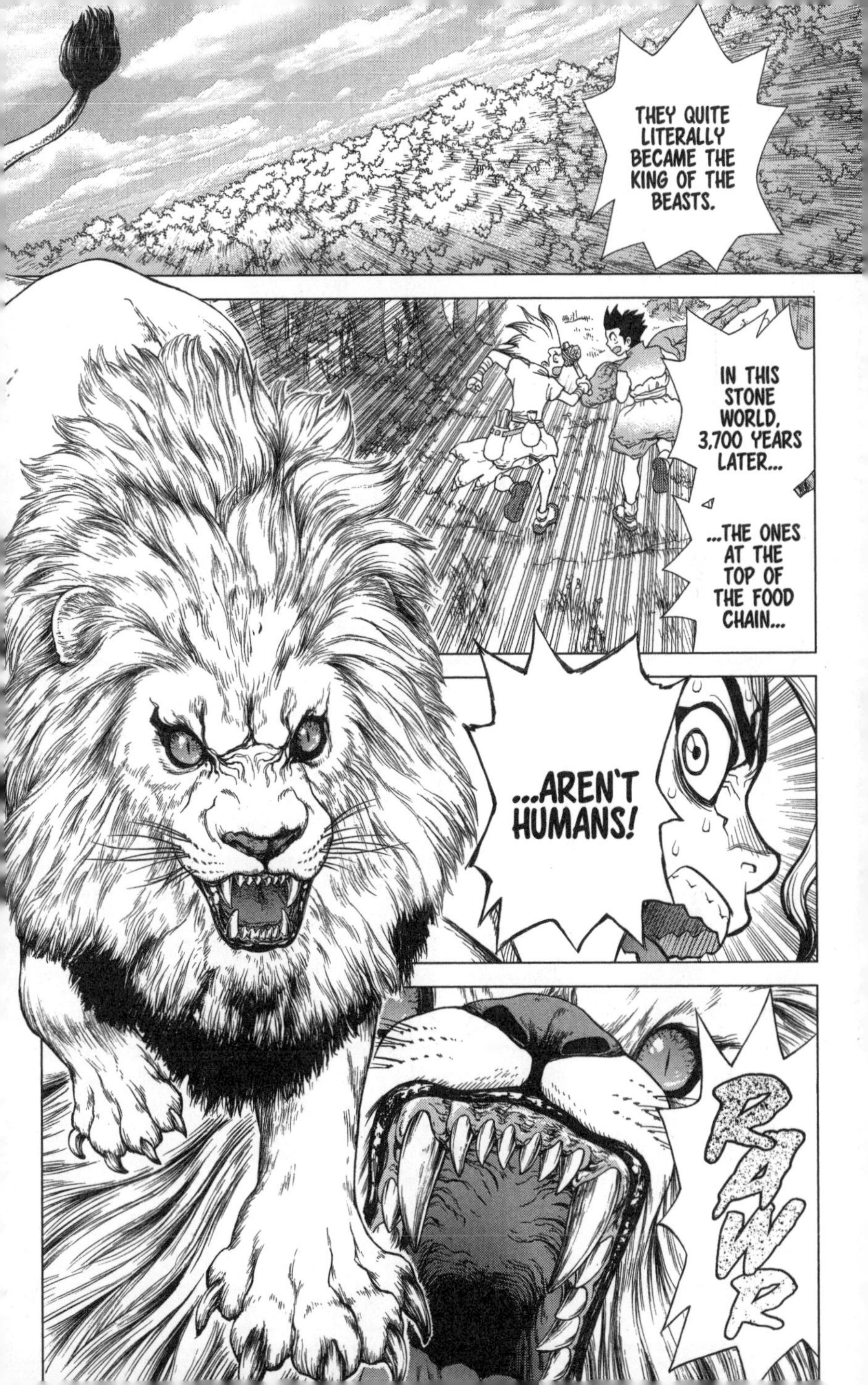
THEY QUITE LITERALLY BECAME THE KING OF THE BEASTS.
IN THIS STONE WORLD, 3,700 YEARS LATER...
...THE ONES AT THE TOP OF THE FOOD CHAIN...
...AREN'T HUMANS!
RAWR

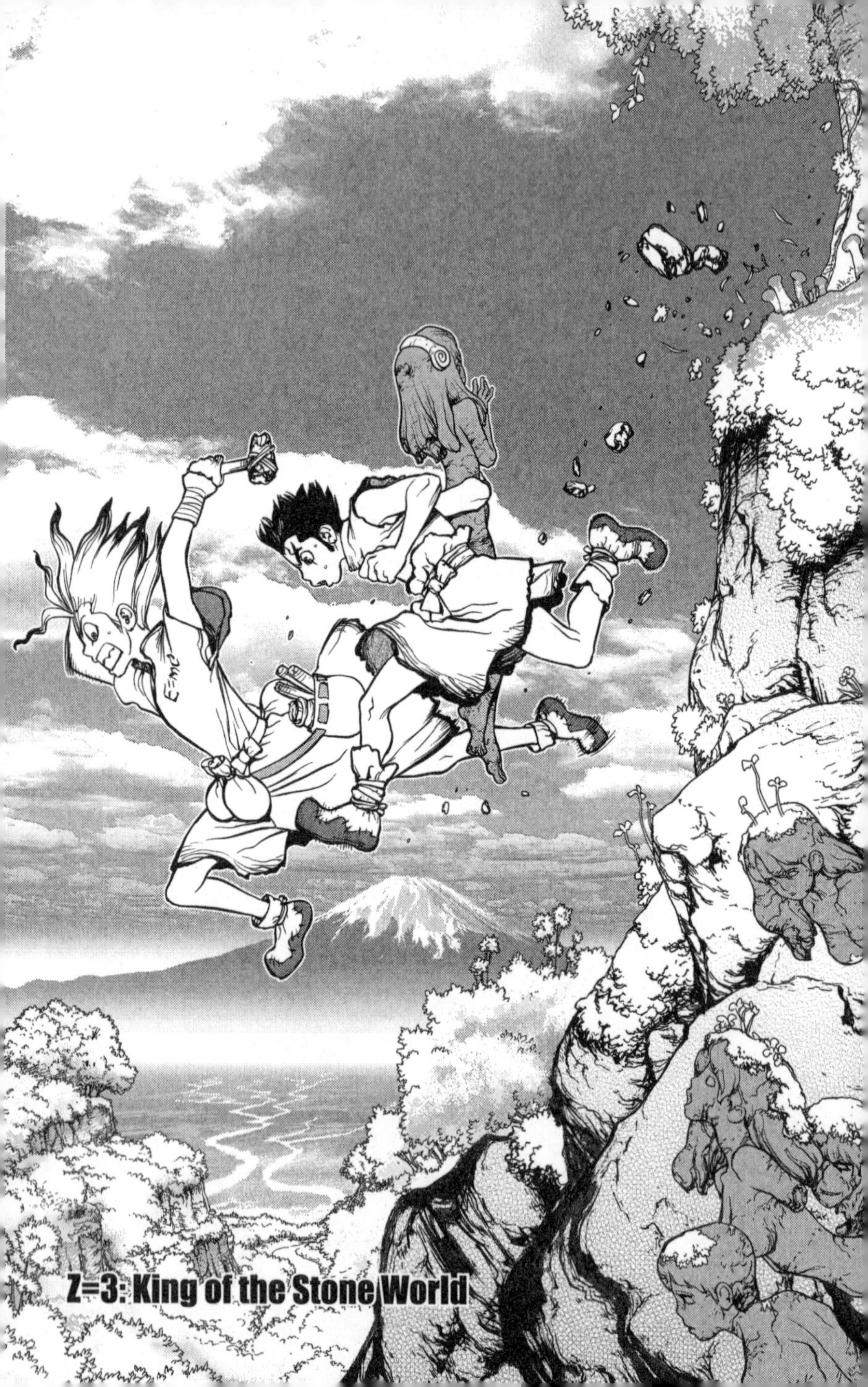

Z=3: King of the Stone World

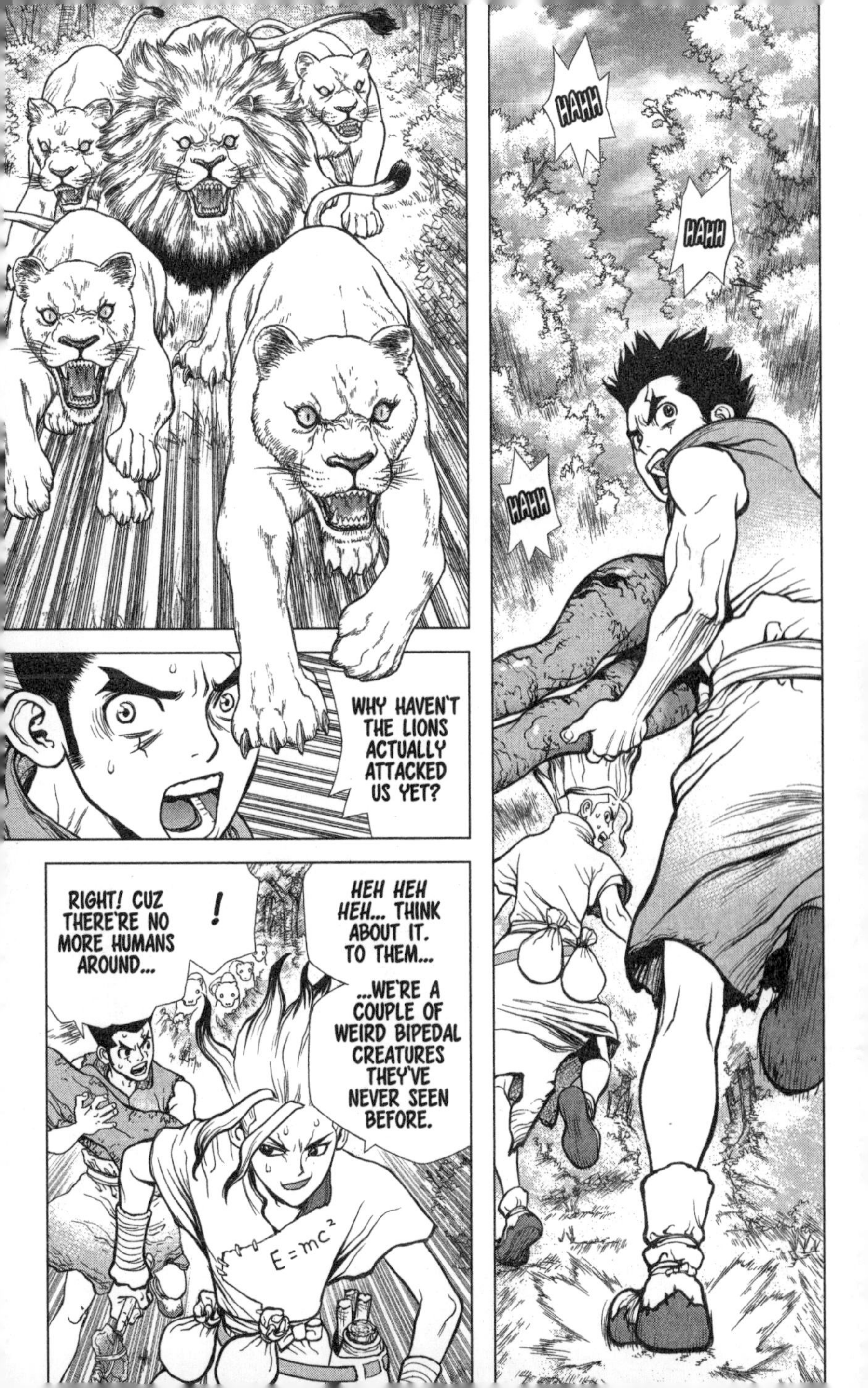
HAHH
HAHH
HAHH
WHY HAVEN'T THE LIONS ACTUALLY ATTACKED US YET?
HEH HEH HEH... THINK ABOUT IT. TO THEM...
...WE'RE A COUPLE OF WEIRD BIPEDAL CREATURES THEY'VE NEVER SEEN BEFORE.
!
RIGHT! CUZ THERE'RE NO MORE HUMANS AROUND...
E = mc²

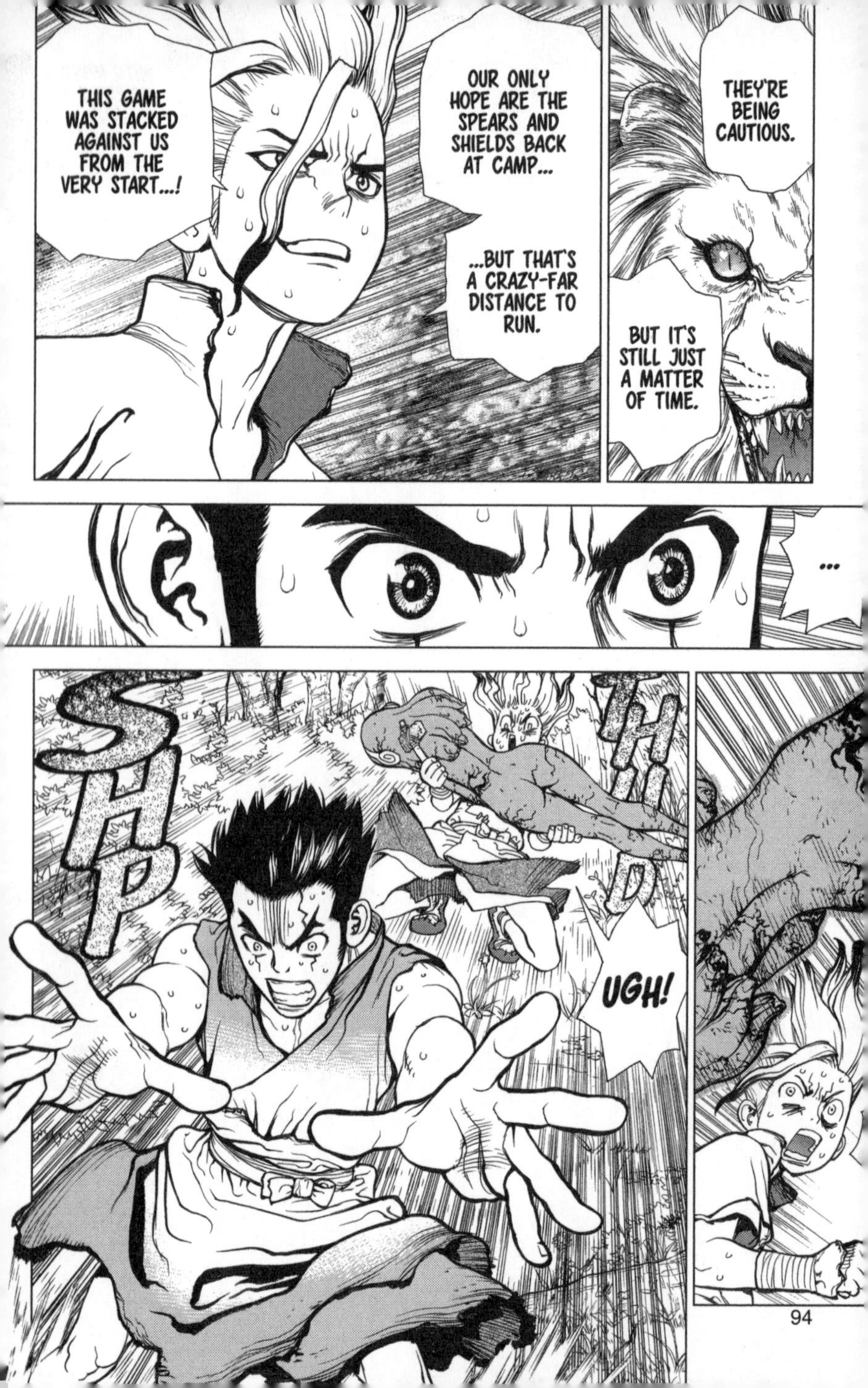
THEY'RE BEING CAUTIOUS.
BUT IT'S STILL JUST A MATTER OF TIME.
OUR ONLY HOPE ARE THE SPEARS AND SHIELDS BACK AT CAMP...
...BUT THAT'S A CRAZY-FAR DISTANCE TO RUN.
THIS GAME WAS STACKED AGAINST US FROM THE VERY START...!
...
THUD
UGH!
SHP

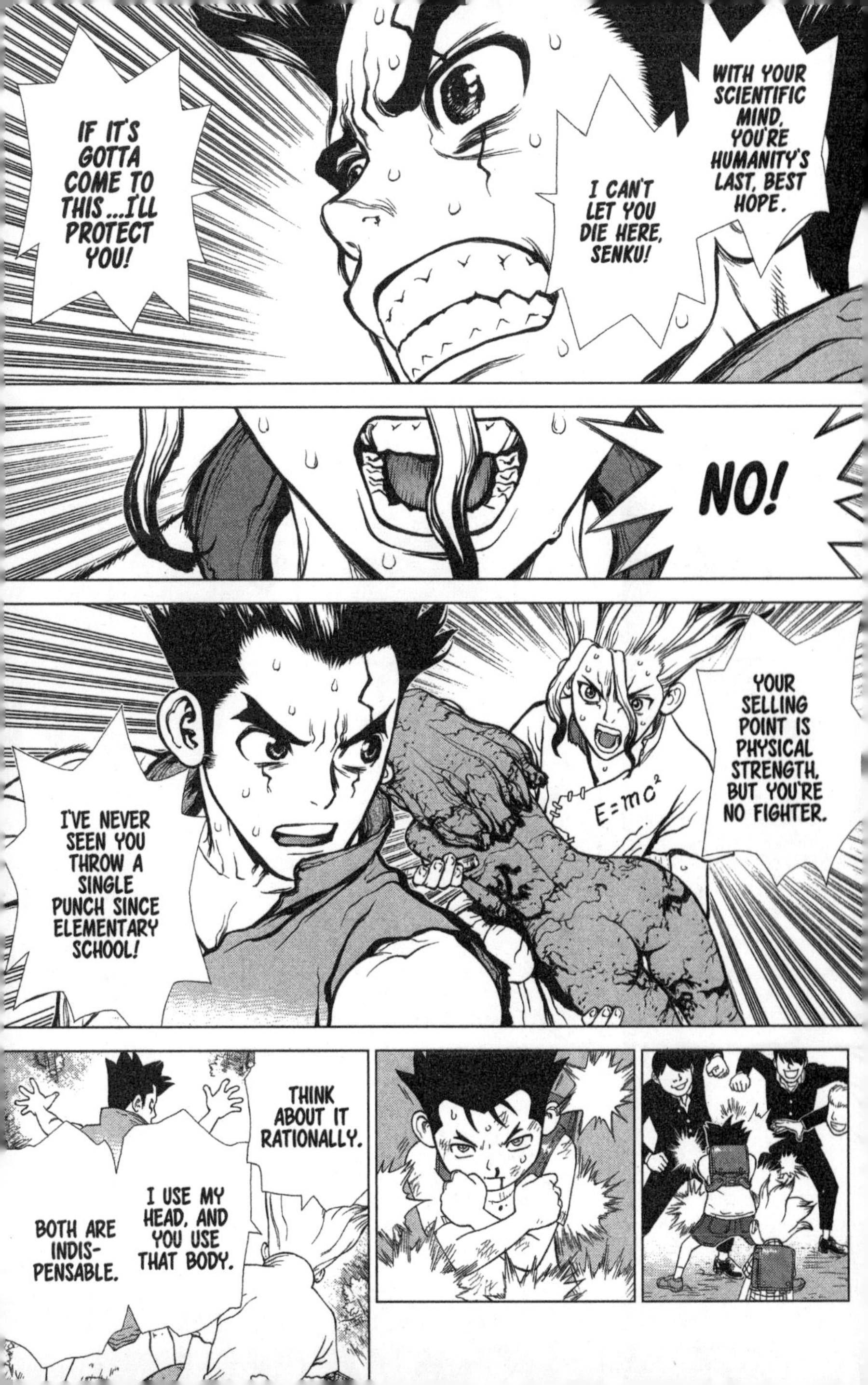
WITH YOUR SCIENTIFIC MIND, YOU'RE HUMANITY'S LAST, BEST HOPE.
I CAN'T LET YOU DIE HERE, SENKU!
IF IT'S GOTTA COME TO THIS...I'LL PROTECT YOU!
NO!
YOUR SELLING POINT IS PHYSICAL STRENGTH, BUT YOU'RE NO FIGHTER.
$E=mc^2$
I'VE NEVER SEEN YOU THROW A SINGLE PUNCH SINCE ELEMENTARY SCHOOL!
THINK ABOUT IT RATIONALLY.
I USE MY HEAD, AND YOU USE THAT BODY.
BOTH ARE INDIS-PENSABLE.

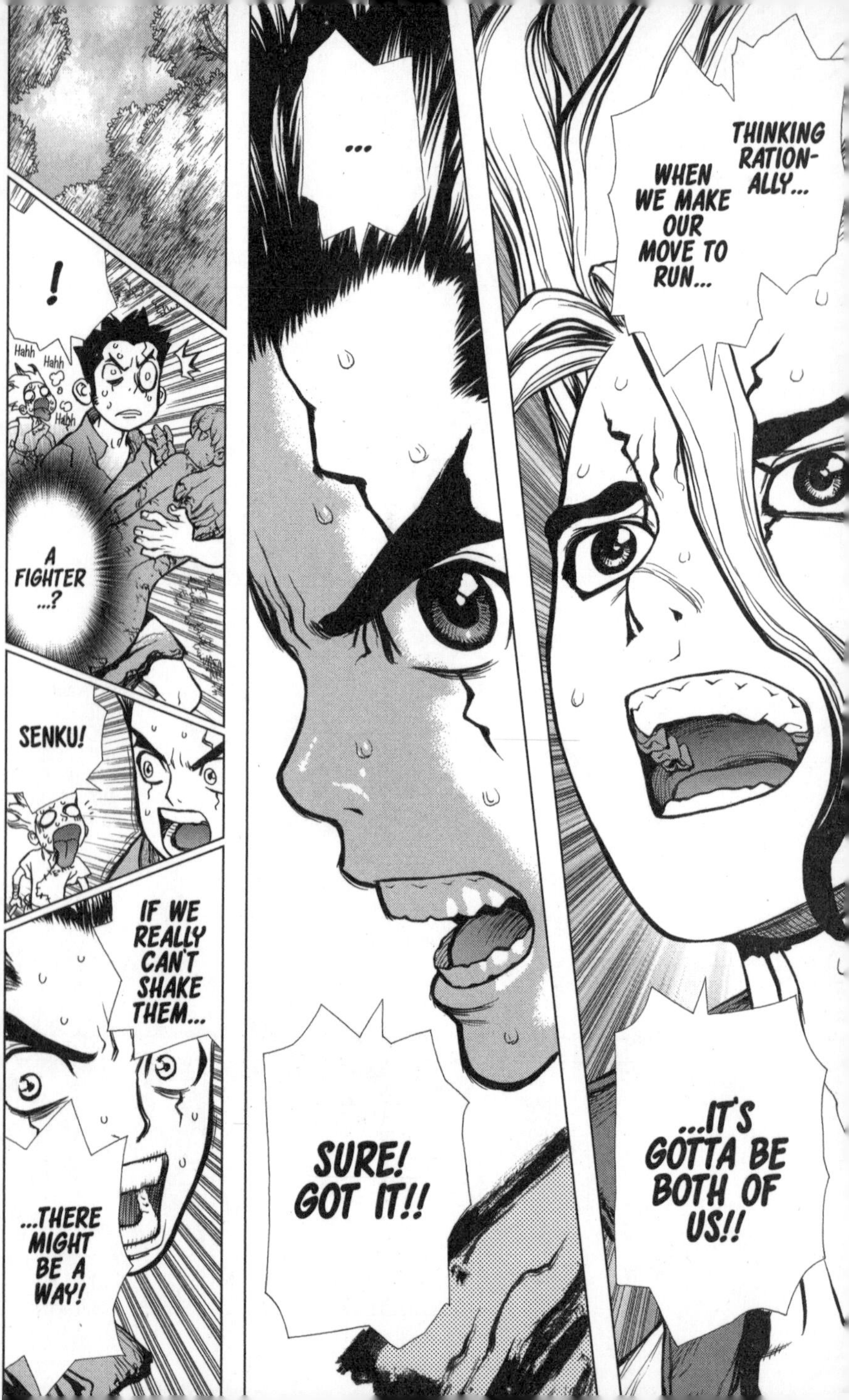
THINKING RATIONALLY...
WHEN WE MAKE OUR MOVE TO RUN...
...IT'S GOTTA BE BOTH OF US!!
...
SURE! GOT IT!!
!
Hahh Hahh Hahh
A FIGHTER ...?
SENKU!
IF WE REALLY CAN'T SHAKE THEM...
...THERE MIGHT BE A WAY!

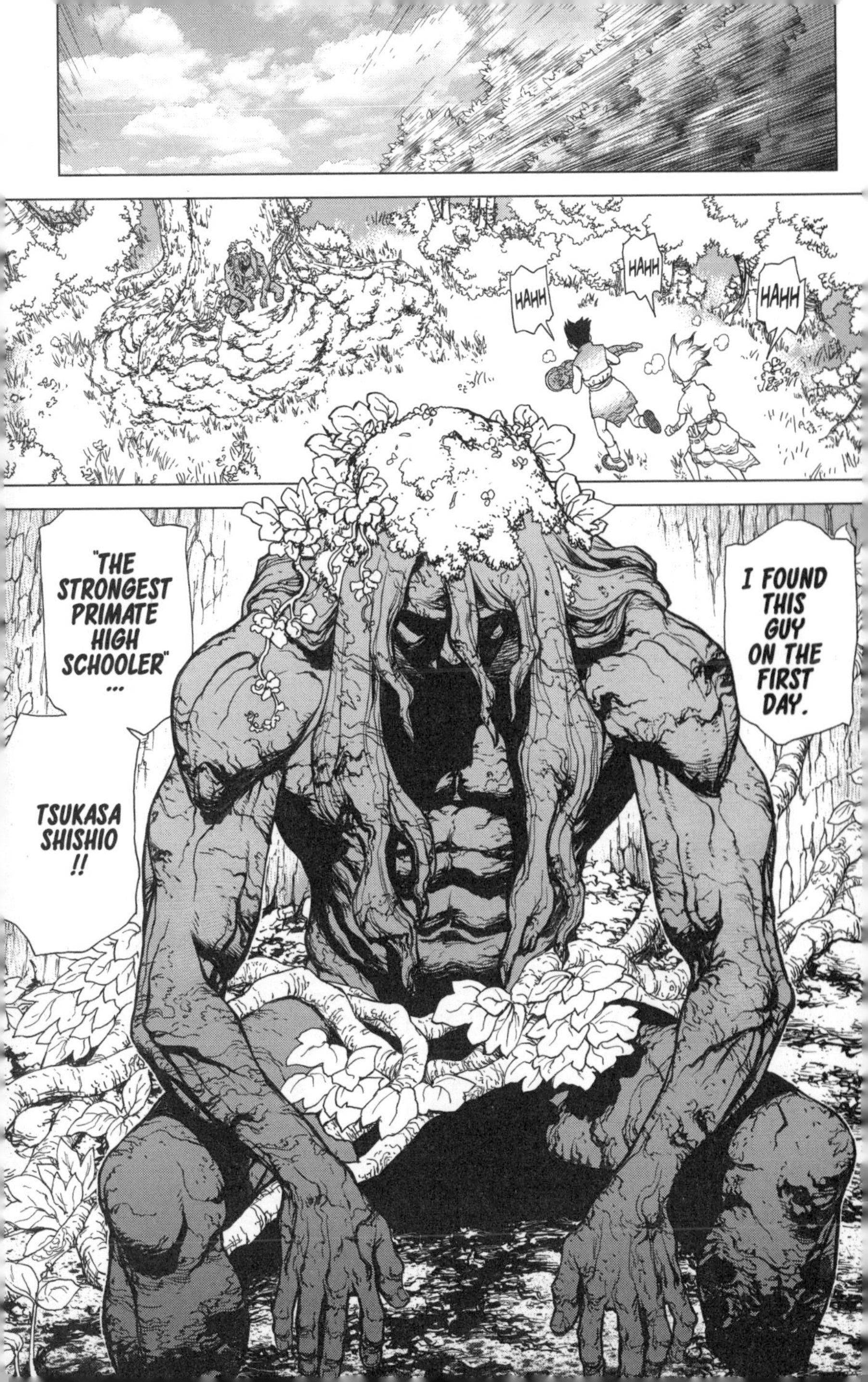
HAHH
HAHH
HAHH
I FOUND THIS GUY ON THE FIRST DAY.
"THE STRONGEST PRIMATE HIGH SCHOOLER"...
TSUKASA SHISHIO !!

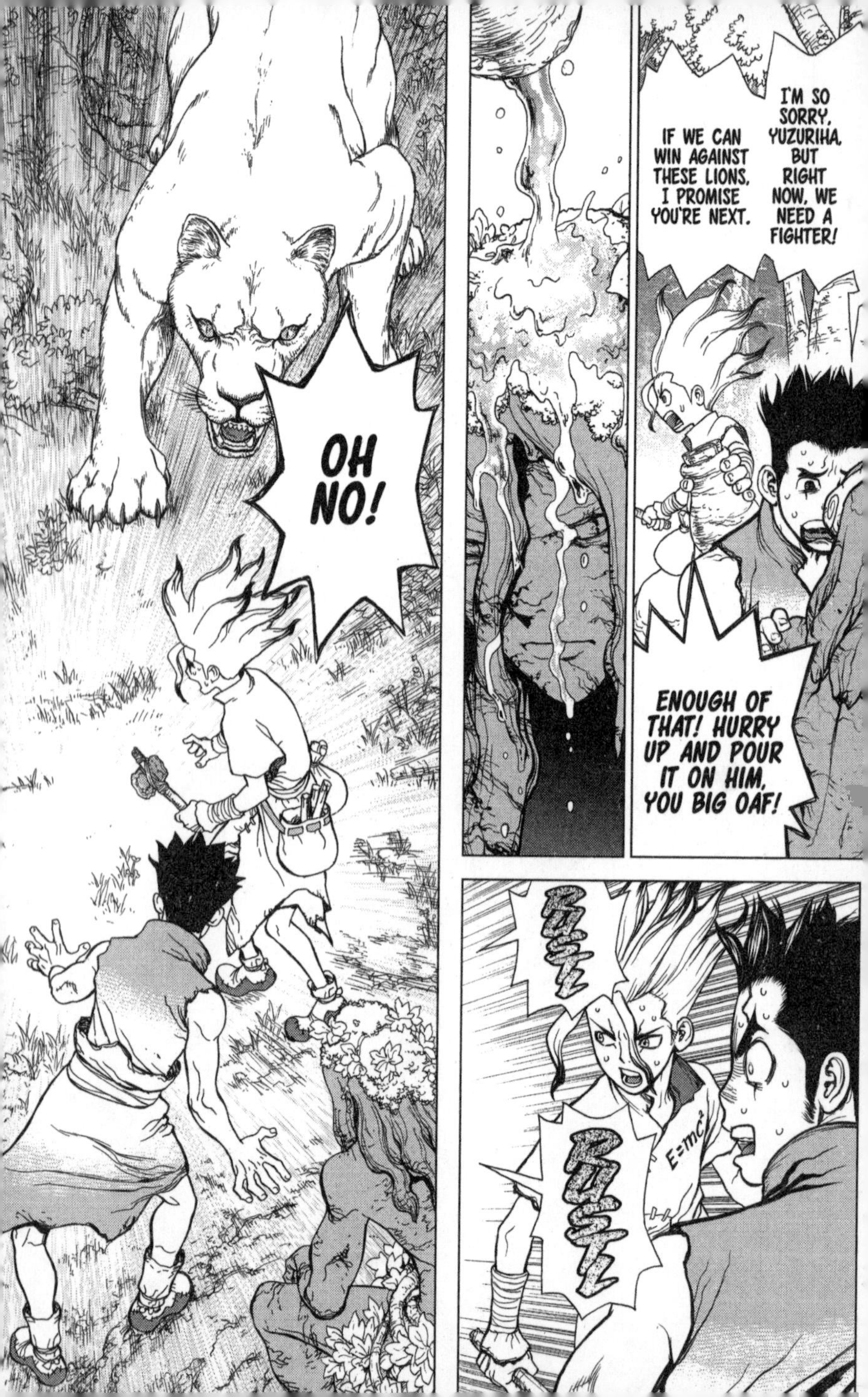
I'M SO SORRY, YUZURIHA, BUT RIGHT NOW, WE NEED A FIGHTER!
IF WE CAN WIN AGAINST THESE LIONS, I PROMISE YOU'RE NEXT.
ENOUGH OF THAT! HURRY UP AND POUR IT ON HIM, YOU BIG OAF!
E=mc²
OH NO!

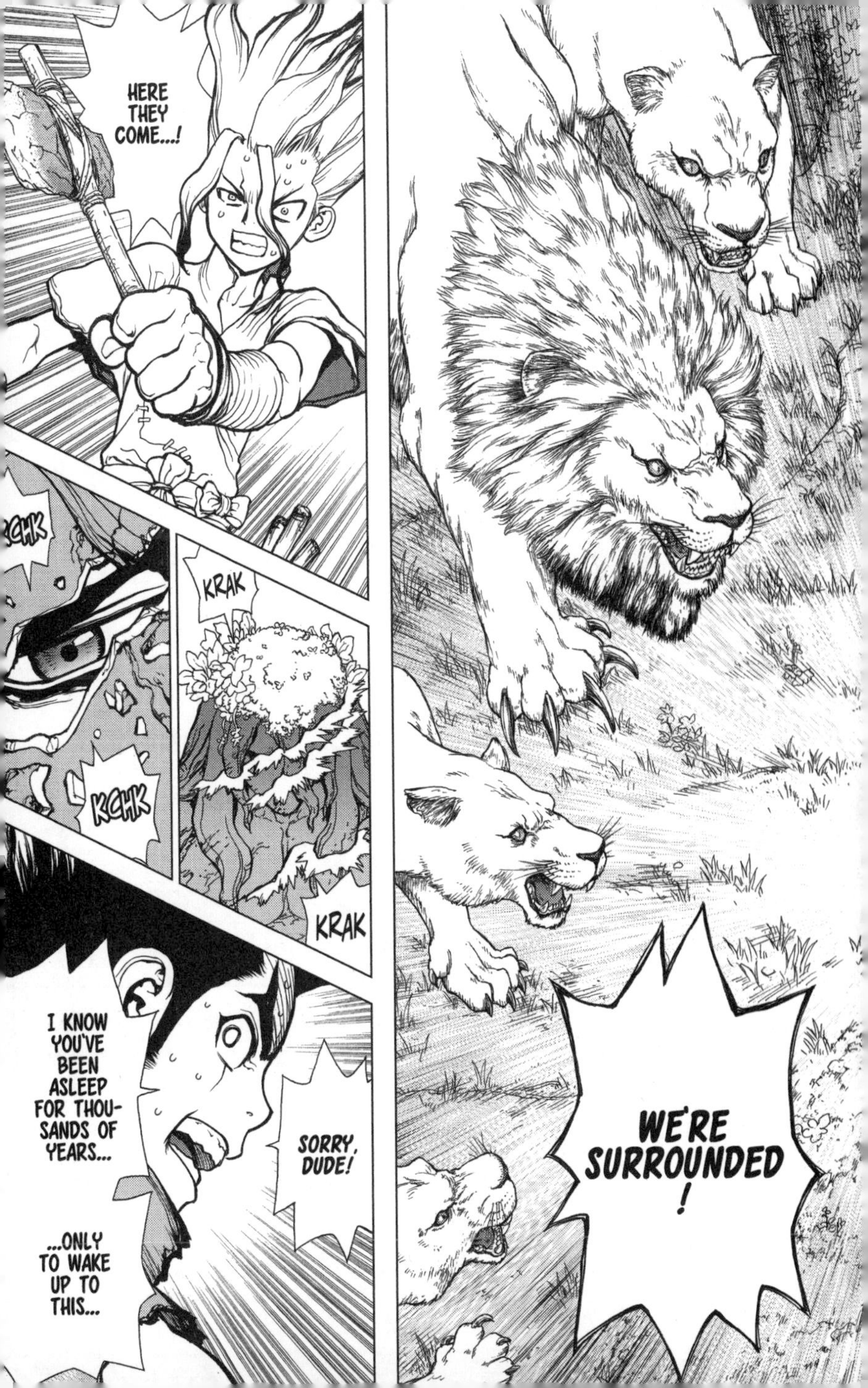
WE'RE SURROUNDED!
HERE THEY COME...!
KCHK
KCHK
KRAK
KRAK
I KNOW YOU'VE BEEN ASLEEP FOR THOUSANDS OF YEARS...
...ONLY TO WAKE UP TO THIS...
SORRY, DUDE!

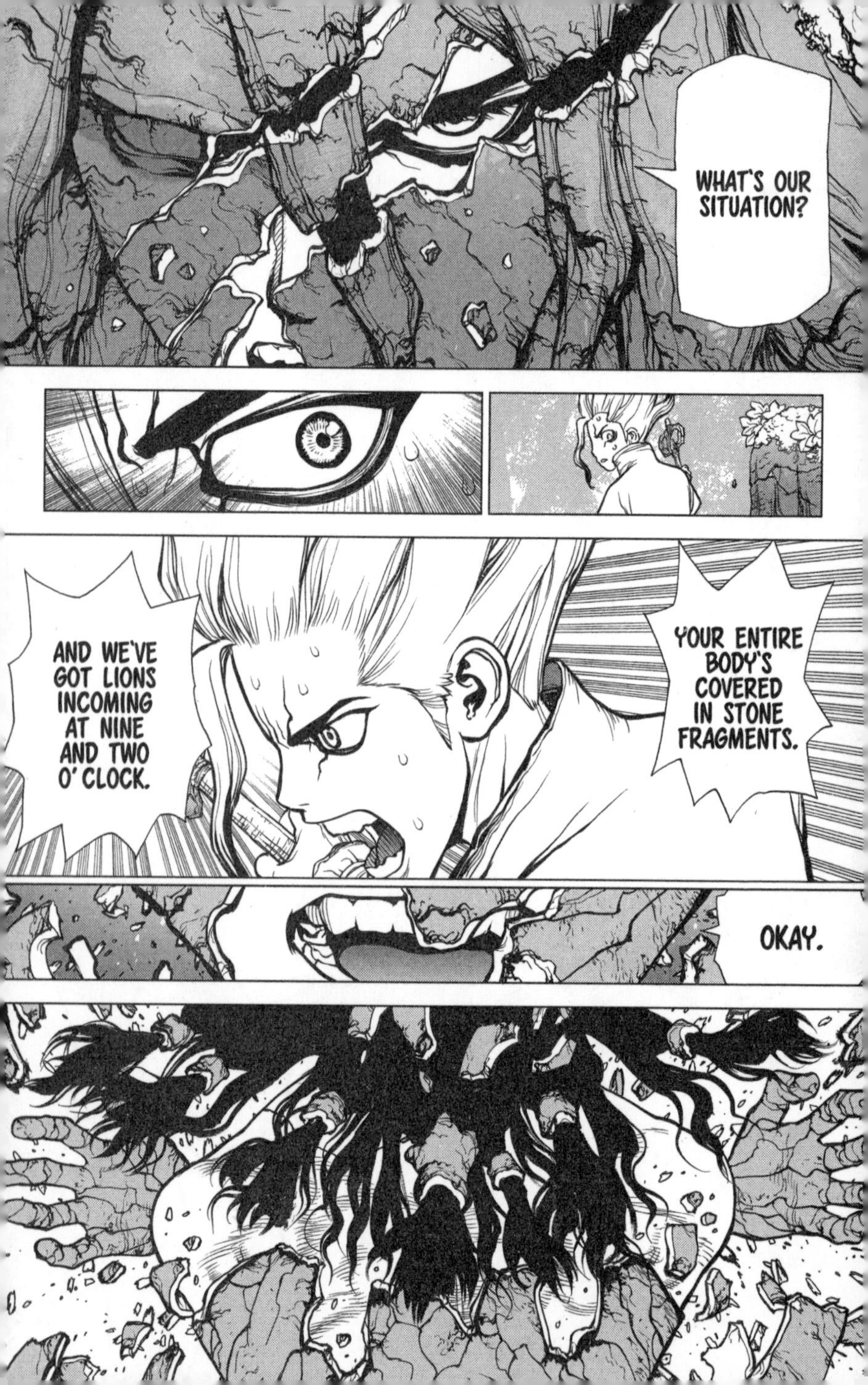
WHAT'S OUR SITUATION?
YOUR ENTIRE BODY'S COVERED IN STONE FRAGMENTS.
AND WE'VE GOT LIONS INCOMING AT NINE AND TWO O' CLOCK.
OKAY.

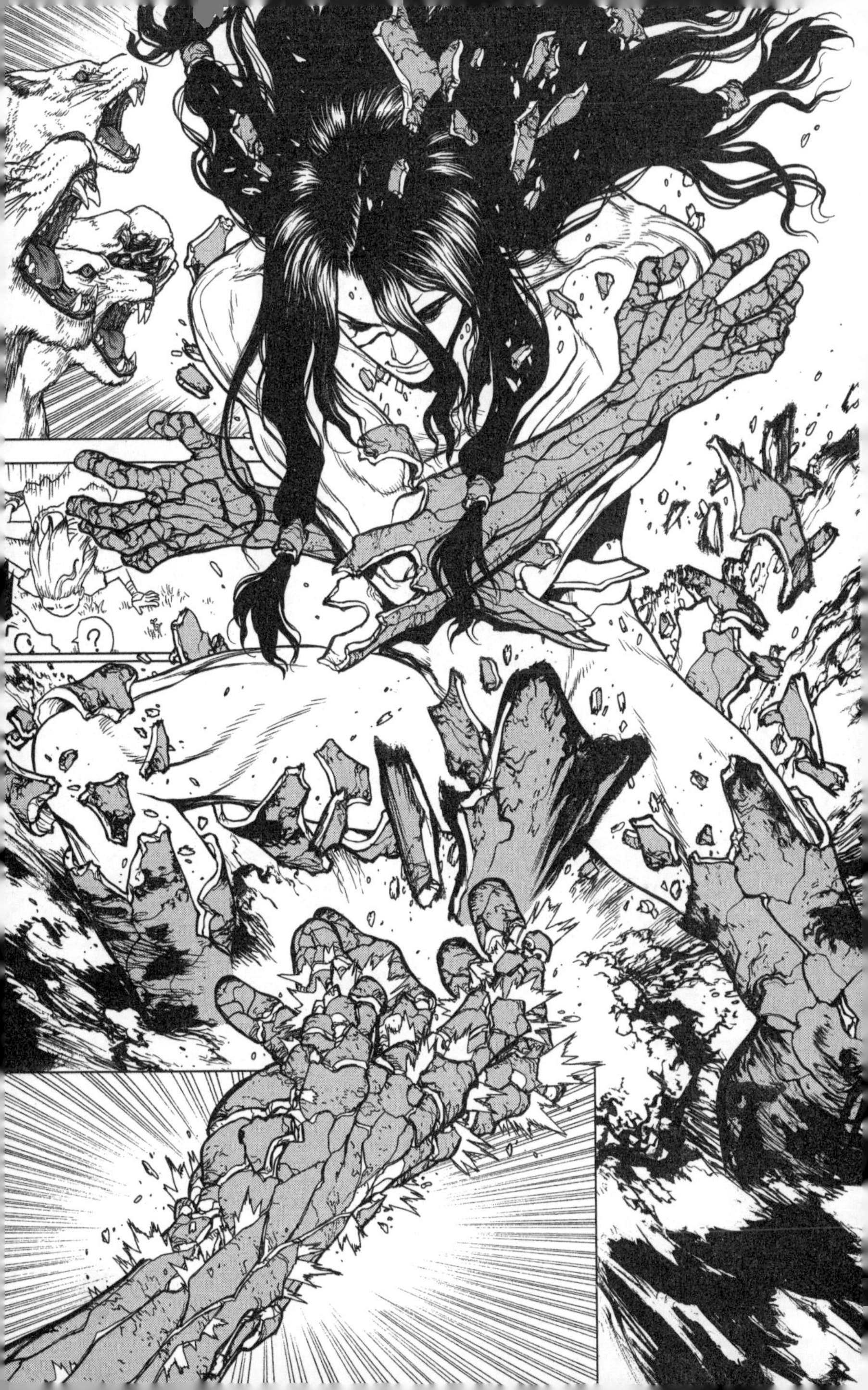
?

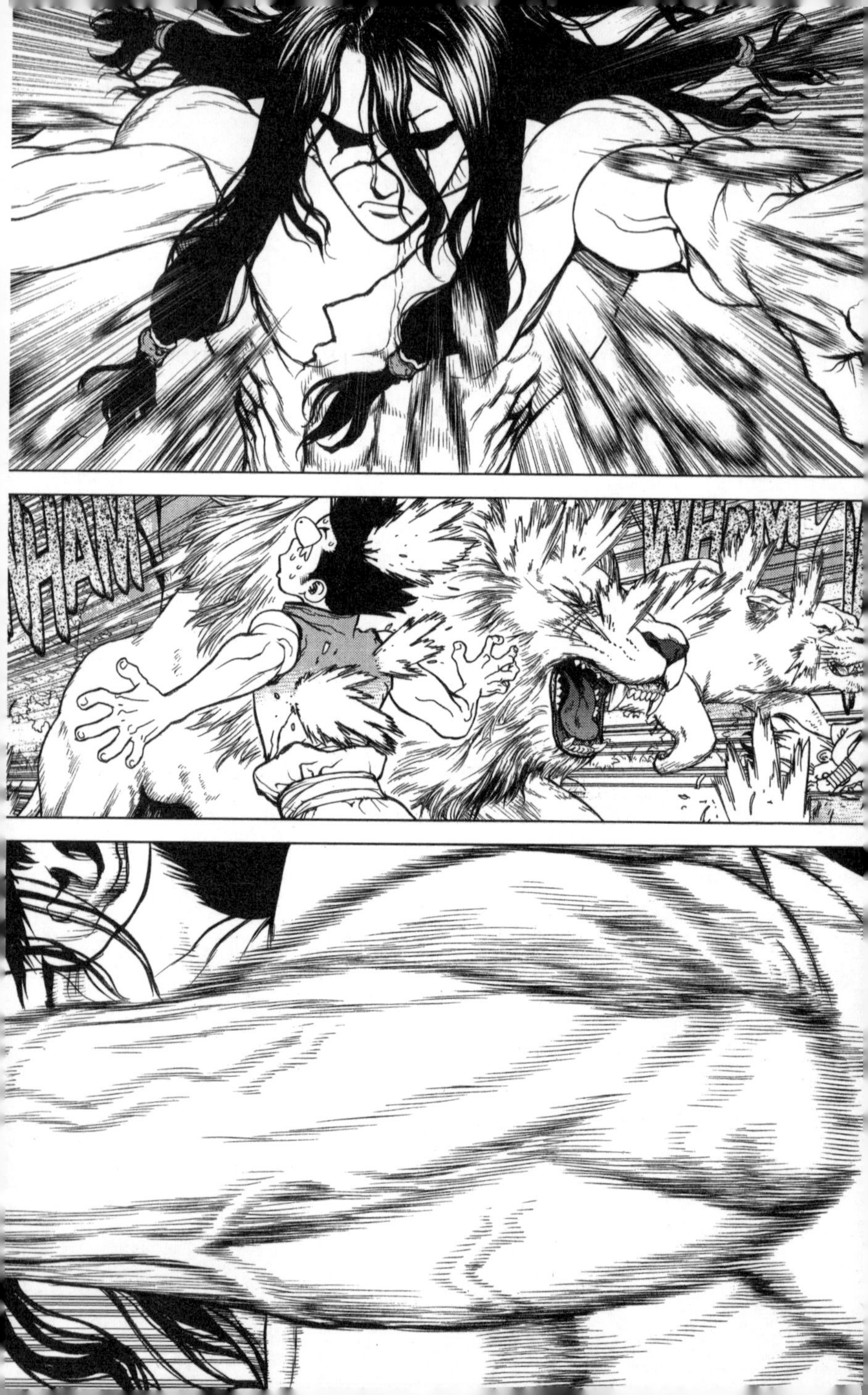
WHAM
HAM

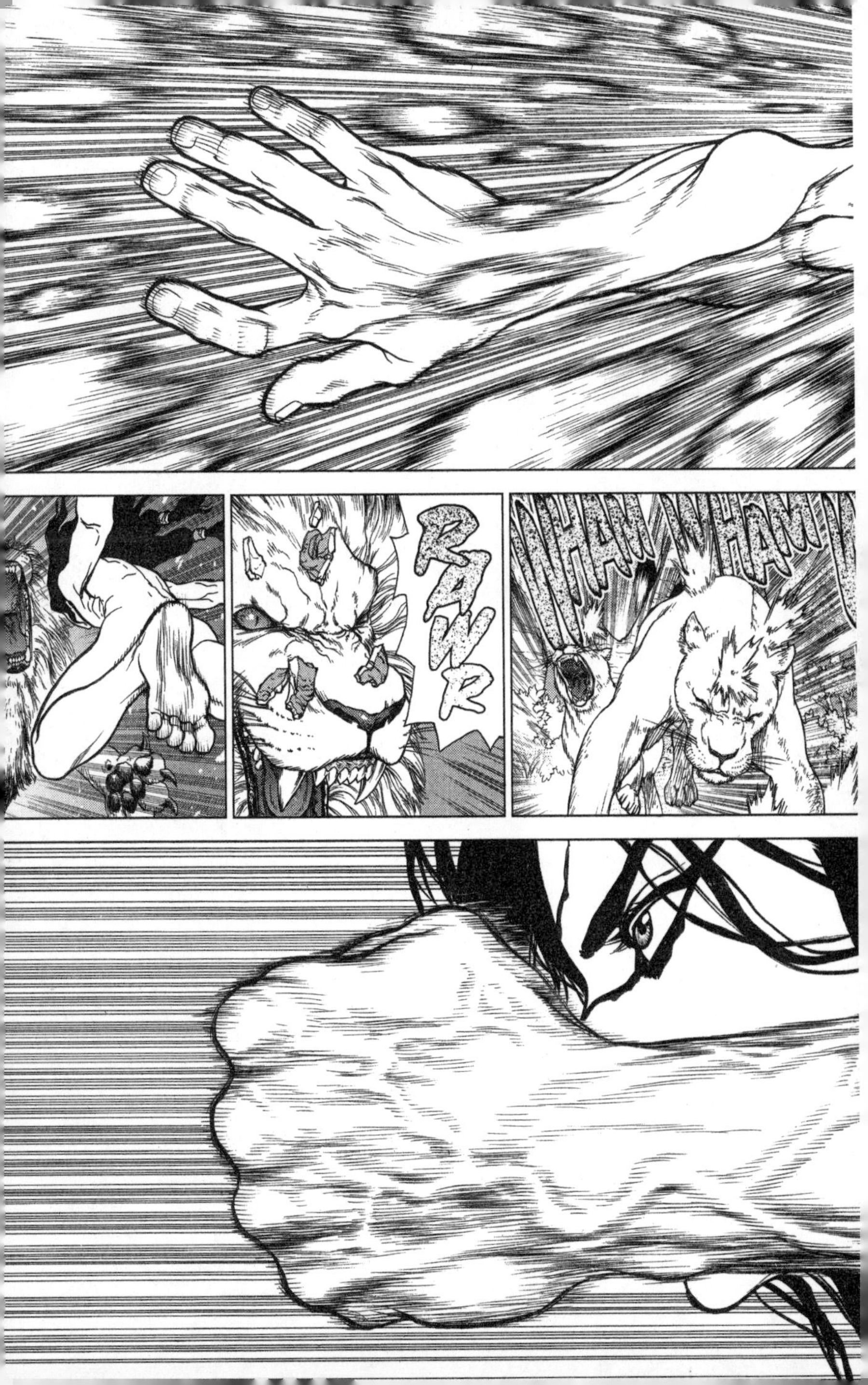
WHAM WHAM
RAWR

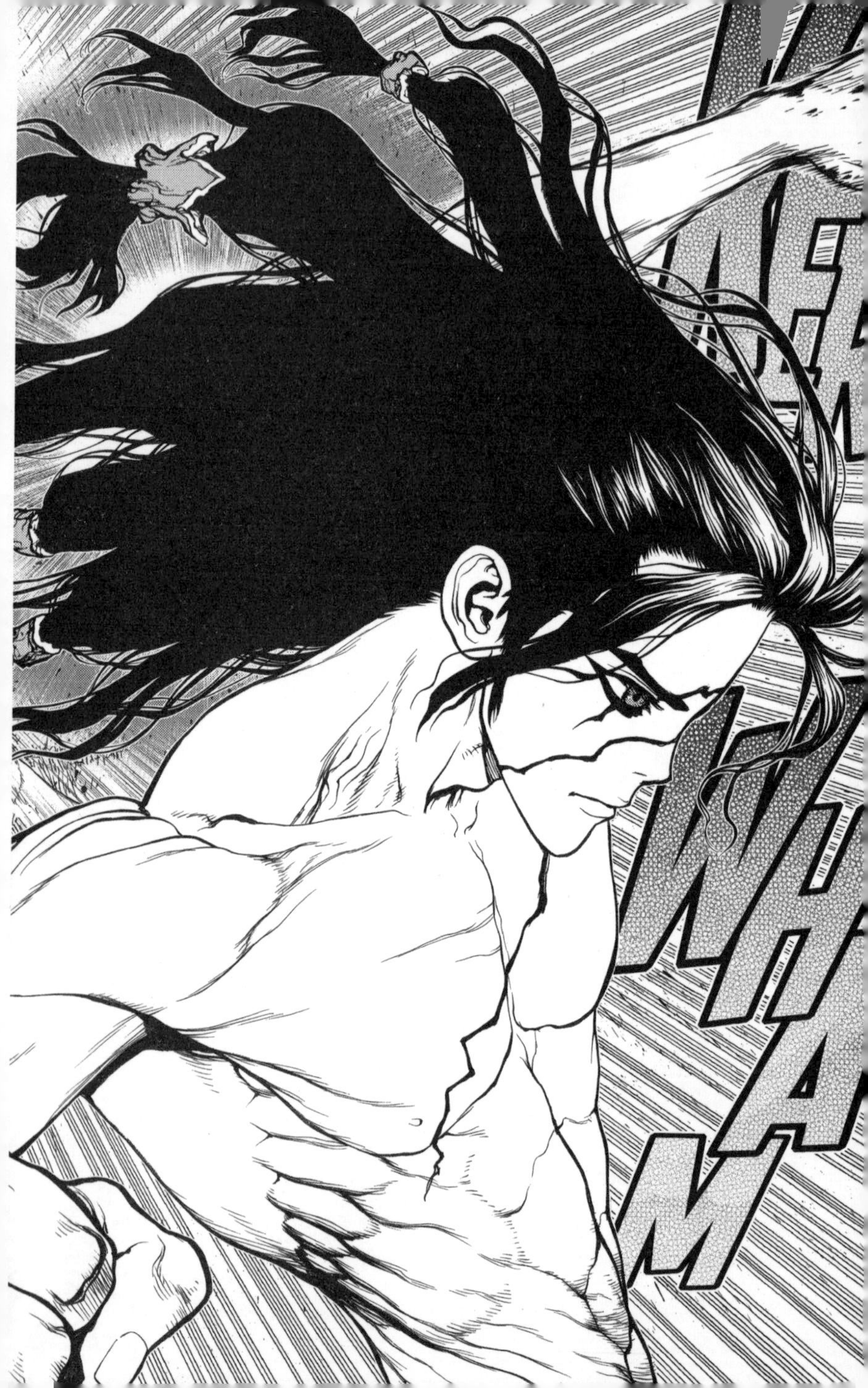
WHAM

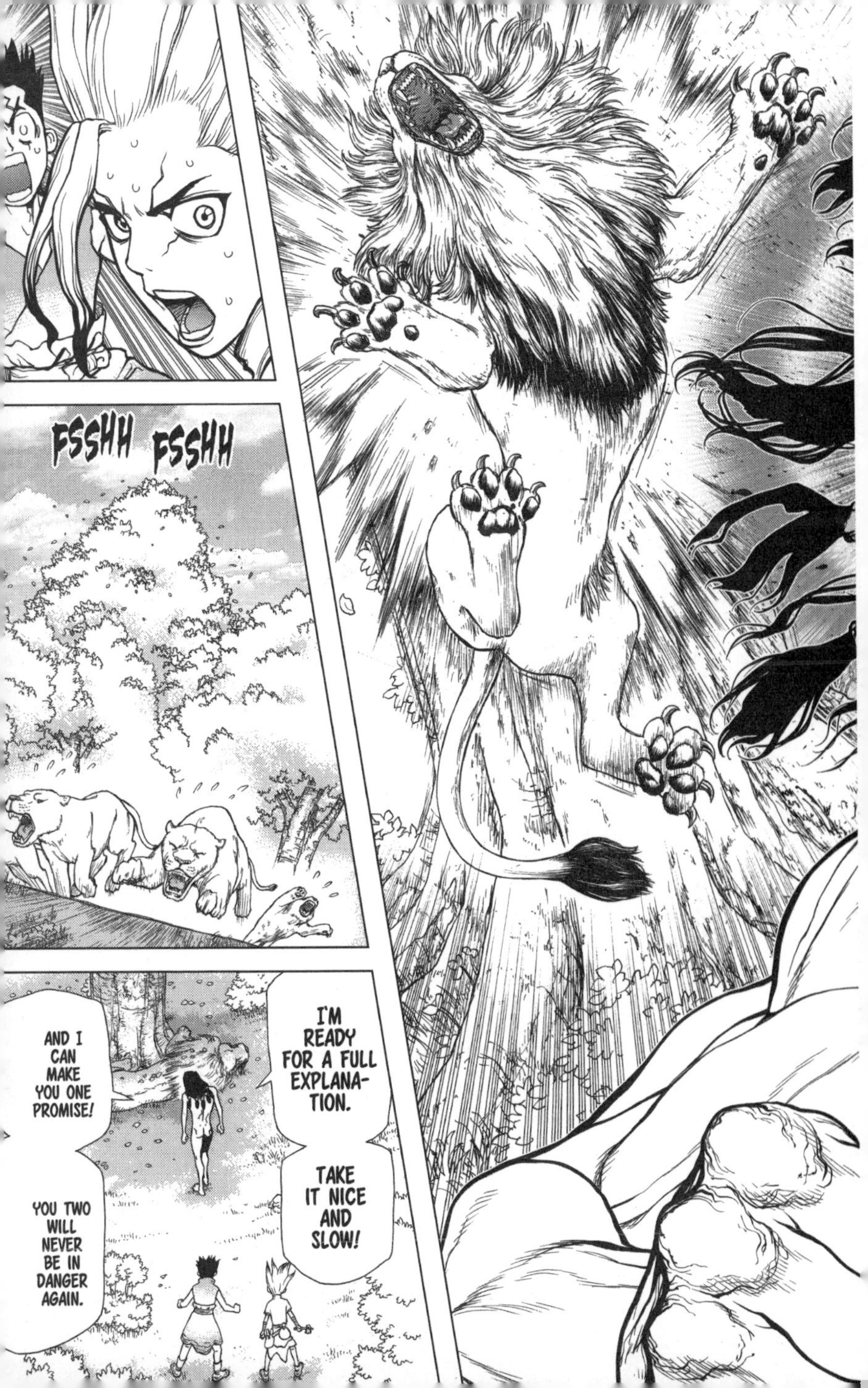
FSSHH FSSHH
I'M READY FOR A FULL EXPLANATION.
TAKE IT NICE AND SLOW!
AND I CAN MAKE YOU ONE PROMISE!
YOU TWO WILL NEVER BE IN DANGER AGAIN.

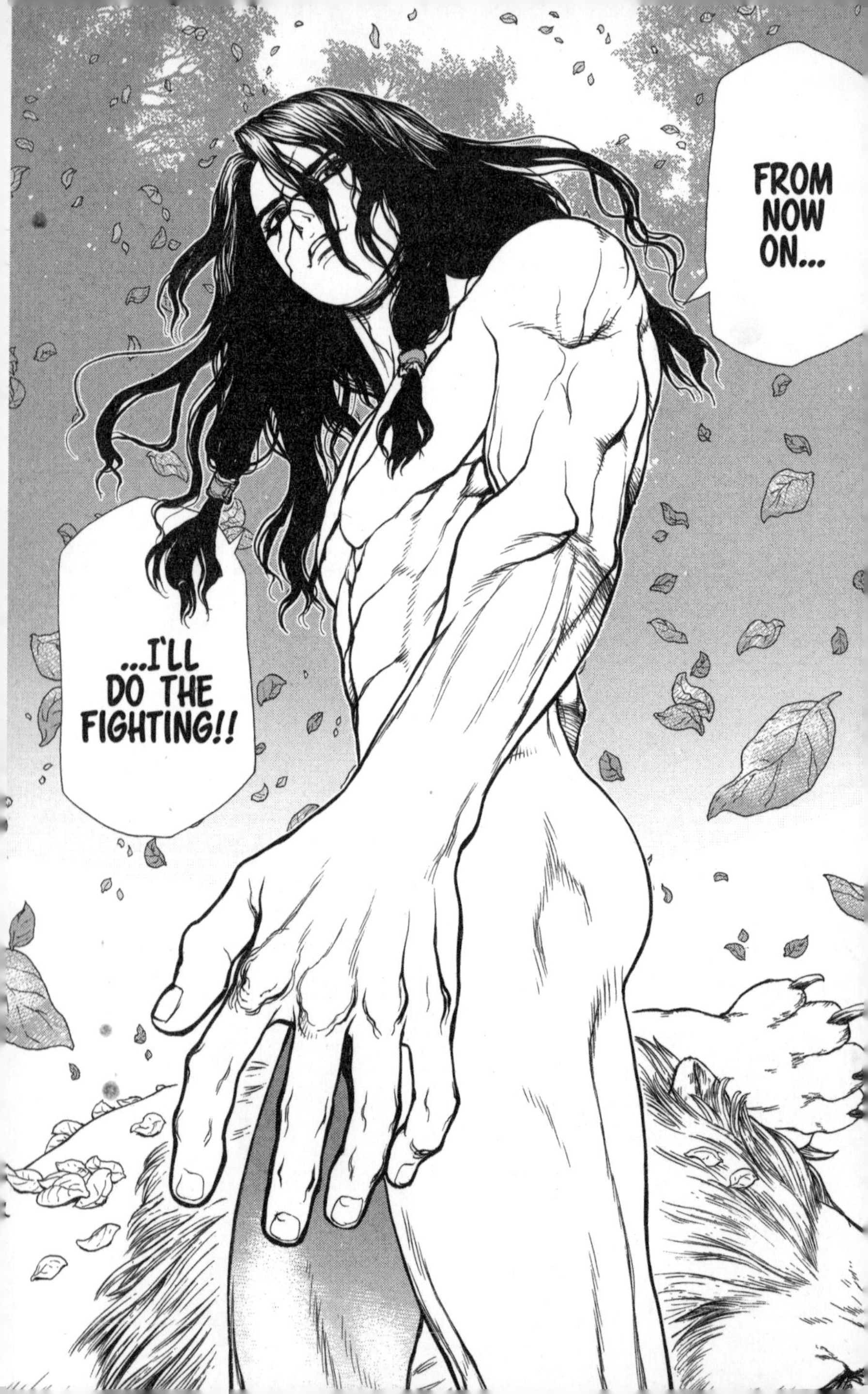
FROM NOW ON...
...I'LL DO THE FIGHTING!!

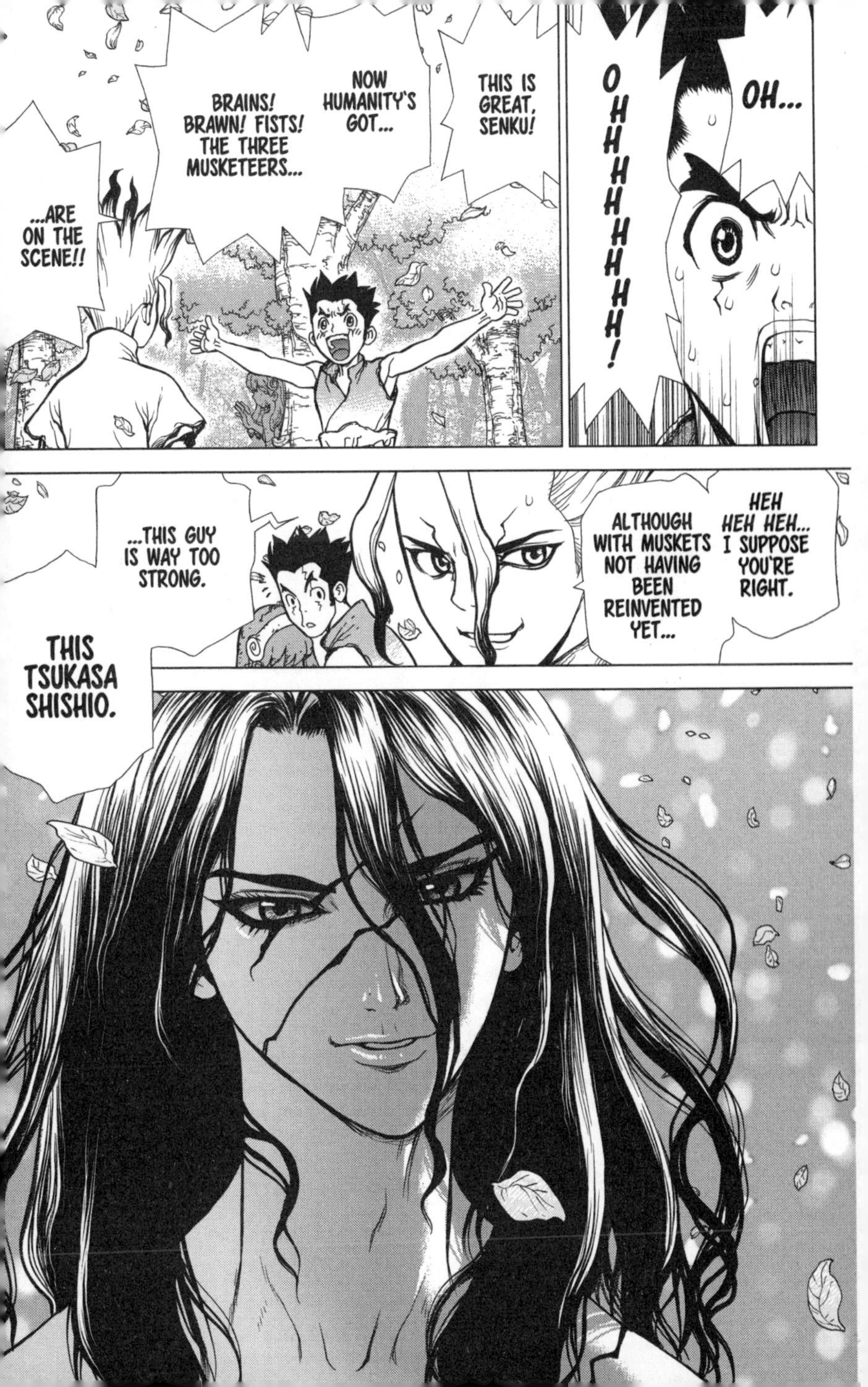
OH...
OHHHHHHHHHH!
THIS IS GREAT, SENKU!
NOW HUMANITY'S GOT...
BRAINS! BRAWN! FISTS! THE THREE MUSKETEERS...
...ARE ON THE SCENE!!
HEH HEH HEH... I SUPPOSE YOU'RE RIGHT.
ALTHOUGH WITH MUSKETS NOT HAVING BEEN REINVENTED YET...
...THIS GUY IS WAY TOO STRONG.
THIS TSUKASA SHISHIO.

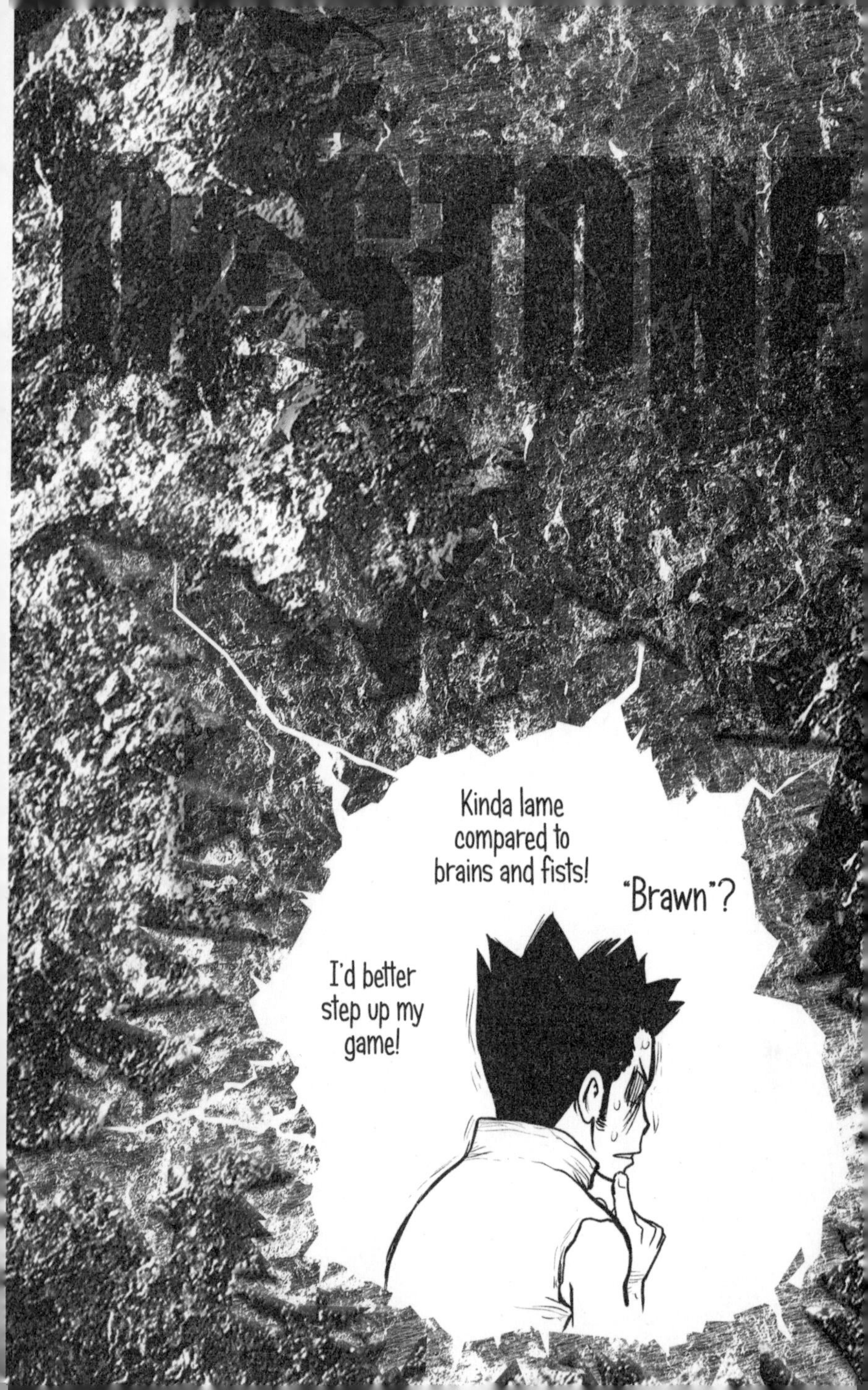
Kinda lame compared to brains and fists!
"Brawn"?
I'd better step up my game!

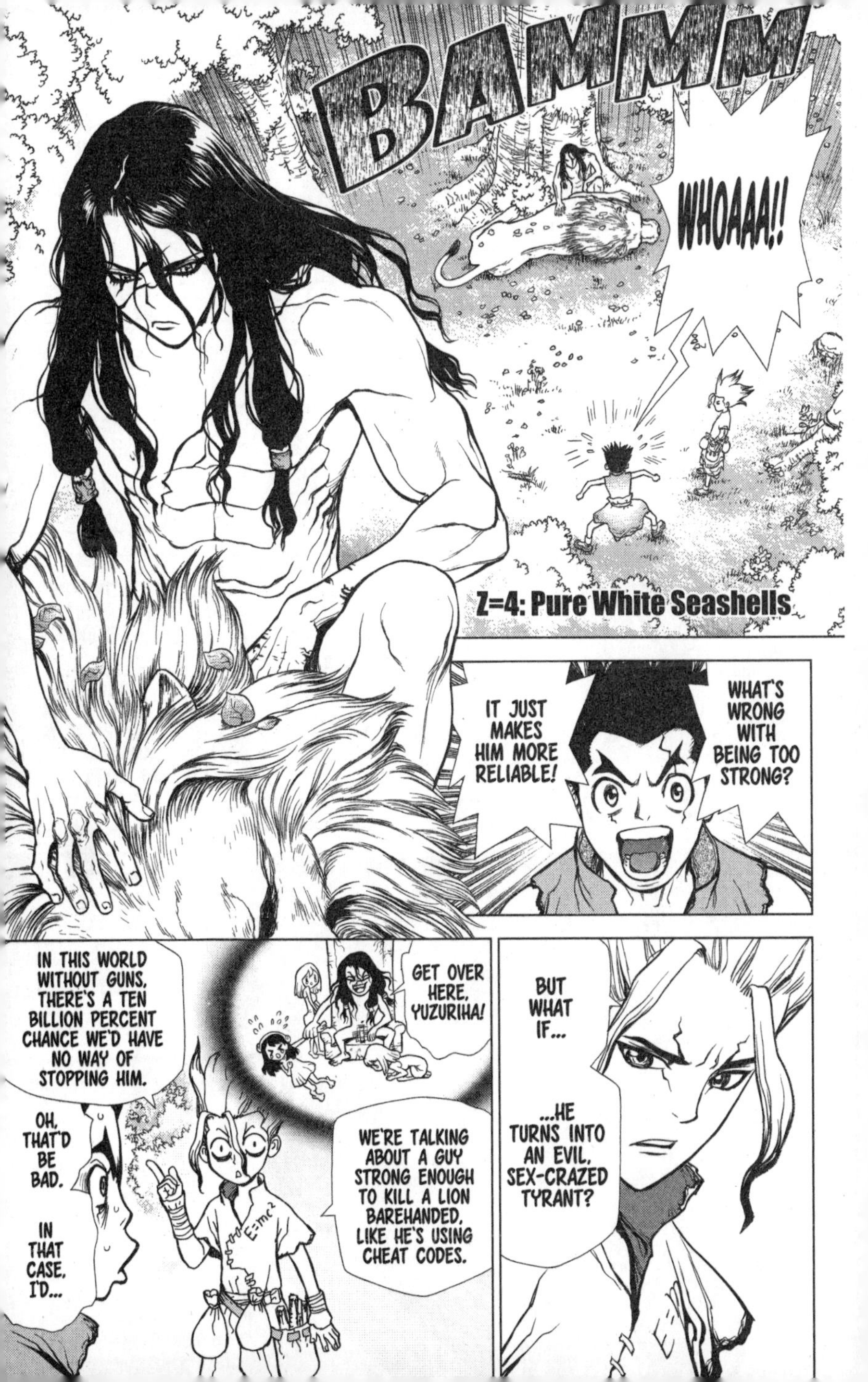
BAMMM
WHOAAA!!
Z=4: Pure White Seashells
WHAT'S WRONG WITH BEING TOO STRONG?
IT JUST MAKES HIM MORE RELIABLE!
BUT WHAT IF...
...HE TURNS INTO AN EVIL, SEX-CRAZED TYRANT?
GET OVER HERE, YUZURIHA!
IN THIS WORLD WITHOUT GUNS, THERE'S A TEN BILLION PERCENT CHANCE WE'D HAVE NO WAY OF STOPPING HIM.
WE'RE TALKING ABOUT A GUY STRONG ENOUGH TO KILL A LION BAREHANDED, LIKE HE'S USING CHEAT CODES.
OH, THAT'D BE BAD.
IN THAT CASE, I'D...

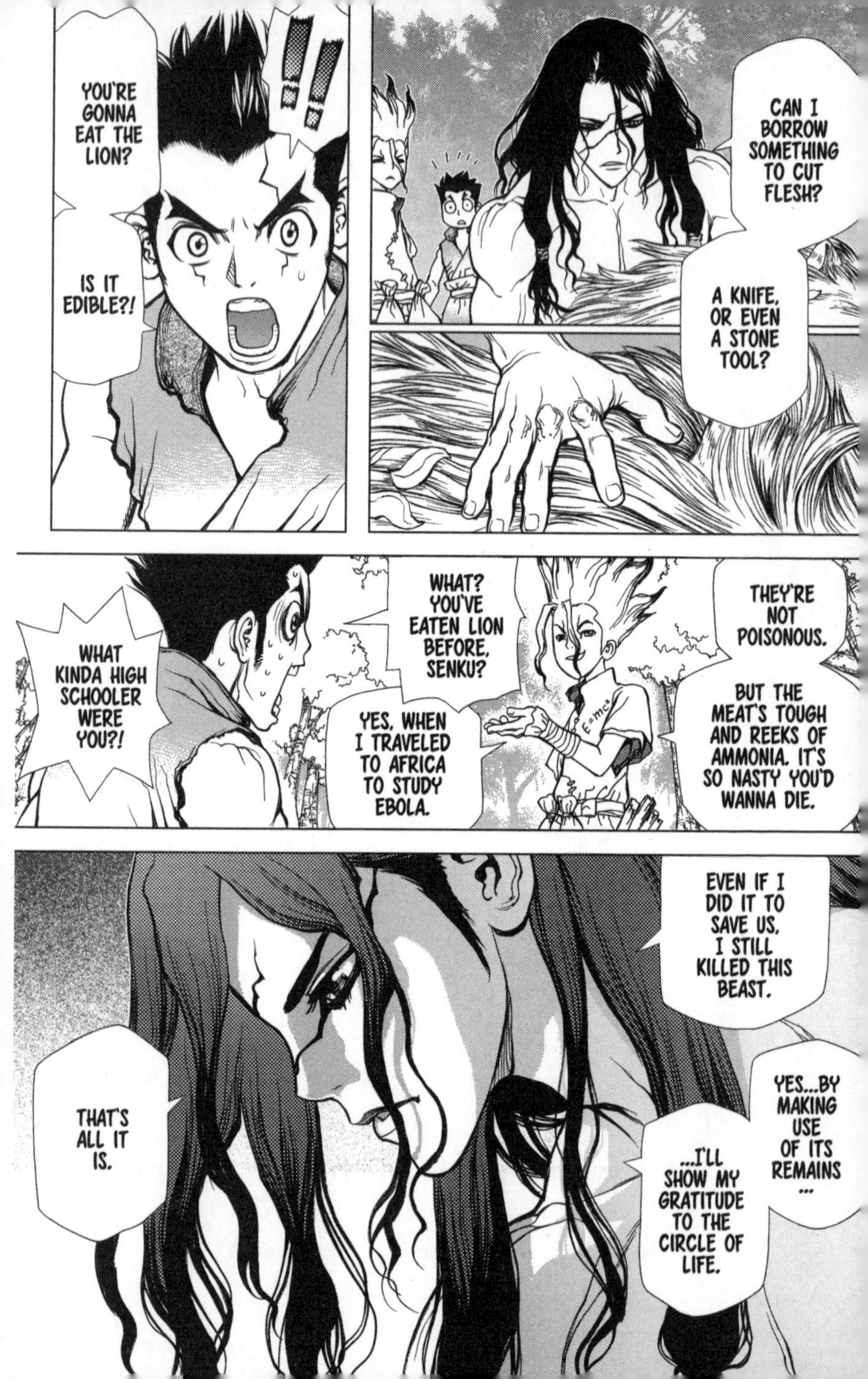
CAN I BORROW SOMETHING TO CUT FLESH?
A KNIFE, OR EVEN A STONE TOOL?
YOU'RE GONNA EAT THE LION?
!!
IS IT EDIBLE?!
THEY'RE NOT POISONOUS.
BUT THE MEAT'S TOUGH AND REEKS OF AMMONIA. IT'S SO NASTY YOU'D WANNA DIE.
WHAT? YOU'VE EATEN LION BEFORE, SENKU?
YES, WHEN I TRAVELED TO AFRICA TO STUDY EBOLA.
WHAT KINDA HIGH SCHOOLER WERE YOU?!
EVEN IF I DID IT TO SAVE US, I STILL KILLED THIS BEAST.
YES...BY MAKING USE OF ITS REMAINS...
...I'LL SHOW MY GRATITUDE TO THE CIRCLE OF LIFE.
THAT'S ALL IT IS.

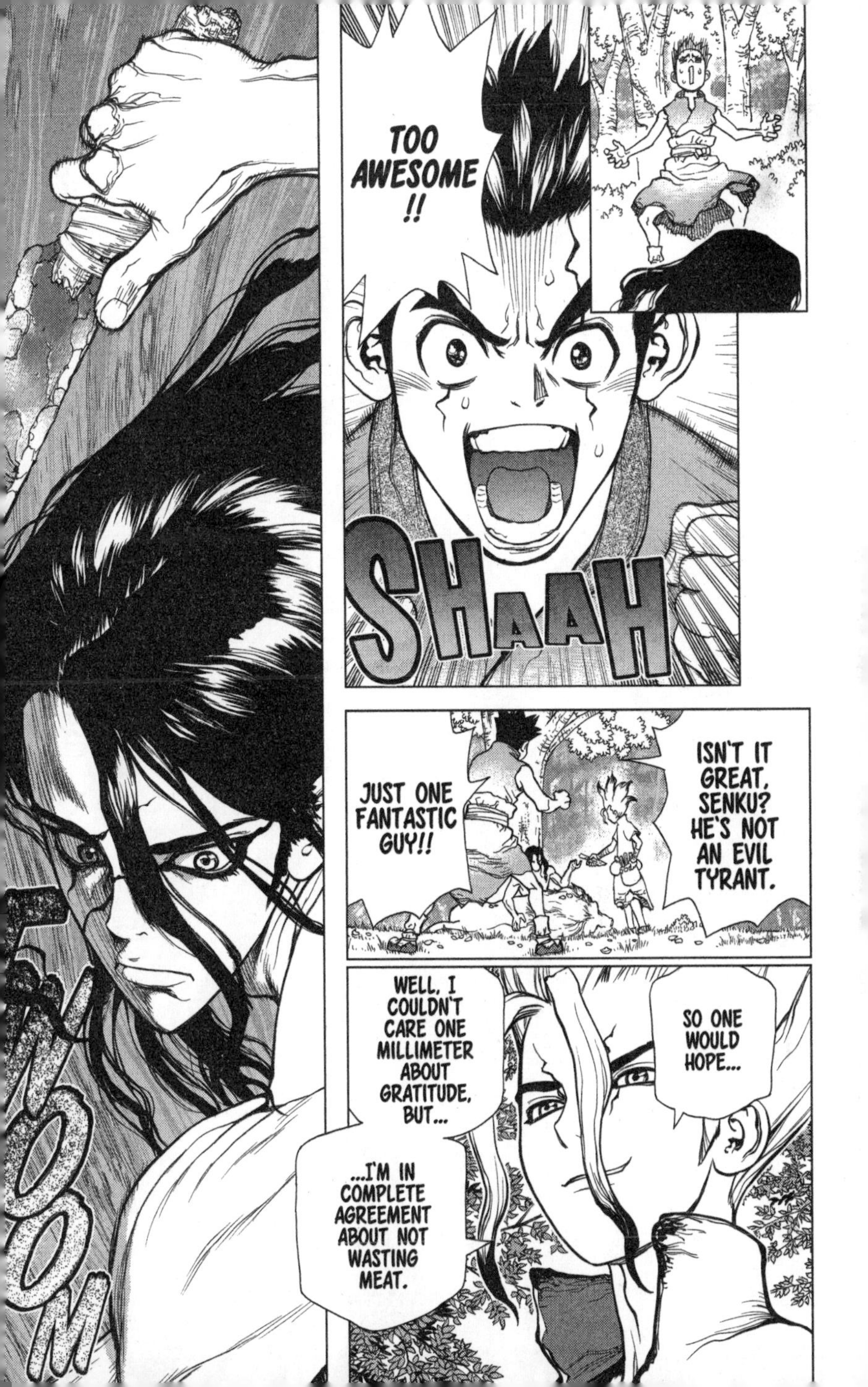
TOO AWESOME !!
SHAAH
ISN'T IT GREAT, SENKU? HE'S NOT AN EVIL TYRANT.
JUST ONE FANTASTIC GUY!!
SO ONE WOULD HOPE...
WELL, I COULDN'T CARE ONE MILLIMETER ABOUT GRATITUDE, BUT...
...I'M IN COMPLETE AGREEMENT ABOUT NOT WASTING MEAT.

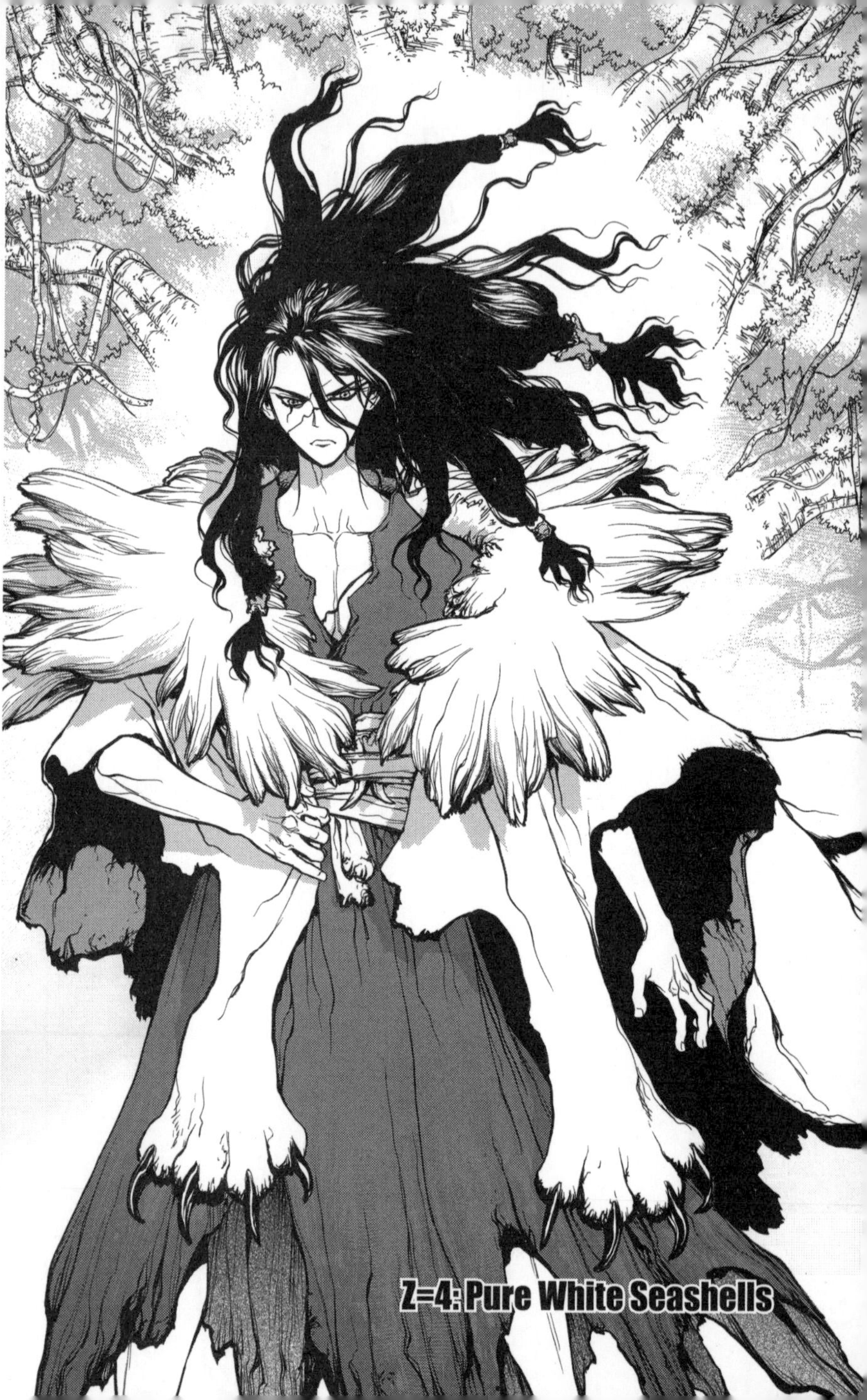
Z=4: Pure White Seashells

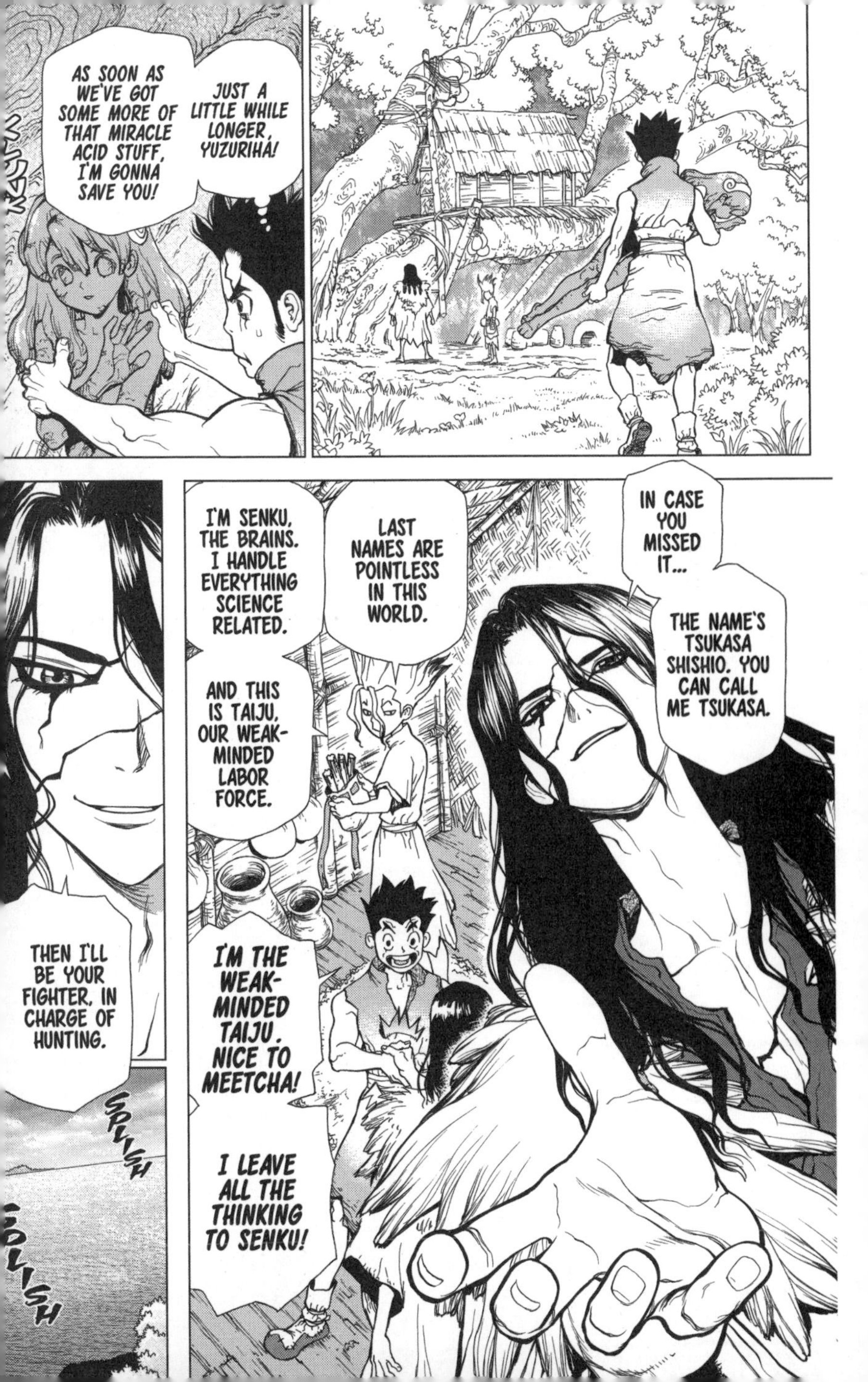
JUST A LITTLE WHILE LONGER, YUZURIHA!
AS SOON AS WE'VE GOT SOME MORE OF THAT MIRACLE ACID STUFF, I'M GONNA SAVE YOU!
IN CASE YOU MISSED IT...
THE NAME'S TSUKASA SHISHIO. YOU CAN CALL ME TSUKASA.
LAST NAMES ARE POINTLESS IN THIS WORLD.
I'M SENKU, THE BRAINS. I HANDLE EVERYTHING SCIENCE RELATED.
AND THIS IS TAIJU, OUR WEAK-MINDED LABOR FORCE.
I'M THE WEAK-MINDED TAIJU. NICE TO MEETCHA!
I LEAVE ALL THE THINKING TO SENKU!
THEN I'LL BE YOUR FIGHTER, IN CHARGE OF HUNTING.
SPLISH
SPLISH

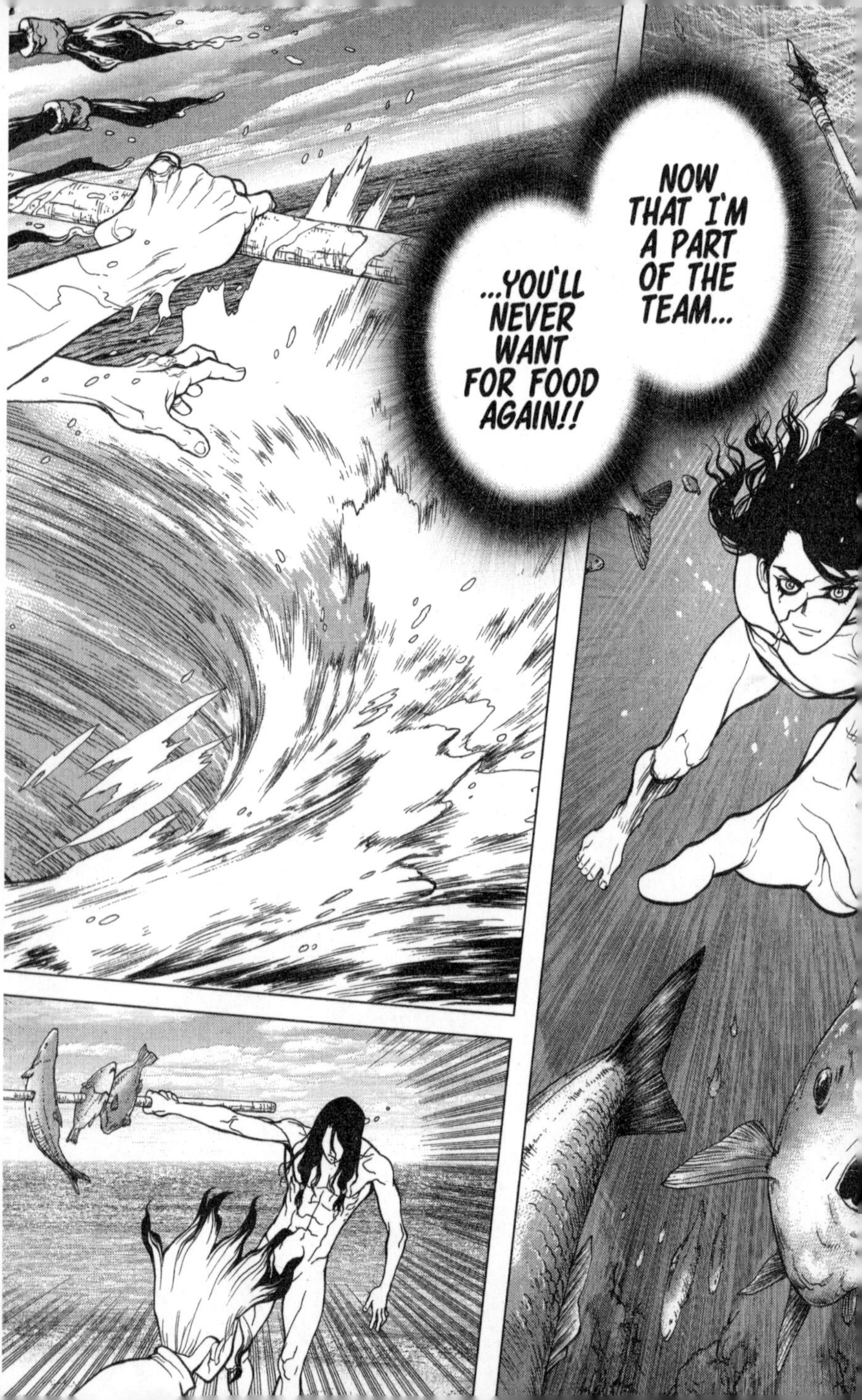
NOW THAT I'M A PART OF THE TEAM...
...YOU'LL NEVER WANT FOR FOOD AGAIN!!

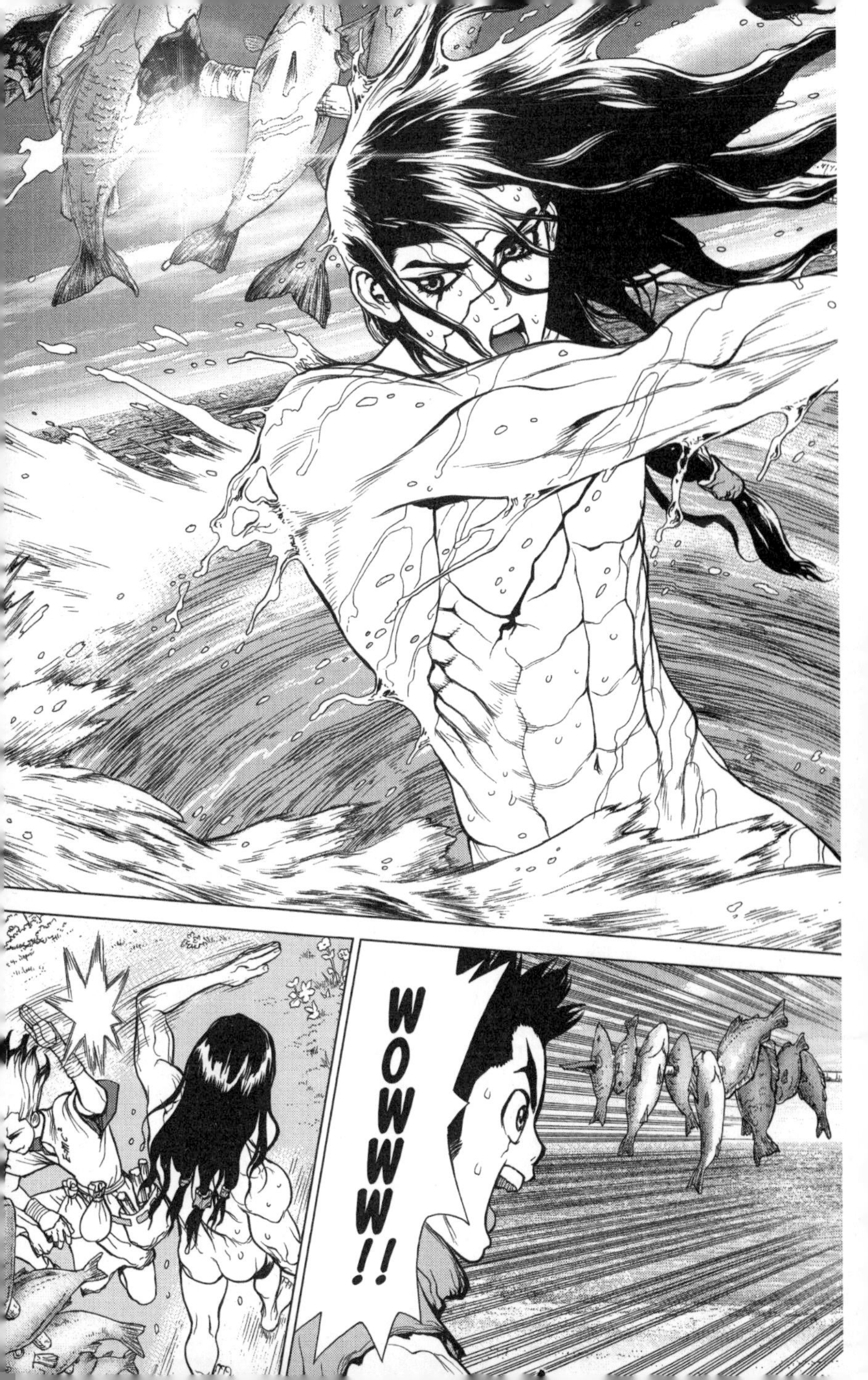
WOWWWW!!

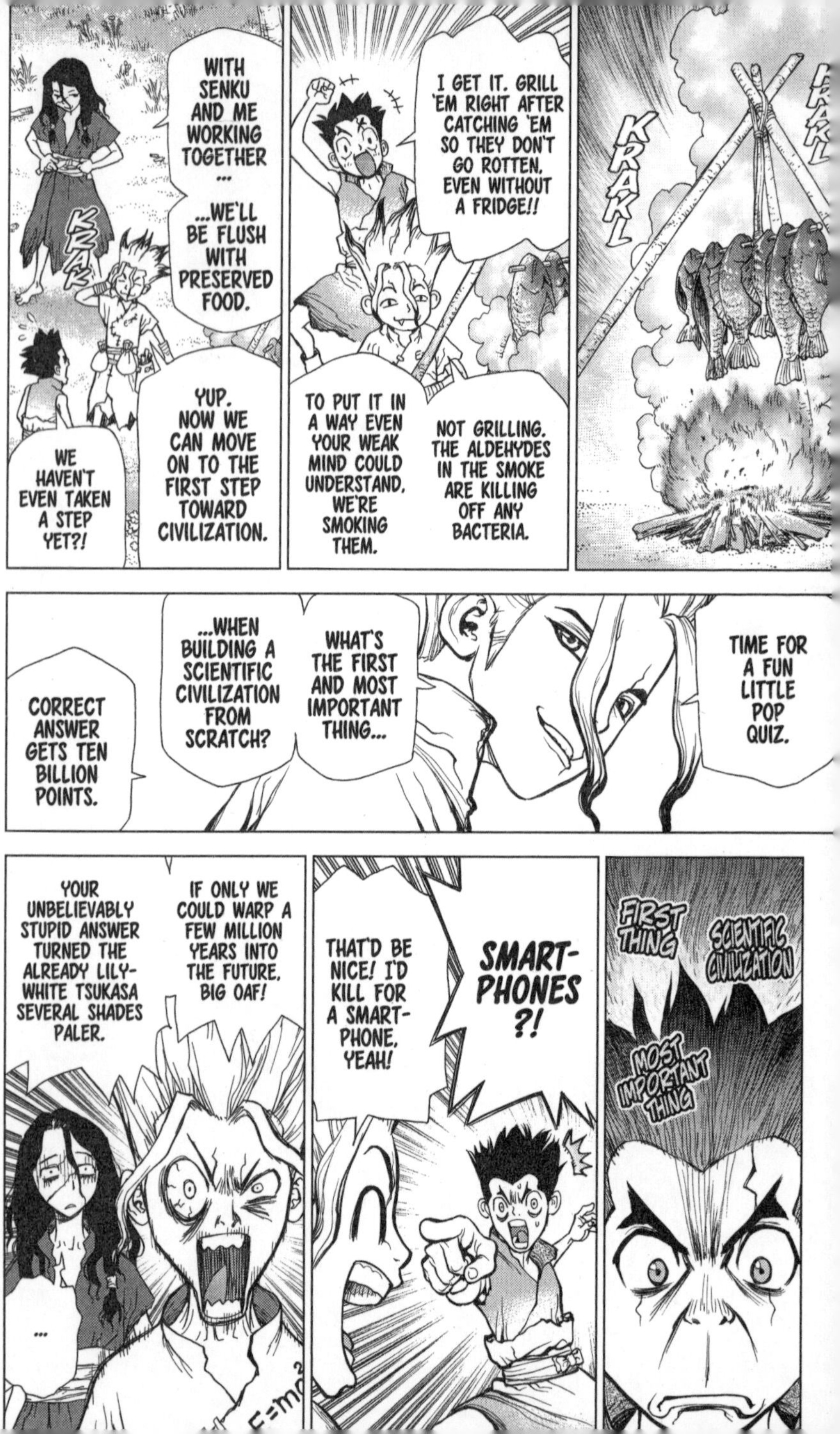
KRAKL
KRAKL
I GET IT. GRILL 'EM RIGHT AFTER CATCHING 'EM SO THEY DON'T GO ROTTEN, EVEN WITHOUT A FRIDGE!!
NOT GRILLING. THE ALDEHYDES IN THE SMOKE ARE KILLING OFF ANY BACTERIA.
TO PUT IT IN A WAY EVEN YOUR WEAK MIND COULD UNDERSTAND, WE'RE SMOKING THEM.
WITH SENKU AND ME WORKING TOGETHER...
...WE'LL BE FLUSH WITH PRESERVED FOOD.
KRAK
YUP. NOW WE CAN MOVE ON TO THE FIRST STEP TOWARD CIVILIZATION.
WE HAVEN'T EVEN TAKEN A STEP YET?!
TIME FOR A FUN LITTLE POP QUIZ.
WHAT'S THE FIRST AND MOST IMPORTANT THING...
...WHEN BUILDING A SCIENTIFIC CIVILIZATION FROM SCRATCH?
CORRECT ANSWER GETS TEN BILLION POINTS.
FIRST THING
SCIENTIFIC CIVILIZATION
MOST IMPORTANT THING
SMART-PHONES?!
THAT'D BE NICE! I'D KILL FOR A SMART-PHONE, YEAH!
IF ONLY WE COULD WARP A FEW MILLION YEARS INTO THE FUTURE, BIG OAF!
YOUR UNBELIEVABLY STUPID ANSWER TURNED THE ALREADY LILY-WHITE TSUKASA SEVERAL SHADES PALER.
...

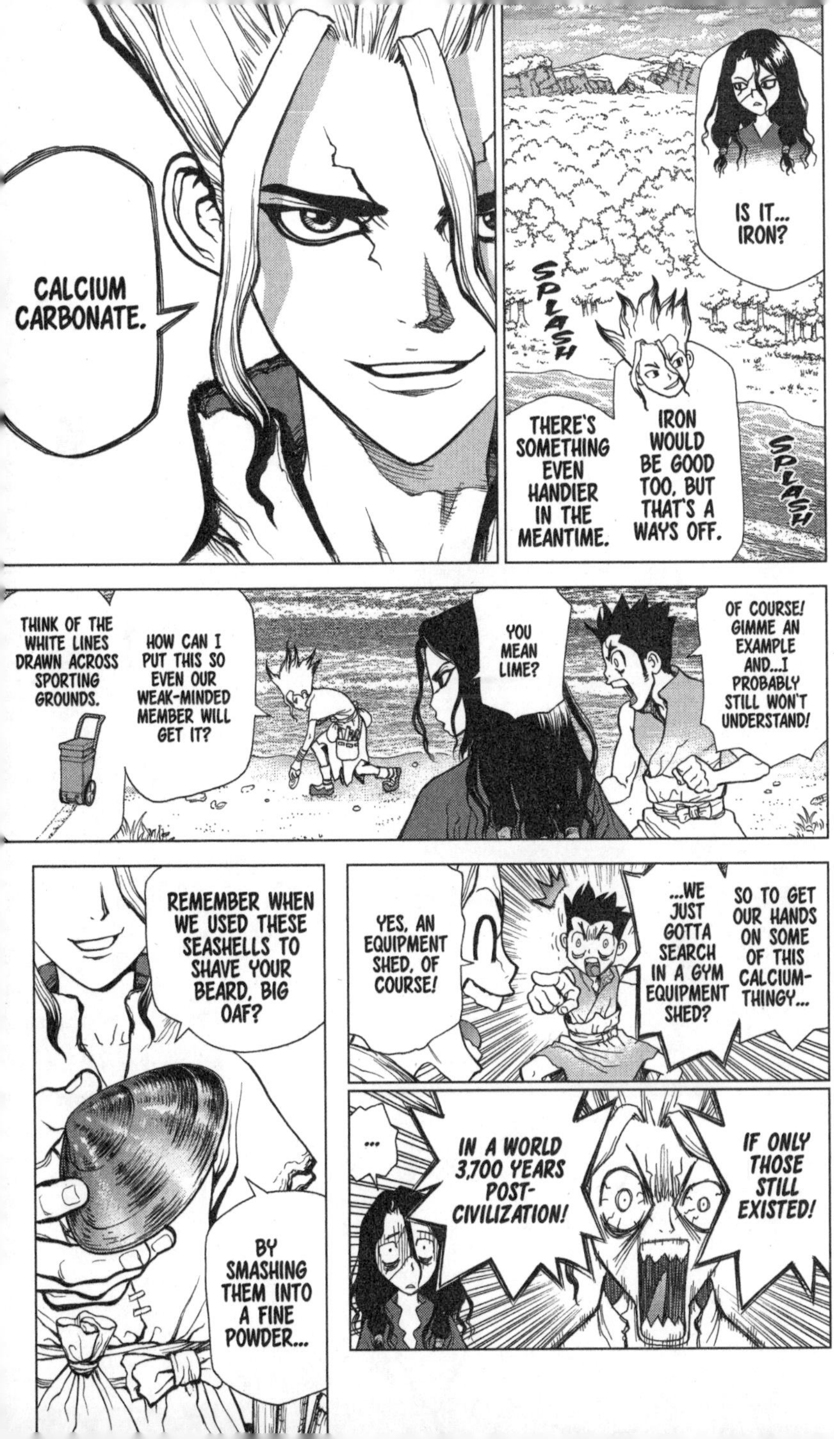
IS IT... IRON?
SPLASH
IRON WOULD BE GOOD TOO, BUT THAT'S A WAYS OFF.
THERE'S SOMETHING EVEN HANDIER IN THE MEANTIME.
SPLASH
CALCIUM CARBONATE.
OF COURSE! GIMME AN EXAMPLE AND...I PROBABLY STILL WON'T UNDERSTAND!
YOU MEAN LIME?
HOW CAN I PUT THIS SO EVEN OUR WEAK-MINDED MEMBER WILL GET IT?
THINK OF THE WHITE LINES DRAWN ACROSS SPORTING GROUNDS.
SO TO GET OUR HANDS ON SOME OF THIS CALCIUM-THINGY...
...WE JUST GOTTA SEARCH IN A GYM EQUIPMENT SHED?
YES, AN EQUIPMENT SHED, OF COURSE!
IF ONLY THOSE STILL EXISTED!
IN A WORLD 3,700 YEARS POST-CIVILIZATION!
...
REMEMBER WHEN WE USED THESE SEASHELLS TO SHAVE YOUR BEARD, BIG OAF?
BY SMASHING THEM INTO A FINE POWDER...

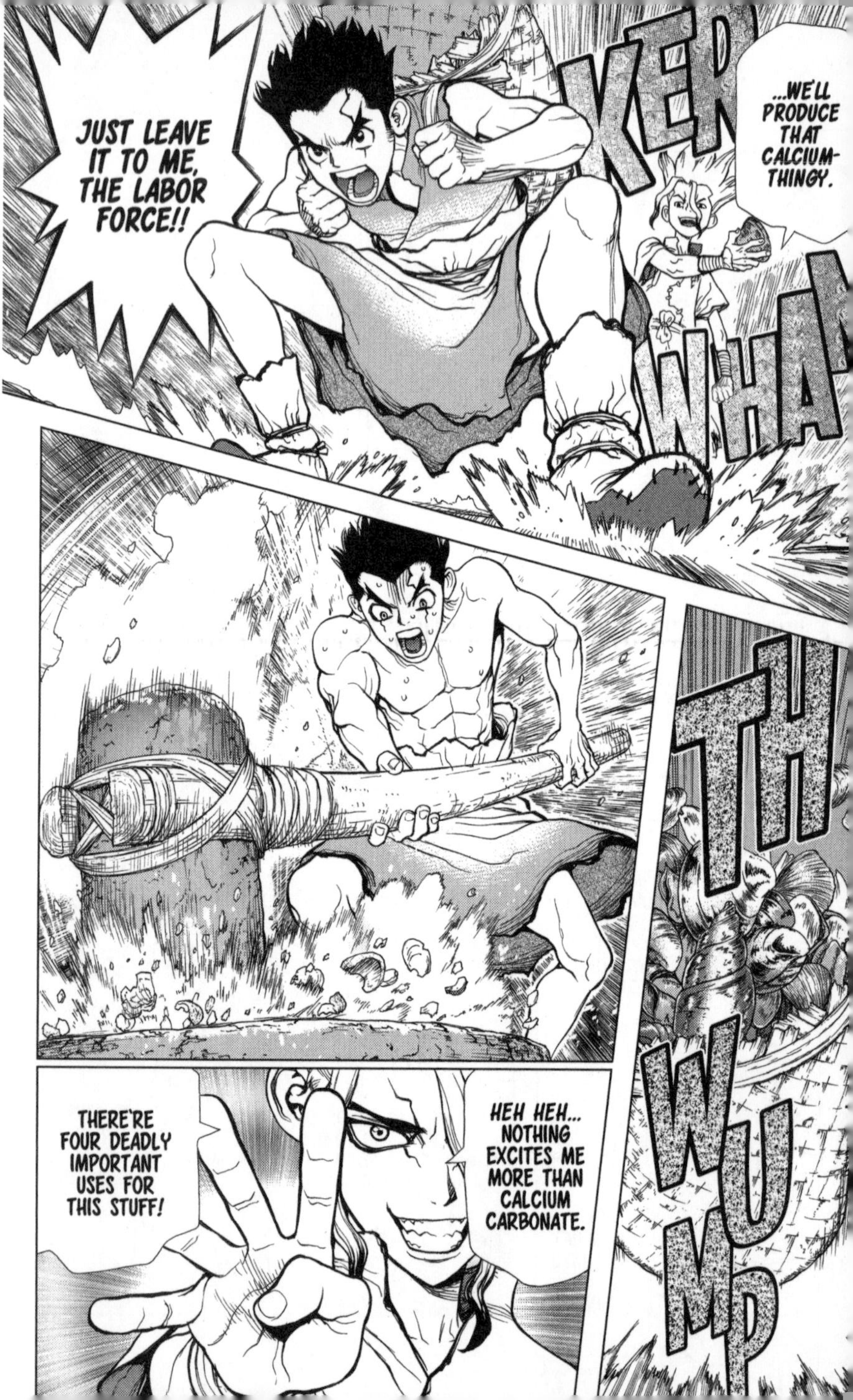
...WE'LL PRODUCE THAT CALCIUM-THINGY.
KER
WHA
JUST LEAVE IT TO ME, THE LABOR FORCE!!
TH
WUMP
HEH HEH... NOTHING EXCITES ME MORE THAN CALCIUM CARBONATE.
THERE'RE FOUR DEADLY IMPORTANT USES FOR THIS STUFF!

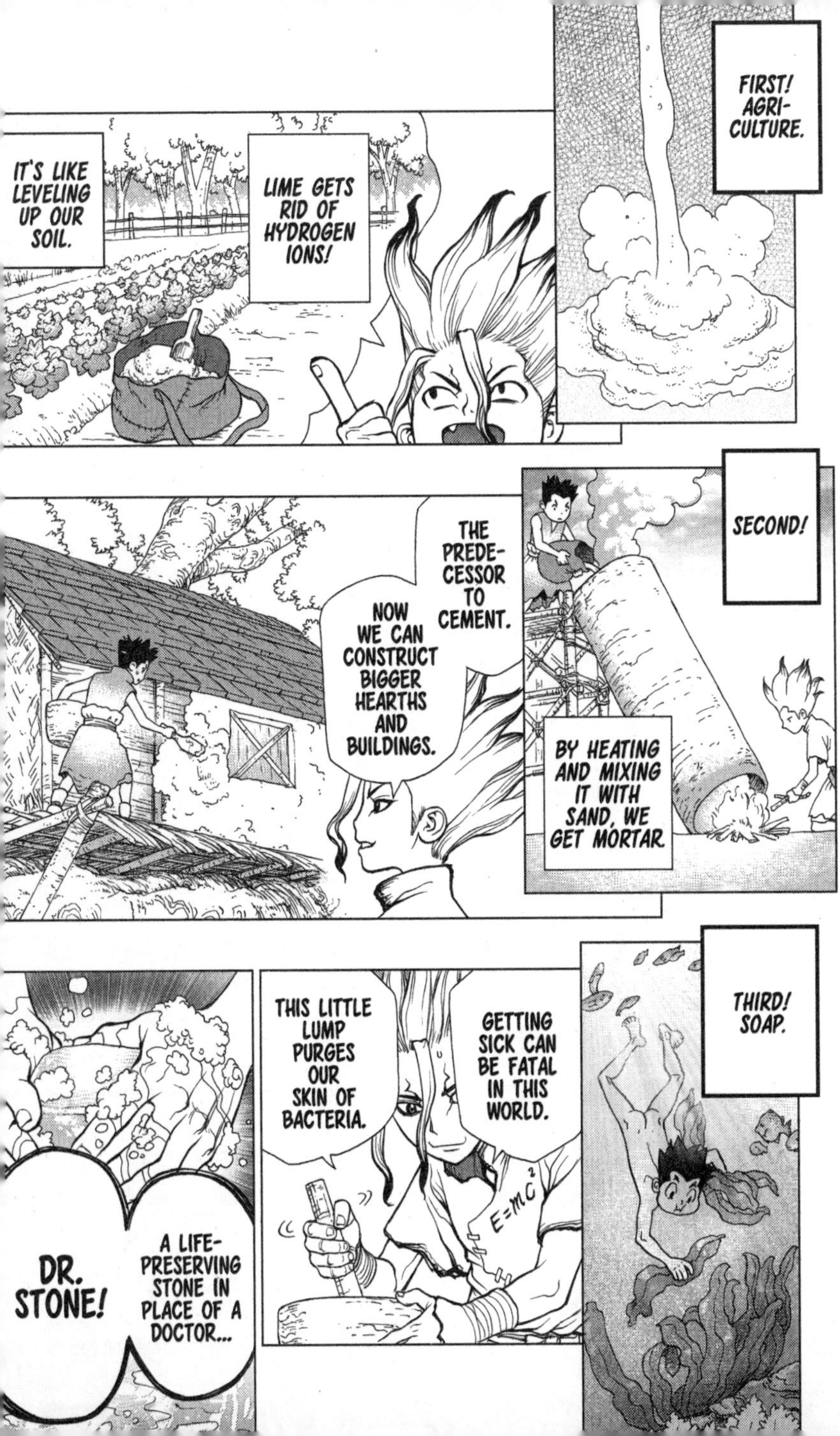
FIRST! AGRI-CULTURE.
LIME GETS RID OF HYDROGEN IONS!
IT'S LIKE LEVELING UP OUR SOIL.
SECOND!
BY HEATING AND MIXING IT WITH SAND, WE GET MORTAR.
THE PREDE-CESSOR TO CEMENT.
NOW WE CAN CONSTRUCT BIGGER HEARTHS AND BUILDINGS.
THIRD! SOAP.
GETTING SICK CAN BE FATAL IN THIS WORLD.
THIS LITTLE LUMP PURGES OUR SKIN OF BACTERIA.
E=MC2
A LIFE-PRESERVING STONE IN PLACE OF A DOCTOR...
DR. STONE!

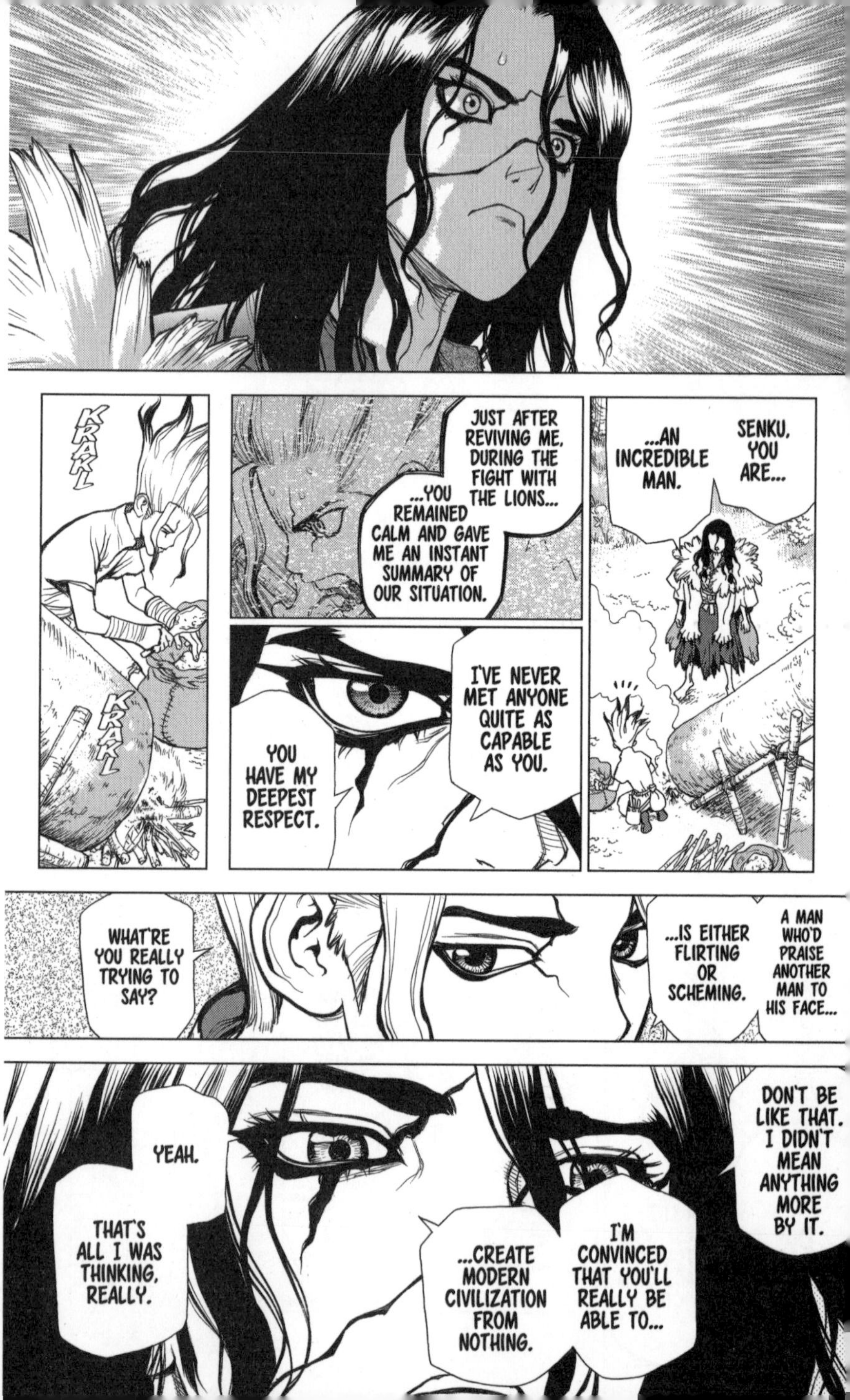

SENKU, YOU ARE...
...AN INCREDIBLE MAN.
JUST AFTER REVIVING ME, DURING THE FIGHT WITH THE LIONS...
...YOU REMAINED CALM AND GAVE ME AN INSTANT SUMMARY OF OUR SITUATION.
I'VE NEVER MET ANYONE QUITE AS CAPABLE AS YOU.
YOU HAVE MY DEEPEST RESPECT.
KRAKL
KRAKL
A MAN WHO'D PRAISE ANOTHER MAN TO HIS FACE...
...IS EITHER FLIRTING OR SCHEMING.
WHAT'RE YOU REALLY TRYING TO SAY?
DON'T BE LIKE THAT. I DIDN'T MEAN ANYTHING MORE BY IT.
I'M CONVINCED THAT YOU'LL REALLY BE ABLE TO...
...CREATE MODERN CIVILIZATION FROM NOTHING.
YEAH.
THAT'S ALL I WAS THINKING, REALLY.

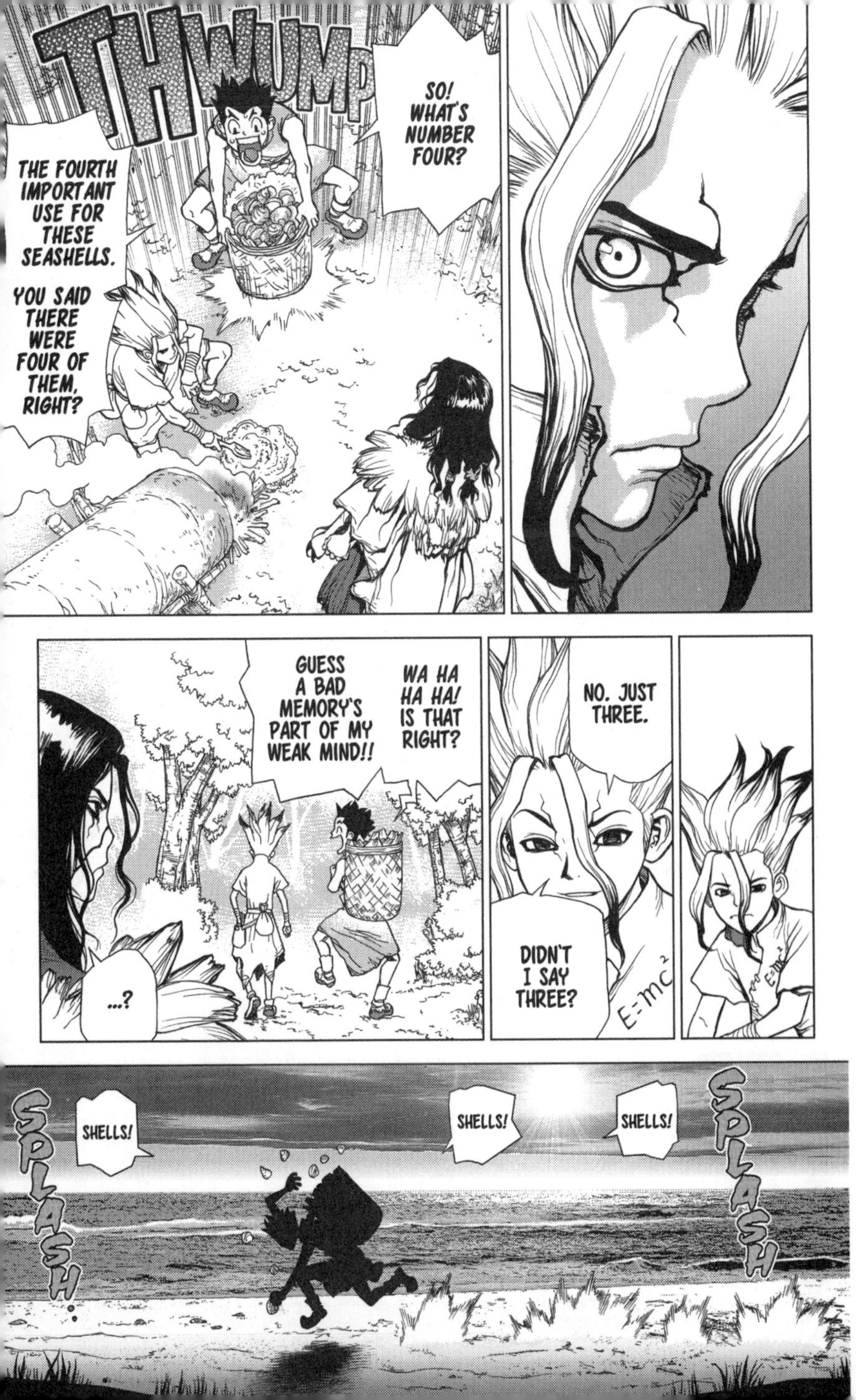
THWUMP
SO! WHAT'S NUMBER FOUR?
THE FOURTH IMPORTANT USE FOR THESE SEASHELLS.
YOU SAID THERE WERE FOUR OF THEM, RIGHT?
NO. JUST THREE.
DIDN'T I SAY THREE?
E=mc2
WA HA HA HA! IS THAT RIGHT?
GUESS A BAD MEMORY'S PART OF MY WEAK MIND!!
...?
SPLASH
SHELLS!
SHELLS!
SHELLS!
SPLASH

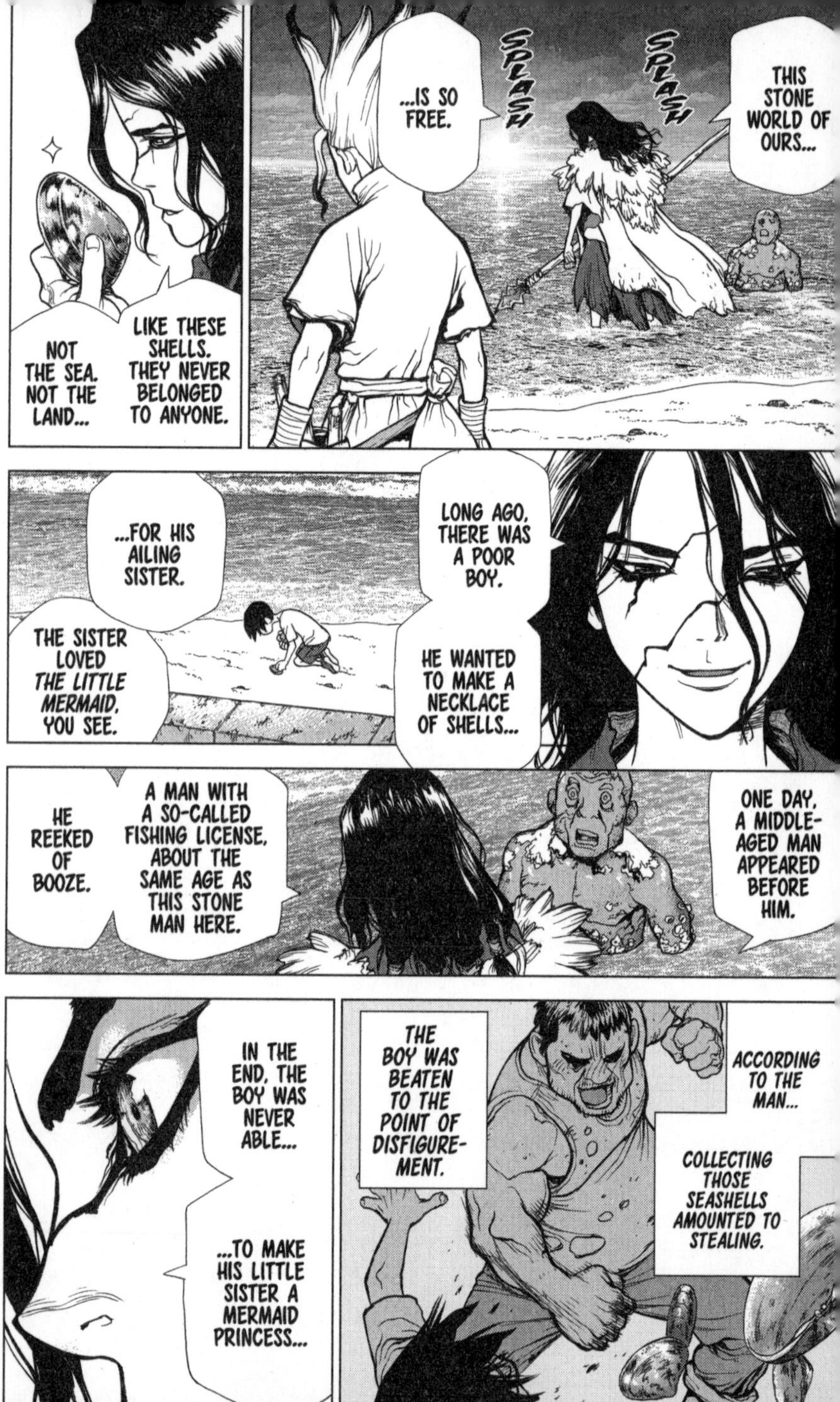
THIS STONE WORLD OF OURS...
SPLASH
SPLASH
...IS SO FREE.
LIKE THESE SHELLS. THEY NEVER BELONGED TO ANYONE.
NOT THE SEA. NOT THE LAND...
LONG AGO, THERE WAS A POOR BOY.
HE WANTED TO MAKE A NECKLACE OF SHELLS...
...FOR HIS AILING SISTER.
THE SISTER LOVED *THE LITTLE MERMAID*, YOU SEE.
ONE DAY, A MIDDLE-AGED MAN APPEARED BEFORE HIM.
A MAN WITH A SO-CALLED FISHING LICENSE, ABOUT THE SAME AGE AS THIS STONE MAN HERE.
HE REEKED OF BOOZE.
ACCORDING TO THE MAN...
COLLECTING THOSE SEASHELLS AMOUNTED TO STEALING.
THE BOY WAS BEATEN TO THE POINT OF DISFIGUREMENT.
IN THE END, THE BOY WAS NEVER ABLE...
...TO MAKE HIS LITTLE SISTER A MERMAID PRINCESS...

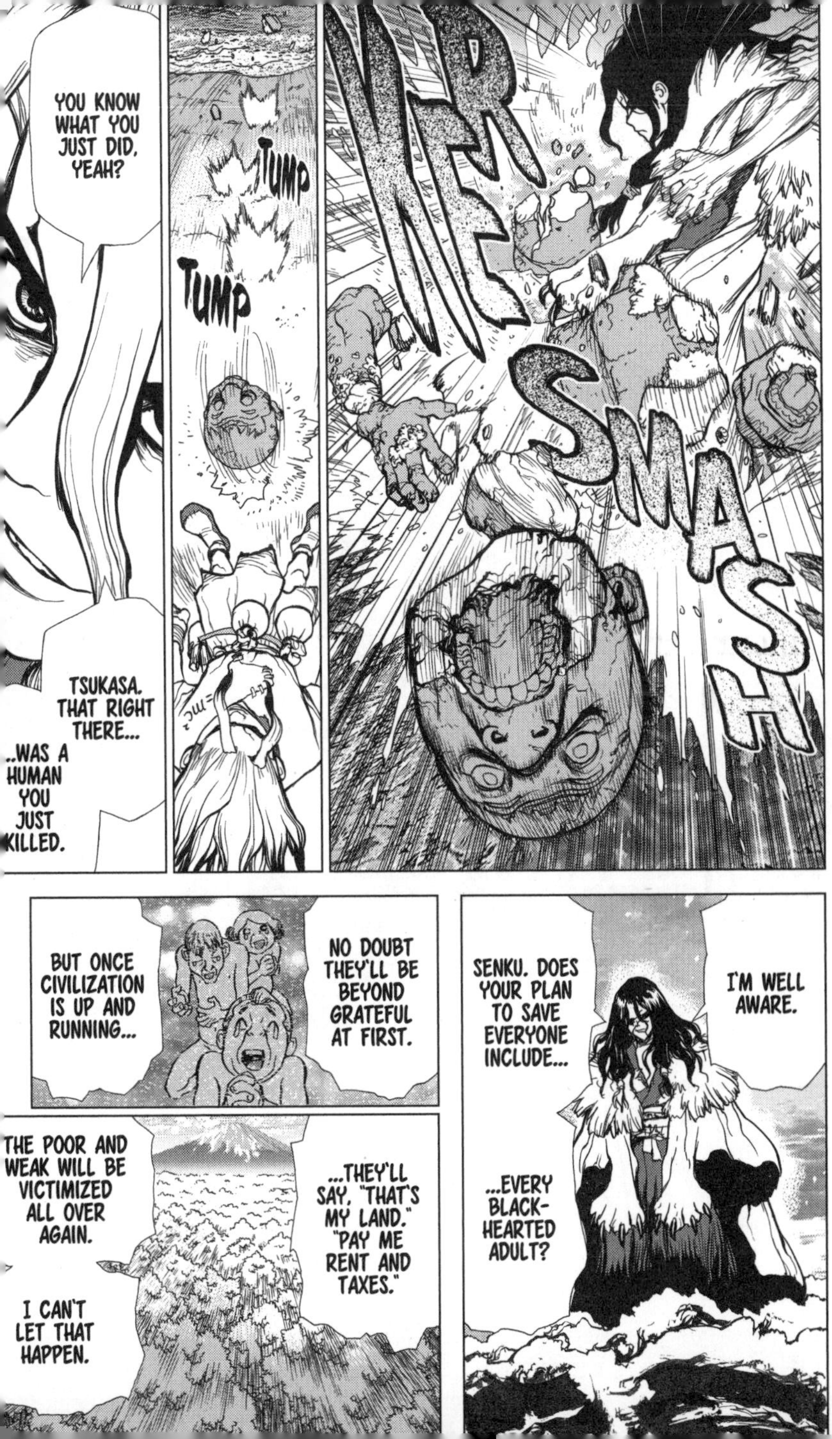
SMASH
TUMP
TUMP
YOU KNOW WHAT YOU JUST DID, YEAH?
TSUKASA. THAT RIGHT THERE...
..WAS A HUMAN YOU JUST KILLED.
I'M WELL AWARE.
SENKU. DOES YOUR PLAN TO SAVE EVERYONE INCLUDE...
...EVERY BLACK-HEARTED ADULT?
NO DOUBT THEY'LL BE BEYOND GRATEFUL AT FIRST.
BUT ONCE CIVILIZATION IS UP AND RUNNING...
...THEY'LL SAY, "THAT'S MY LAND." "PAY ME RENT AND TAXES."
THE POOR AND WEAK WILL BE VICTIMIZED ALL OVER AGAIN.
I CAN'T LET THAT HAPPEN.

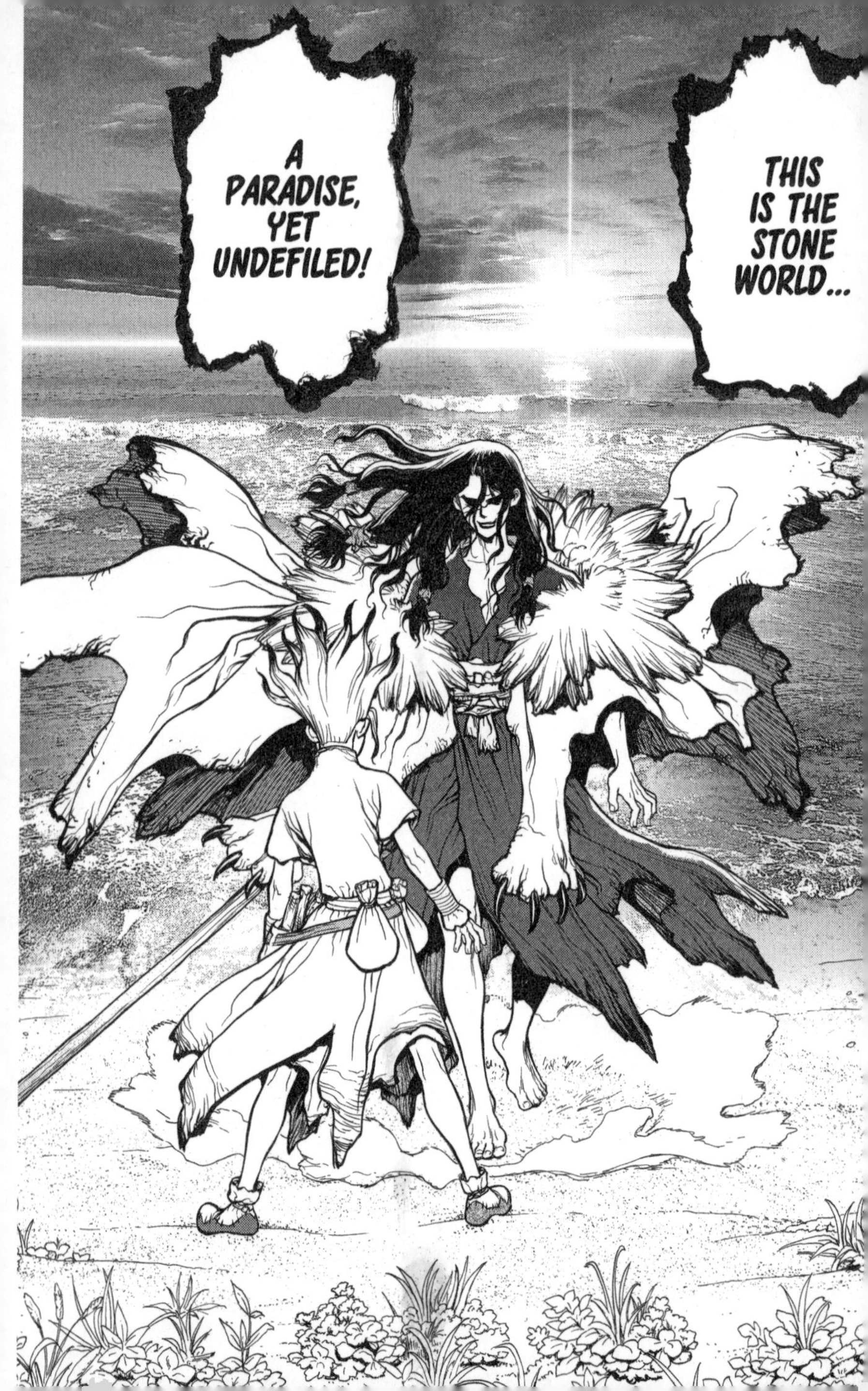
THIS IS THE STONE WORLD...
A PARADISE, YET UNDEFILED!

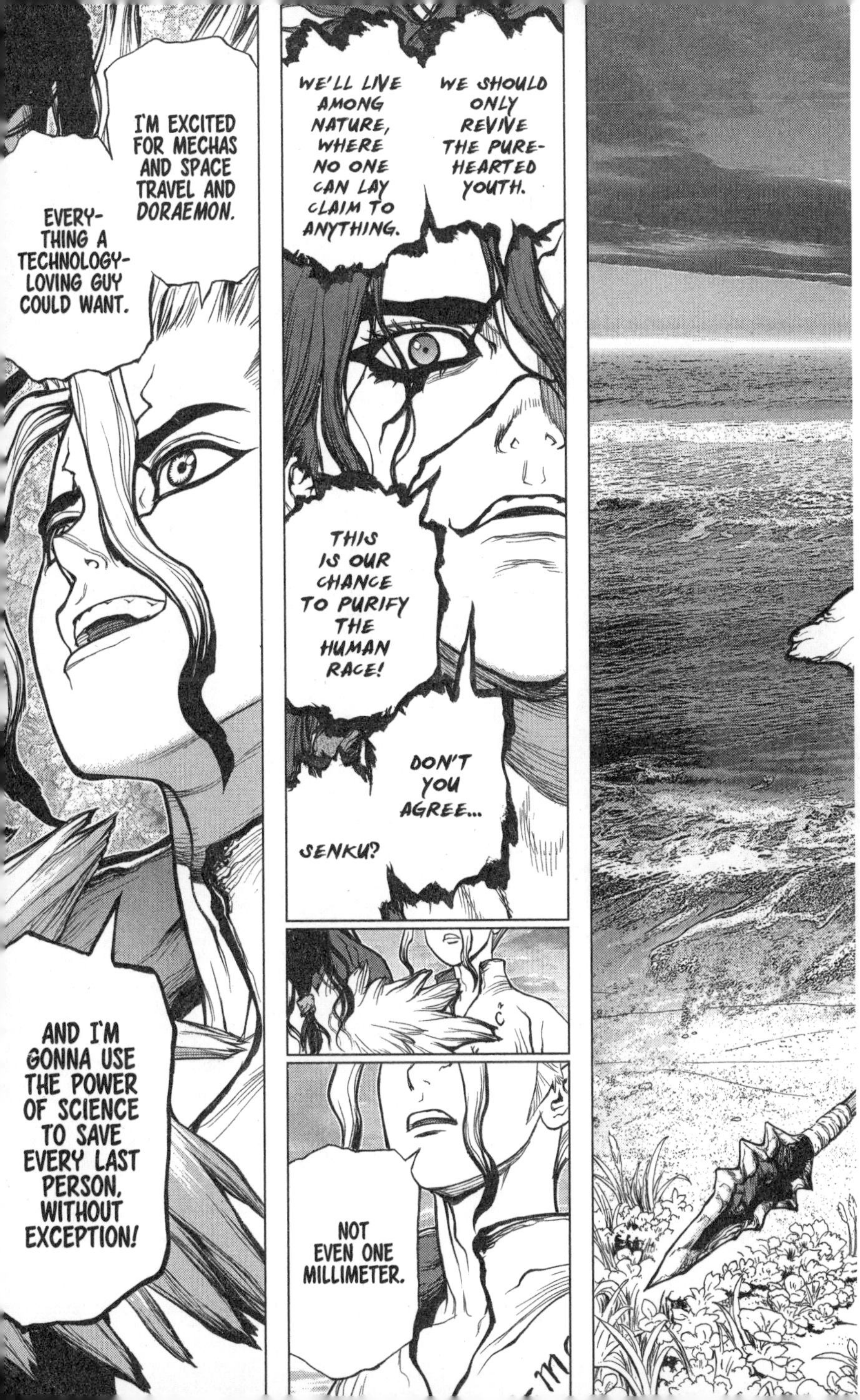
WE SHOULD ONLY REVIVE THE PURE-HEARTED YOUTH.
WE'LL LIVE AMONG NATURE, WHERE NO ONE CAN LAY CLAIM TO ANYTHING.
THIS IS OUR CHANCE TO PURIFY THE HUMAN RACE!
DON'T YOU AGREE... SENKU?
NOT EVEN ONE MILLIMETER.
I'M EXCITED FOR MECHAS AND SPACE TRAVEL AND DORAEMON.
EVERY-THING A TECHNOLOGY-LOVING GUY COULD WANT.
AND I'M GONNA USE THE POWER OF SCIENCE TO SAVE EVERY LAST PERSON, WITHOUT EXCEPTION!

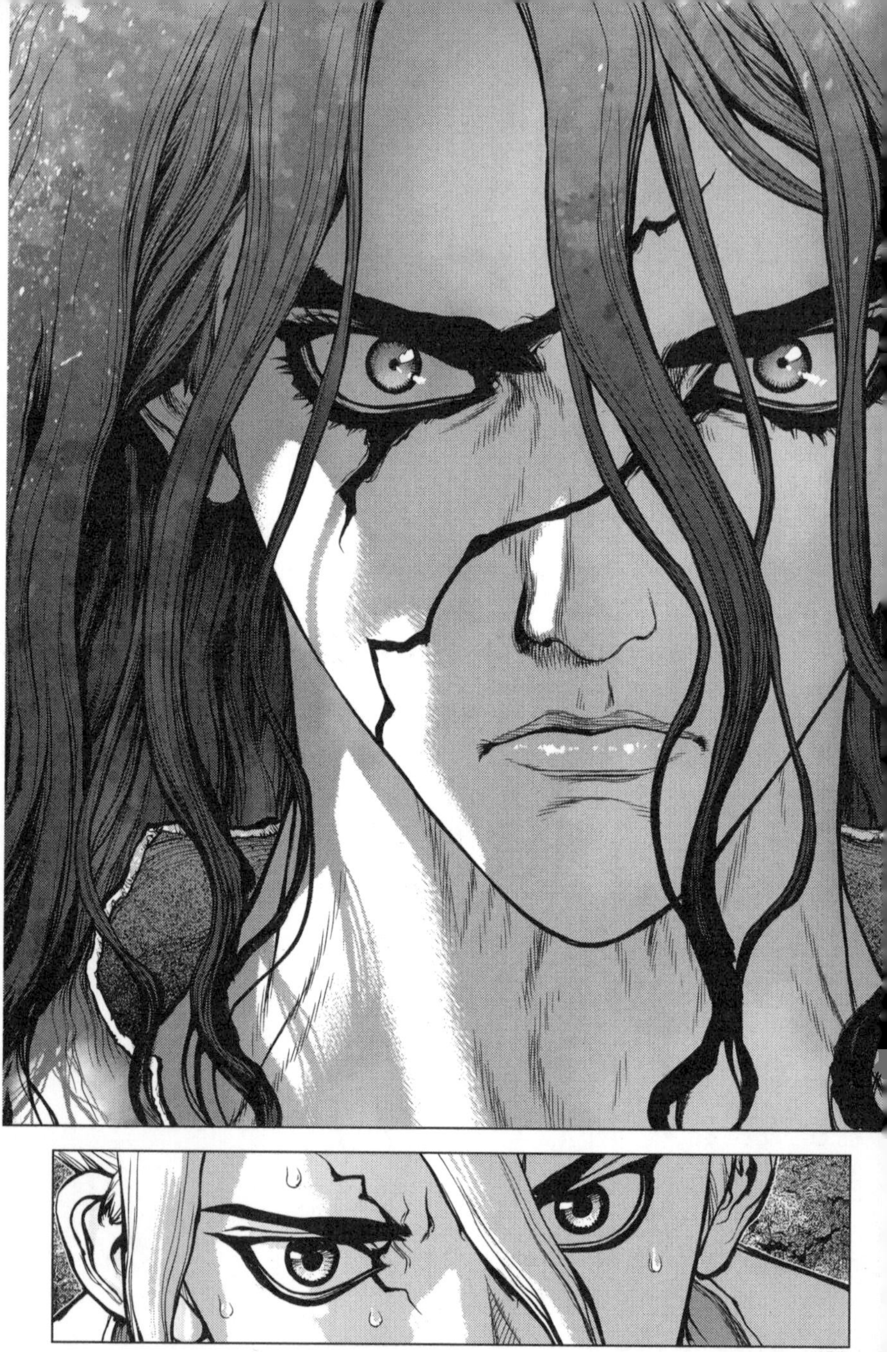

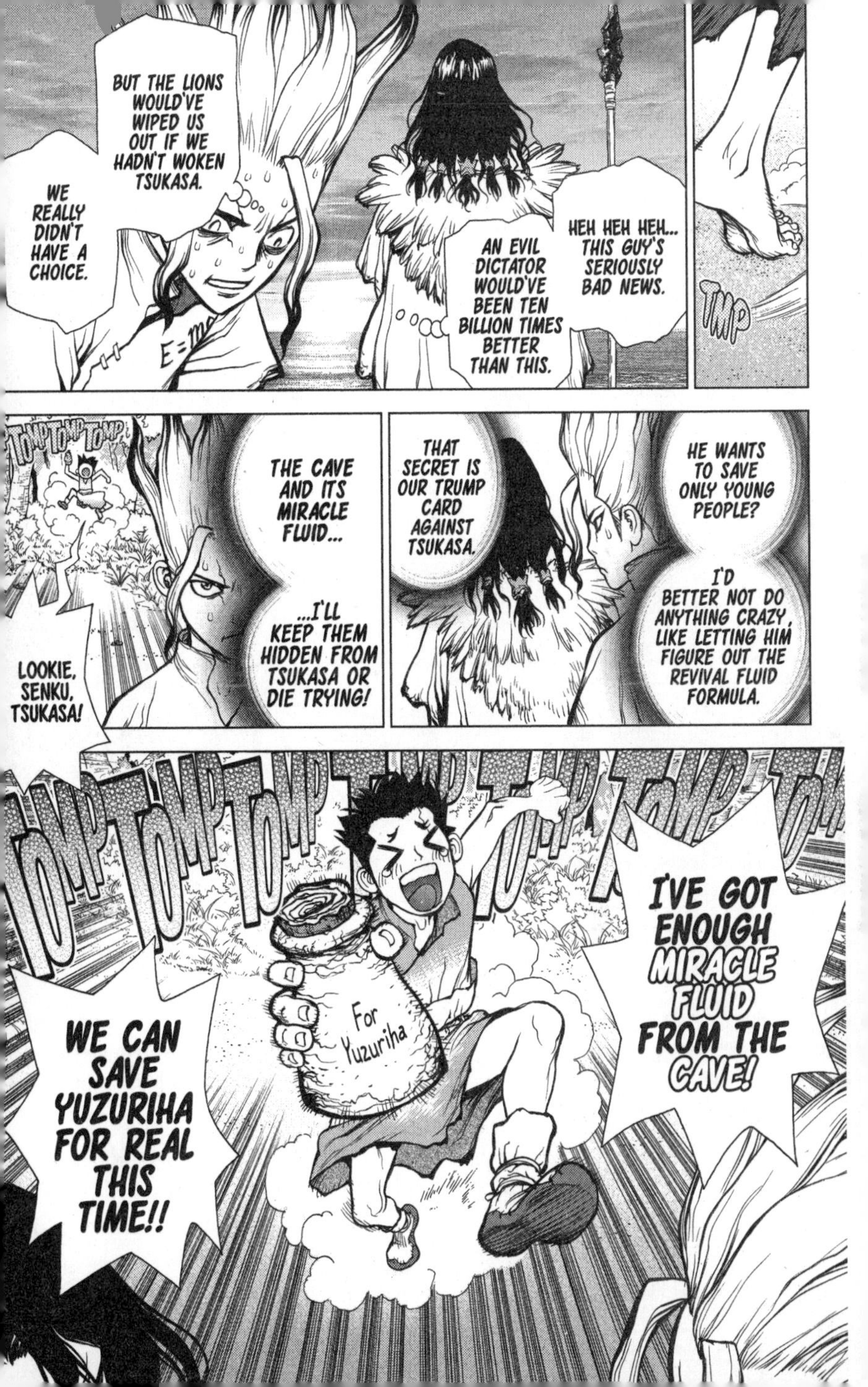
TMP
HEH HEH HEH... THIS GUY'S SERIOUSLY BAD NEWS.
AN EVIL DICTATOR WOULD'VE BEEN TEN BILLION TIMES BETTER THAN THIS.
BUT THE LIONS WOULD'VE WIPED US OUT IF WE HADN'T WOKEN TSUKASA.
WE REALLY DIDN'T HAVE A CHOICE.
E=mc
HE WANTS TO SAVE ONLY YOUNG PEOPLE?
THAT SECRET IS OUR TRUMP CARD AGAINST TSUKASA.
I'D BETTER NOT DO ANYTHING CRAZY, LIKE LETTING HIM FIGURE OUT THE REVIVAL FLUID FORMULA.
THE CAVE AND ITS MIRACLE FLUID...
...I'LL KEEP THEM HIDDEN FROM TSUKASA OR DIE TRYING!
TOMP TOMP TOMP
LOOKIE, SENKU, TSUKASA!
TOMP TOMP TOMP TOMP TOMP TOMP TOMP
I'VE GOT ENOUGH MIRACLE FLUID FROM THE CAVE!
WE CAN SAVE YUZURIHA FOR REAL THIS TIME!!
For Yuzuriha

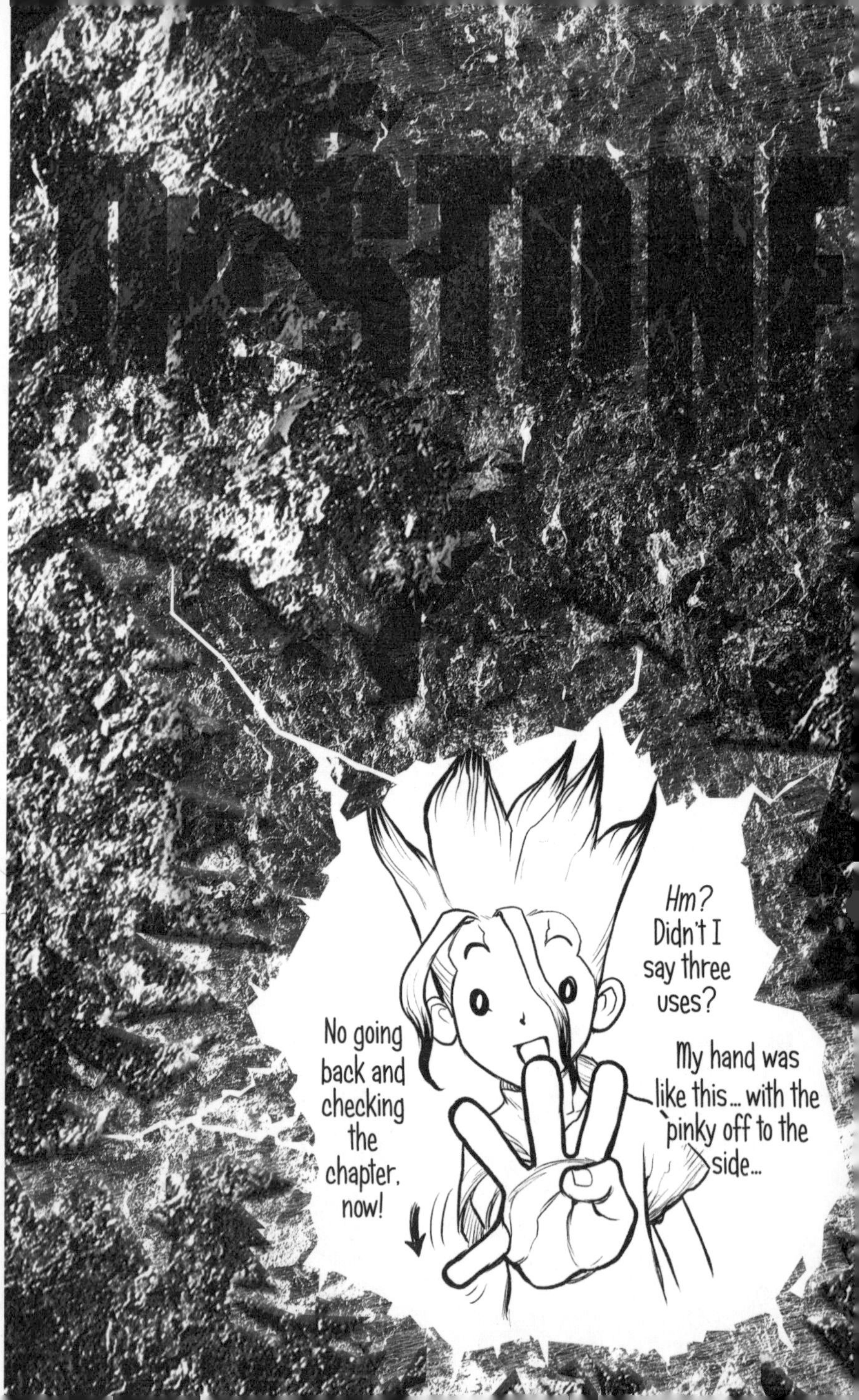
DR. STONE
Hm? Didn't I say three uses?
My hand was like this... with the pinky off to the side...
No going back and checking the chapter, now!

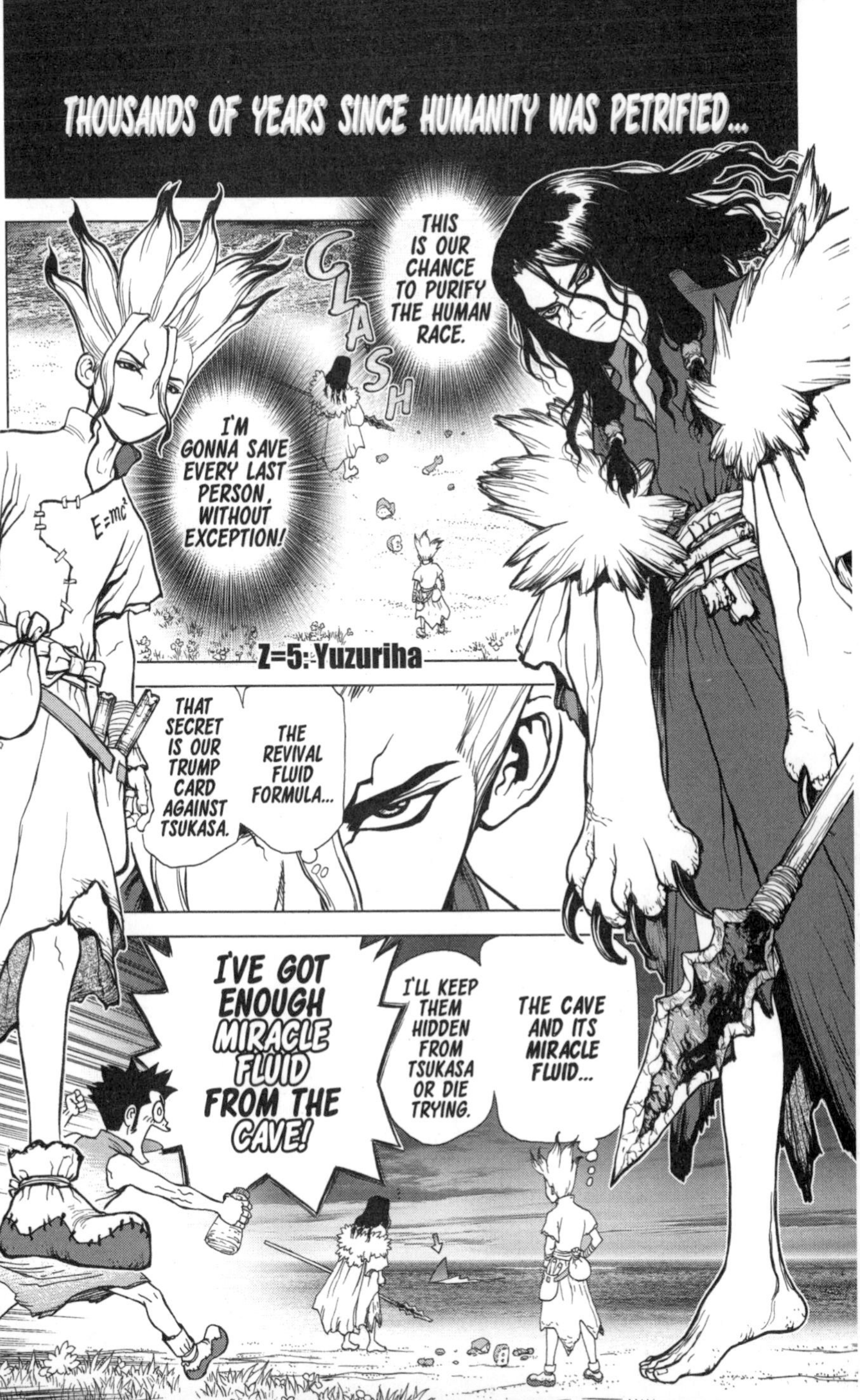
THOUSANDS OF YEARS SINCE HUMANITY WAS PETRIFIED...
THIS IS OUR CHANCE TO PURIFY THE HUMAN RACE.
CLASH
I'M GONNA SAVE EVERY LAST PERSON, WITHOUT EXCEPTION!
E=mc²
Z=5: Yuzuriha
THE REVIVAL FLUID FORMULA...
THAT SECRET IS OUR TRUMP CARD AGAINST TSUKASA.
THE CAVE AND ITS MIRACLE FLUID...
I'LL KEEP THEM HIDDEN FROM TSUKASA OR DIE TRYING.
I'VE GOT ENOUGH MIRACLE FLUID FROM THE CAVE!

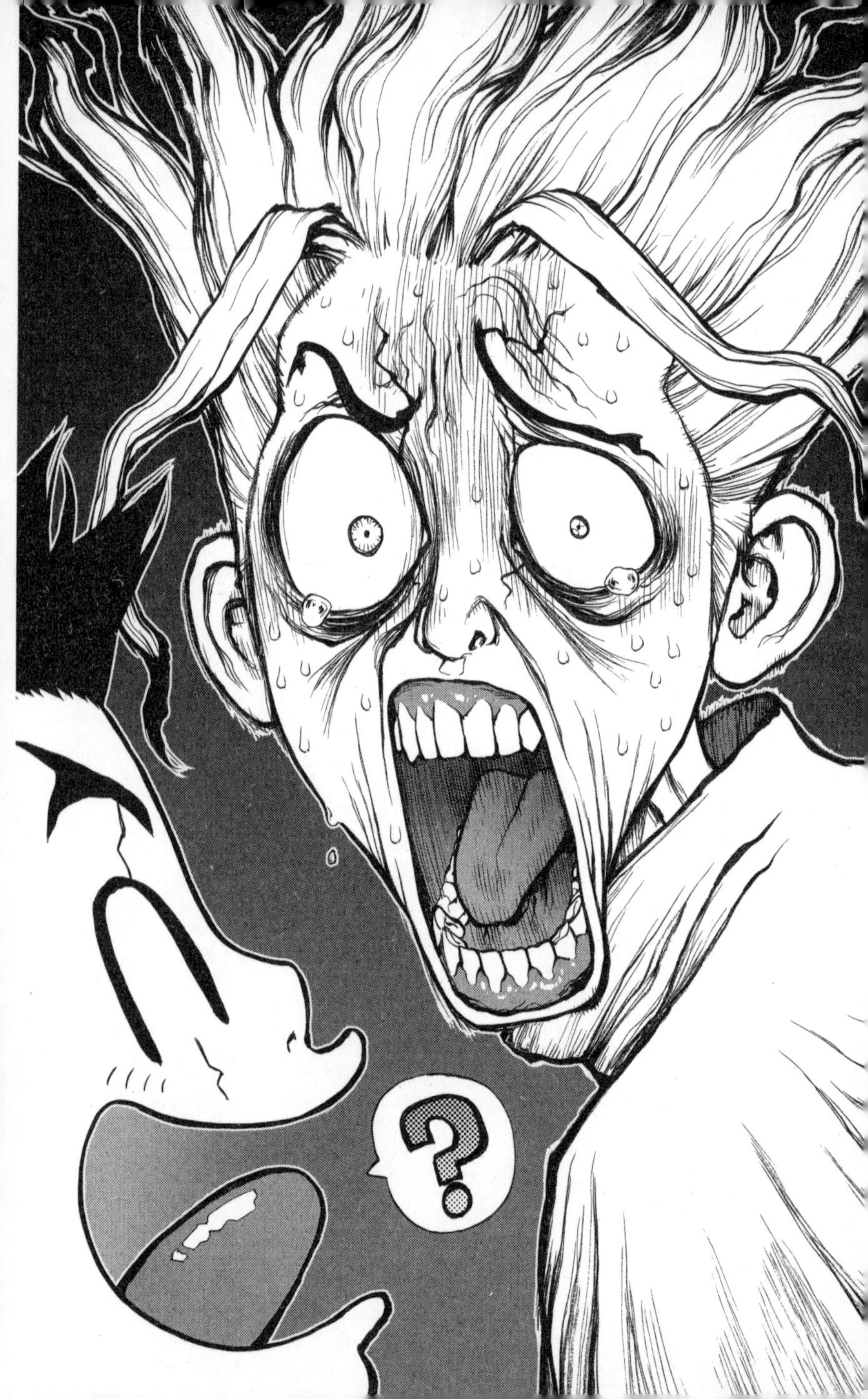
?

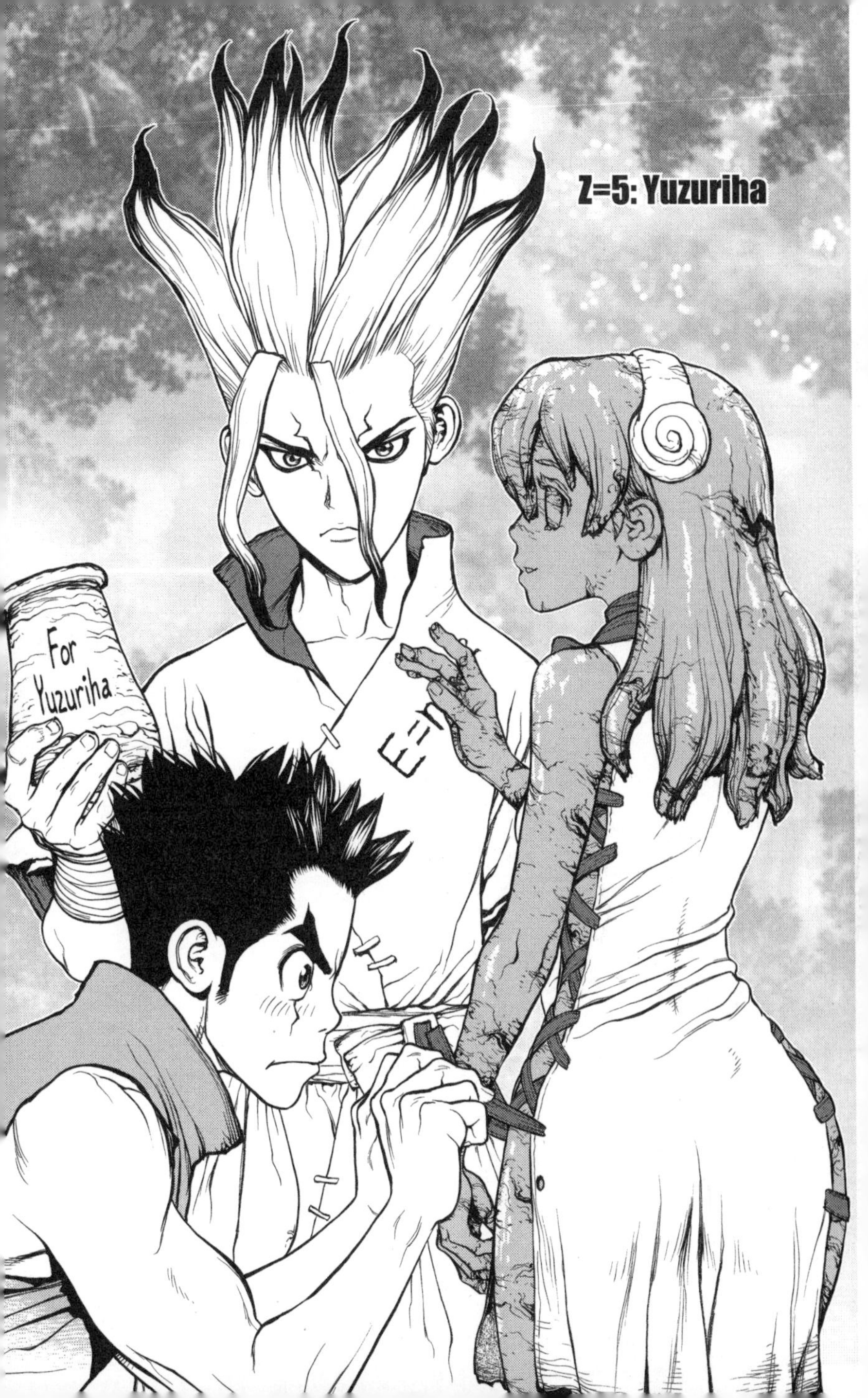
Z=5: Yuzuriha
For Yuzuriha

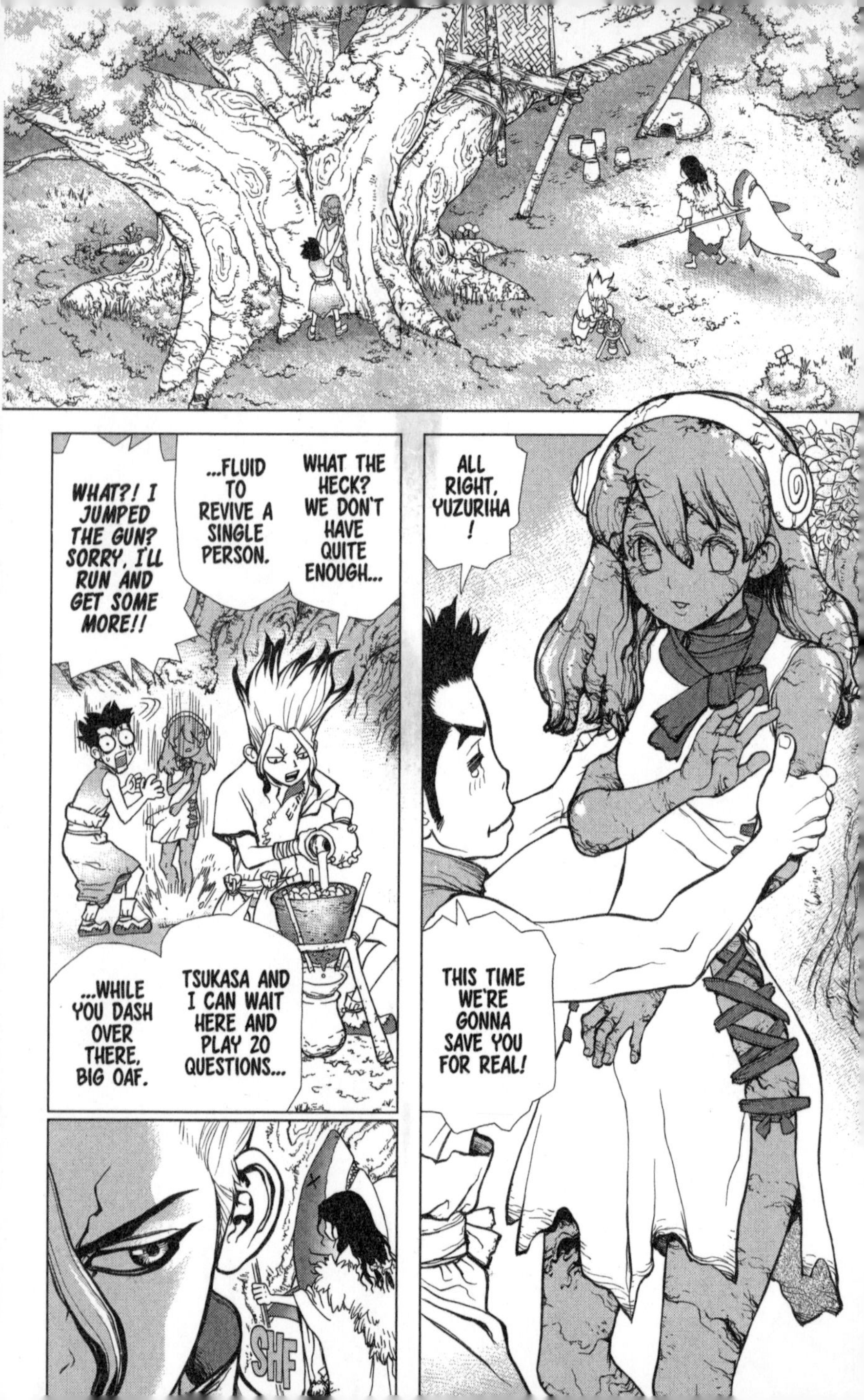
ALL RIGHT, YUZURIHA!
THIS TIME WE'RE GONNA SAVE YOU FOR REAL!
WHAT THE HECK? WE DON'T HAVE QUITE ENOUGH...
...FLUID TO REVIVE A SINGLE PERSON.
WHAT?! I JUMPED THE GUN? SORRY, I'LL RUN AND GET SOME MORE!!
TSUKASA AND I CAN WAIT HERE AND PLAY 20 QUESTIONS...
...WHILE YOU DASH OVER THERE, BIG OAF.
SHF

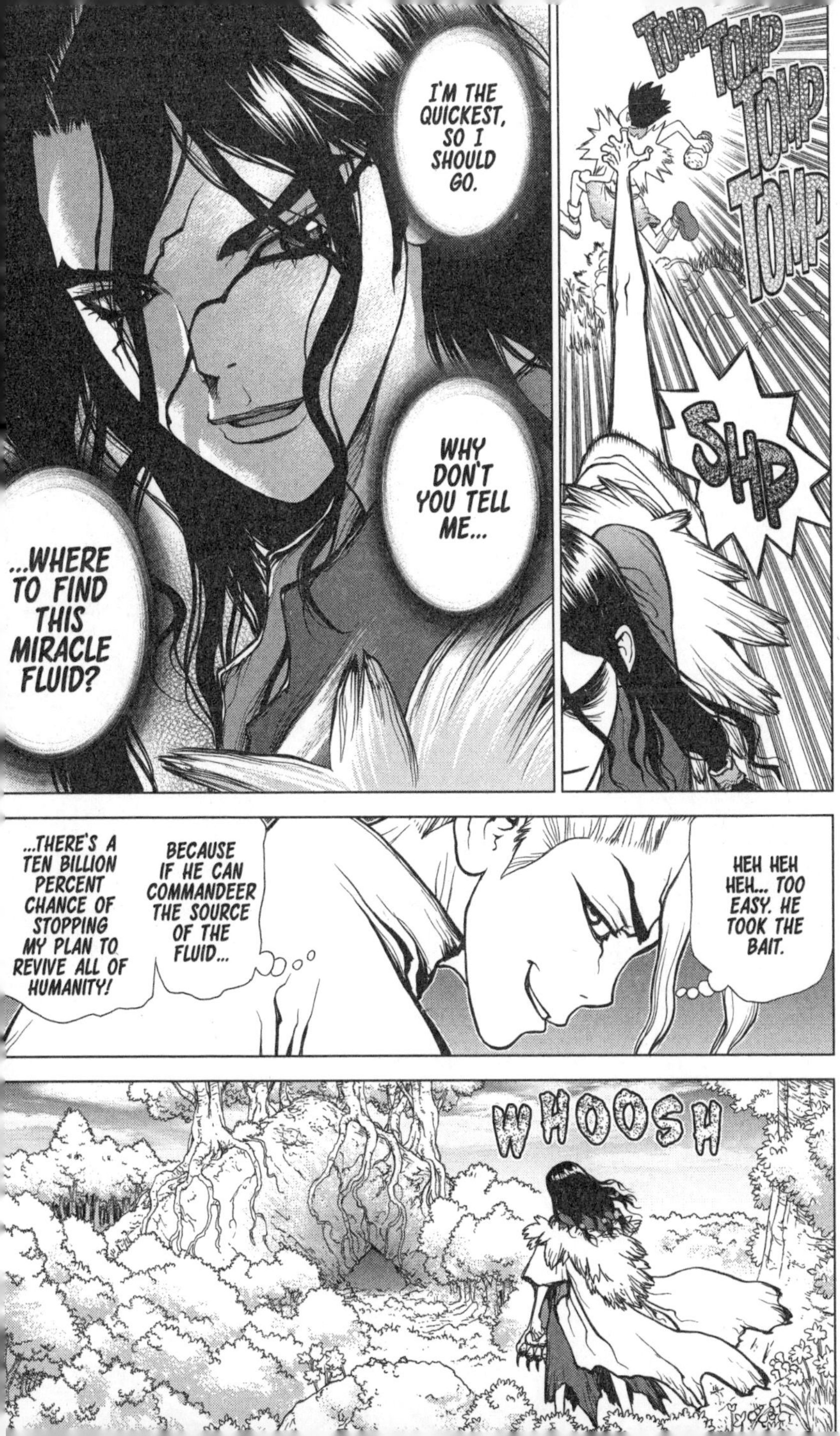
TOMP TOMP TOMP TOMP TOMP
SHP
I'M THE QUICKEST, SO I SHOULD GO.
WHY DON'T YOU TELL ME...
...WHERE TO FIND THIS MIRACLE FLUID?
HEH HEH HEH... TOO EASY. HE TOOK THE BAIT.
BECAUSE IF HE CAN COMMANDEER THE SOURCE OF THE FLUID...
...THERE'S A TEN BILLION PERCENT CHANCE OF STOPPING MY PLAN TO REVIVE ALL OF HUMANITY!
WHOOSH

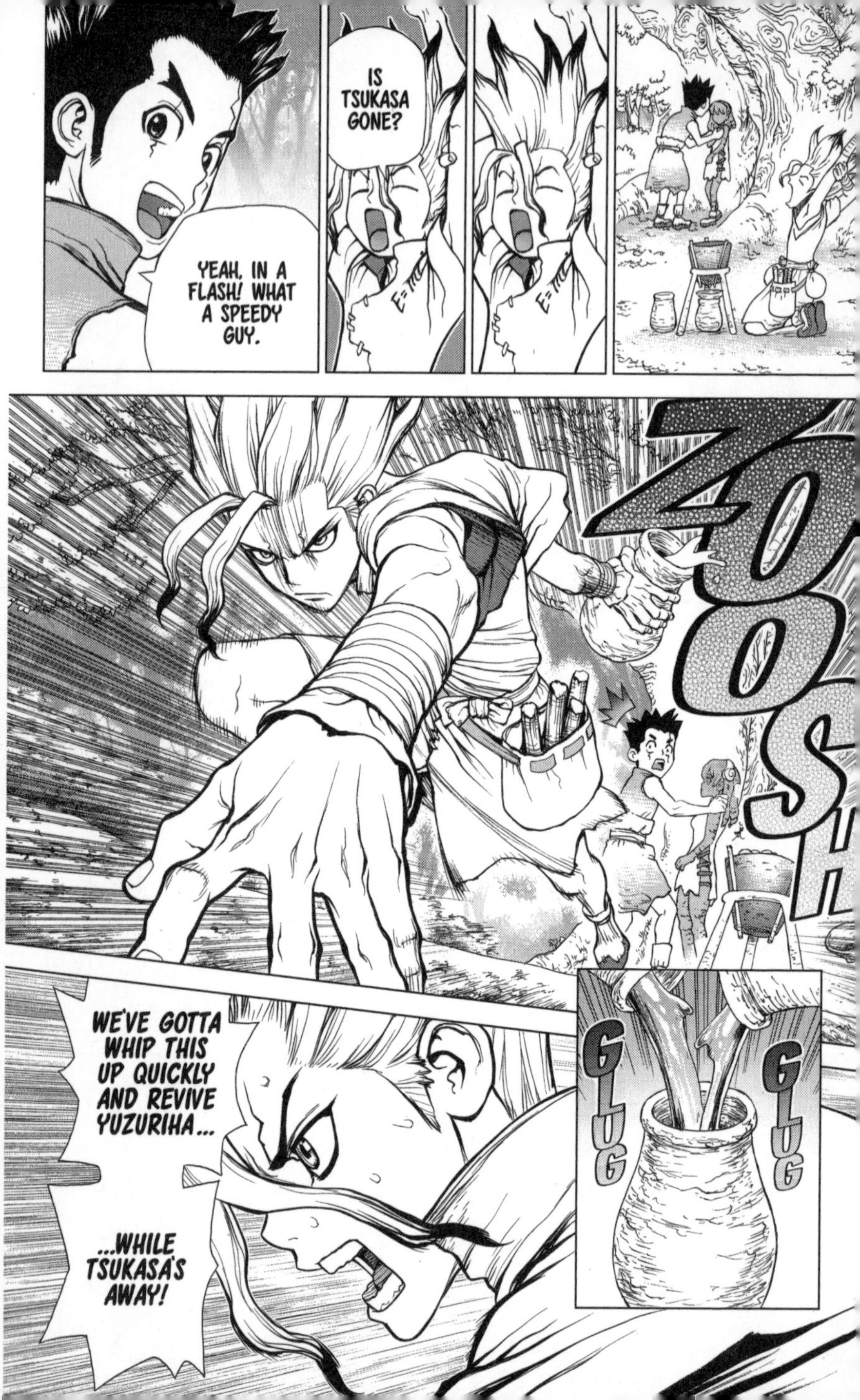
IS TSUKASA GONE?
YEAH, IN A FLASH! WHAT A SPEEDY GUY.
ZOOOSH
GLUG GLUG
WE'VE GOTTA WHIP THIS UP QUICKLY AND REVIVE YUZURIHA...
...WHILE TSUKASA'S AWAY!

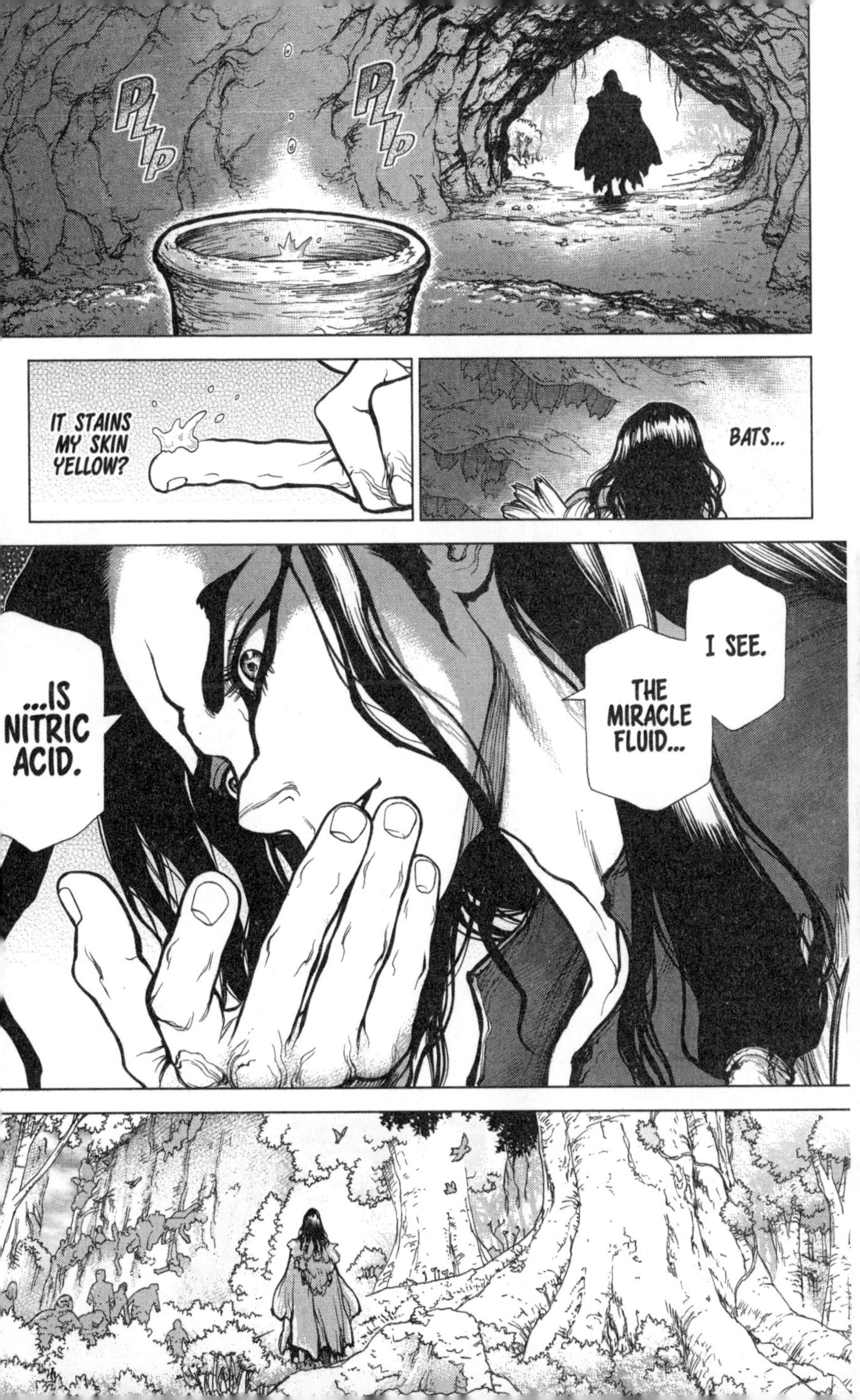
PLIP
PLIP
BATS...
IT STAINS MY SKIN YELLOW?
I SEE.
THE MIRACLE FLUID...
...IS NITRIC ACID.

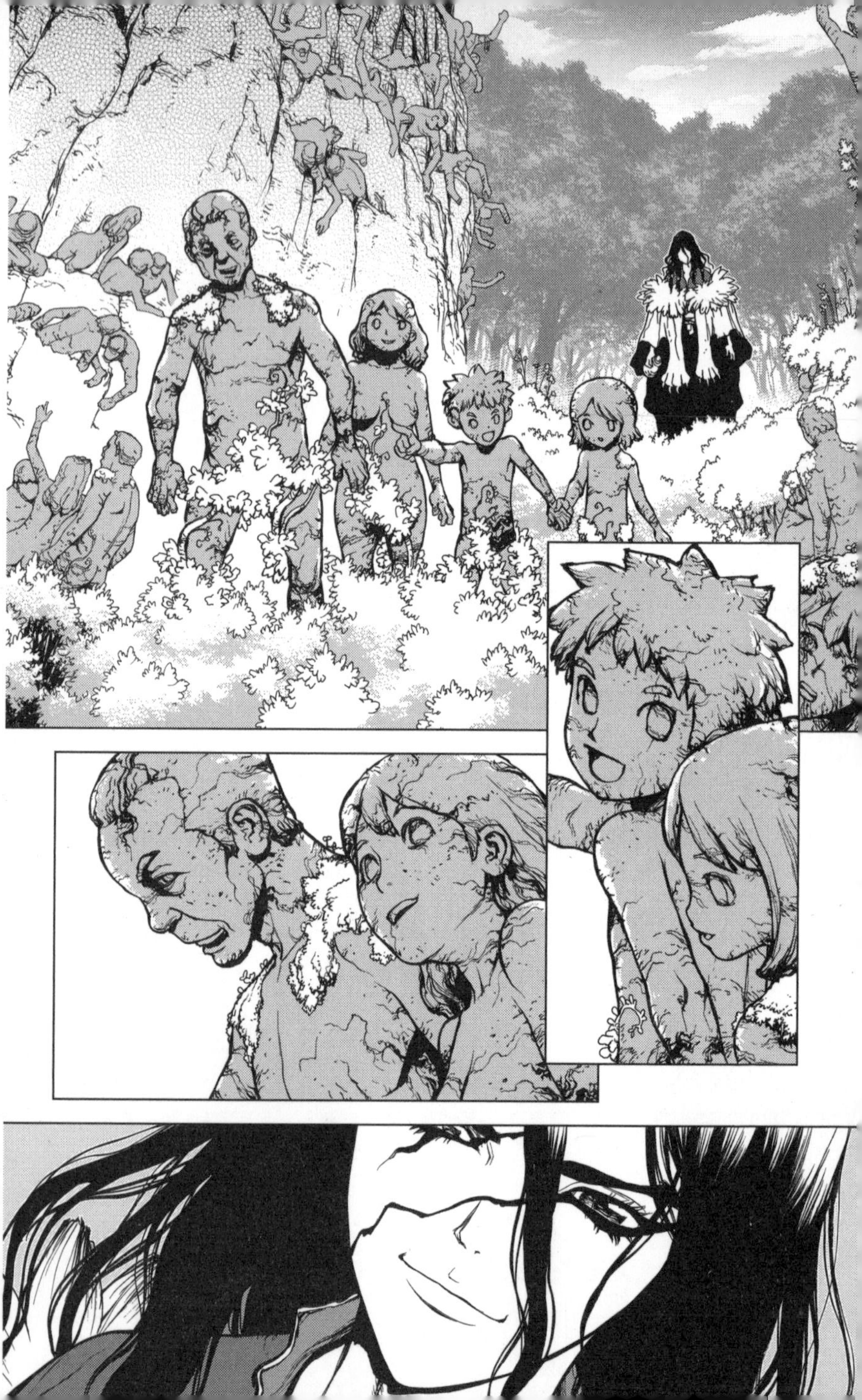

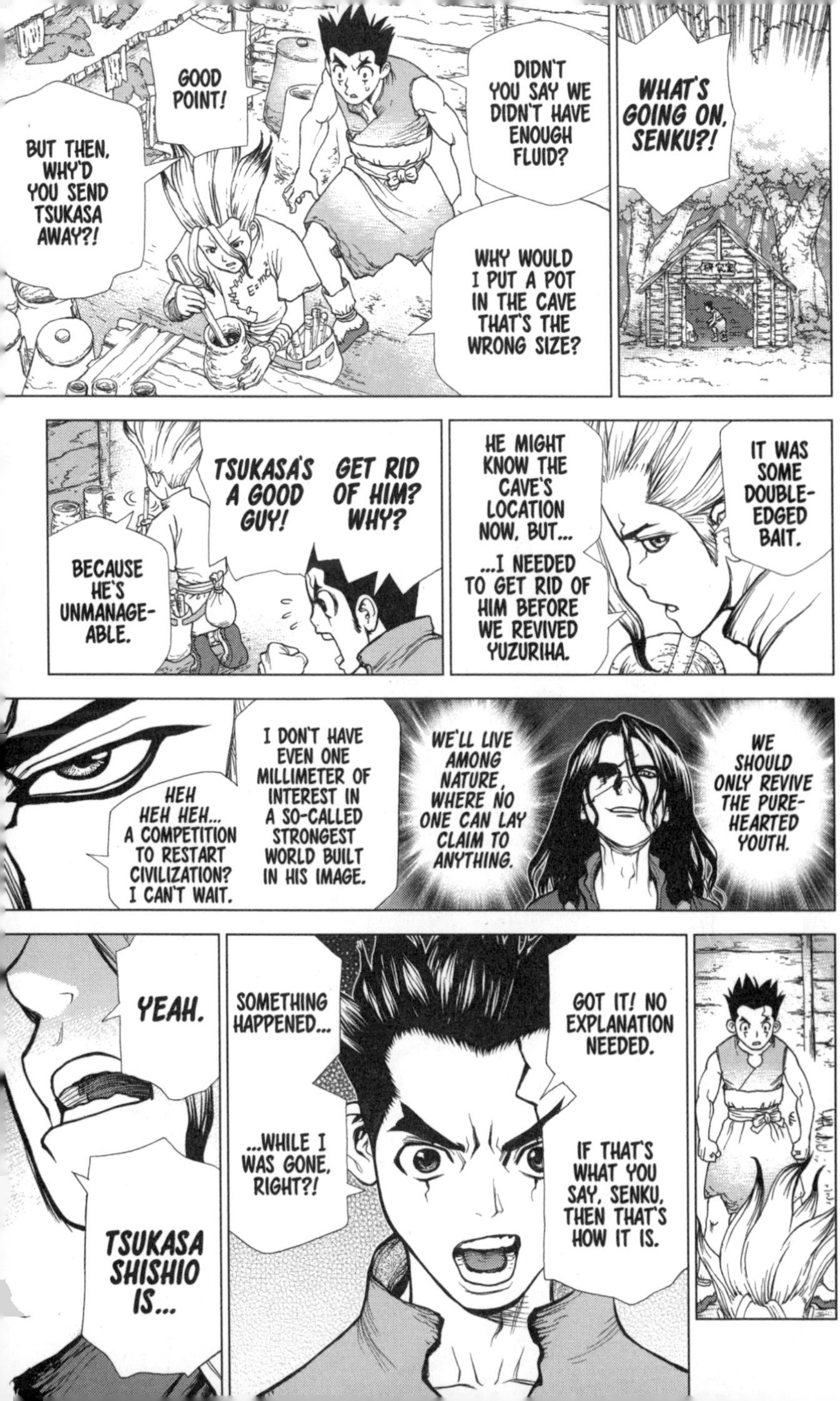
WHAT'S GOING ON, SENKU?!
DIDN'T YOU SAY WE DIDN'T HAVE ENOUGH FLUID?
WHY WOULD I PUT A POT IN THE CAVE THAT'S THE WRONG SIZE?
GOOD POINT!
BUT THEN, WHY'D YOU SEND TSUKASA AWAY?!
IT WAS SOME DOUBLE-EDGED BAIT.
HE MIGHT KNOW THE CAVE'S LOCATION NOW, BUT...
...I NEEDED TO GET RID OF HIM BEFORE WE REVIVED YUZURIHA.
GET RID OF HIM? WHY?
TSUKASA'S A GOOD GUY!
BECAUSE HE'S UNMANAGE-ABLE.
WE SHOULD ONLY REVIVE THE PURE-HEARTED YOUTH.
WE'LL LIVE AMONG NATURE, WHERE NO ONE CAN LAY CLAIM TO ANYTHING.
I DON'T HAVE EVEN ONE MILLIMETER OF INTEREST IN A SO-CALLED STRONGEST WORLD BUILT IN HIS IMAGE.
HEH HEH HEH... A COMPETITION TO RESTART CIVILIZATION? I CAN'T WAIT.
GOT IT! NO EXPLANATION NEEDED.
IF THAT'S WHAT YOU SAY, SENKU, THEN THAT'S HOW IT IS.
SOMETHING HAPPENED...
...WHILE I WAS GONE, RIGHT?!
YEAH.
TSUKASA SHISHIO IS...

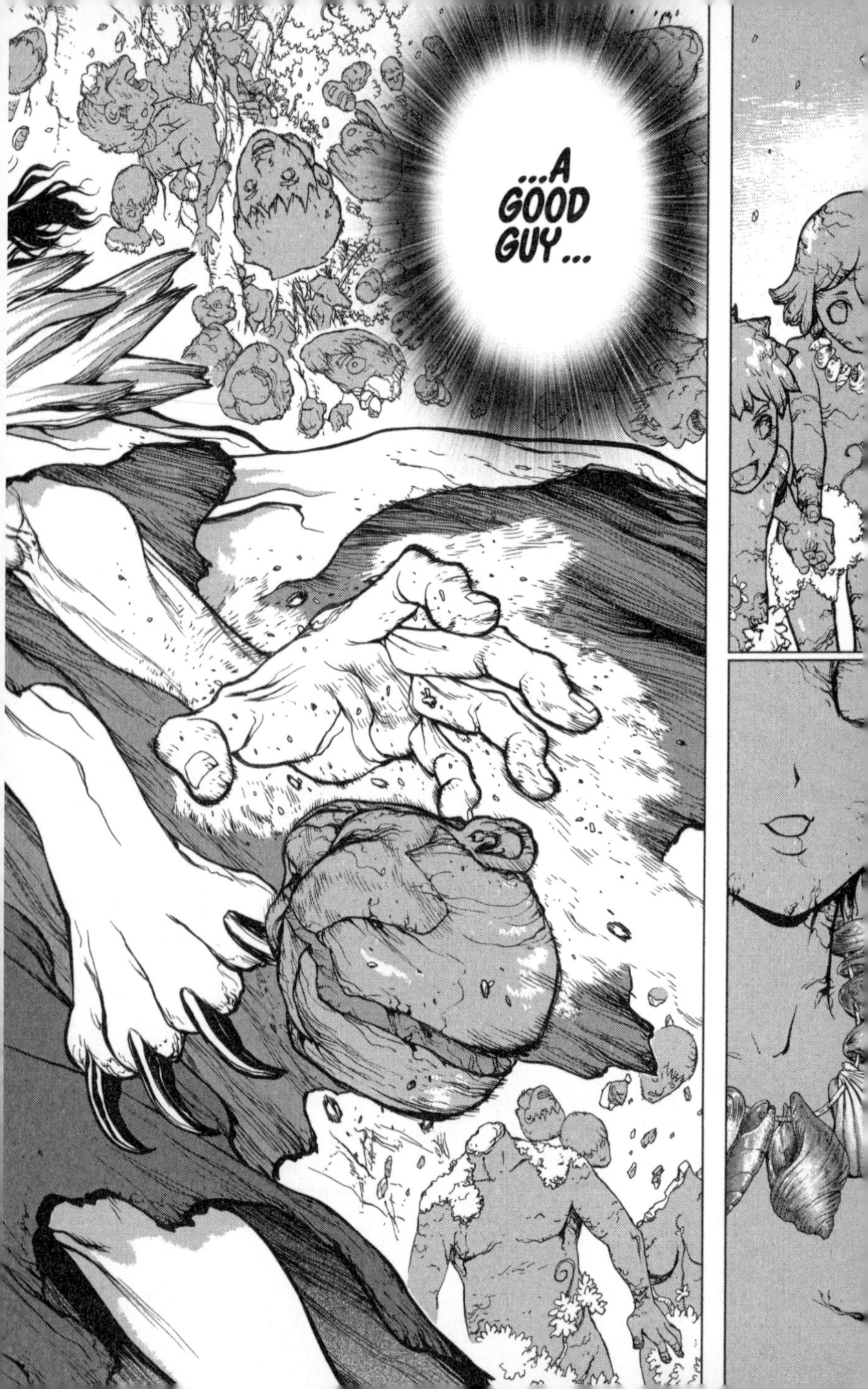
...A GOOD GUY...

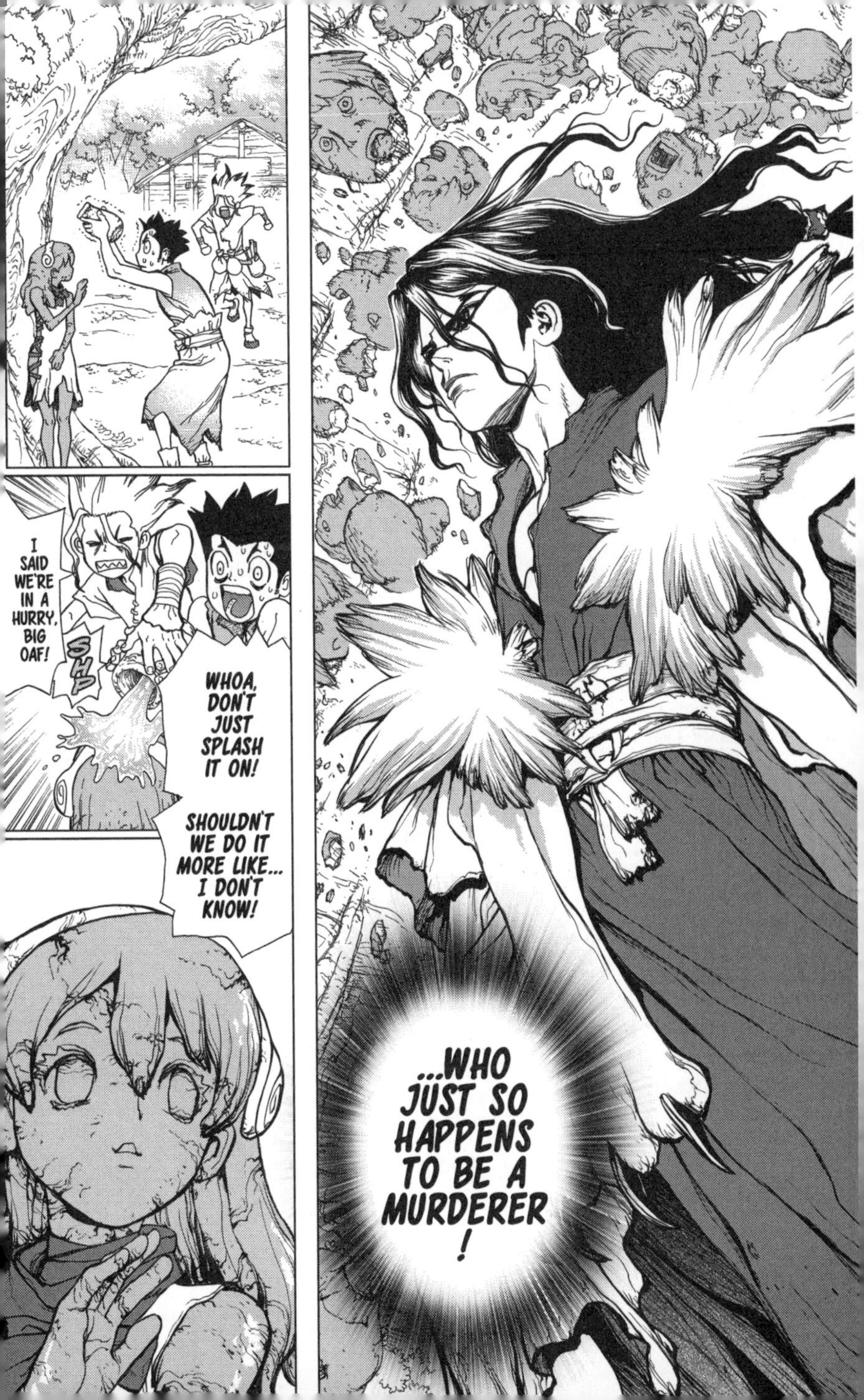
...WHO JUST SO HAPPENS TO BE A MURDERER!
I SAID WE'RE IN A HURRY, BIG OAF!
SHP
WHOA, DON'T JUST SPLASH IT ON!
SHOULDN'T WE DO IT MORE LIKE... I DON'T KNOW!

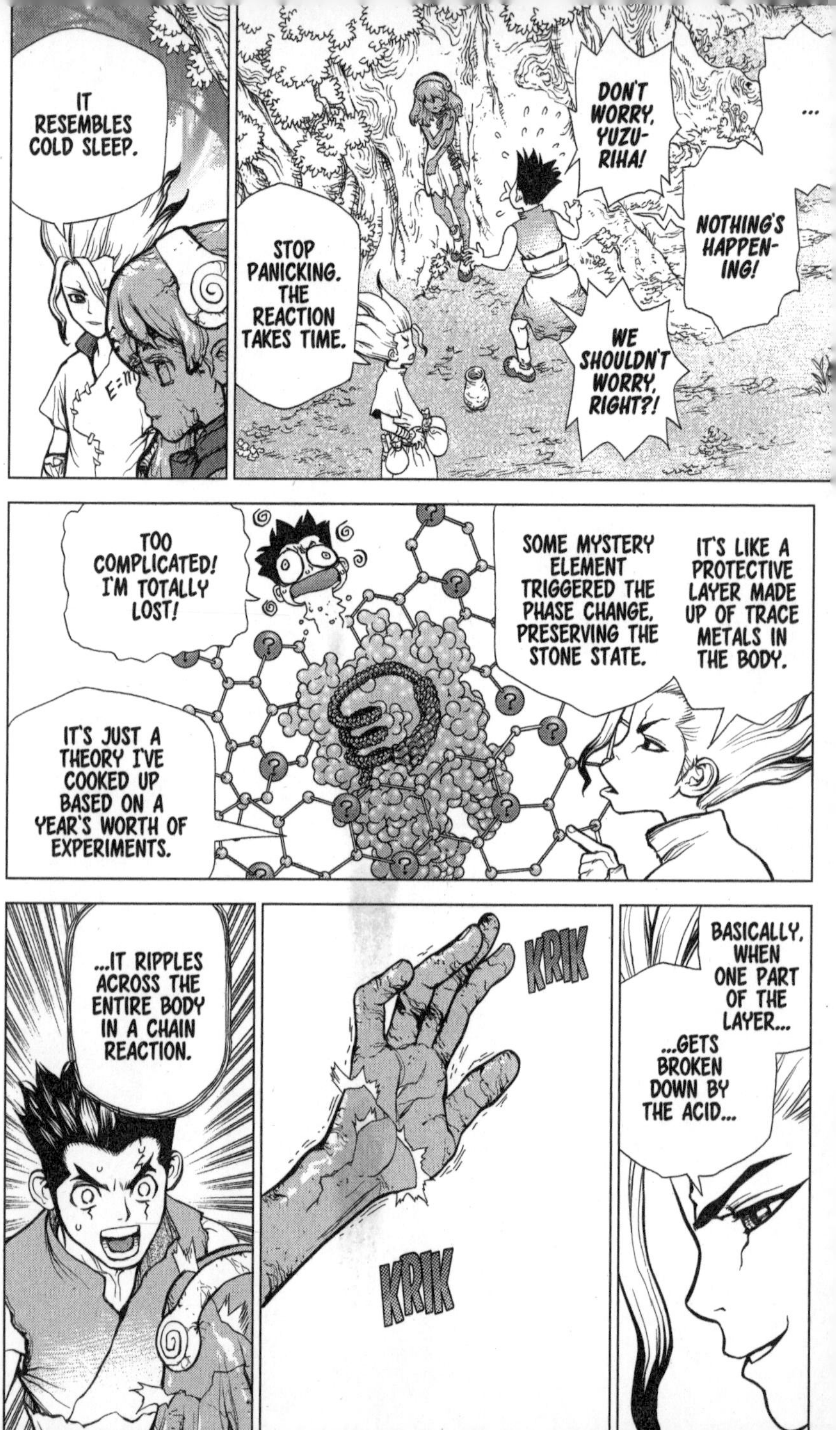
...
DON'T WORRY, YUZURIHA!
NOTHING'S HAPPENING!
WE SHOULDN'T WORRY, RIGHT?!
STOP PANICKING. THE REACTION TAKES TIME.
IT RESEMBLES COLD SLEEP.
IT'S LIKE A PROTECTIVE LAYER MADE UP OF TRACE METALS IN THE BODY.
SOME MYSTERY ELEMENT TRIGGERED THE PHASE CHANGE, PRESERVING THE STONE STATE.
TOO COMPLICATED! I'M TOTALLY LOST!
IT'S JUST A THEORY I'VE COOKED UP BASED ON A YEAR'S WORTH OF EXPERIMENTS.
BASICALLY, WHEN ONE PART OF THE LAYER...
...GETS BROKEN DOWN BY THE ACID...
KRIK
KRIK
...IT RIPPLES ACROSS THE ENTIRE BODY IN A CHAIN REACTION.

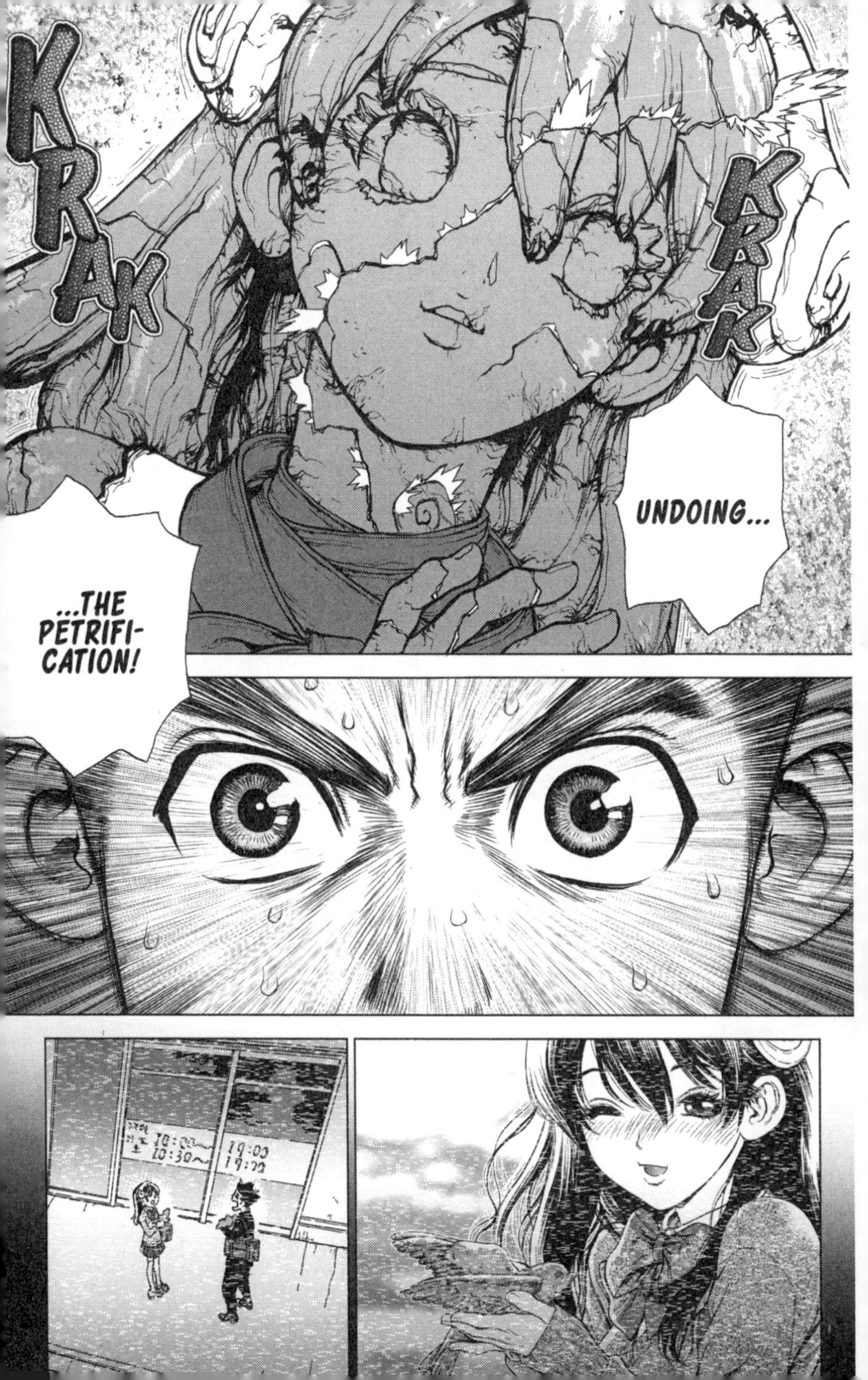
KRAK
UNDOING...
KRAK
...THE PETRIFI-
CATION!

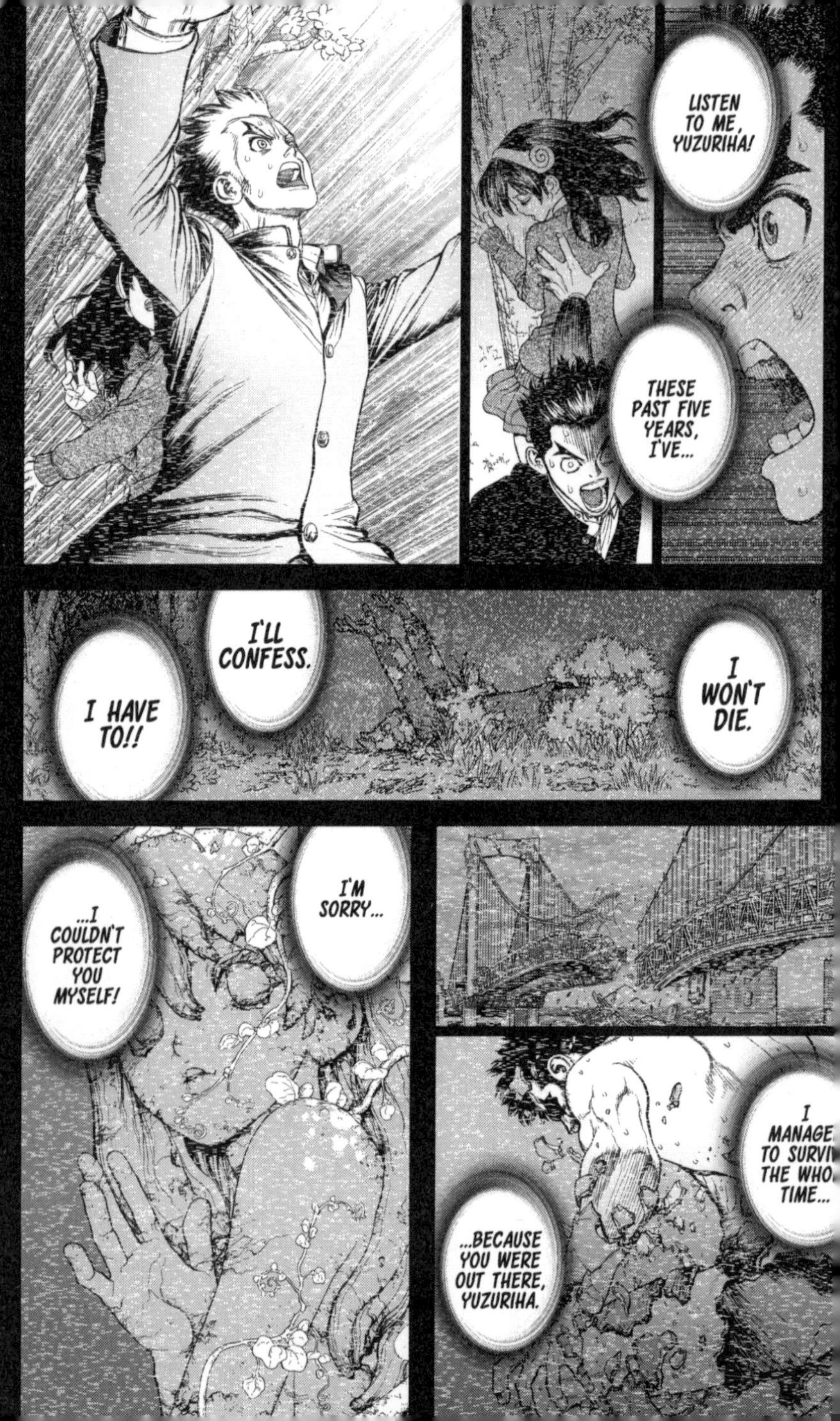
LISTEN TO ME, YUZURIHA!
THESE PAST FIVE YEARS, I'VE...
I WON'T DIE.
I'LL CONFESS.
I HAVE TO!!
I MANAGE TO SURVIV THE WHO TIME...
...BECAUSE YOU WERE OUT THERE, YUZURIHA.
I'M SORRY...
...I COULDN'T PROTECT YOU MYSELF!

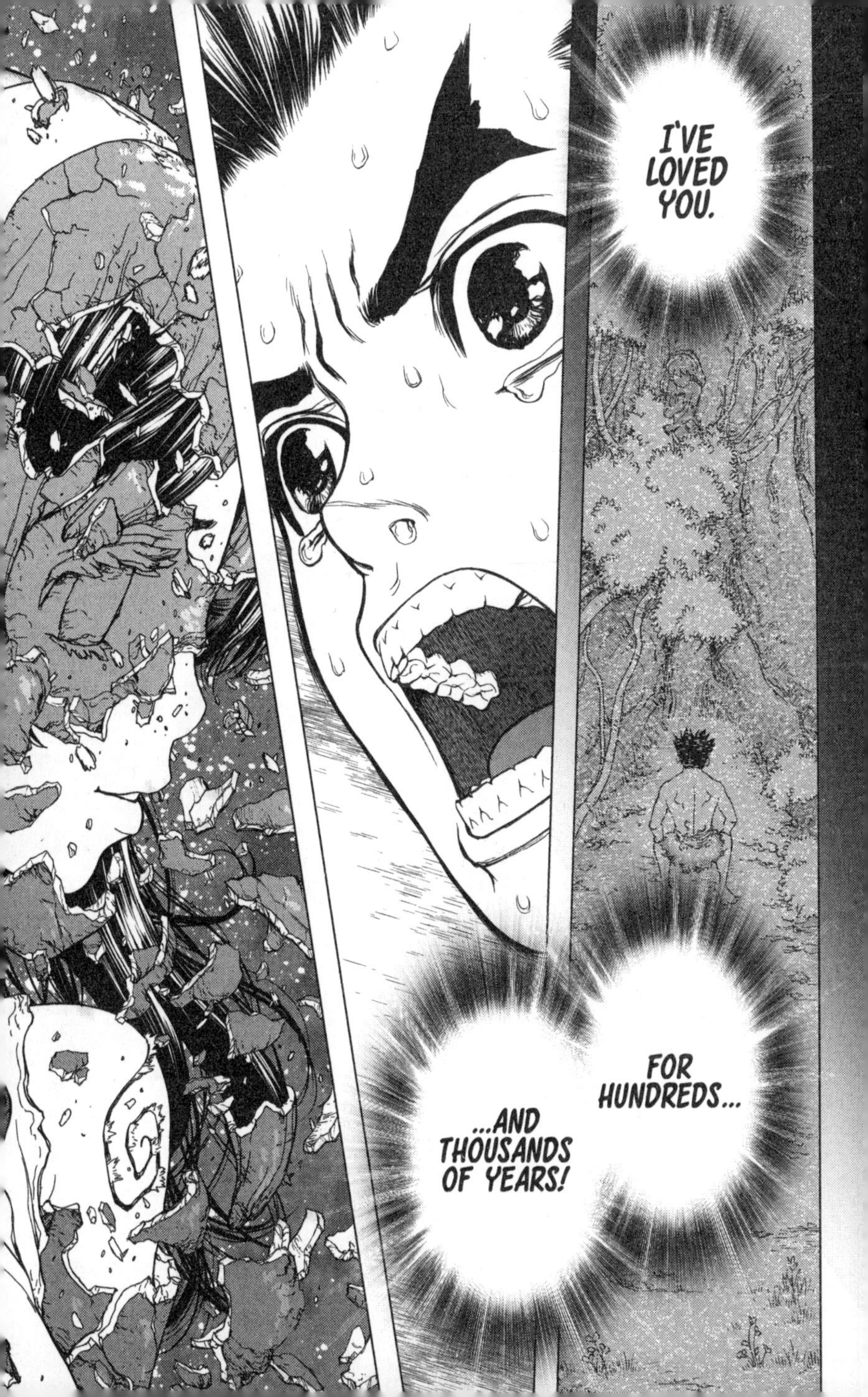
I'VE LOVED YOU.
FOR HUNDREDS...
...AND THOUSANDS OF YEARS!

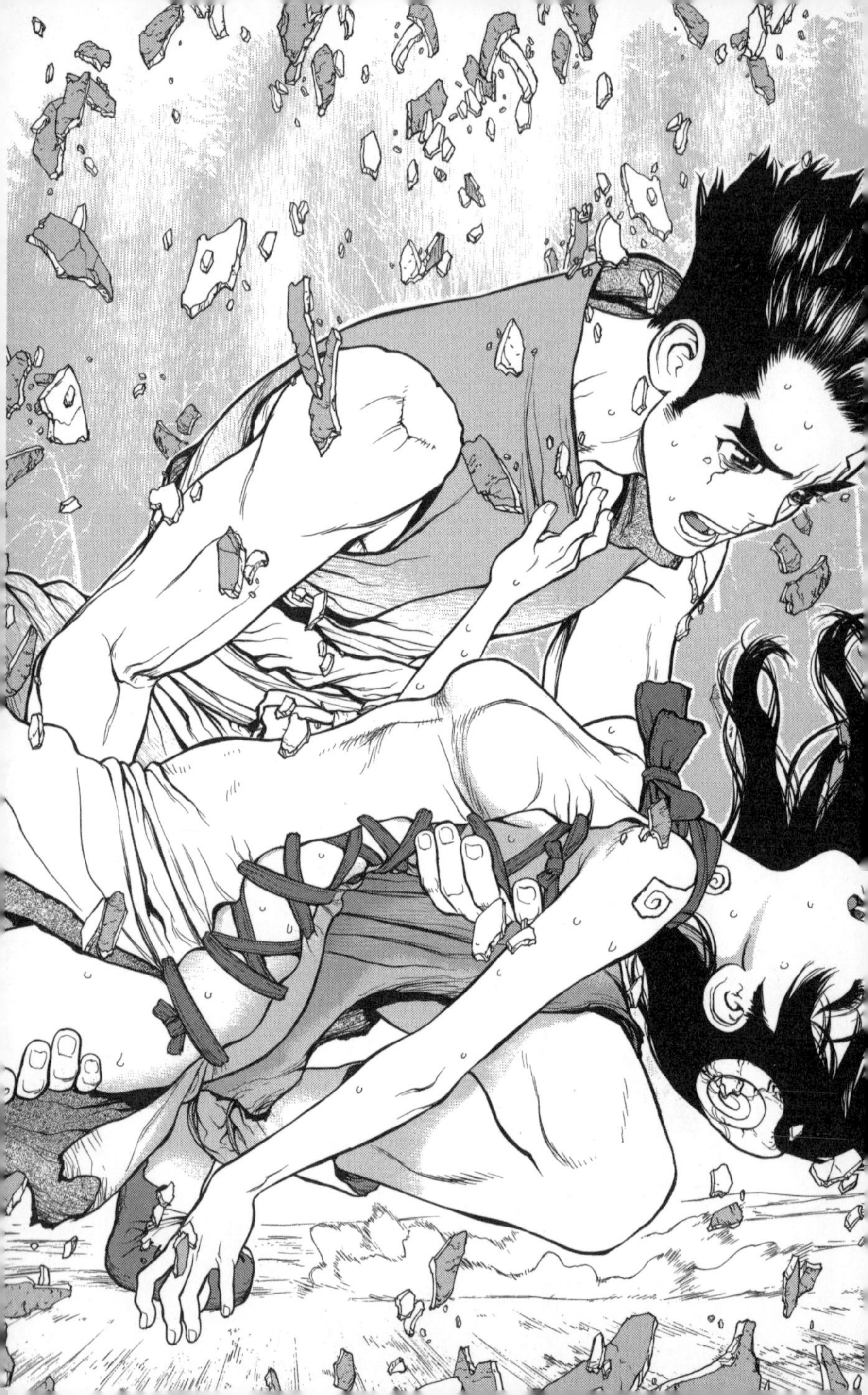

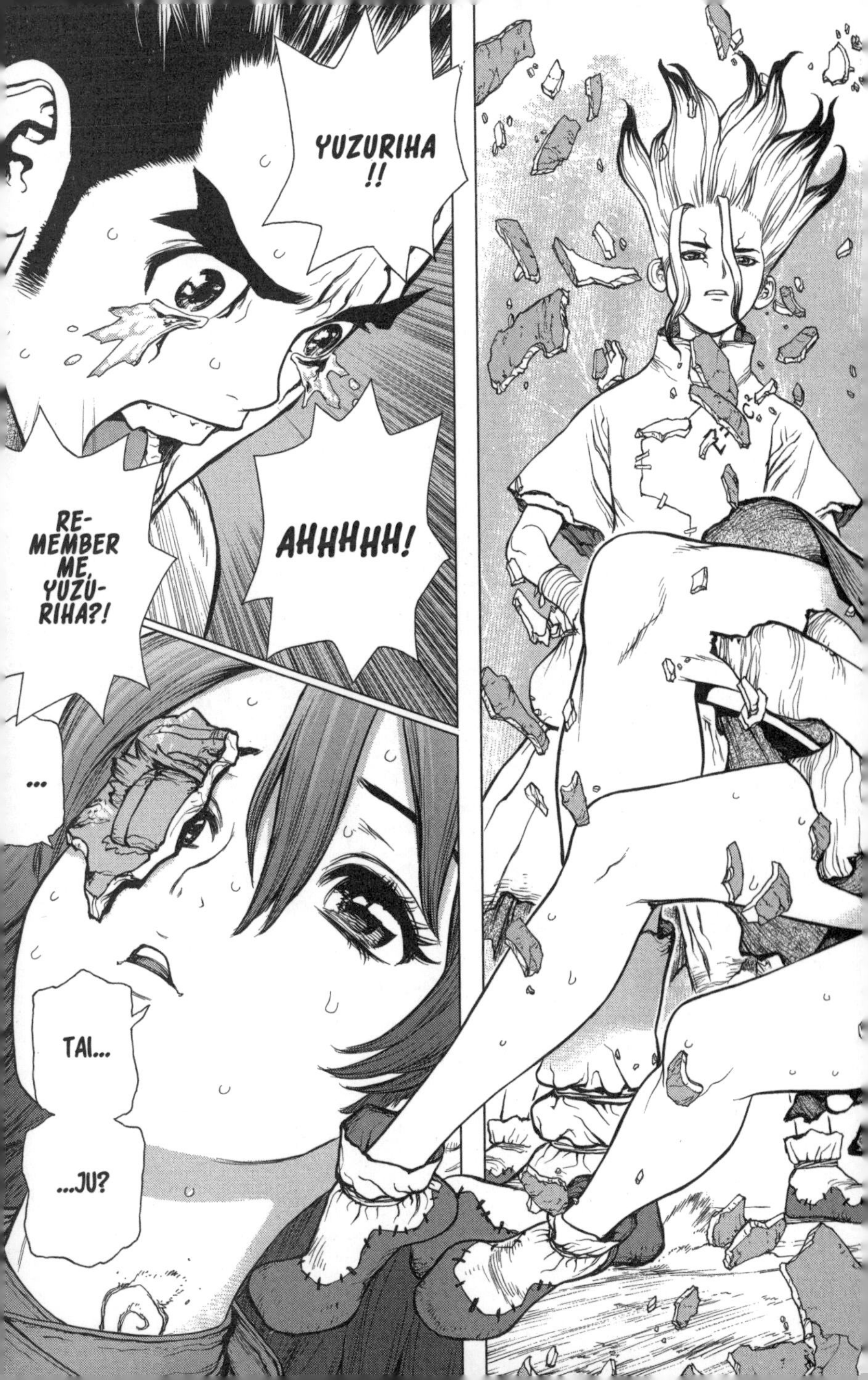
YUZURIHA !!
AHHHHH!
RE-MEMBER ME, YUZU-RIHA?!
...
TAI...
...JU?

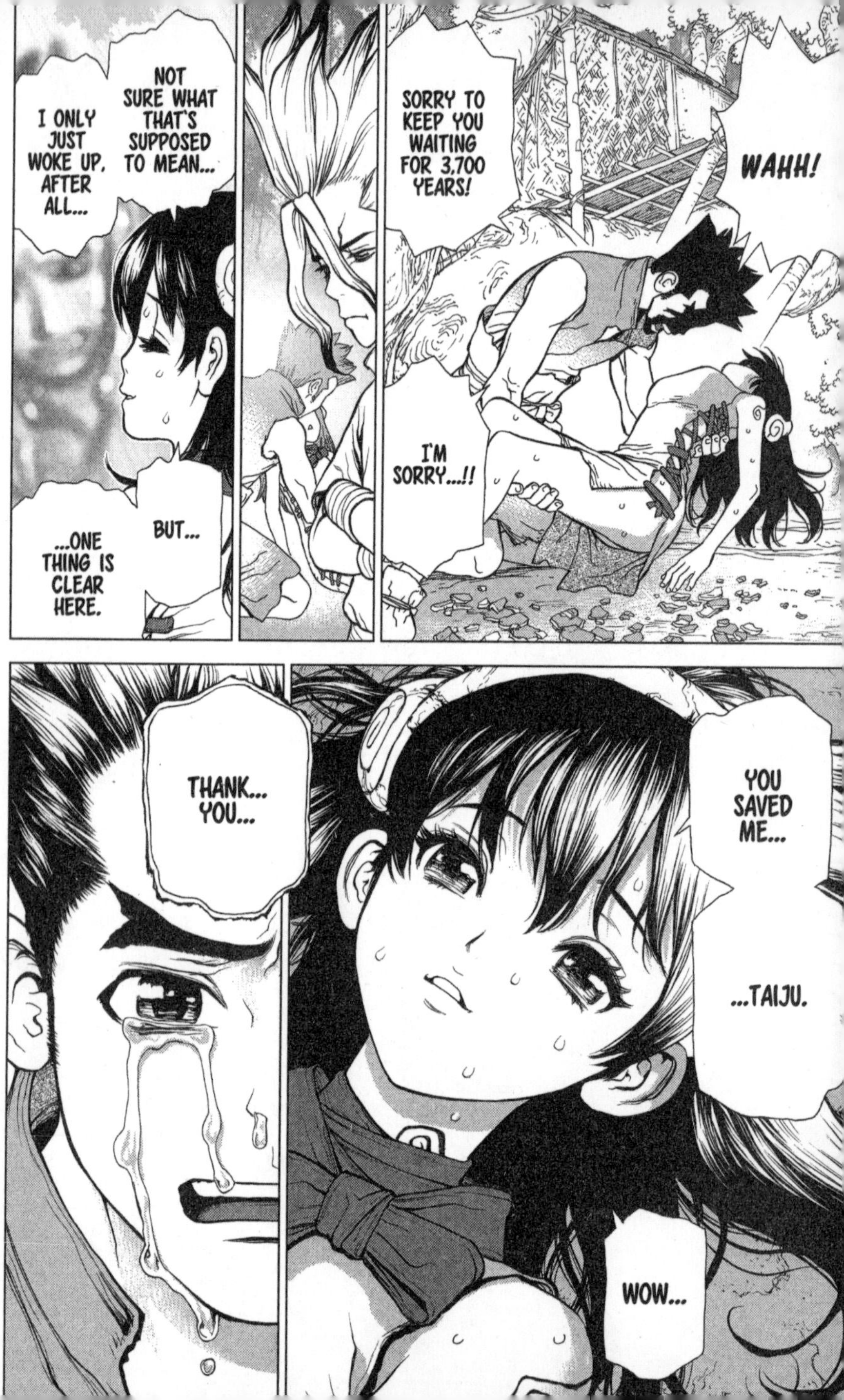
WAHH!
SORRY TO KEEP YOU WAITING FOR 3,700 YEARS!
I'M SORRY...!!
NOT SURE WHAT THAT'S SUPPOSED TO MEAN...
I ONLY JUST WOKE UP, AFTER ALL...
BUT...
...ONE THING IS CLEAR HERE.
YOU SAVED ME...
...TAIJU.
WOW...
THANK... YOU...

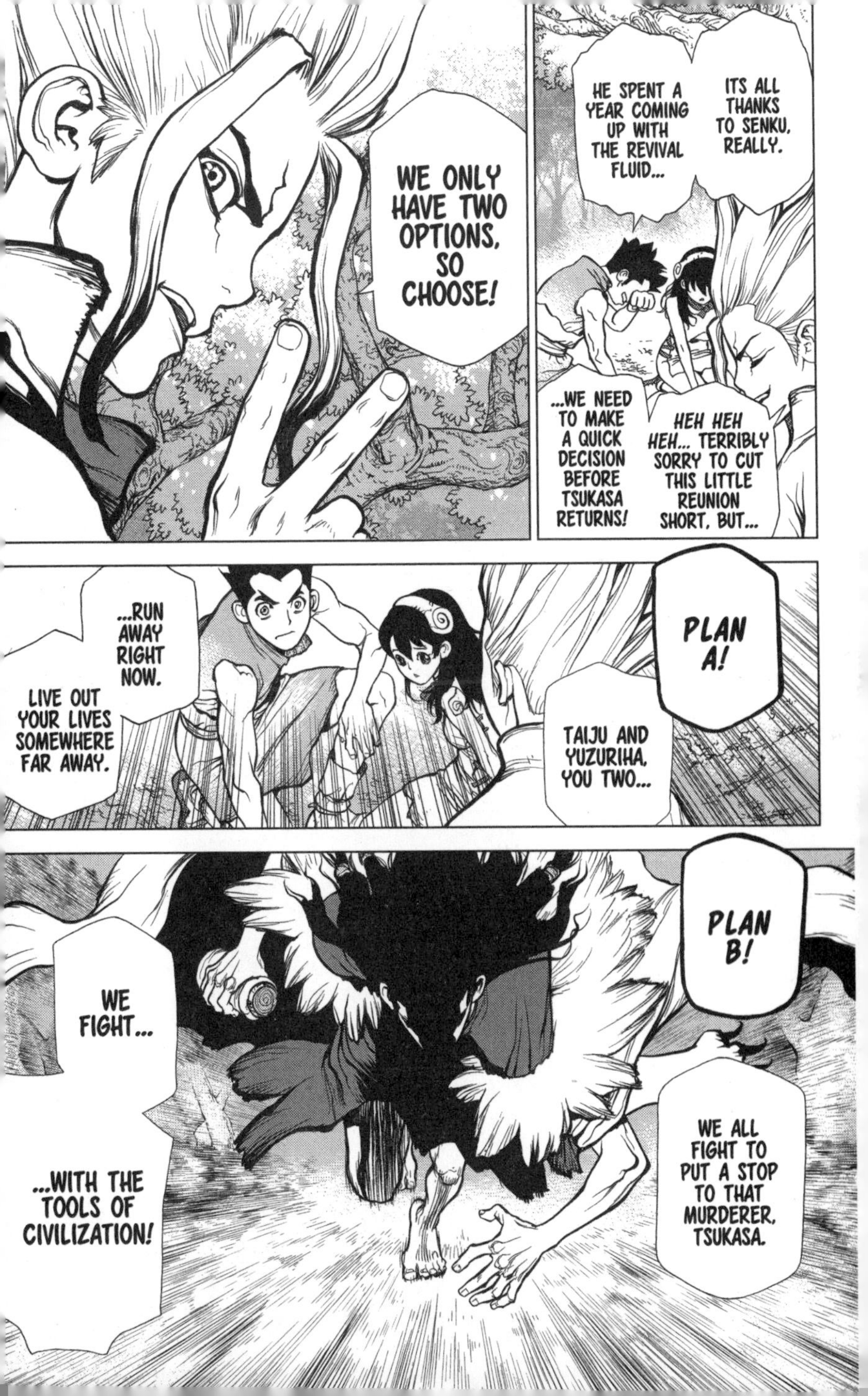
ITS ALL THANKS TO SENKU, REALLY.
HE SPENT A YEAR COMING UP WITH THE REVIVAL FLUID...
HEH HEH HEH... TERRIBLY SORRY TO CUT THIS LITTLE REUNION SHORT, BUT...
...WE NEED TO MAKE A QUICK DECISION BEFORE TSUKASA RETURNS!
WE ONLY HAVE TWO OPTIONS, SO CHOOSE!
PLAN A!
TAIJU AND YUZURIHA, YOU TWO...
...RUN AWAY RIGHT NOW.
LIVE OUT YOUR LIVES SOMEWHERE FAR AWAY.
PLAN B!
WE ALL FIGHT TO PUT A STOP TO THAT MURDERER, TSUKASA.
WE FIGHT...
...WITH THE TOOLS OF CIVILIZATION!

Dr.STONE

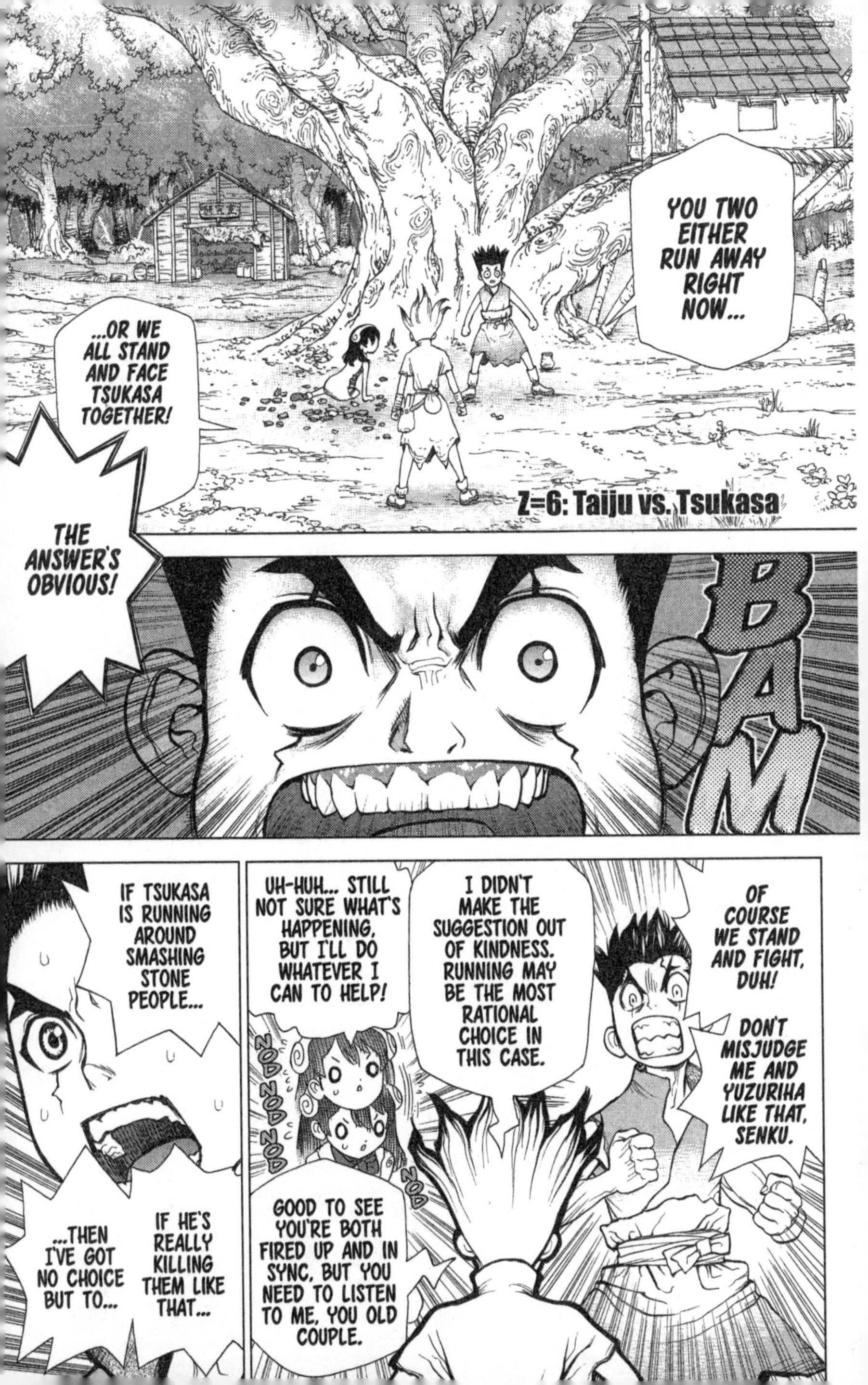
YOU TWO EITHER RUN AWAY RIGHT NOW...
...OR WE ALL STAND AND FACE TSUKASA TOGETHER!
Z=6: Taiju vs. Tsukasa
THE ANSWER'S OBVIOUS!
BAM
OF COURSE WE STAND AND FIGHT, DUH!
DON'T MISJUDGE ME AND YUZURIHA LIKE THAT, SENKU.
I DIDN'T MAKE THE SUGGESTION OUT OF KINDNESS. RUNNING MAY BE THE MOST RATIONAL CHOICE IN THIS CASE.
UH-HUH... STILL NOT SURE WHAT'S HAPPENING, BUT I'LL DO WHATEVER I CAN TO HELP!
NOD NOD NOD NOD
GOOD TO SEE YOU'RE BOTH FIRED UP AND IN SYNC, BUT YOU NEED TO LISTEN TO ME, YOU OLD COUPLE.
IF TSUKASA IS RUNNING AROUND SMASHING STONE PEOPLE...
IF HE'S REALLY KILLING THEM LIKE THAT...
...THEN I'VE GOT NO CHOICE BUT TO...

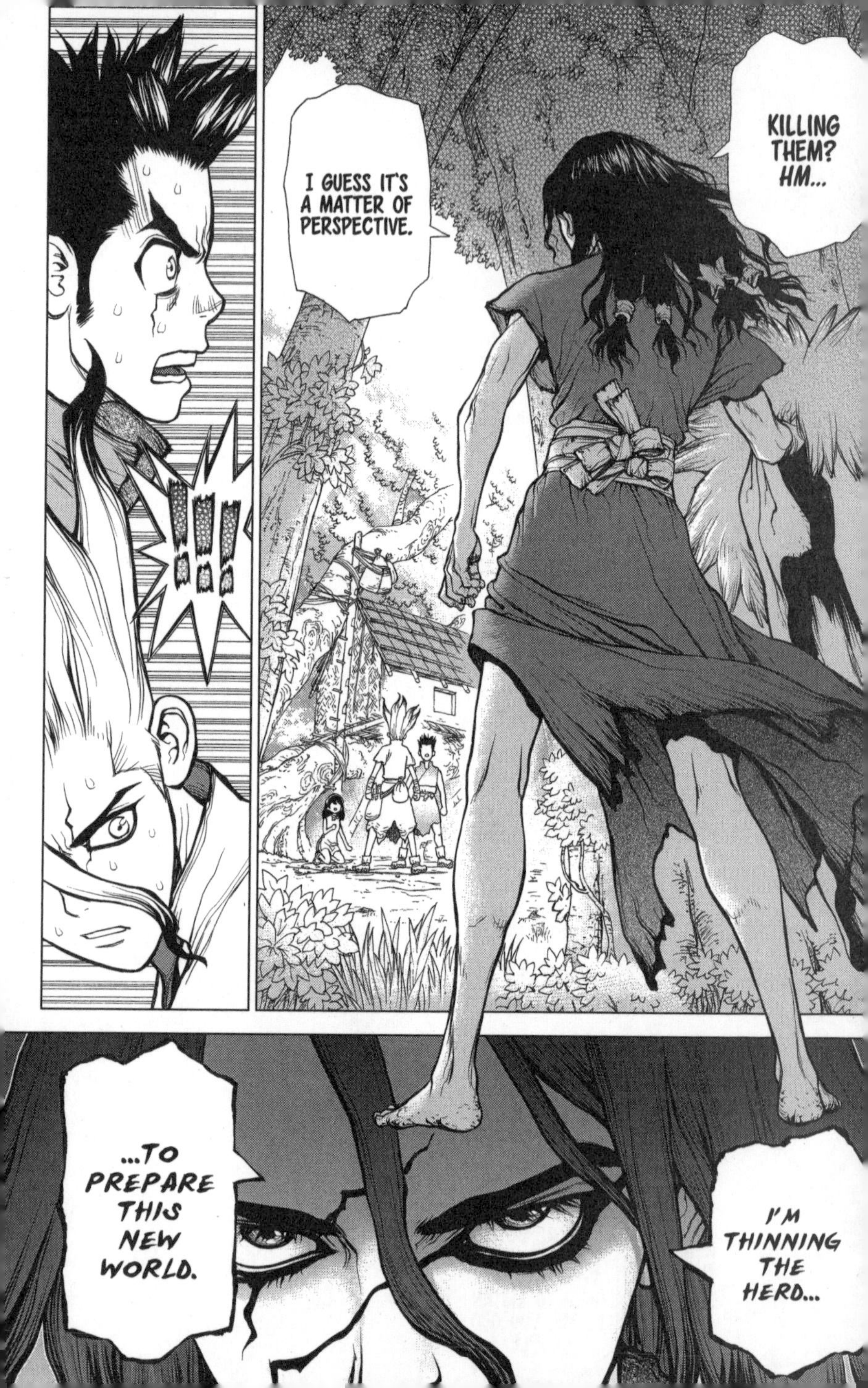
KILLING THEM? HM...
I GUESS IT'S A MATTER OF PERSPECTIVE.
!!!
I'M THINNING THE HERD...
...TO PREPARE THIS NEW WORLD.

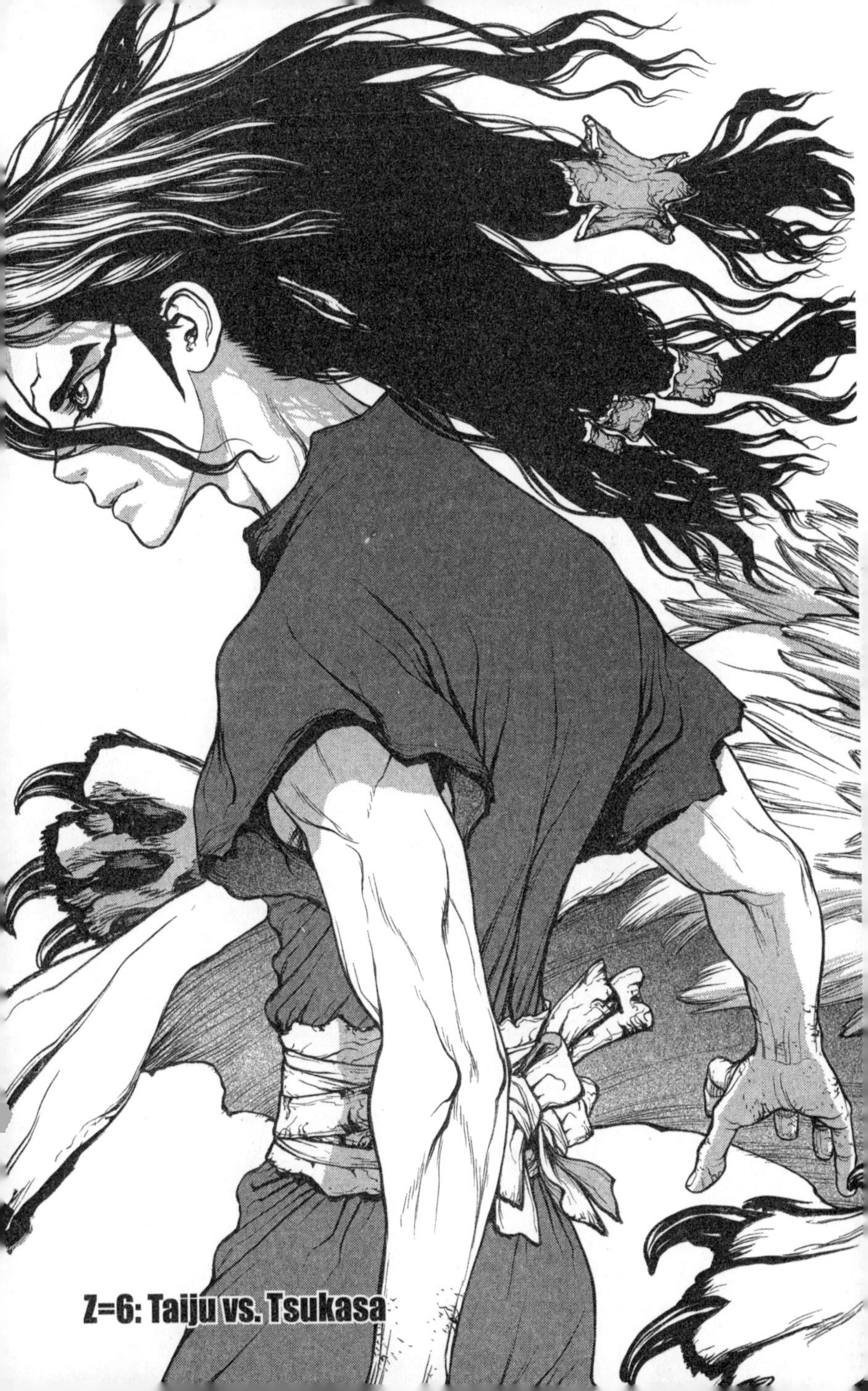

Z=6: Taiju vs. Tsukasa

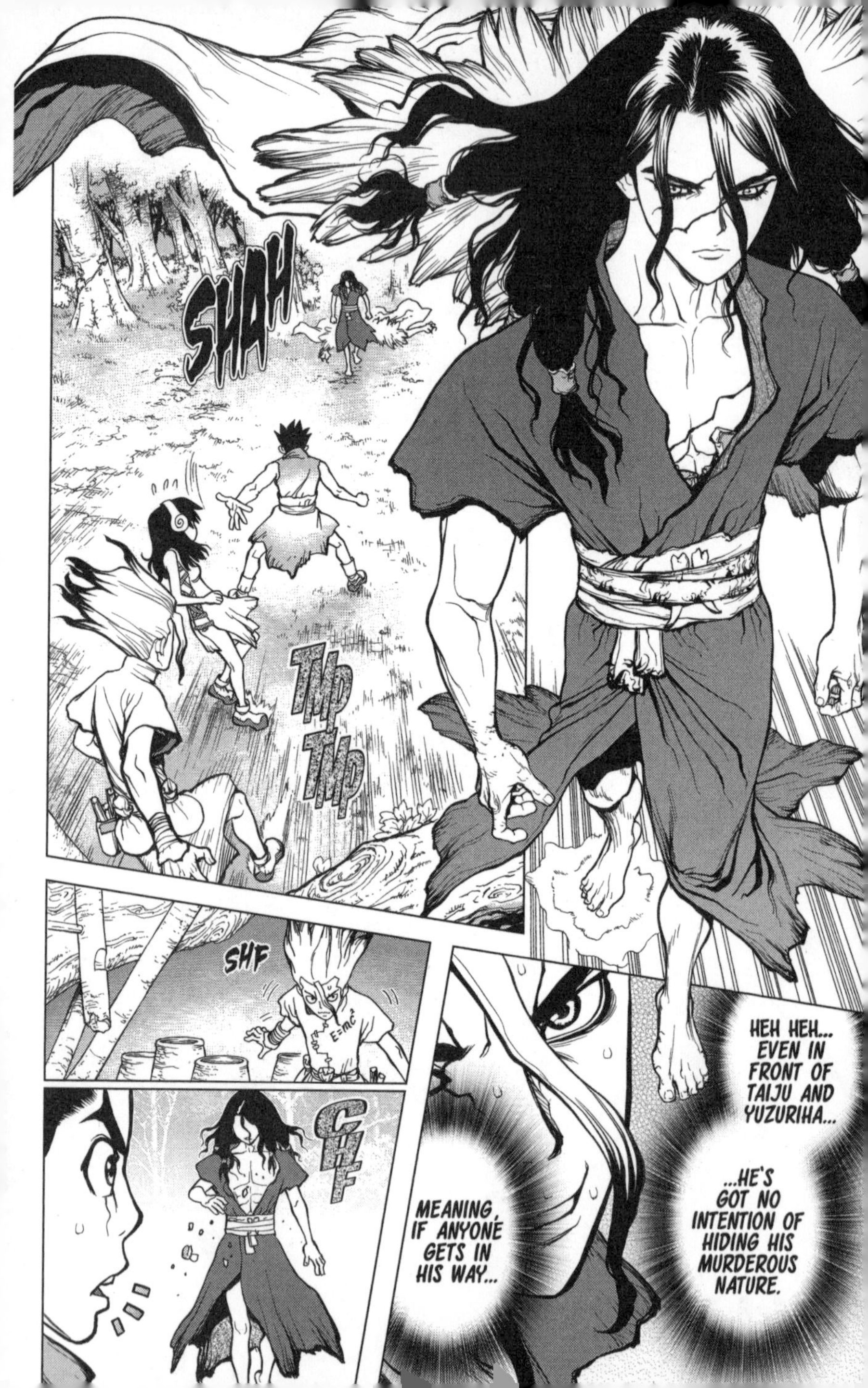
SHAH
TMP TMP
HEH HEH... EVEN IN FRONT OF TAIJU AND YUZURIHA...
...HE'S GOT NO INTENTION OF HIDING HIS MURDEROUS NATURE.
MEANING, IF ANYONE GETS IN HIS WAY...
SHF
E=mc²
CHF

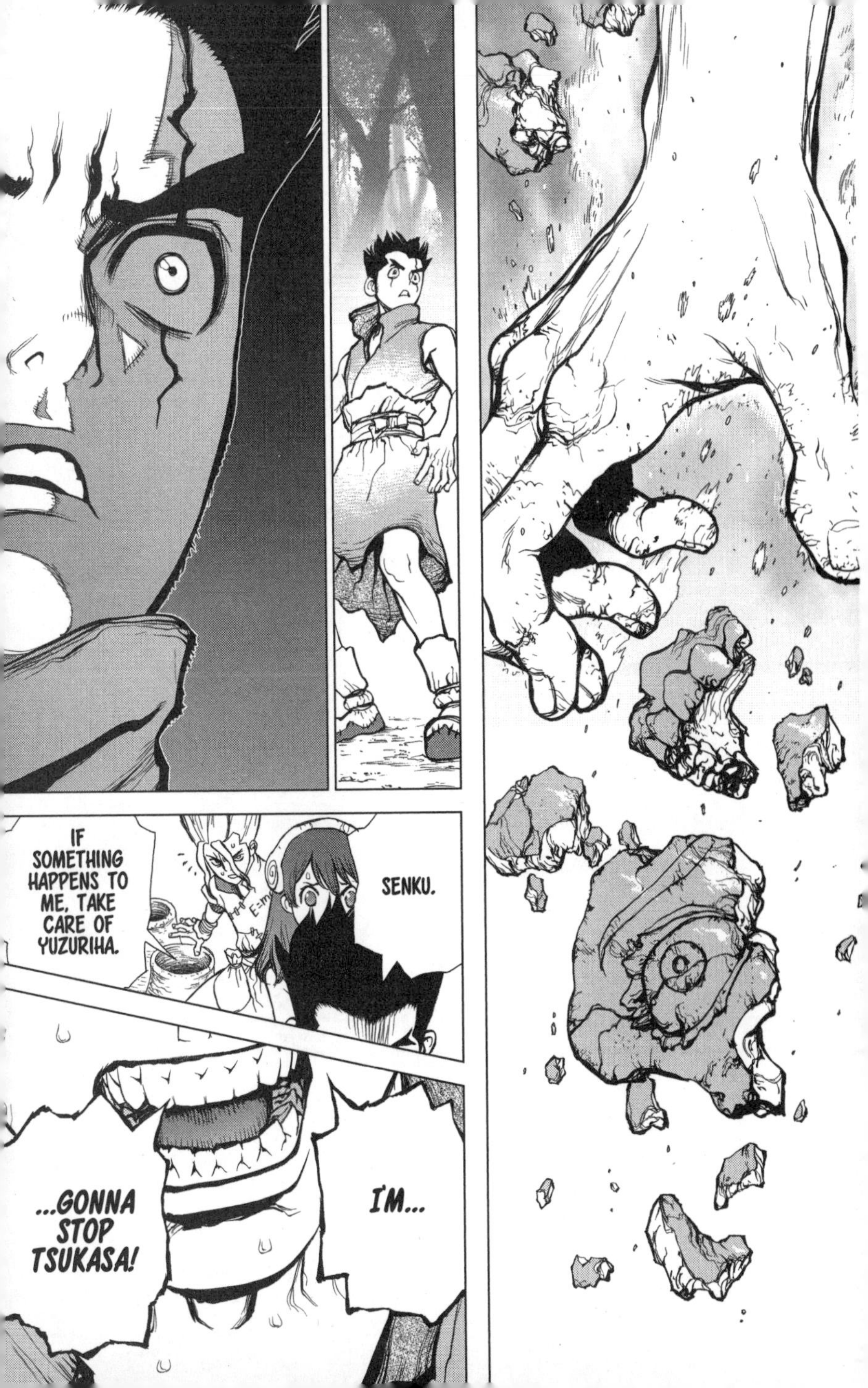
SENKU.
IF SOMETHING HAPPENS TO ME, TAKE CARE OF YUZURIHA.
I'M...
...GONNA STOP TSUKASA!

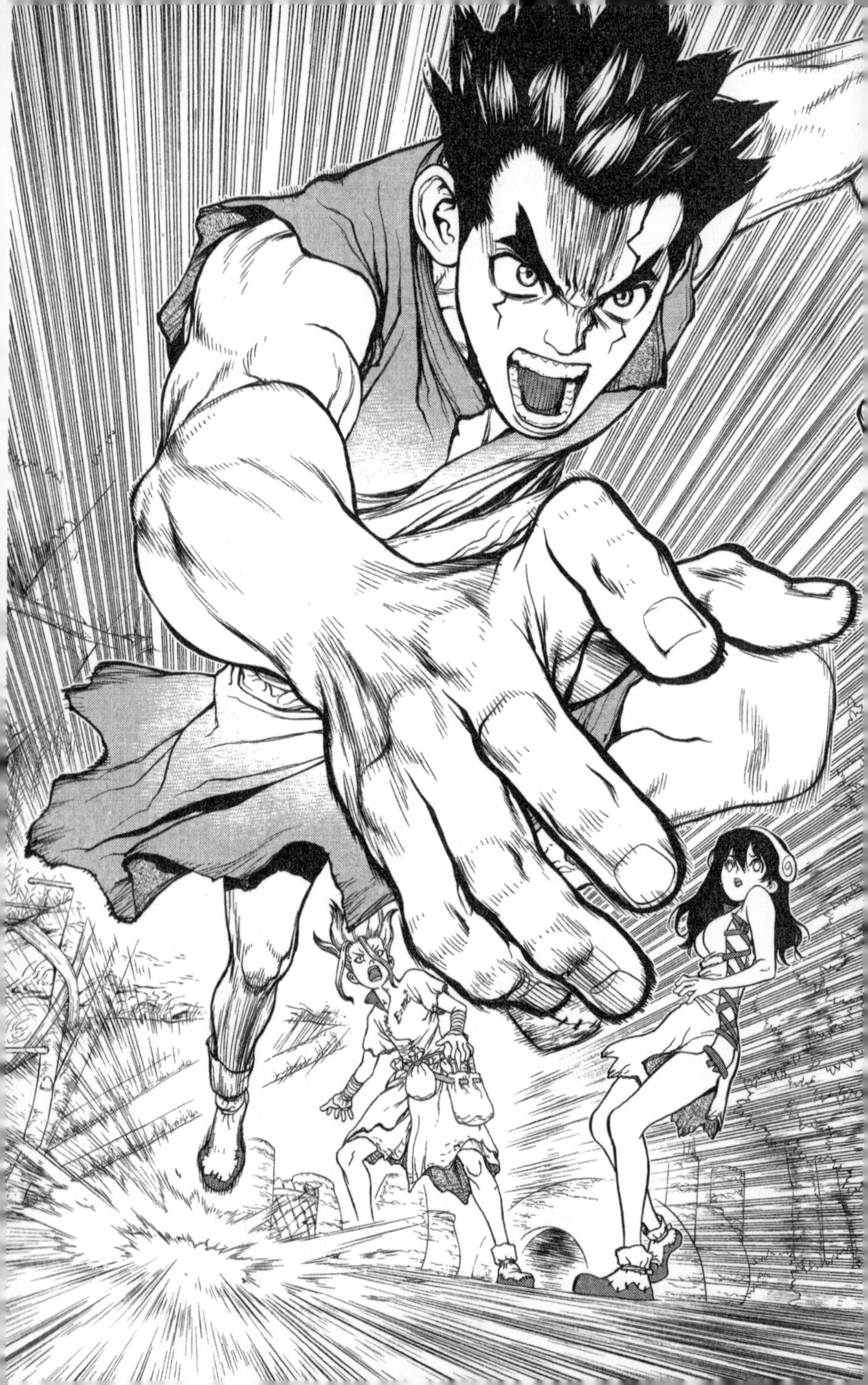

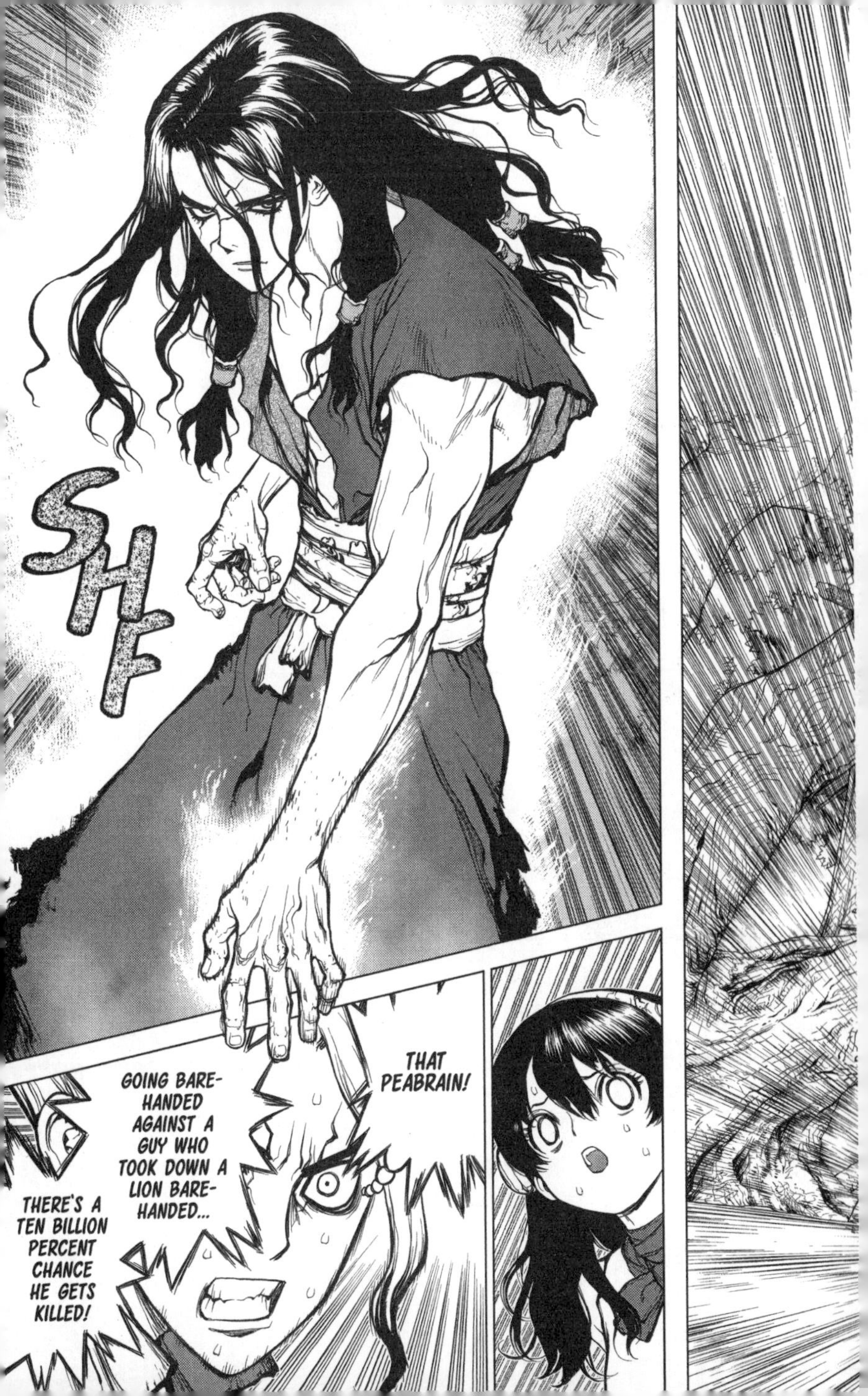
SHF
THAT PEABRAIN!
GOING BARE-HANDED AGAINST A GUY WHO TOOK DOWN A LION BARE-HANDED...
THERE'S A TEN BILLION PERCENT CHANCE HE GETS KILLED!

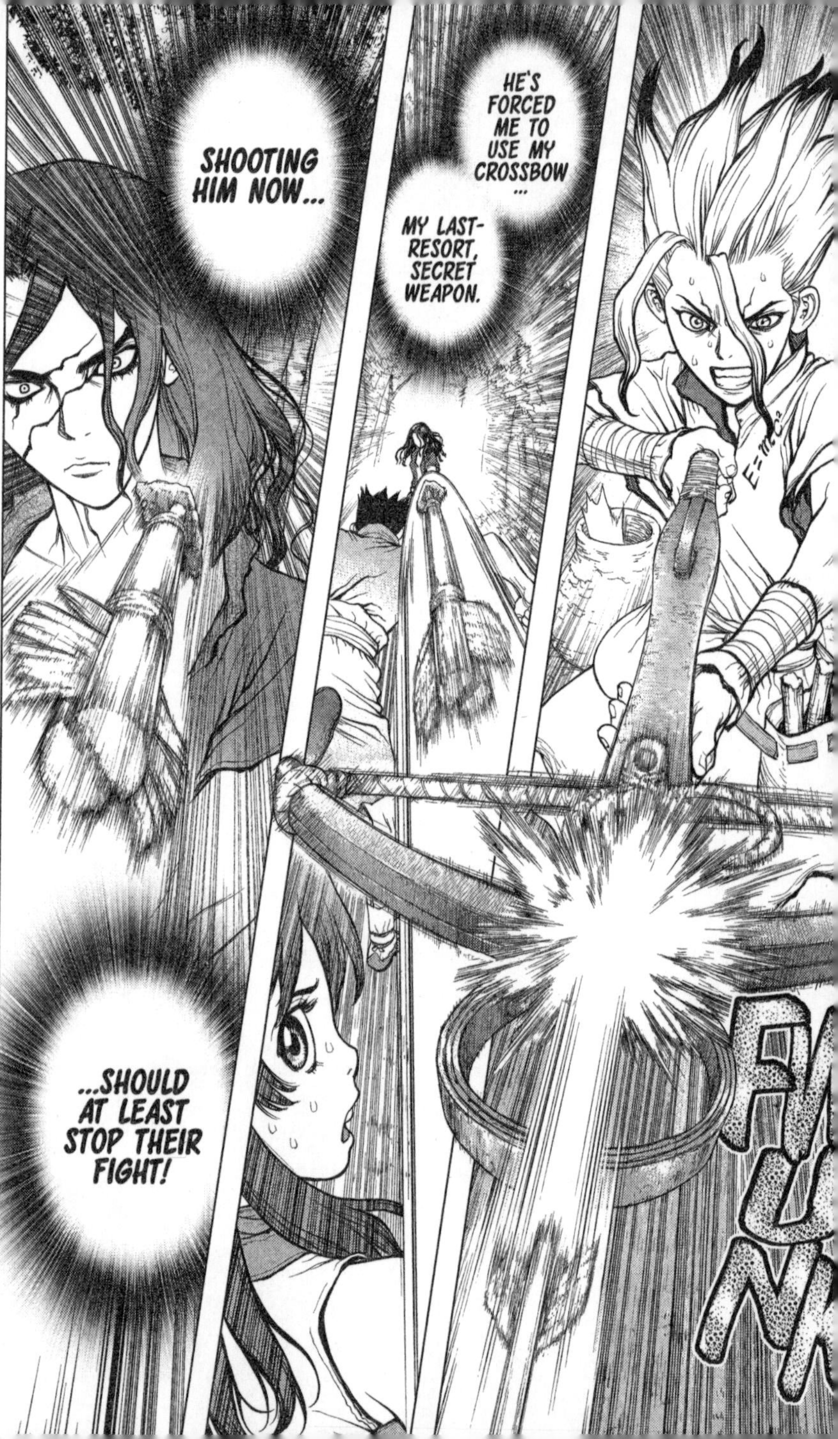
HE'S FORCED ME TO USE MY CROSSBOW...
MY LAST-RESORT, SECRET WEAPON.
SHOOTING HIM NOW...
...SHOULD AT LEAST STOP THEIR FIGHT!

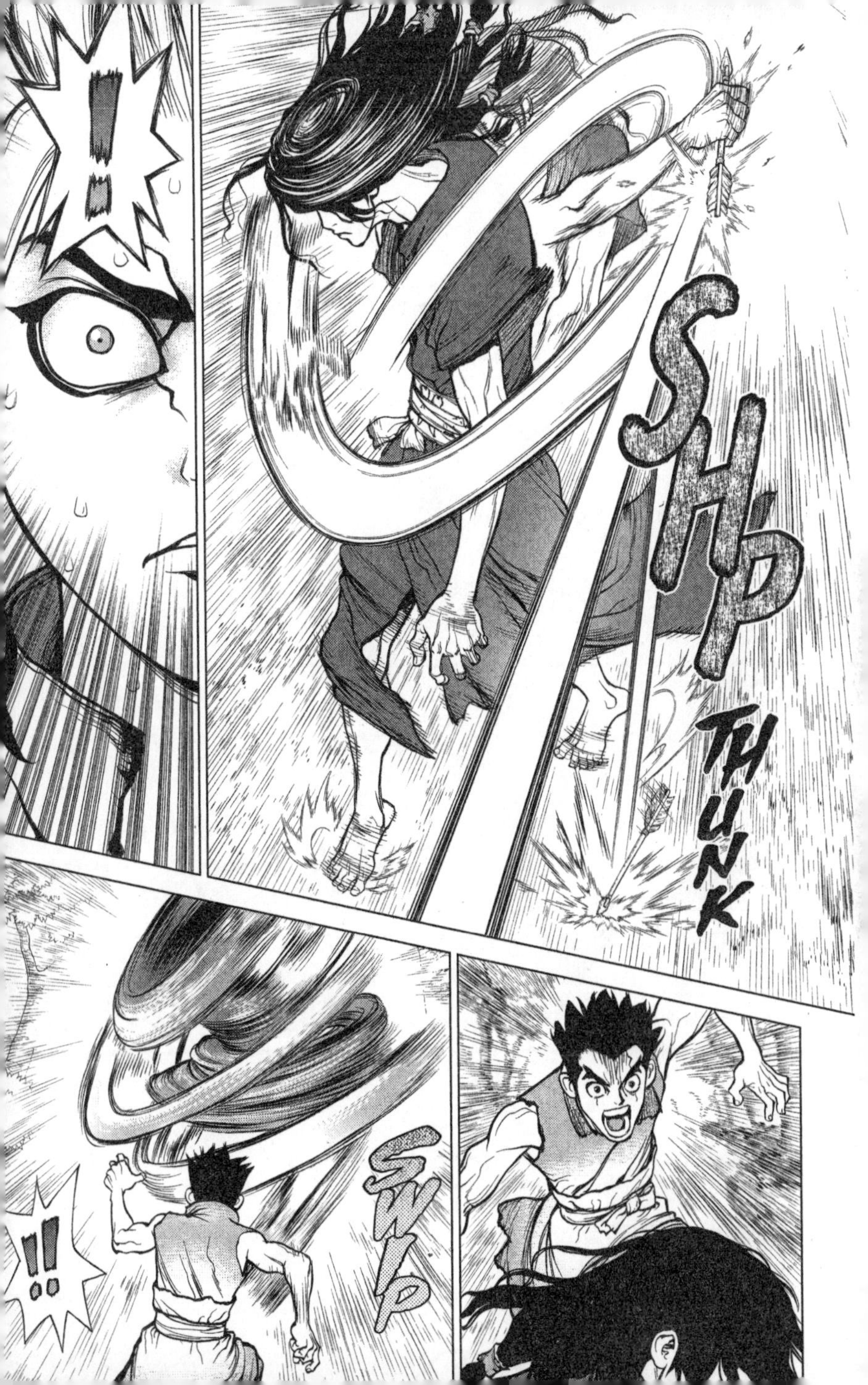
SHP
THUNK
!
SWIP
!!

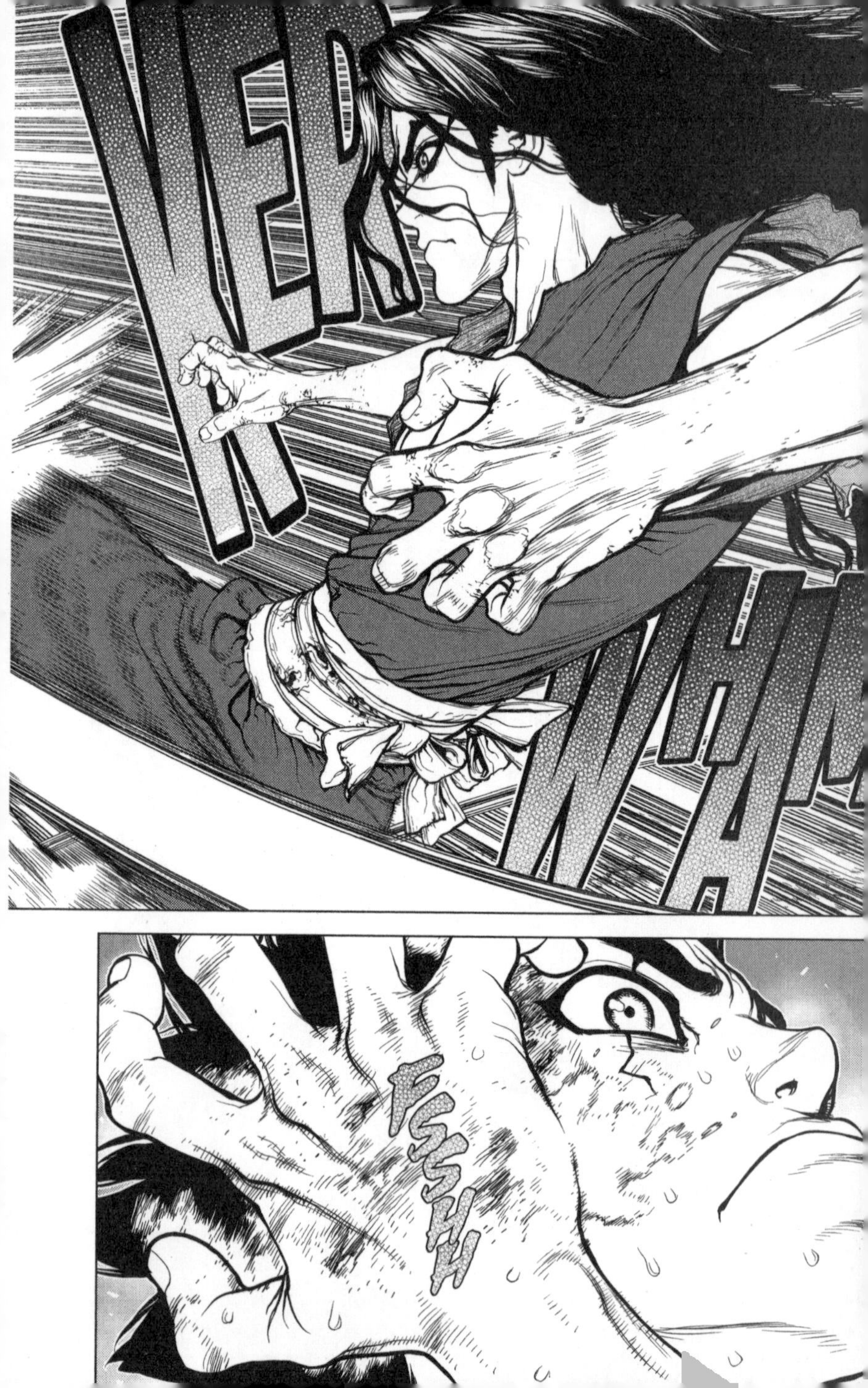
WHAM
FSSH

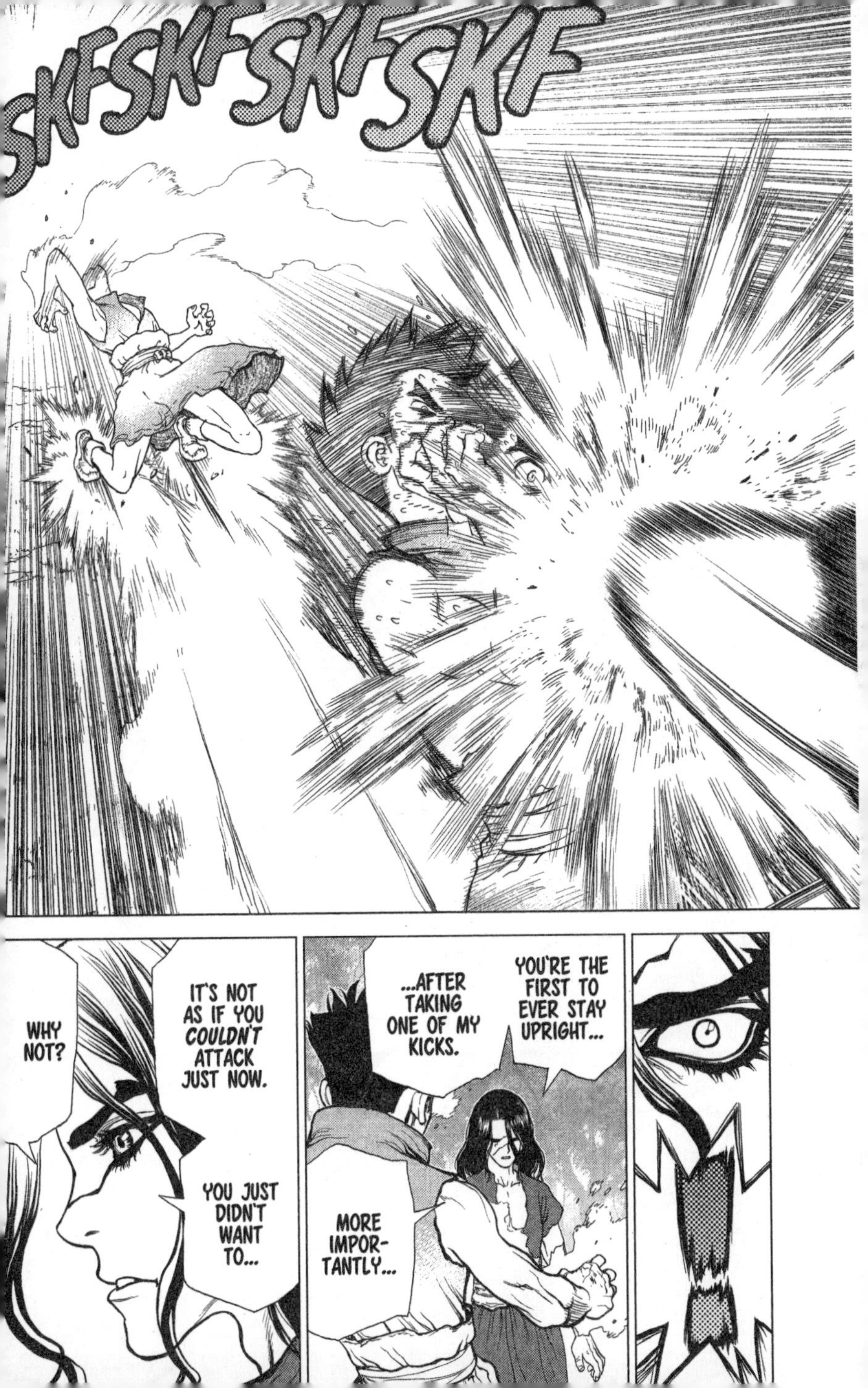
SKFSKFSKFSKF
YOU'RE THE FIRST TO EVER STAY UPRIGHT...
...AFTER TAKING ONE OF MY KICKS.
MORE IMPOR-TANTLY...
IT'S NOT AS IF YOU COULDN'T ATTACK JUST NOW.
WHY NOT?
YOU JUST DIDN'T WANT TO...

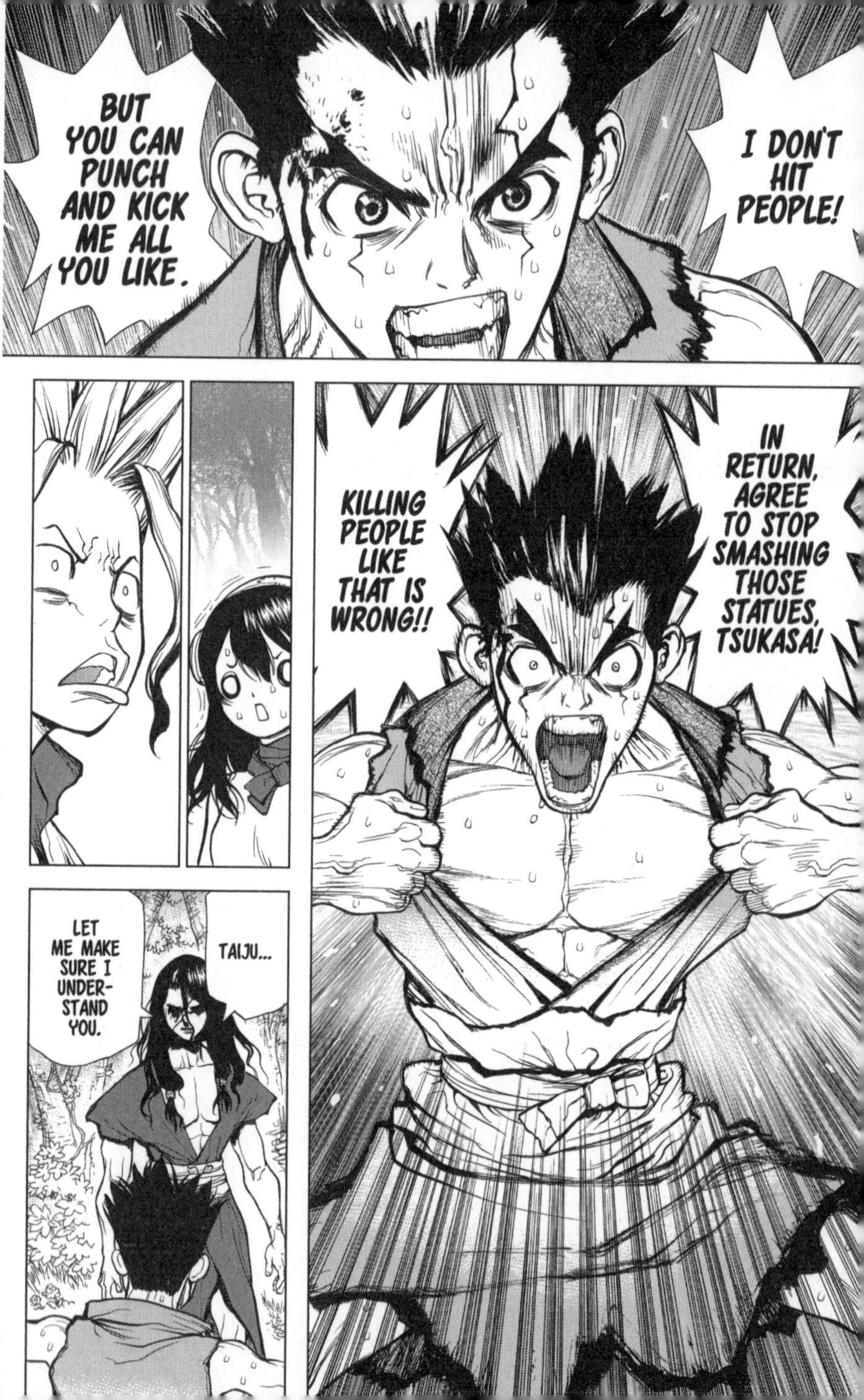
I DON'T HIT PEOPLE!
BUT YOU CAN PUNCH AND KICK ME ALL YOU LIKE.
IN RETURN, AGREE TO STOP SMASHING THOSE STATUES, TSUKASA!
KILLING PEOPLE LIKE THAT IS WRONG!!
TAIJU...
LET ME MAKE SURE I UNDER-STAND YOU.

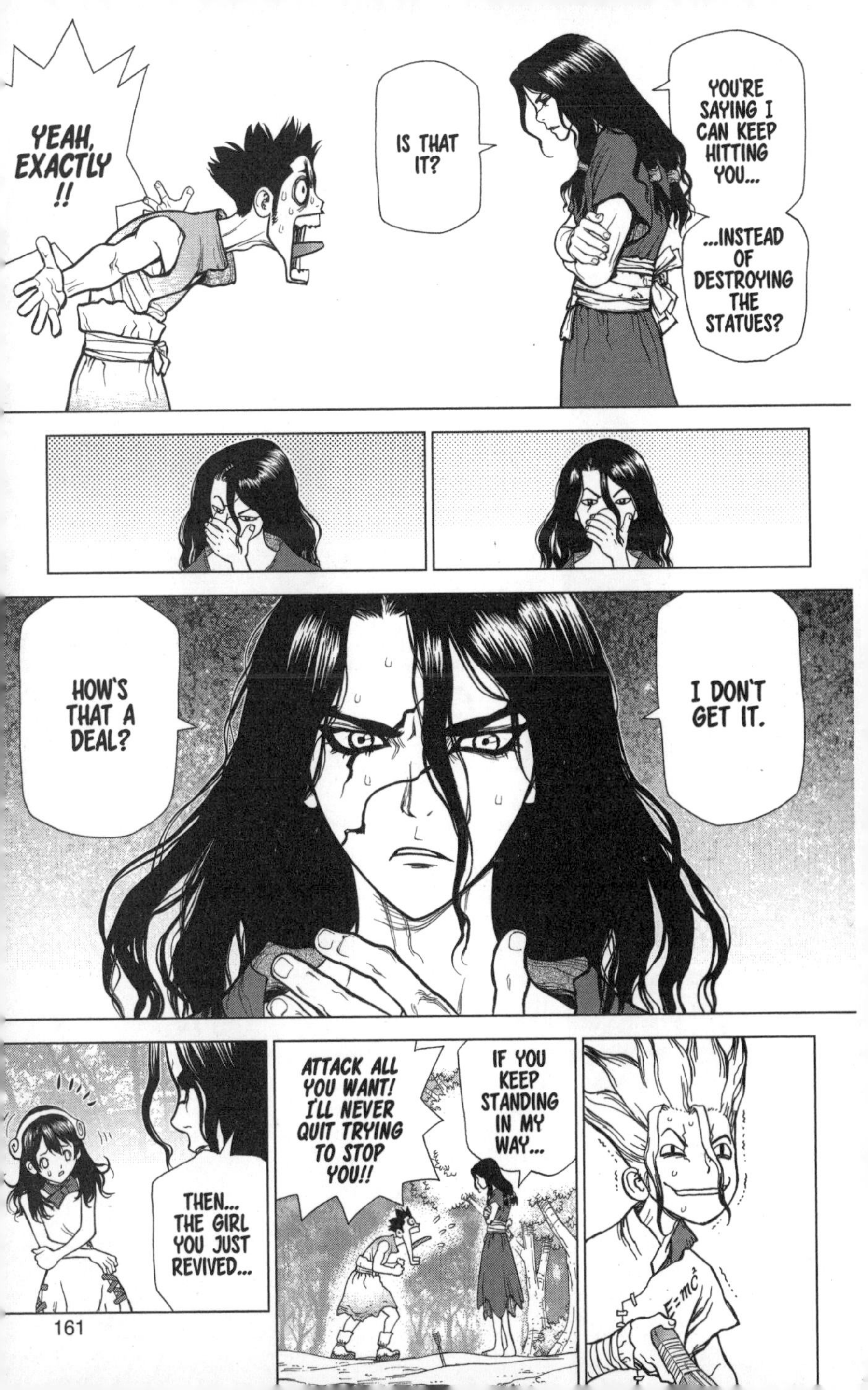
YOU'RE SAYING I CAN KEEP HITTING YOU...
...INSTEAD OF DESTROYING THE STATUES?
IS THAT IT?
YEAH, EXACTLY!!
I DON'T GET IT.
HOW'S THAT A DEAL?
IF YOU KEEP STANDING IN MY WAY...
ATTACK ALL YOU WANT! I'LL NEVER QUIT TRYING TO STOP YOU!!
THEN... THE GIRL YOU JUST REVIVED...

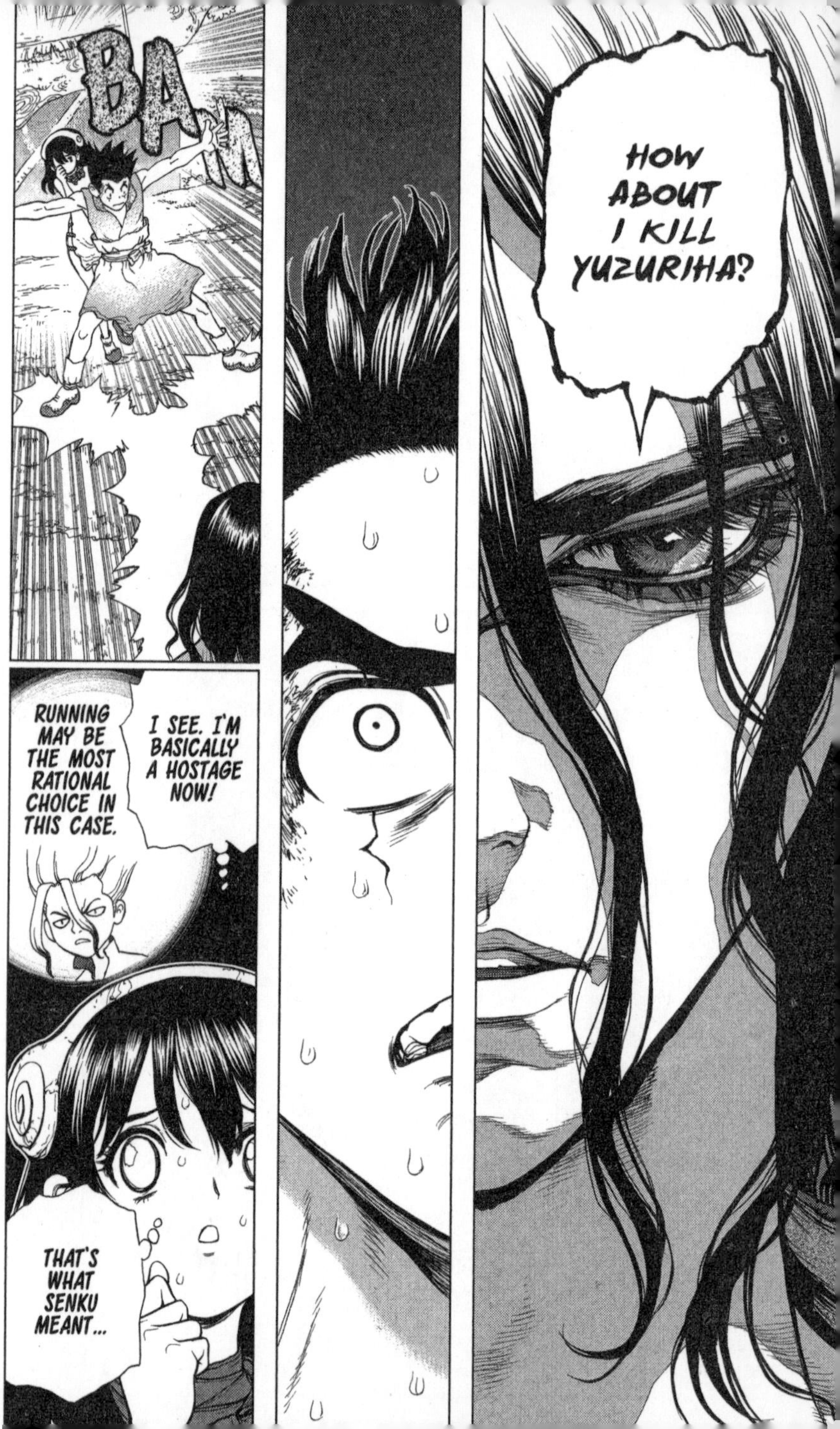
HOW ABOUT I KILL YUZURIHA?
BAM
I SEE. I'M BASICALLY A HOSTAGE NOW!
RUNNING MAY BE THE MOST RATIONAL CHOICE IN THIS CASE.
THAT'S WHAT SENKU MEANT...

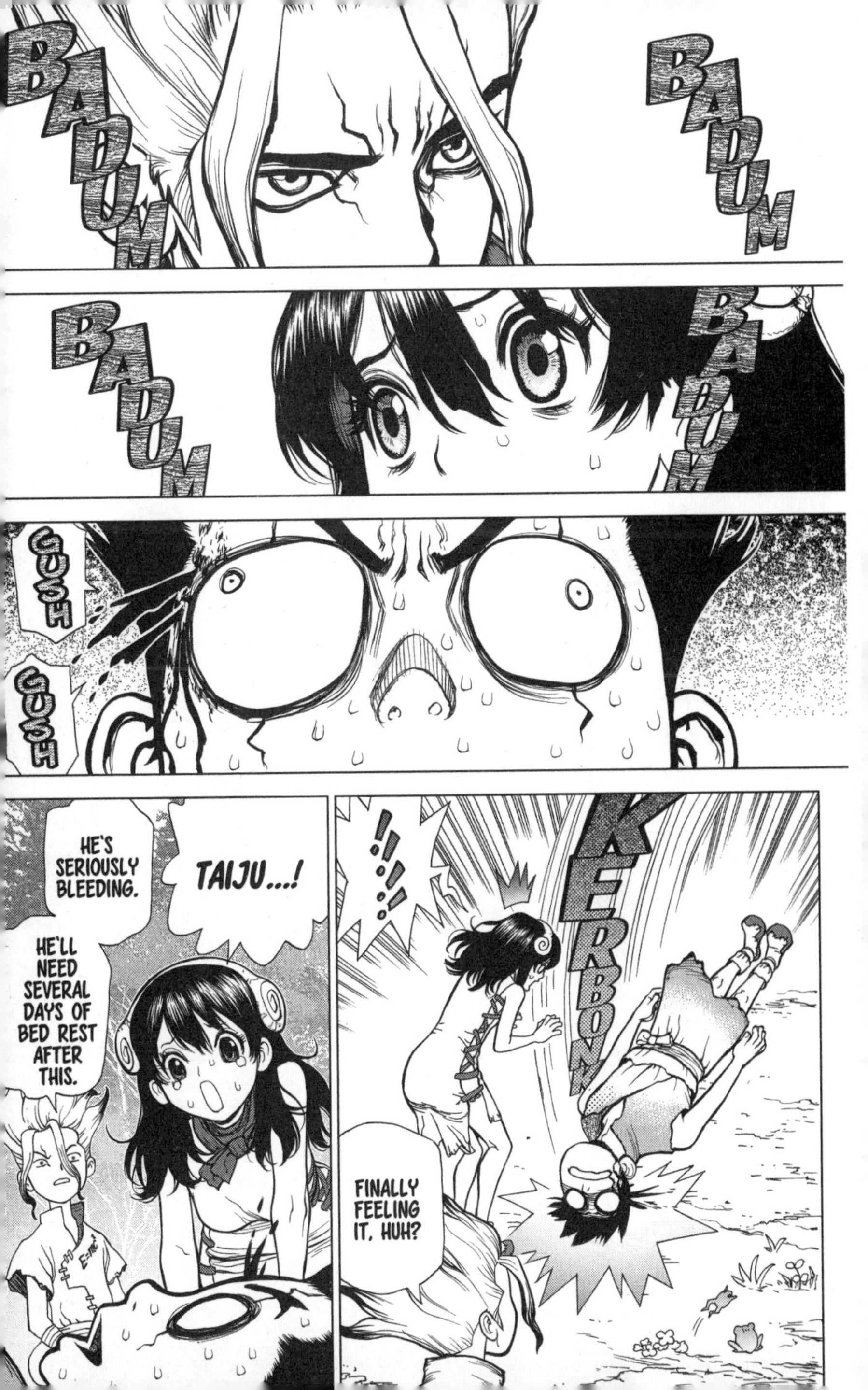
BADUM
BADUM
BADUM
BADUM
GUSH
GUSH
!!...!!
KERBOM
FINALLY FEELING IT, HUH?
TAIJU...!
HE'S SERIOUSLY BLEEDING.
HE'LL NEED SEVERAL DAYS OF BED REST AFTER THIS.

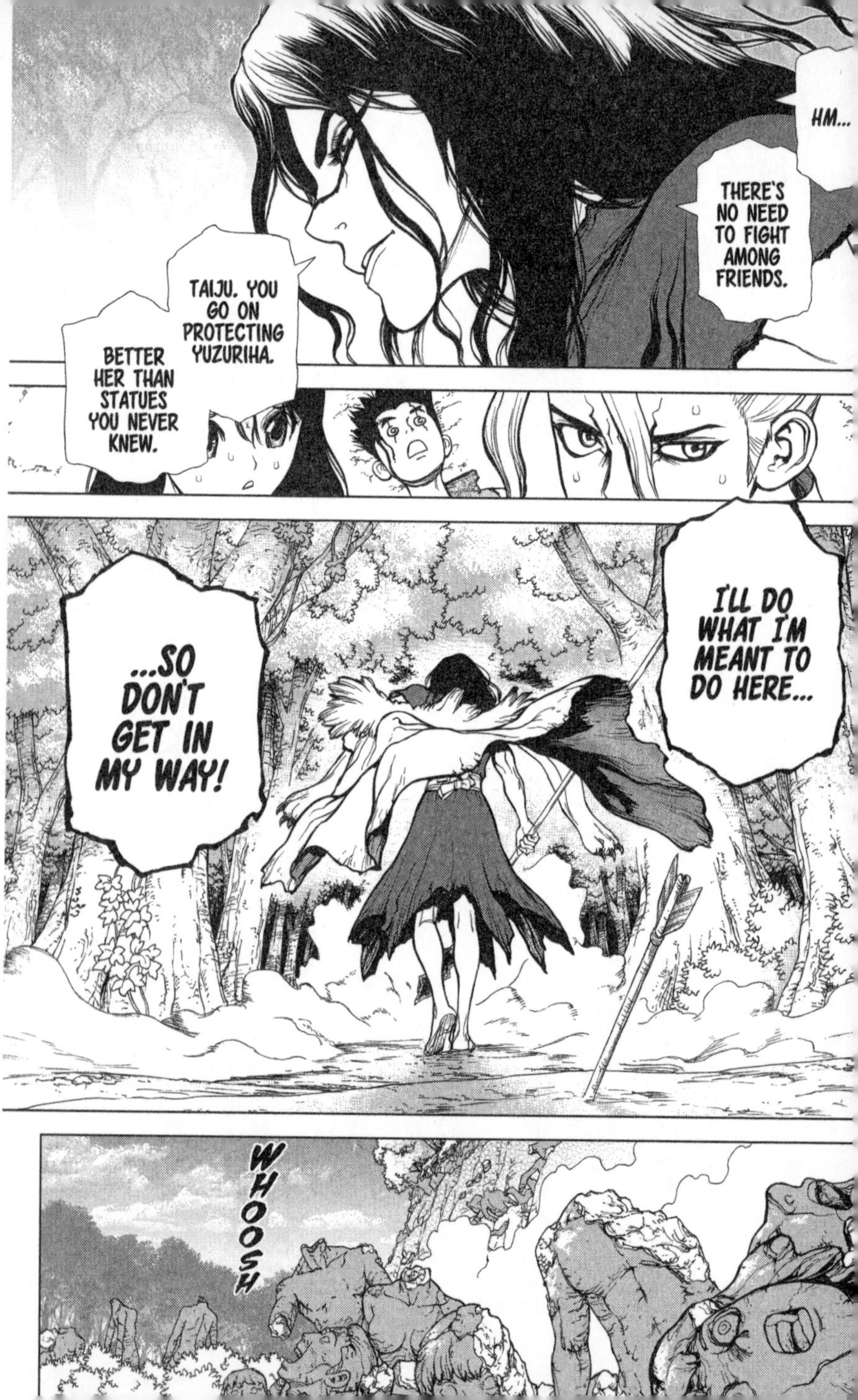
HM...
THERE'S NO NEED TO FIGHT AMONG FRIENDS.
TAIJU. YOU GO ON PROTECTING YUZURIHA.
BETTER HER THAN STATUES YOU NEVER KNEW.
I'LL DO WHAT I'M MEANT TO DO HERE...
...SO DON'T GET IN MY WAY!
WHOOOSH

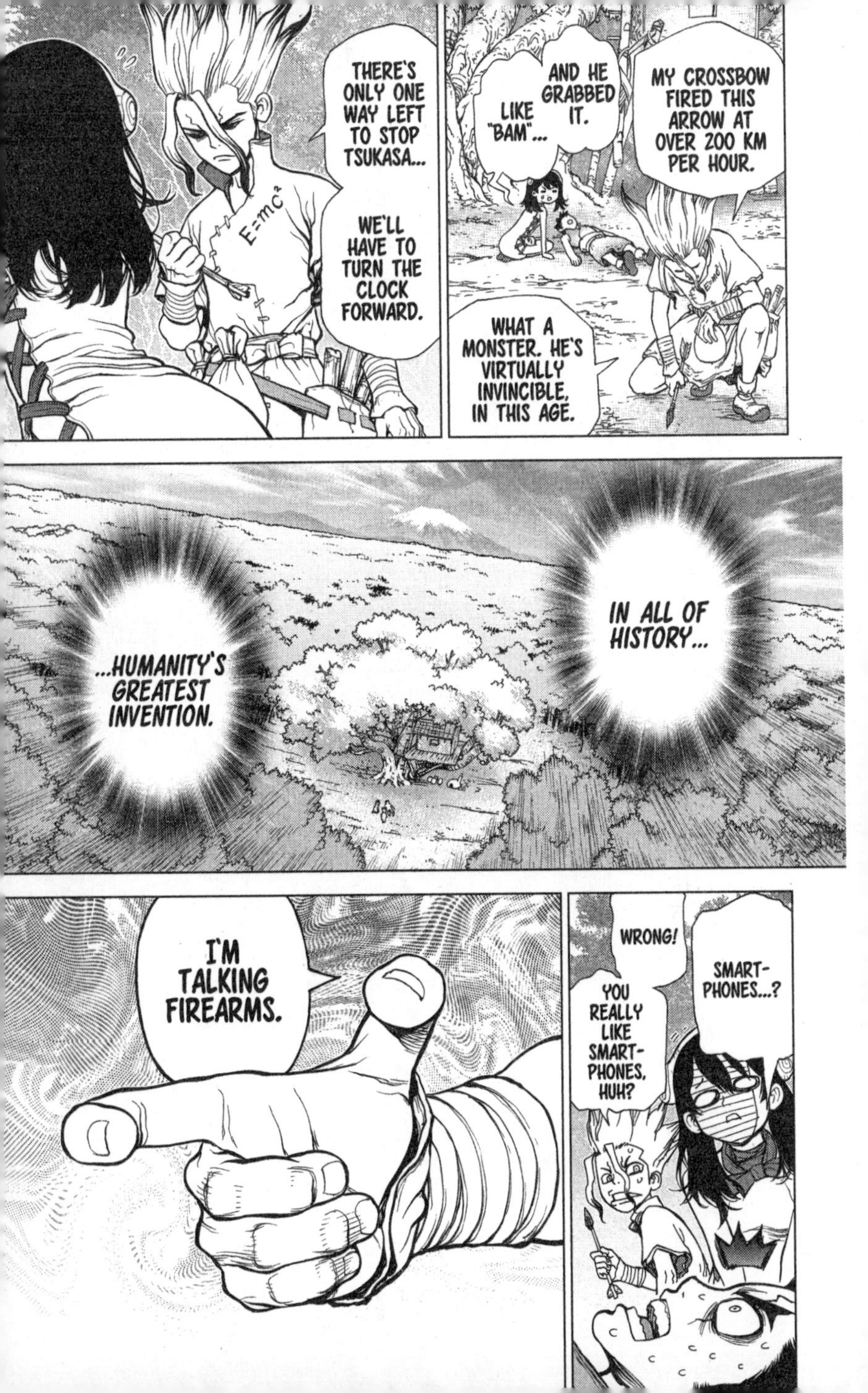
MY CROSSBOW FIRED THIS ARROW AT OVER 200 KM PER HOUR.
AND HE GRABBED IT.
LIKE "BAM"...
WHAT A MONSTER. HE'S VIRTUALLY INVINCIBLE, IN THIS AGE.
THERE'S ONLY ONE WAY LEFT TO STOP TSUKASA...
WE'LL HAVE TO TURN THE CLOCK FORWARD.
IN ALL OF HISTORY...
...HUMANITY'S GREATEST INVENTION.
SMART-PHONES...?
WRONG!
YOU REALLY LIKE SMART-PHONES, HUH?
I'M TALKING FIREARMS.

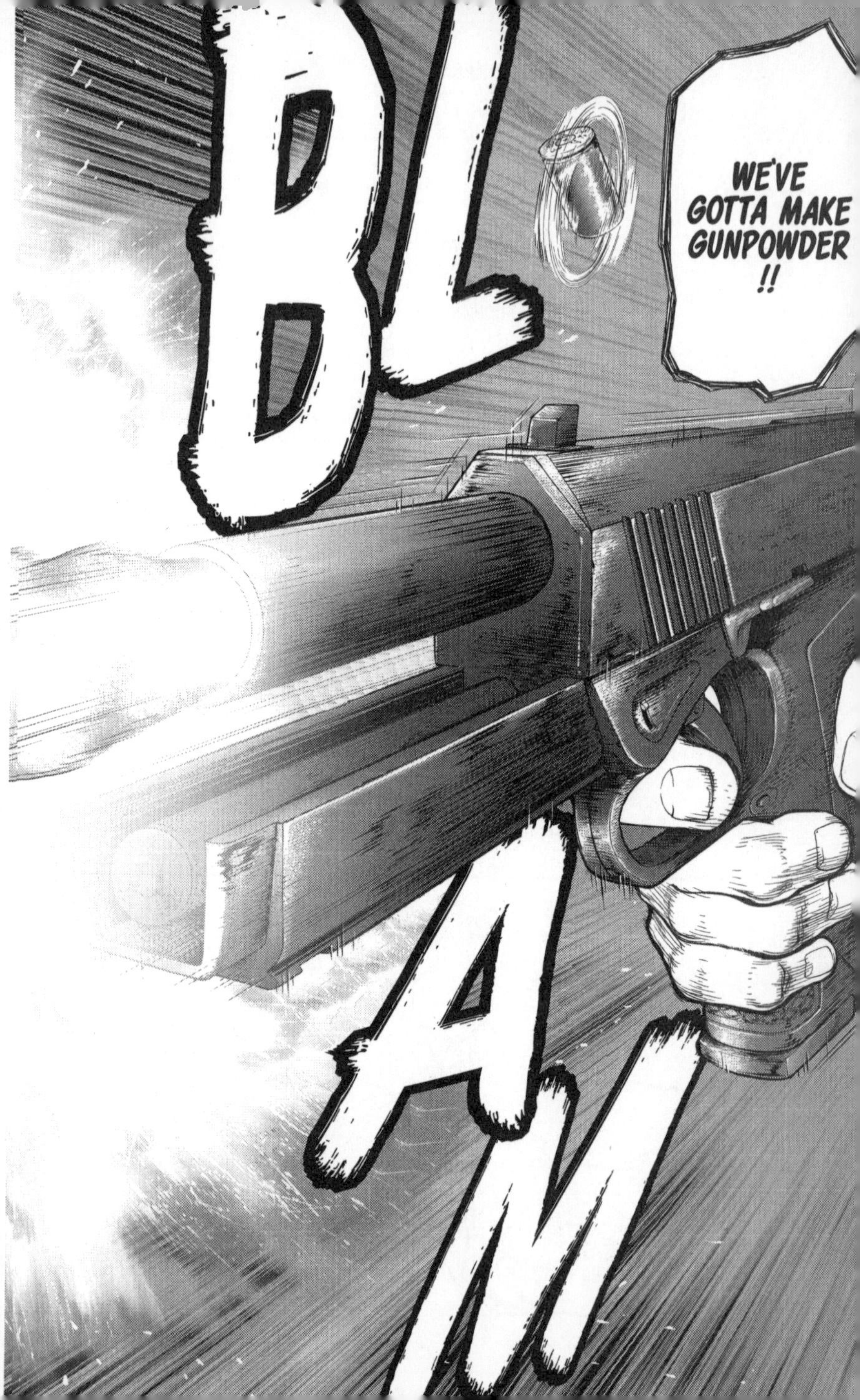
WE'VE GOTTA MAKE GUNPOWDER !!
BLAM

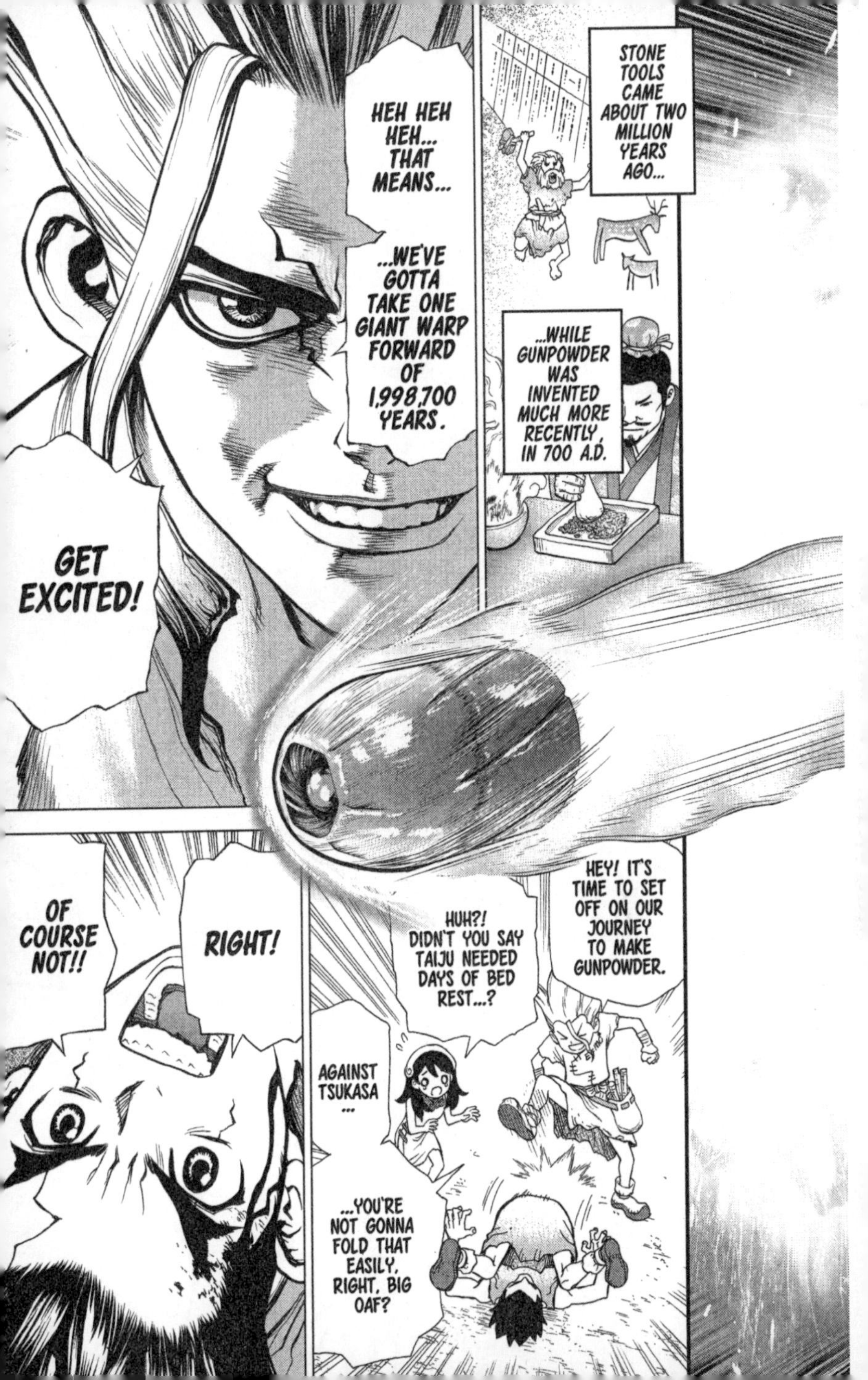
STONE TOOLS CAME ABOUT TWO MILLION YEARS AGO...
...WHILE GUNPOWDER WAS INVENTED MUCH MORE RECENTLY, IN 700 A.D.
HEH HEH HEH... THAT MEANS...
...WE'VE GOTTA TAKE ONE GIANT WARP FORWARD OF 1,998,700 YEARS.
GET EXCITED!
HEY! IT'S TIME TO SET OFF ON OUR JOURNEY TO MAKE GUNPOWDER.
HUH?! DIDN'T YOU SAY TAIJU NEEDED DAYS OF BED REST...?
AGAINST TSUKASA...
...YOU'RE NOT GONNA FOLD THAT EASILY, RIGHT, BIG OAF?
RIGHT!
OF COURSE NOT!!

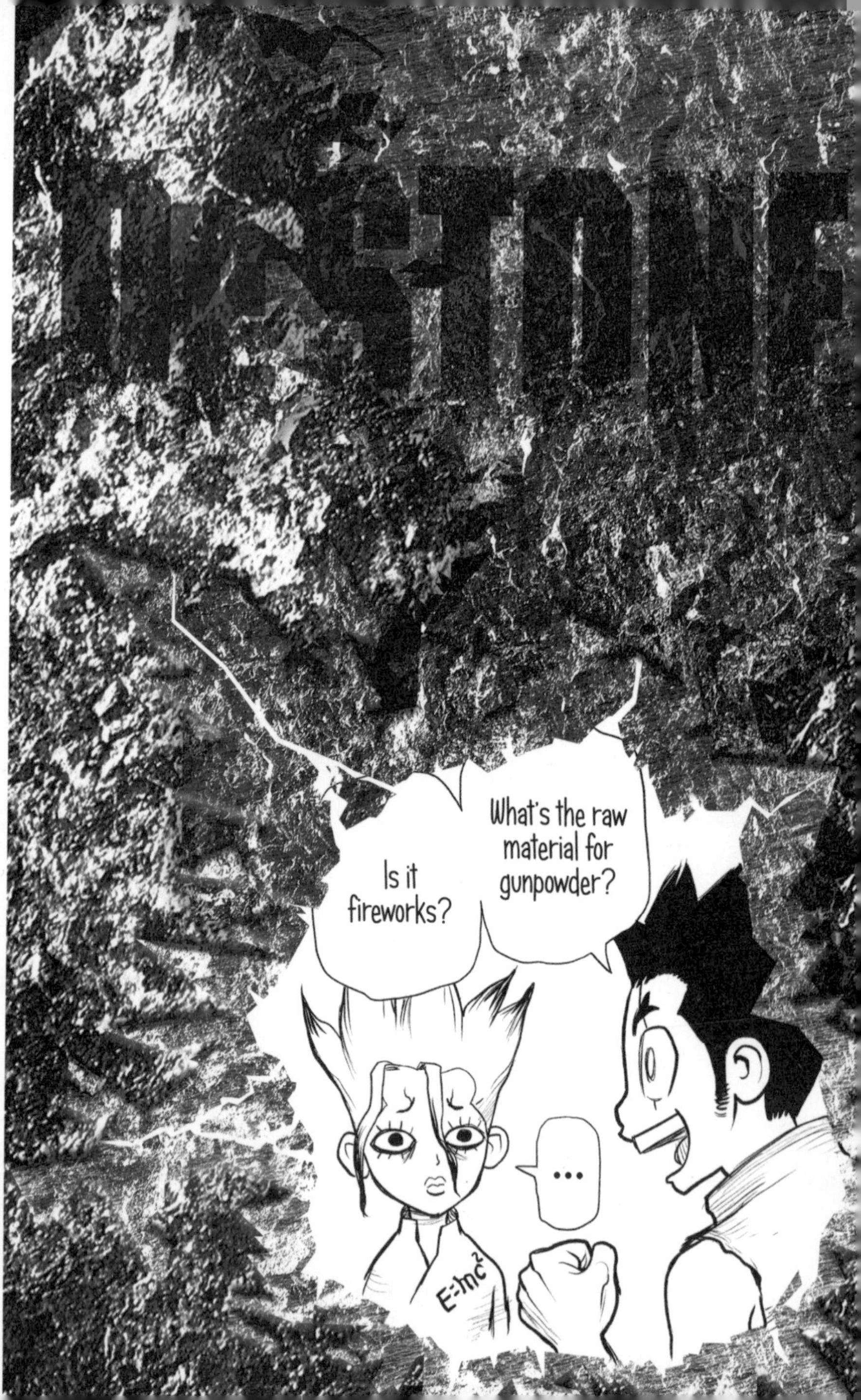
What's the raw material for gunpowder?
Is it fireworks?
...
E=mc²

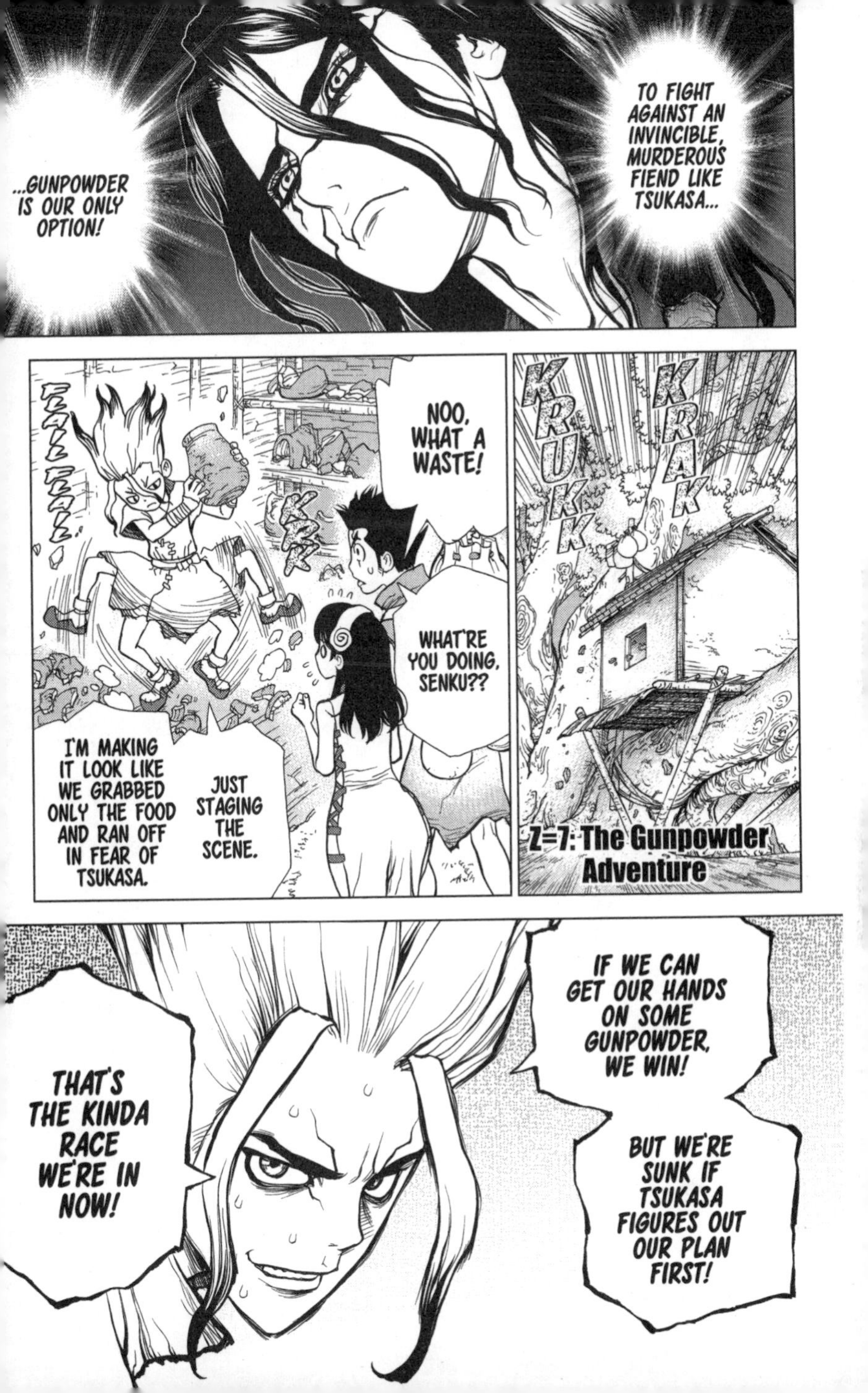
TO FIGHT AGAINST AN INVINCIBLE, MURDEROUS FIEND LIKE TSUKASA...
...GUNPOWDER IS OUR ONLY OPTION!
KRUK
KRAK
Z=7: The Gunpowder Adventure
NOO, WHAT A WASTE!
FLAIL FLAIL
WHAT'RE YOU DOING, SENKU??
JUST STAGING THE SCENE.
I'M MAKING IT LOOK LIKE WE GRABBED ONLY THE FOOD AND RAN OFF IN FEAR OF TSUKASA.
IF WE CAN GET OUR HANDS ON SOME GUNPOWDER, WE WIN!
BUT WE'RE SUNK IF TSUKASA FIGURES OUT OUR PLAN FIRST!
THAT'S THE KINDA RACE WE'RE IN NOW!

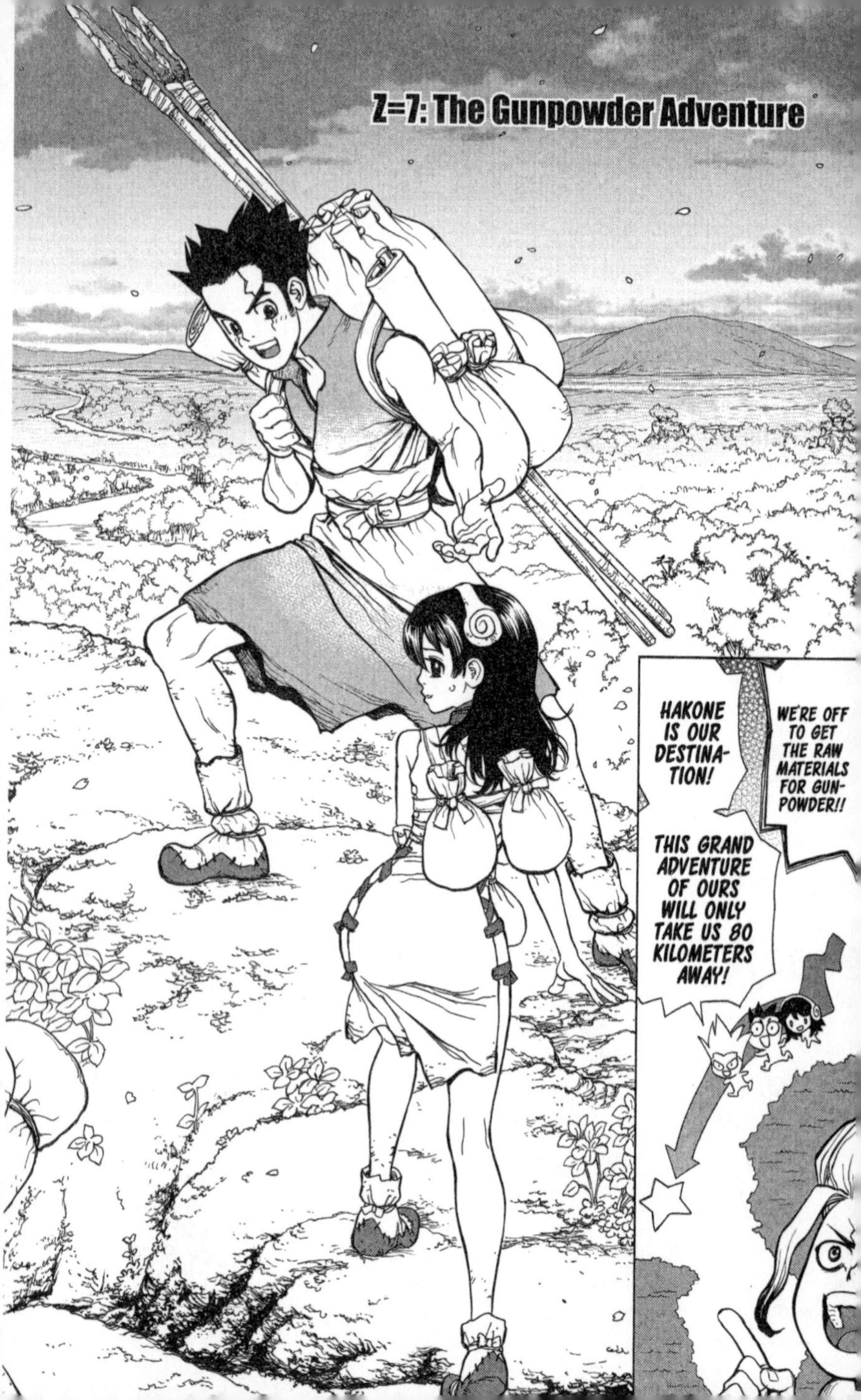
Z=7: The Gunpowder Adventure
WE'RE OFF TO GET THE RAW MATERIALS FOR GUNPOWDER!!
HAKONE IS OUR DESTINATION!
THIS GRAND ADVENTURE OF OURS WILL ONLY TAKE US 80 KILOMETERS AWAY!

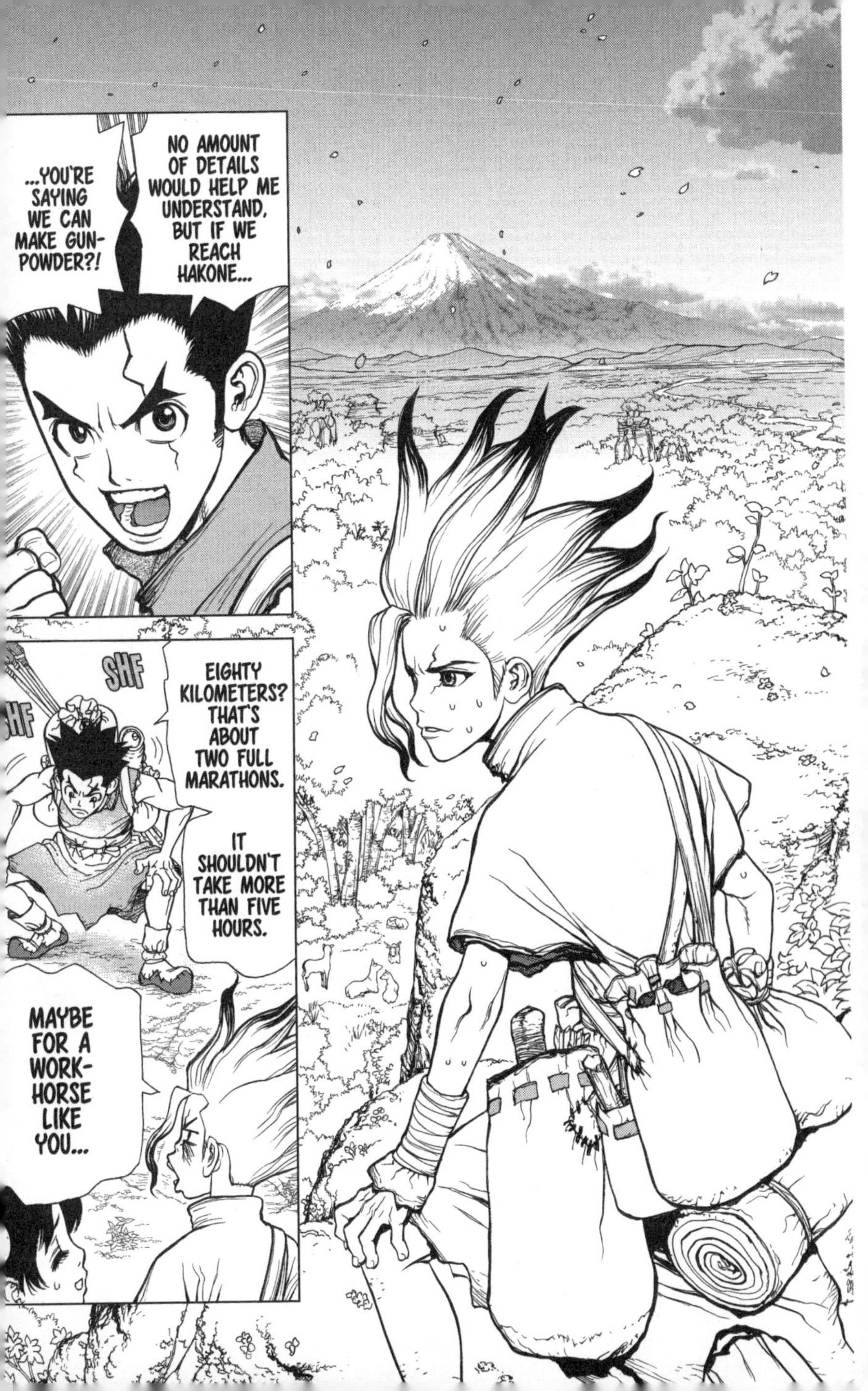
NO AMOUNT OF DETAILS WOULD HELP ME UNDERSTAND, BUT IF WE REACH HAKONE...
...YOU'RE SAYING WE CAN MAKE GUN-POWDER?!
SHF
SHF
EIGHTY KILOMETERS? THAT'S ABOUT TWO FULL MARATHONS.
IT SHOULDN'T TAKE MORE THAN FIVE HOURS.
MAYBE FOR A WORK-HORSE LIKE YOU...

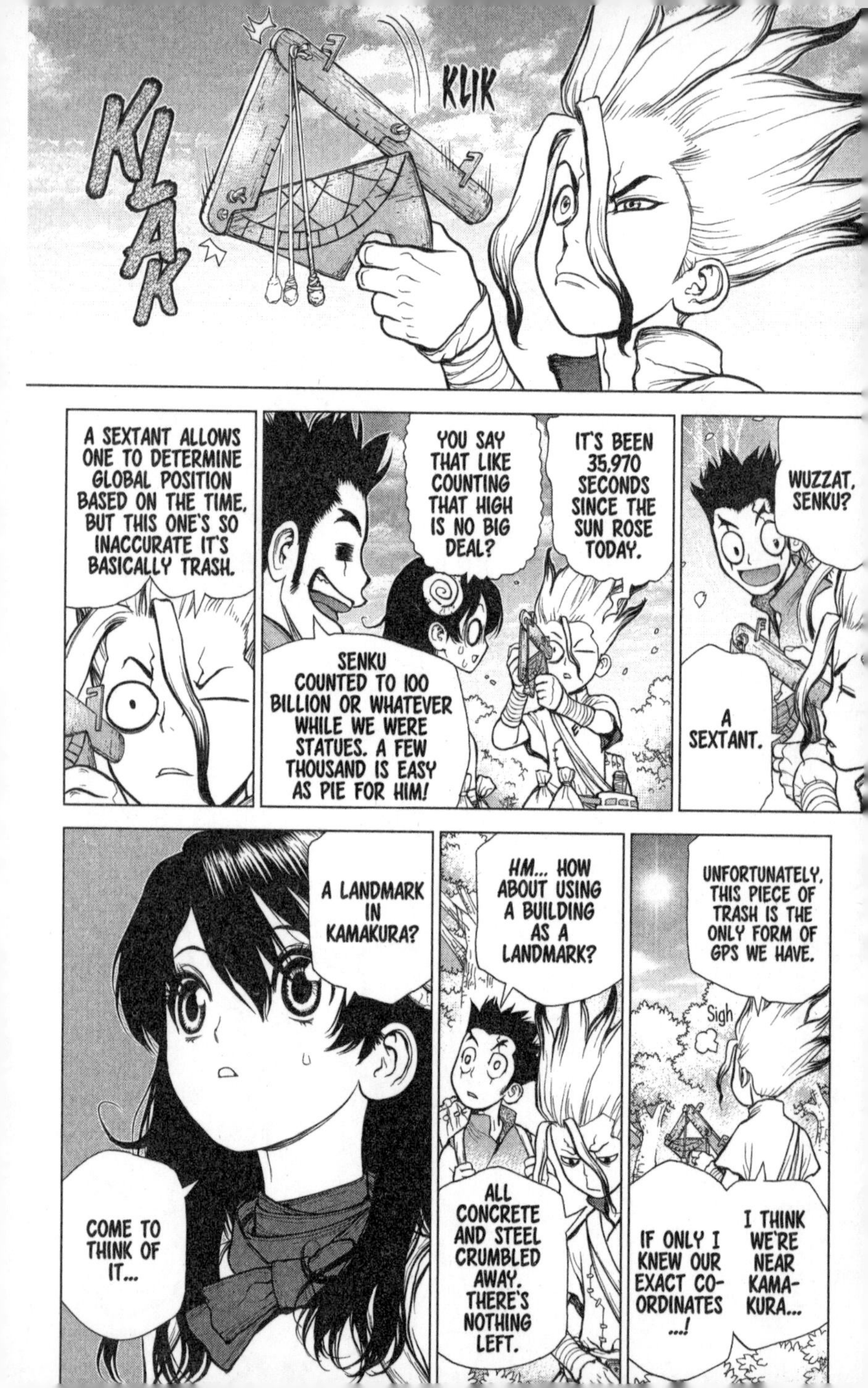
KLIK
KLAK
WUZZAT, SENKU?
A SEXTANT.
IT'S BEEN 35,970 SECONDS SINCE THE SUN ROSE TODAY.
YOU SAY THAT LIKE COUNTING THAT HIGH IS NO BIG DEAL?
SENKU COUNTED TO 100 BILLION OR WHATEVER WHILE WE WERE STATUES. A FEW THOUSAND IS EASY AS PIE FOR HIM!
A SEXTANT ALLOWS ONE TO DETERMINE GLOBAL POSITION BASED ON THE TIME, BUT THIS ONE'S SO INACCURATE IT'S BASICALLY TRASH.
UNFORTUNATELY, THIS PIECE OF TRASH IS THE ONLY FORM OF GPS WE HAVE.
Sigh
I THINK WE'RE NEAR KAMA-KURA...
IF ONLY I KNEW OUR EXACT CO-ORDINATES ...!
HM... HOW ABOUT USING A BUILDING AS A LANDMARK?
ALL CONCRETE AND STEEL CRUMBLED AWAY. THERE'S NOTHING LEFT.
A LANDMARK IN KAMAKURA?
COME TO THINK OF IT...

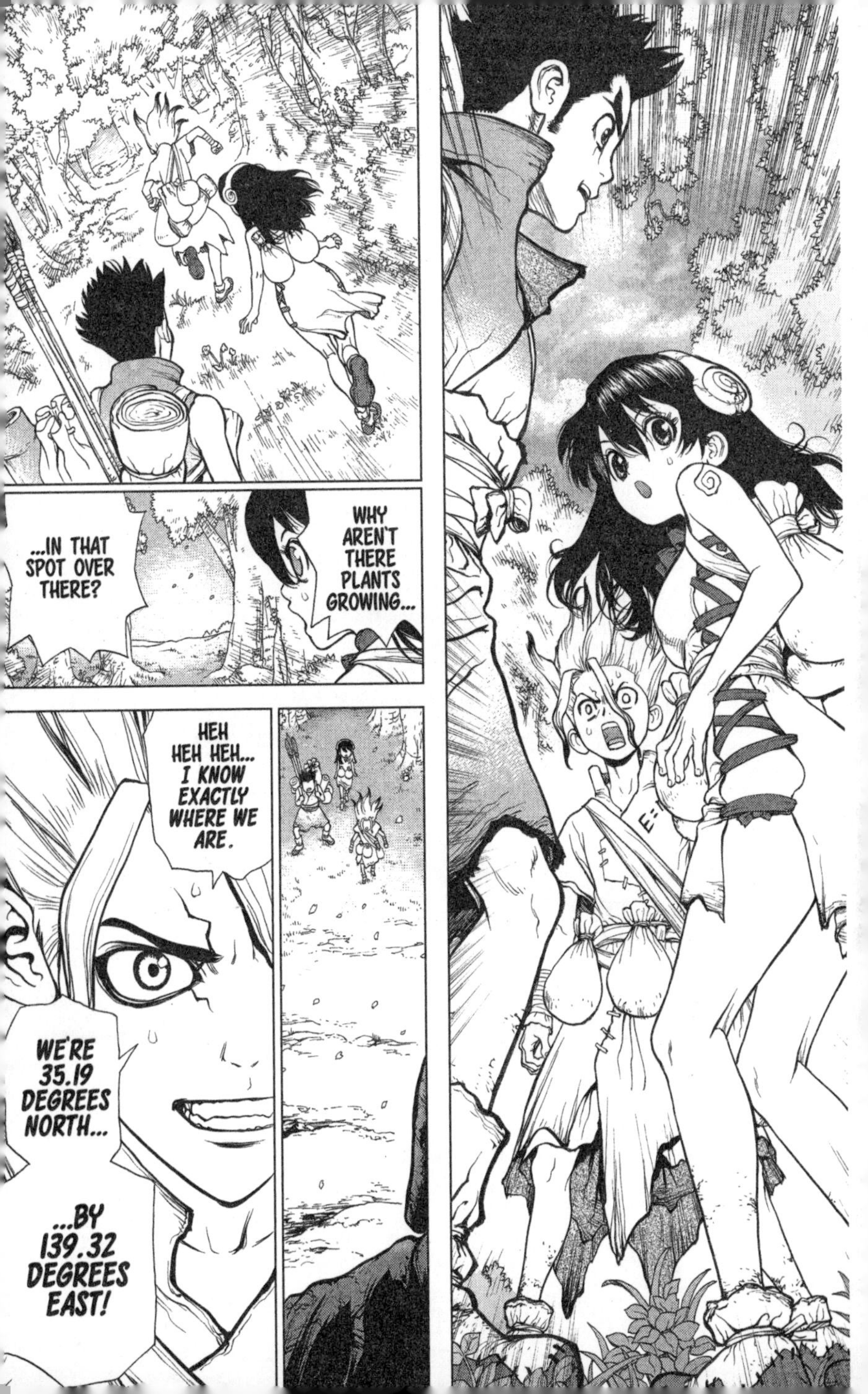
WHY AREN'T THERE PLANTS GROWING...
...IN THAT SPOT OVER THERE?
HEH HEH HEH... I KNOW EXACTLY WHERE WE ARE.
WE'RE 35.19 DEGREES NORTH...
...BY 139.32 DEGREES EAST!

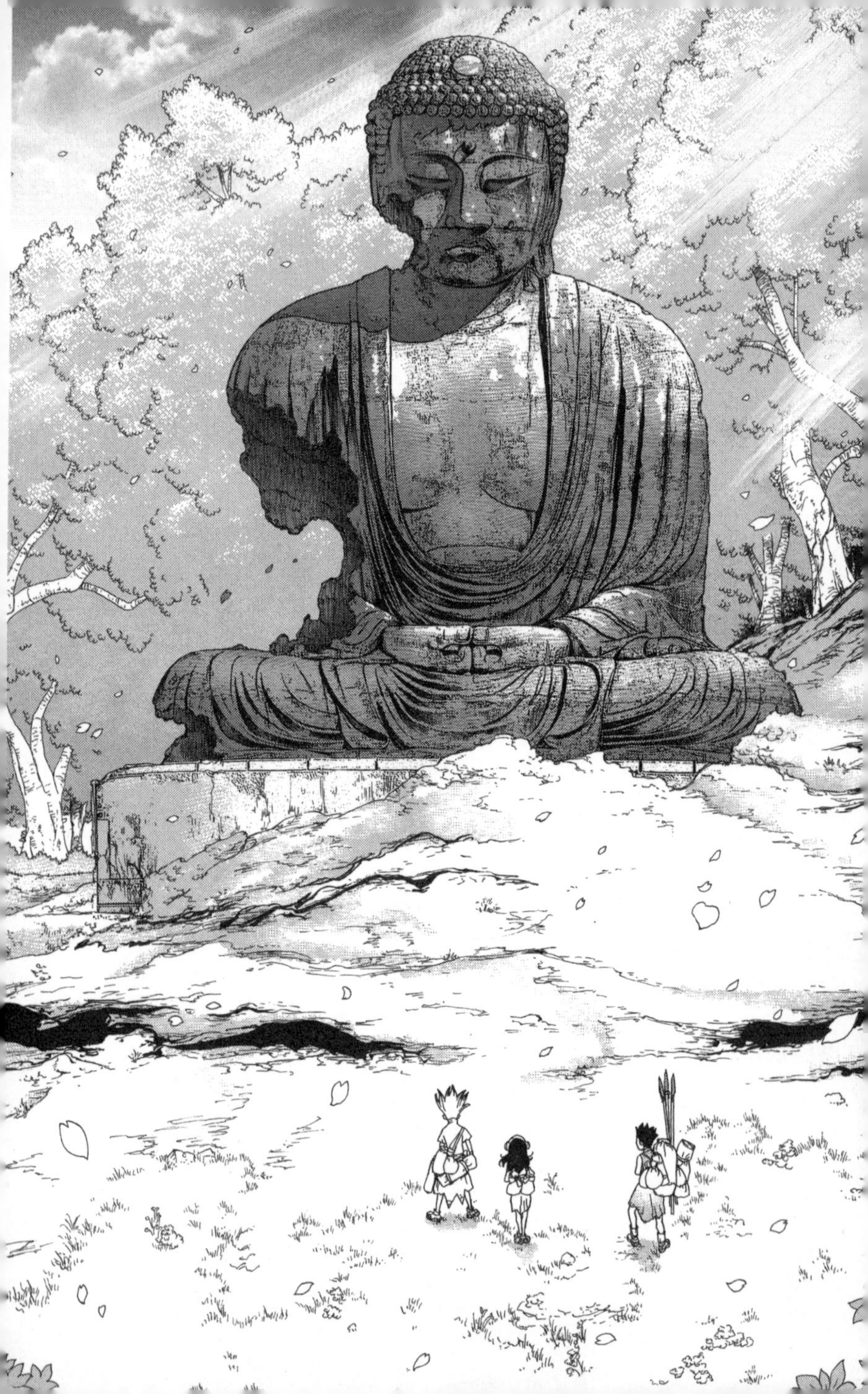

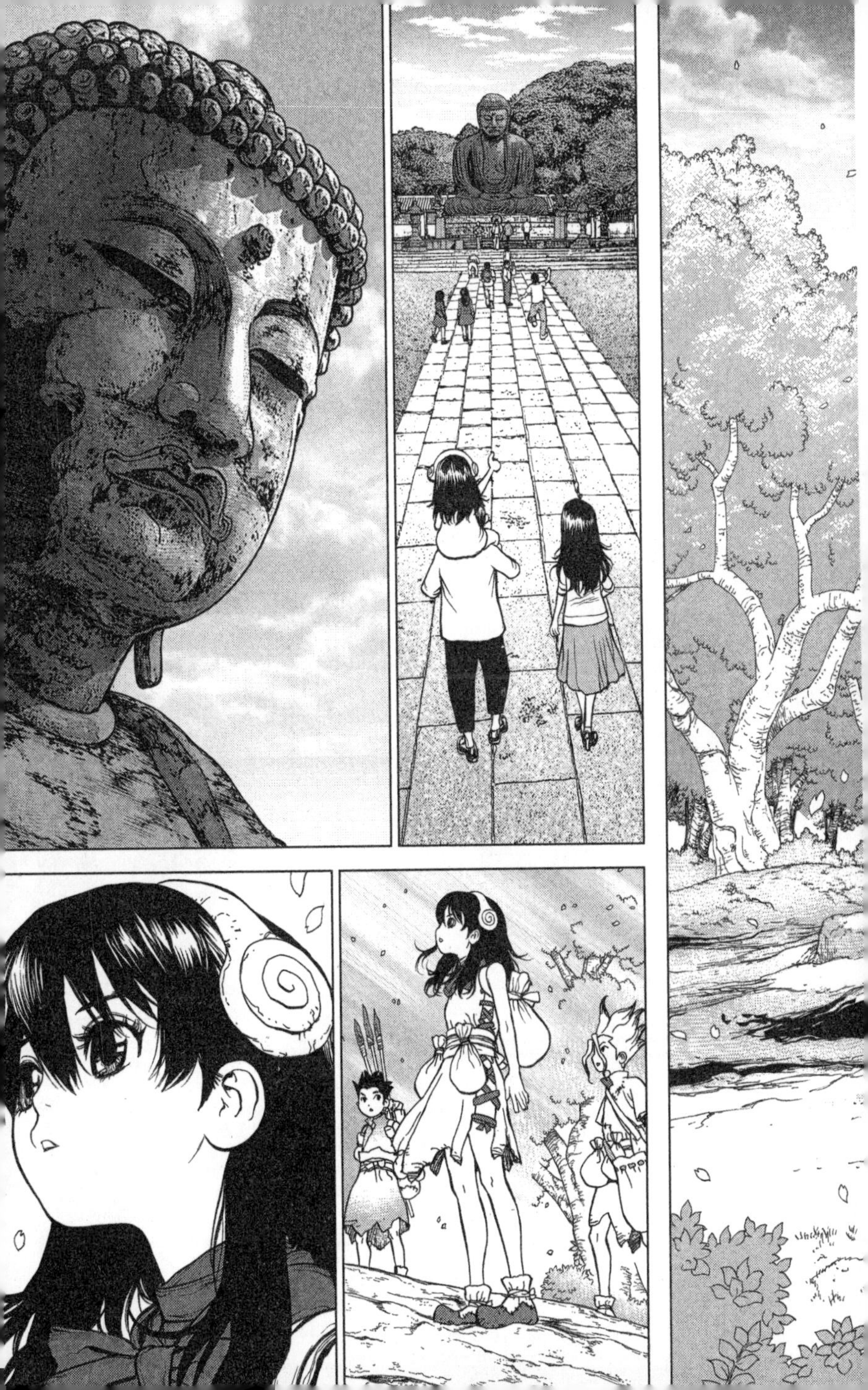

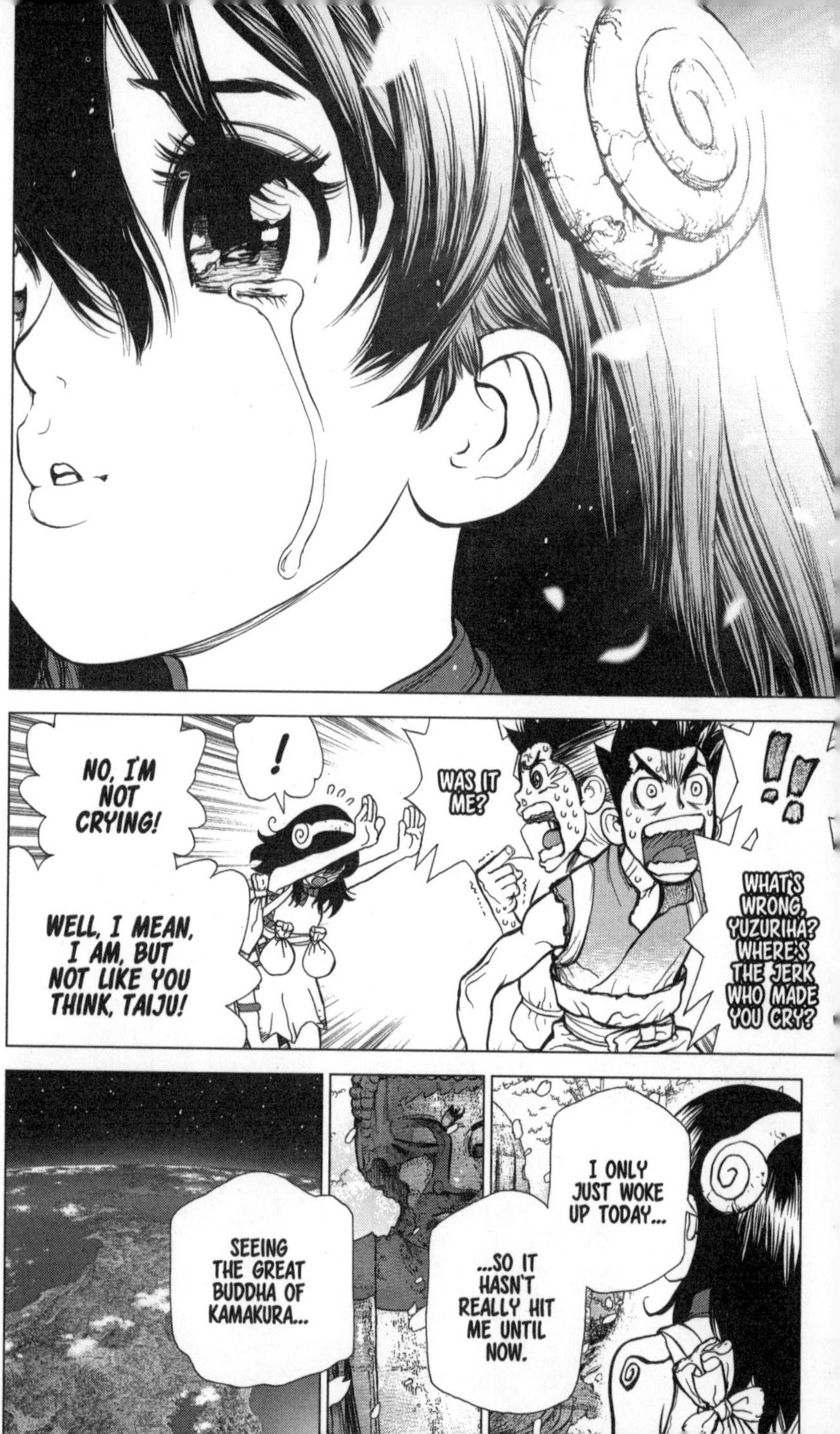
WHAT'S WRONG, YUZURIHA? WHERE'S THE JERK WHO MADE YOU CRY?
WAS IT ME?
!
NO, I'M NOT CRYING!
WELL, I MEAN, I AM, BUT NOT LIKE YOU THINK, TAIJU!
I ONLY JUST WOKE UP TODAY...
...SO IT HASN'T REALLY HIT ME UNTIL NOW.
SEEING THE GREAT BUDDHA OF KAMAKURA...

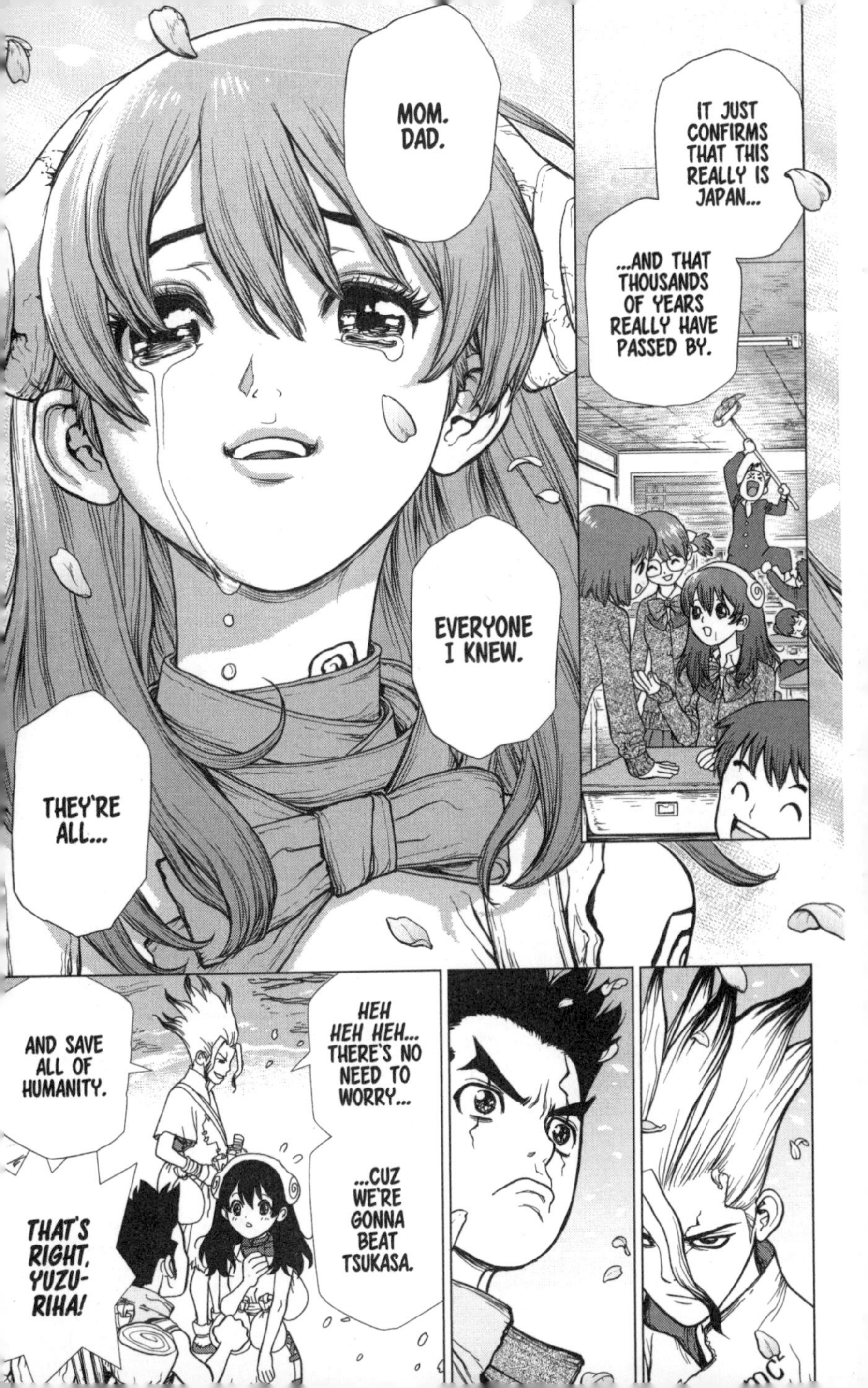
IT JUST CONFIRMS THAT THIS REALLY IS JAPAN...
...AND THAT THOUSANDS OF YEARS REALLY HAVE PASSED BY.
MOM. DAD.
EVERYONE I KNEW.
THEY'RE ALL...
HEH HEH HEH... THERE'S NO NEED TO WORRY...
...CUZ WE'RE GONNA BEAT TSUKASA.
AND SAVE ALL OF HUMANITY.
THAT'S RIGHT, YUZURIHA!

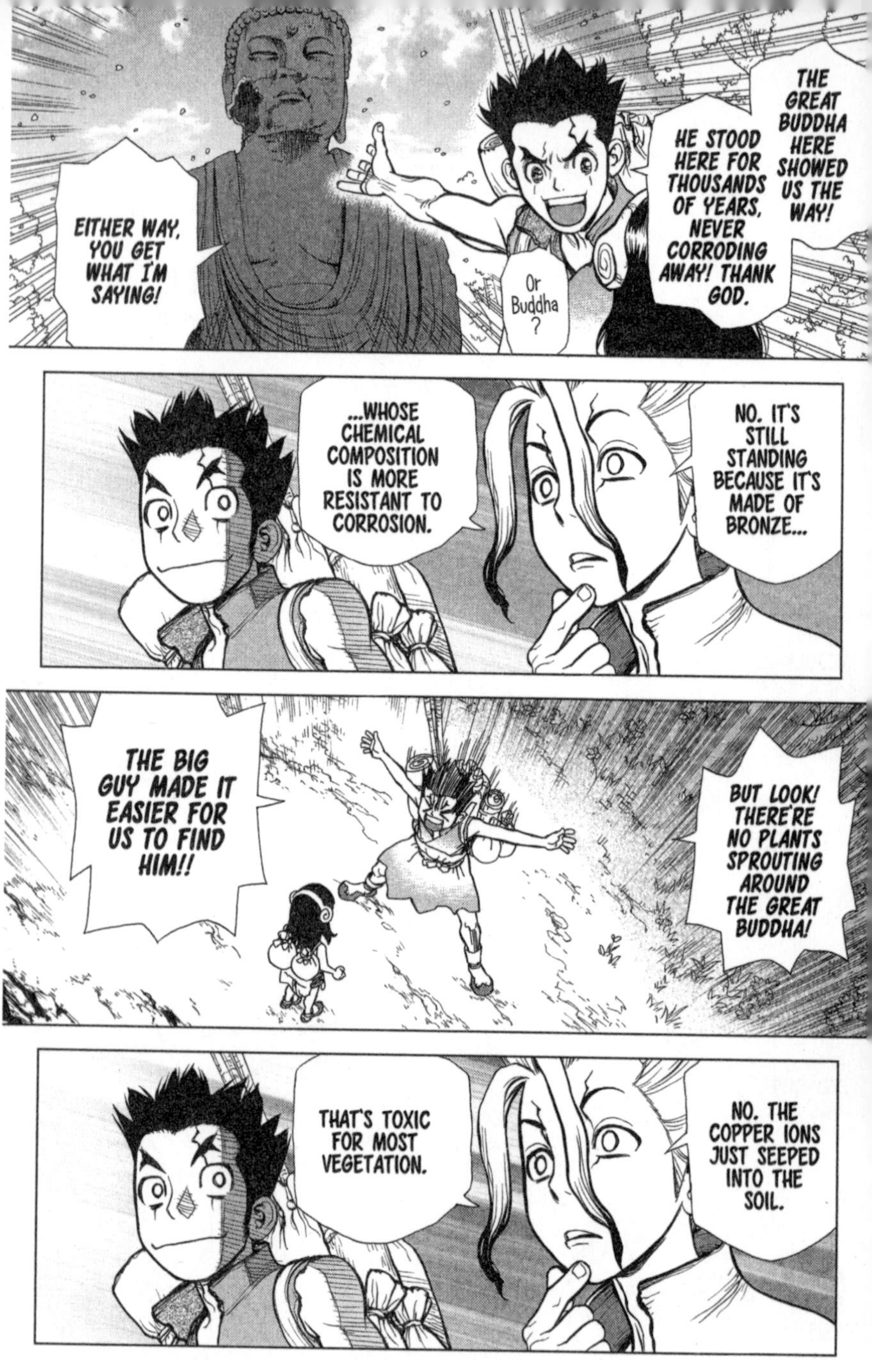
THE GREAT BUDDHA HERE SHOWED US THE WAY!
HE STOOD HERE FOR THOUSANDS OF YEARS, NEVER CORRODING AWAY! THANK GOD.
Or Buddha?
EITHER WAY, YOU GET WHAT I'M SAYING!
NO. IT'S STILL STANDING BECAUSE IT'S MADE OF BRONZE...
...WHOSE CHEMICAL COMPOSITION IS MORE RESISTANT TO CORROSION.
BUT LOOK! THERE'RE NO PLANTS SPROUTING AROUND THE GREAT BUDDHA!
THE BIG GUY MADE IT EASIER FOR US TO FIND HIM!!
NO. THE COPPER IONS JUST SEEPED INTO THE SOIL.
THAT'S TOXIC FOR MOST VEGETATION.

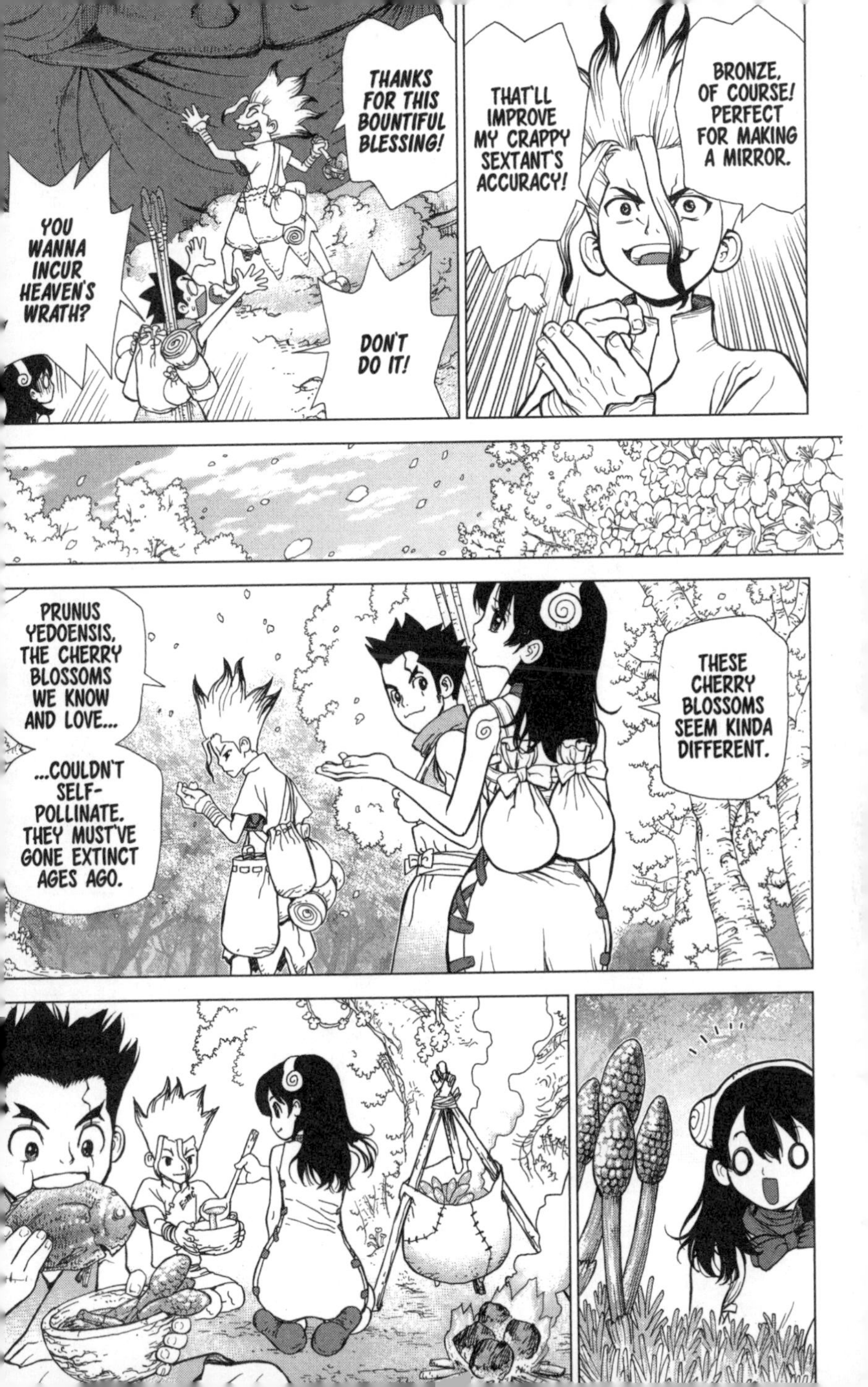
BRONZE, OF COURSE! PERFECT FOR MAKING A MIRROR.
THAT'LL IMPROVE MY CRAPPY SEXTANT'S ACCURACY!
THANKS FOR THIS BOUNTIFUL BLESSING!
YOU WANNA INCUR HEAVEN'S WRATH?
DON'T DO IT!
THESE CHERRY BLOSSOMS SEEM KINDA DIFFERENT.
PRUNUS YEDOENSIS, THE CHERRY BLOSSOMS WE KNOW AND LOVE...
...COULDN'T SELF-POLLINATE. THEY MUST'VE GONE EXTINCT AGES AGO.

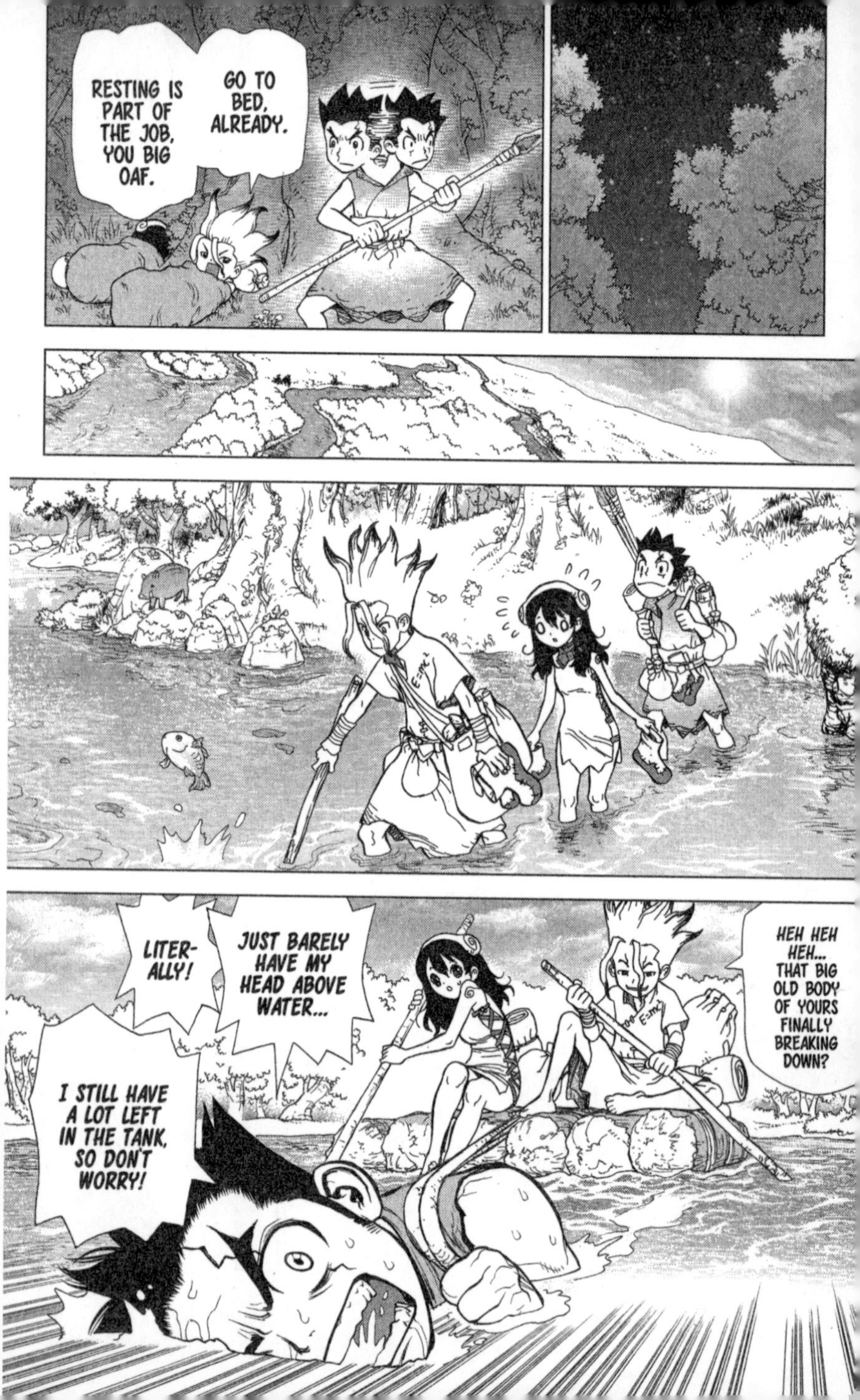
GO TO BED, ALREADY.
RESTING IS PART OF THE JOB, YOU BIG OAF.
HEH HEH HEH... THAT BIG OLD BODY OF YOURS FINALLY BREAKING DOWN?
I STILL HAVE A LOT LEFT IN THE TANK, SO DON'T WORRY!
JUST BARELY HAVE MY HEAD ABOVE WATER...
LITER-ALLY!

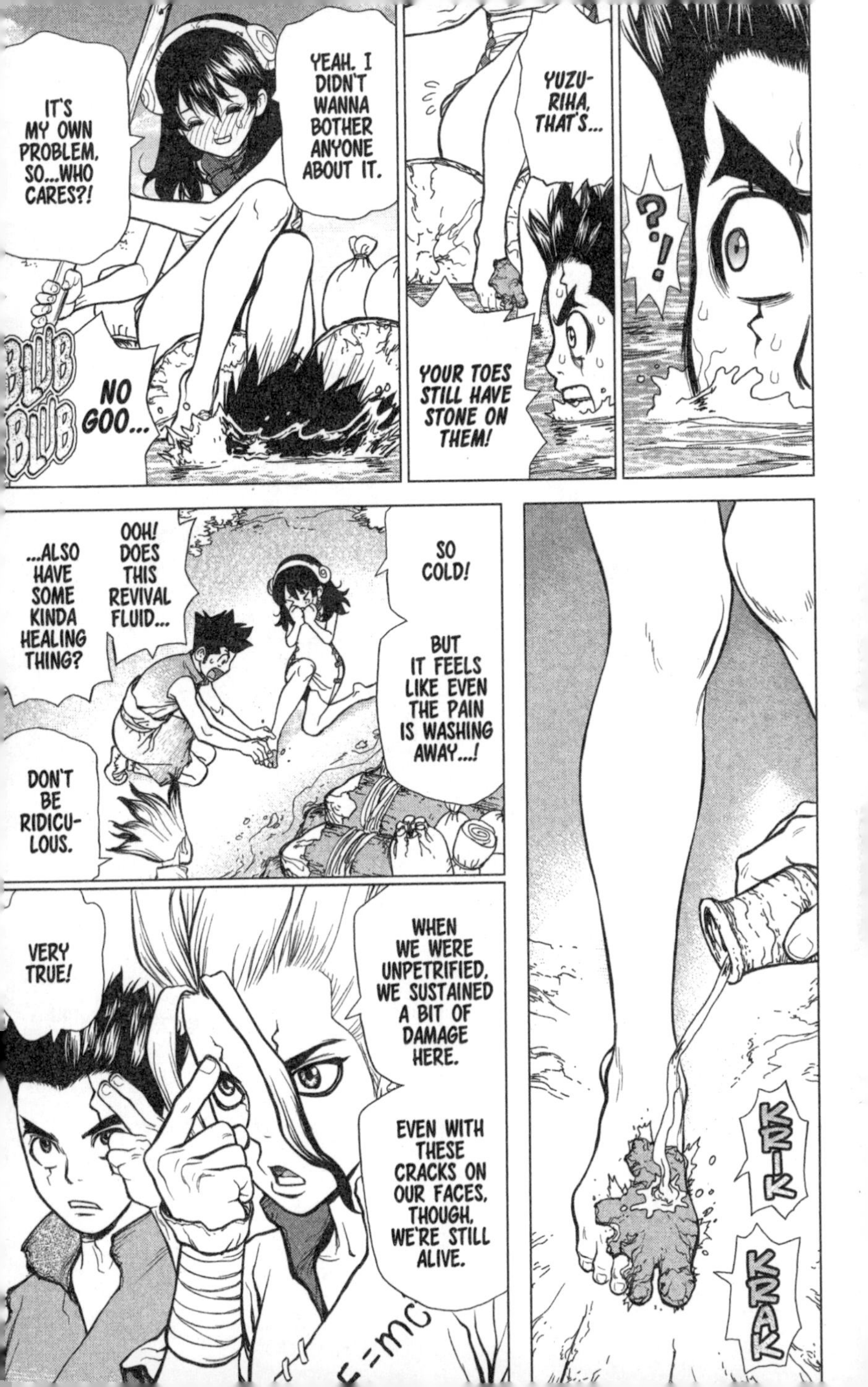
?!
YUZU-RIHA, THAT'S...
YOUR TOES STILL HAVE STONE ON THEM!
YEAH. I DIDN'T WANNA BOTHER ANYONE ABOUT IT.
IT'S MY OWN PROBLEM, SO...WHO CARES?!
NO GOO...
BLUB BLUB
KRIK
KRAK
SO COLD!
BUT IT FEELS LIKE EVEN THE PAIN IS WASHING AWAY...!
OOH! DOES THIS REVIVAL FLUID...
...ALSO HAVE SOME KINDA HEALING THING?
DON'T BE RIDICULOUS.
WHEN WE WERE UNPETRIFIED, WE SUSTAINED A BIT OF DAMAGE HERE.
EVEN WITH THESE CRACKS ON OUR FACES, THOUGH, WE'RE STILL ALIVE.
VERY TRUE!

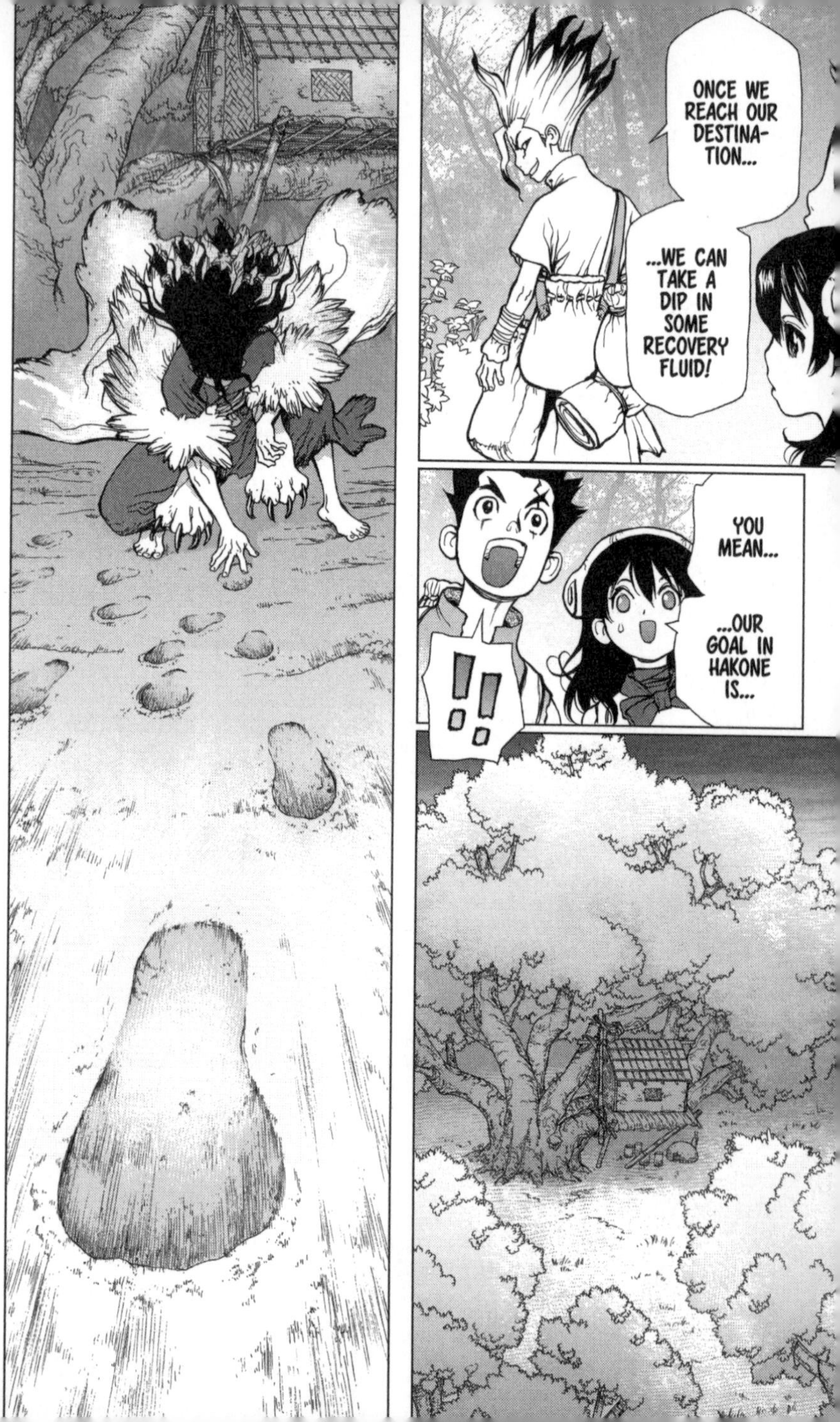
ONCE WE REACH OUR DESTINATION...
...WE CAN TAKE A DIP IN SOME RECOVERY FLUID!
YOU MEAN...
...OUR GOAL IN HAKONE IS...
!!

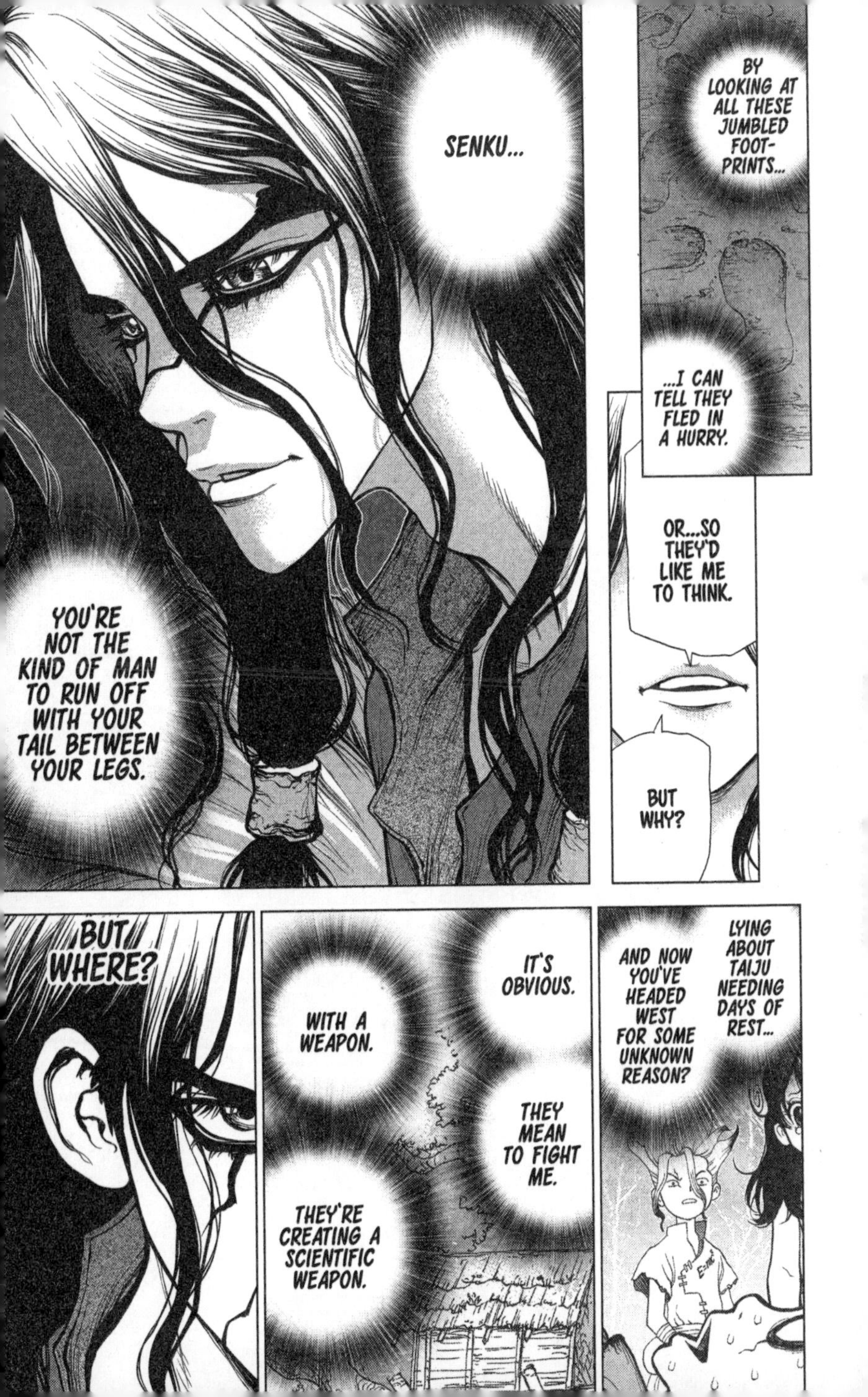
BY LOOKING AT ALL THESE JUMBLED FOOT-PRINTS...
...I CAN TELL THEY FLED IN A HURRY.
OR...SO THEY'D LIKE ME TO THINK.
BUT WHY?
SENKU...
YOU'RE NOT THE KIND OF MAN TO RUN OFF WITH YOUR TAIL BETWEEN YOUR LEGS.
LYING ABOUT TAIJU NEEDING DAYS OF REST...
AND NOW YOU'VE HEADED WEST FOR SOME UNKNOWN REASON?
IT'S OBVIOUS.
THEY MEAN TO FIGHT ME.
WITH A WEAPON.
THEY'RE CREATING A SCIENTIFIC WEAPON.
BUT WHERE?

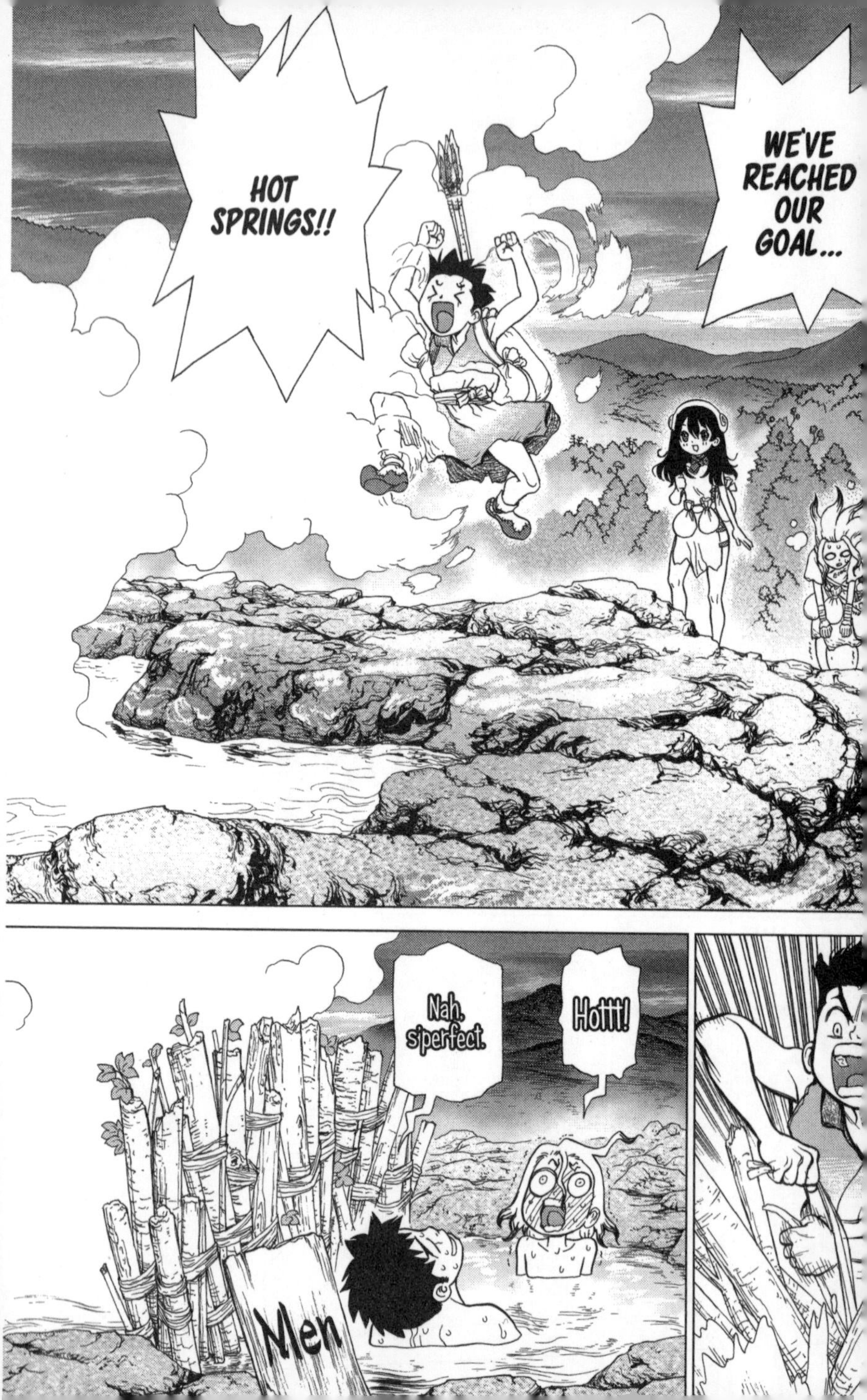
WE'VE REACHED OUR GOAL...
HOT SPRINGS!!
Hottt!
Nah, s'perfect.
Men

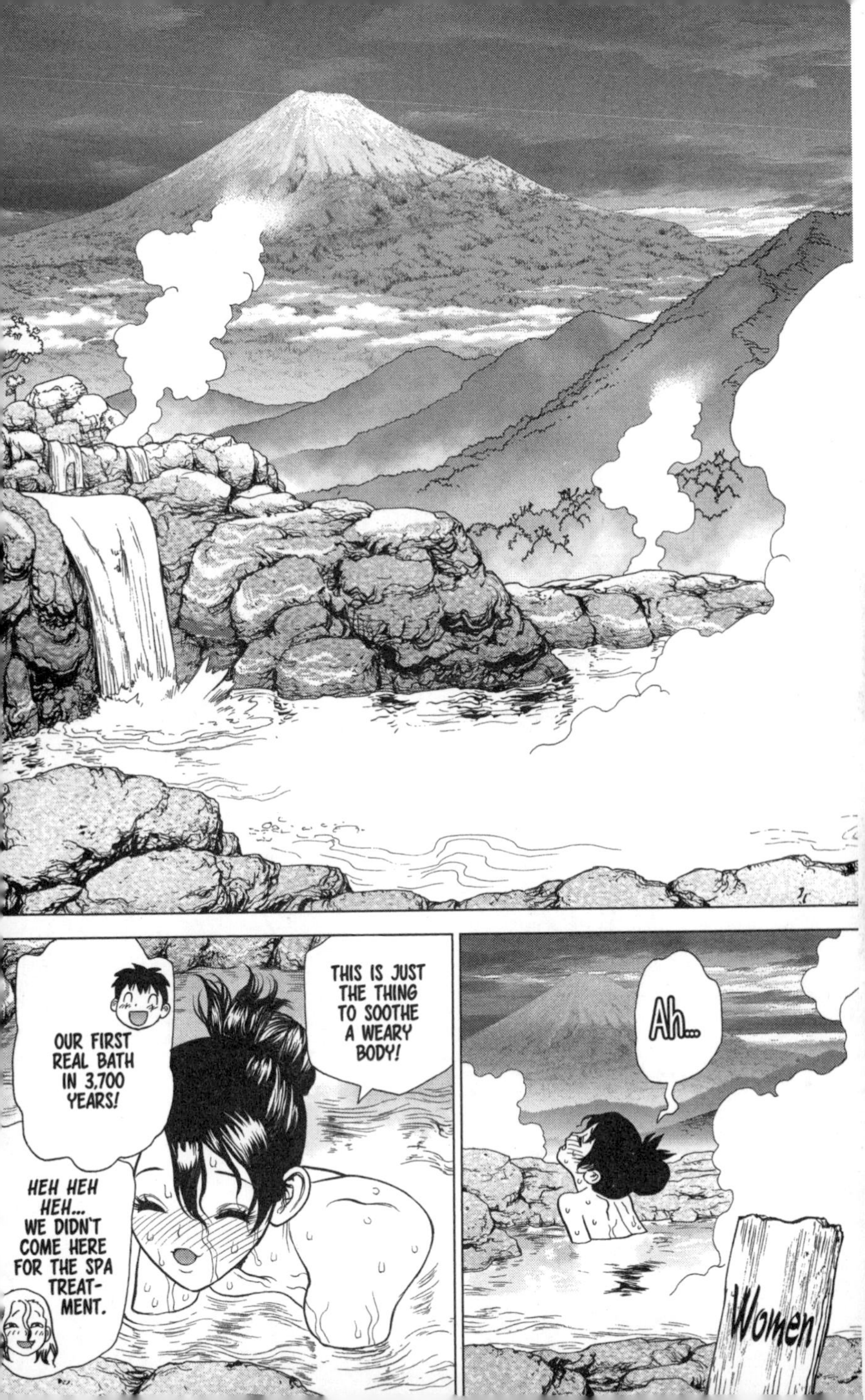
Ah...
Women
THIS IS JUST THE THING TO SOOTHE A WEARY BODY!
OUR FIRST REAL BATH IN 3,700 YEARS!
HEH HEH HEH... WE DIDN'T COME HERE FOR THE SPA TREATMENT.

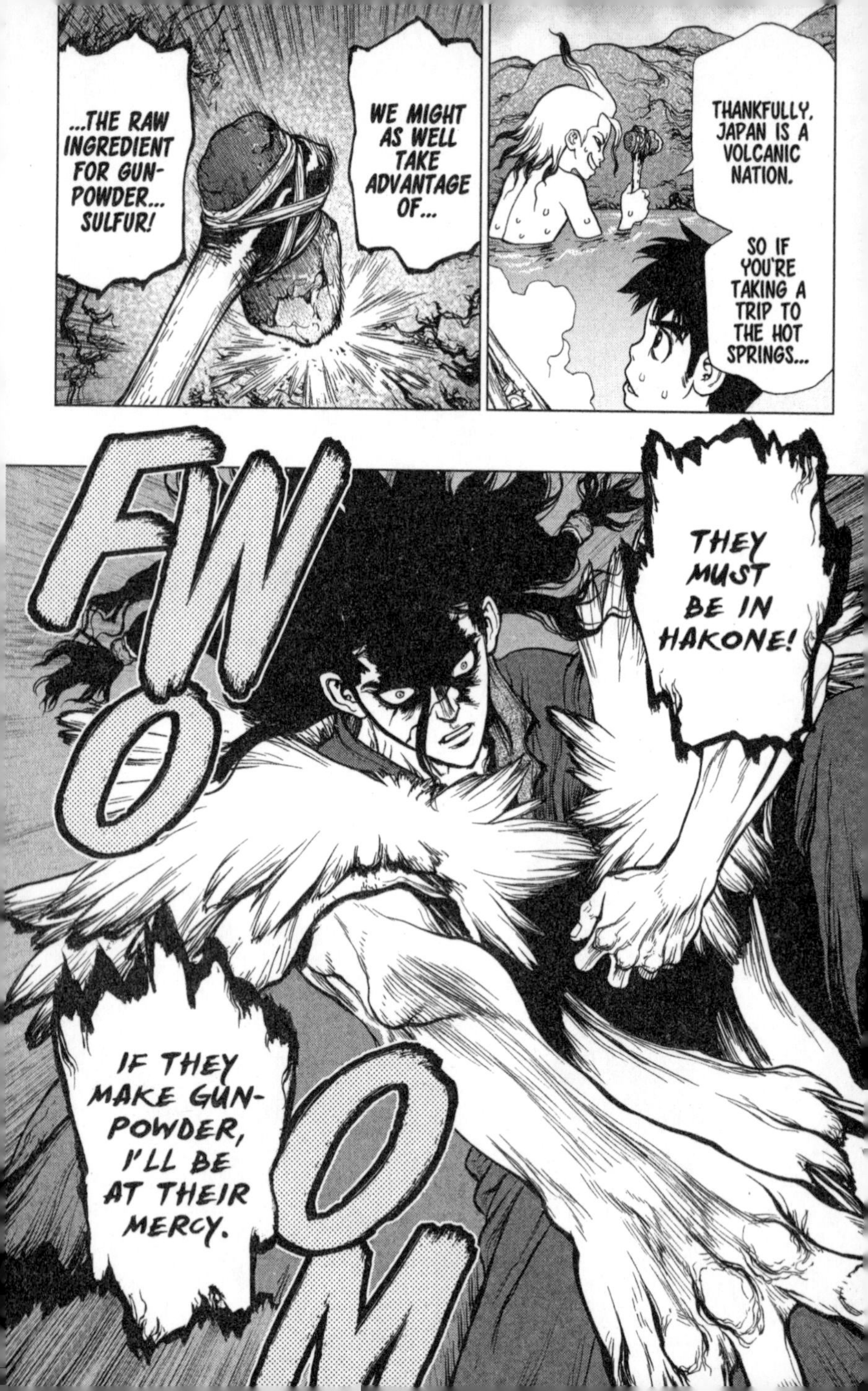
THANKFULLY, JAPAN IS A VOLCANIC NATION.
SO IF YOU'RE TAKING A TRIP TO THE HOT SPRINGS...
WE MIGHT AS WELL TAKE ADVANTAGE OF...
...THE RAW INGREDIENT FOR GUN-POWDER... SULFUR!
THEY MUST BE IN HAKONE!
FWOOM
IF THEY MAKE GUN-POWDER, I'LL BE AT THEIR MERCY.

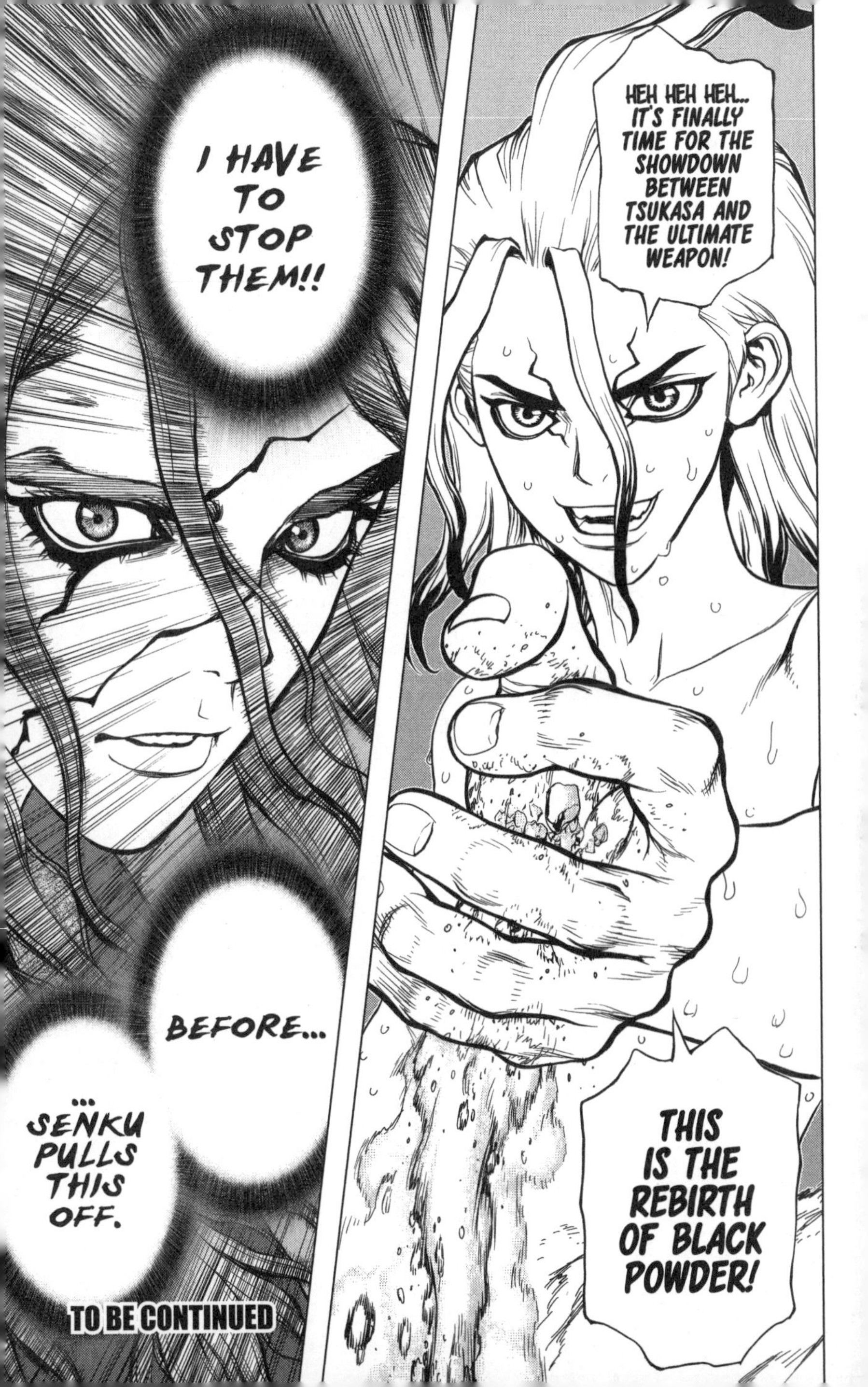
HEH HEH HEH... IT'S FINALLY TIME FOR THE SHOWDOWN BETWEEN TSUKASA AND THE ULTIMATE WEAPON!
THIS IS THE REBIRTH OF BLACK POWDER!
I HAVE TO STOP THEM!!
BEFORE...
...SENKU PULLS THIS OFF.
TO BE CONTINUED

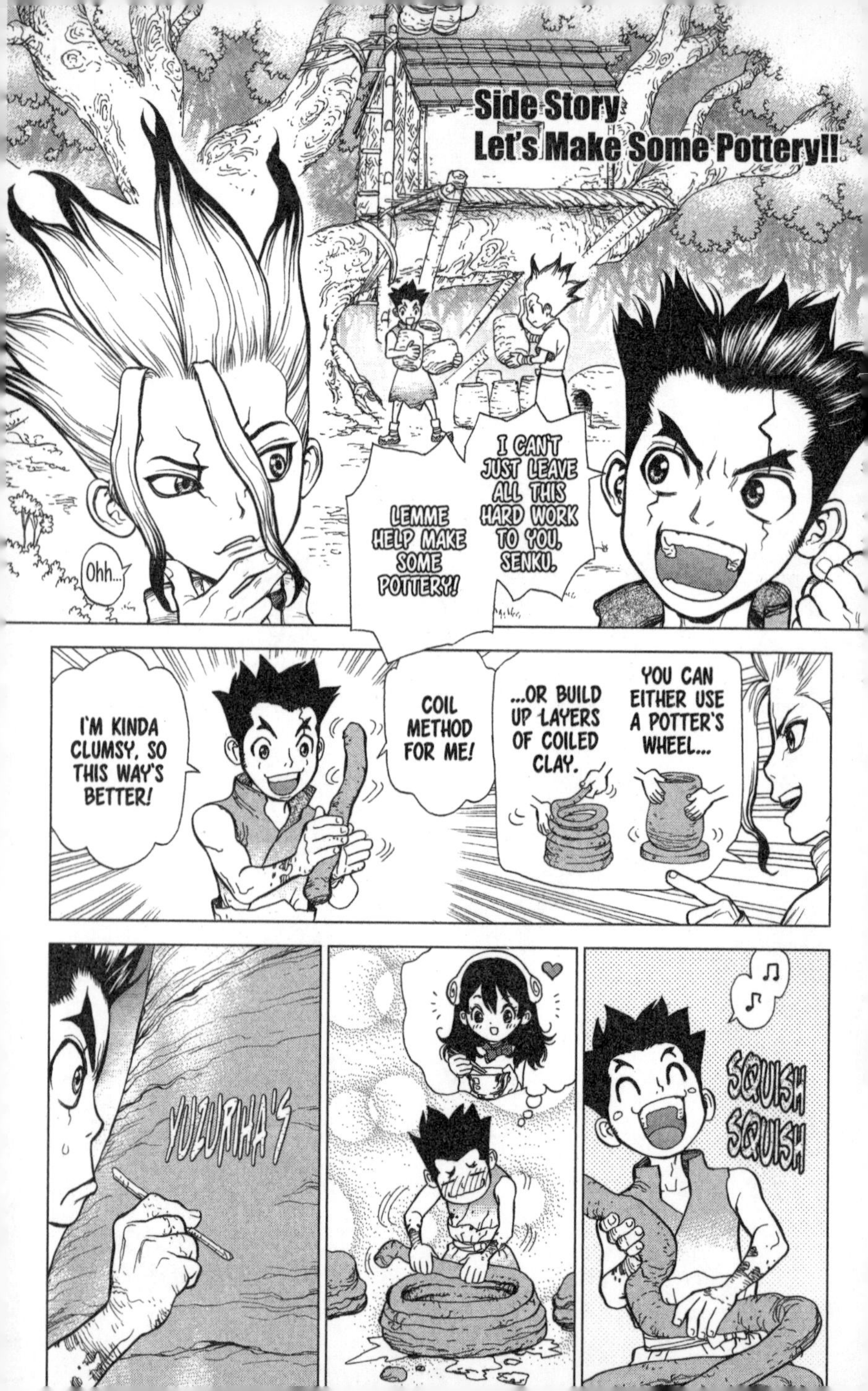
Side Story
Let's Make Some Pottery!!
I CAN'T JUST LEAVE ALL THIS HARD WORK TO YOU, SENKU.
LEMME HELP MAKE SOME POTTERY!
Ohh...
YOU CAN EITHER USE A POTTER'S WHEEL...
...OR BUILD UP LAYERS OF COILED CLAY.
COIL METHOD FOR ME!
I'M KINDA CLUMSY, SO THIS WAY'S BETTER!
SQUISH SQUISH
YUZURIHA'S

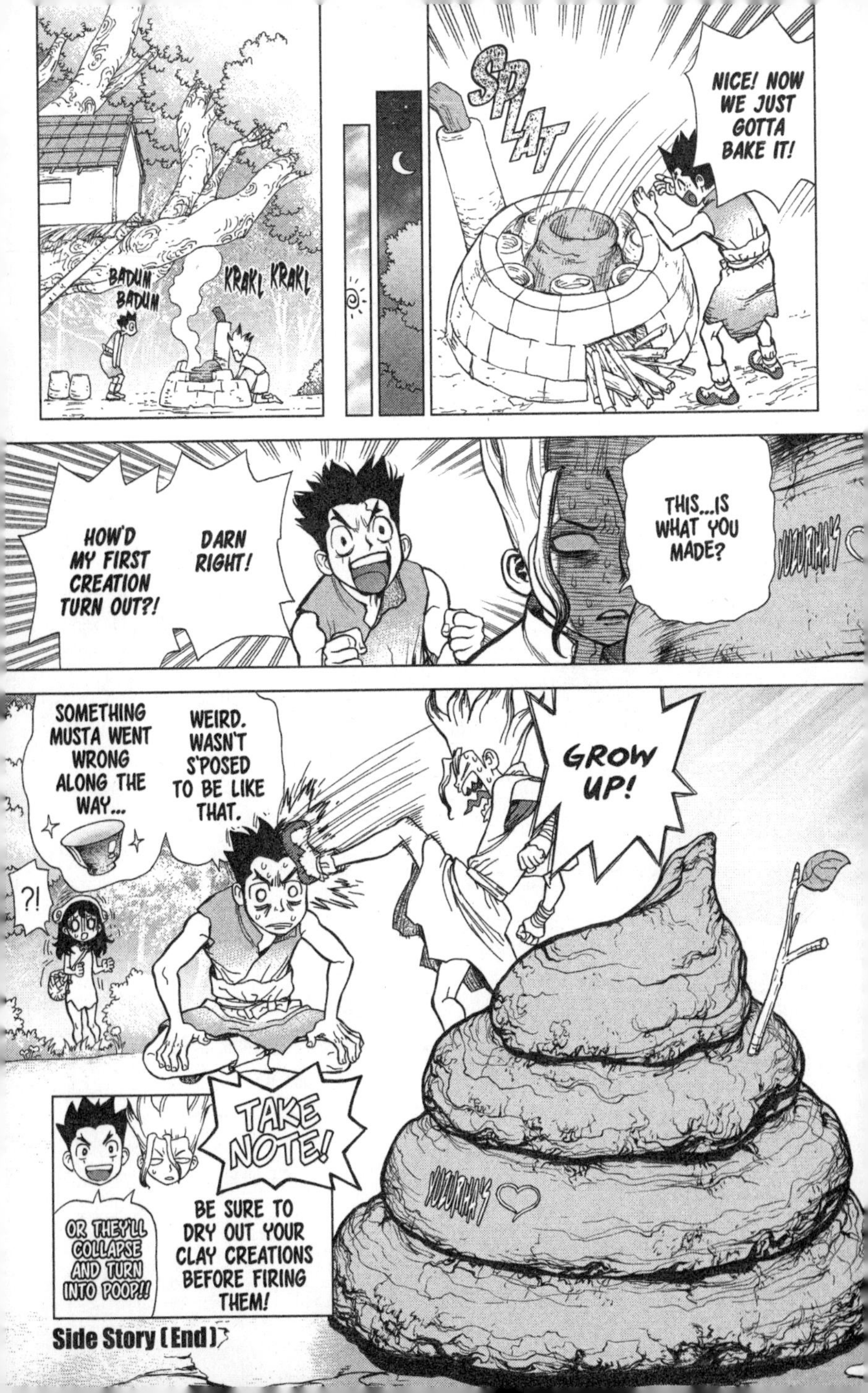
SPLAT
NICE! NOW WE JUST GOTTA BAKE IT!
KRAKL KRAKL
BADUM BADUM
THIS...IS WHAT YOU MADE?
DARN RIGHT!
HOW'D MY FIRST CREATION TURN OUT?!
GROW UP!
WEIRD. WASN'T S'POSED TO BE LIKE THAT.
SOMETHING MUSTA WENT WRONG ALONG THE WAY...
?!
TAKE NOTE!
BE SURE TO DRY OUT YOUR CLAY CREATIONS BEFORE FIRING THEM!
OR THEY'LL COLLAPSE AND TURN INTO POOP!!
Side Story (End)

Black ✤ Clover

STORY & ART BY YŪKI TABATA

Asta is a young boy who dreams of becoming the greatest mage in the kingdom. Only one problem—he can't use any magic! Luckily for Asta, he receives the incredibly rare five-leaf clover grimoire that gives him the power of anti-magic. Can someone who can't use magic really become the Wizard King? One thing's for sure—Asta will never give up!

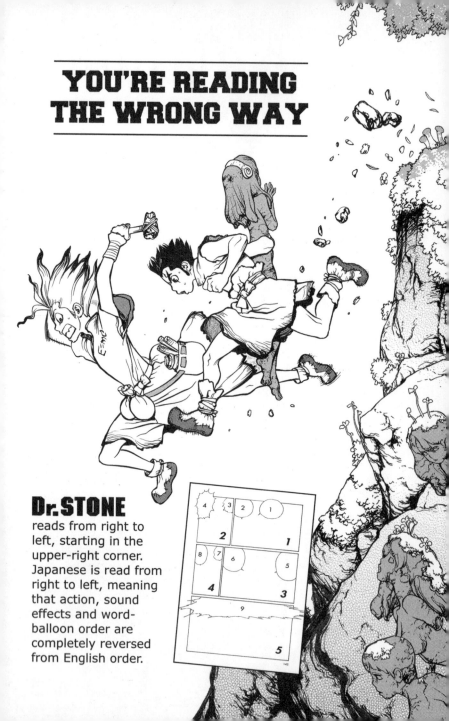

YOU'RE READING THE WRONG WAY

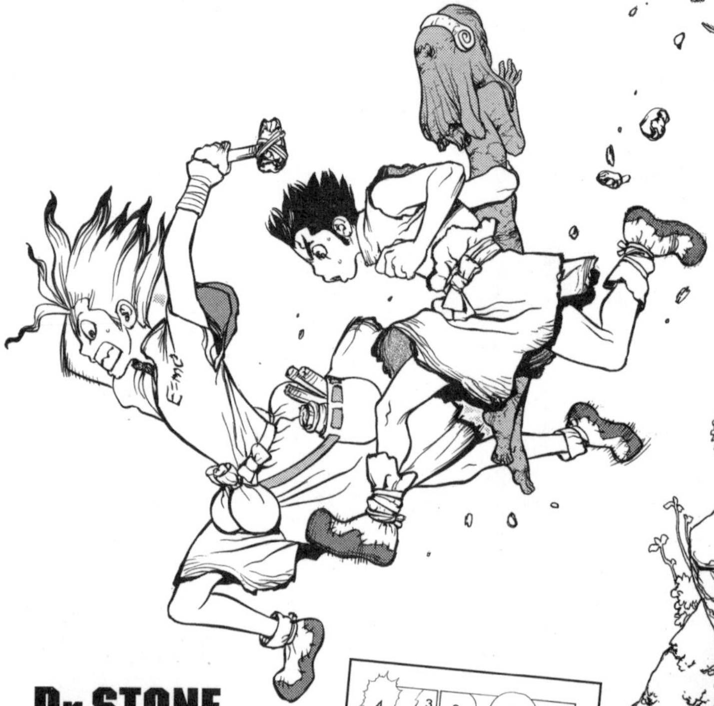

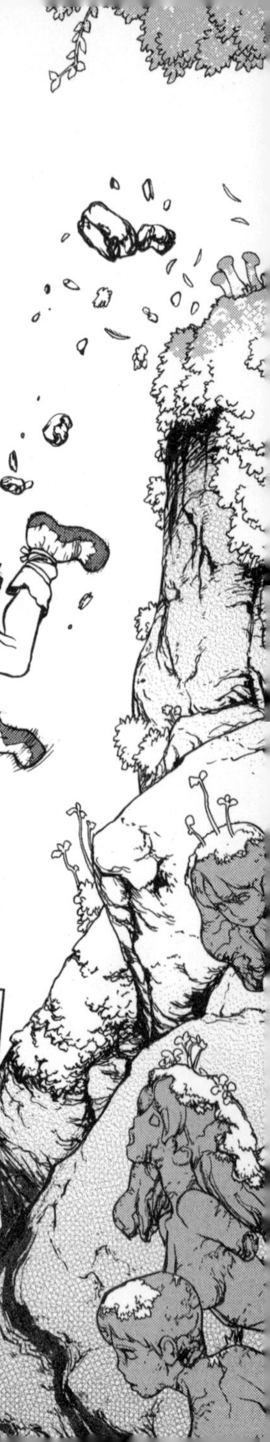

Dr.STONE

reads from right to left, starting in the upper-right corner. Japanese is read from right to left, meaning that action, sound effects and word-balloon order are completely reversed from English order.

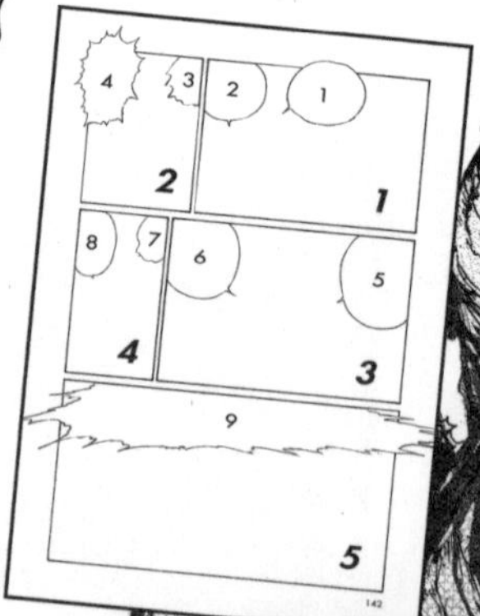

1
2
3
4
1
2
5
6
7
8
3
4
9
5
142